ALITA
Battle Angel
ALITA™
Last Order™
ANGEL ETERNAL

D1267572

3

STORY & ART BY YUKITO KISHIRO

cas of—and replacements for—Alita. Bitter battles ensue, and Lou, the operator who serves as backup support for the TUNED system, is ultimately relieved of duty. Only then is the shocking truth revealed: Tipharean adults have all had their brains replaced by bio-chips!

Alita resists the hacking of her brain by Ouroboros and defeats Nova. It seems as if she has finally won, but a surprising trap awaits her as she makes her way back to Figure—Nova has regenerated himself through nano-technology. Alita is consumed in an explosion, and her brain is taken to Tiphares…

BATTLE ANGEL ALITA: LAST ORDER, VOLS. 1 & 2

Alita is resurrected by Nova, who gives her the ultimate Imaginos body. Upheaval and bloodshed rule Tiphares as its citizens descend into madness after Nova's bio-chip revelation. Jim, the young genius Nova has chosen as his successor, succumbs to despair and activates his monster robot Sachumodo. Alita battles Jim's creation and finally brings calm to the chaos.

In the depths of Tiphares, Alita finds Lou's body—a mere shell without her brain bio-chip. Devastated, Alita finds some hope in Nova's words: Lou could perhaps be brought back to life if they can find her organic brain, long ago taken to the Space City Ketheres. So Alita condescends to ride to Ketheres with Nova and his escort, the TUNED AR series…

BATTLE ANGEL ALITA, VOLS. 1~9

In the near future…the world is divided into the dominated and the dominators. Tiphares, a floating artificial utopia, rules the Scrapyard, the surface, absolutely. But no one knows when or why this floating city was made— or by whom.

Ido, a TiphArean cyber-doctor and denizen of the Scrapyard, finds the head of a cyborg in a pile of rubble, and miraculously rebuilds her. She awakens with no memories, and Ido names her "Alita." Slowly, the harsh life of the Scrapyard stirs the fighting spirit within her, and she begins her path to self-discovery, living as a Hunter-Warrior, or bounty-hunter.

Alita meets and falls in love with Hugo, a boy who idolizes Tiphares. When she loses Hugo, she is heartbroken. Out of desperation, she turns to the pro sport world of Motorball, where she competes against the mighty Jashugan.

In a battle with a vicious cyborg named Zapan, whose body was revamped by evil genius Desty Nova, Alita loses Ido—her only family. Even her own life hangs by a thread.

The TiphArean organization G.I.B. presents Alita with a new path, and she chooses to live the life of a TUNED, a TiphArean agent, so that she can search for Nova, who holds the key to Ido's regeneration.

In the process, Alita becomes acquainted with Figure, a mercenary, and recovers the human soul she almost lost. Still, many seem to stand in her way: Kaos, Nova's son and a master of psychometry; Den, Kaos's alter-ego and the leader of the masses that oppose Tiphares; Koyomi, one of Den's groupies; the TUNED AR series, repli-

**BATTLE ANGEL ALITA:
LAST ORDER VOL. 3**
Angel Eternal
Action Editon

**Story & Art by
Yukito Kishiro**

**English Adaptation by
Fred Burke**

Translation/Lillian Olsen
Touch-up & Lettering/Susan Daigle-Leach
Cover & Graphics Design/Sean Lee
Editor/Annette Roman

Editorial Director/Alvin Lu
Director of Production/Noboru Watanabe
Sr. Director of Licensing & Acquisitions/
Rika Inouye
VP of Sales & Marketing/Liza Coppola
Executive VP/Hyoe Narita
Publisher/Seiji Horibuchi

Printed in Canada.

Published by VIZ, LLC
P.O. Box 77064
San Francisco, CA 94107

Action Edition
10 9 8 7 6 5 4 3 2
First printing, February 2004
Second printing, October 2004

store.viz.com

www.viz.com

CONTENTS

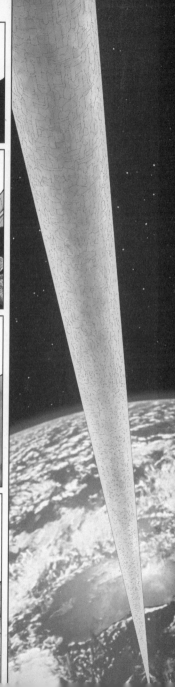

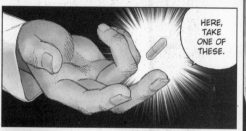

HERE, TAKE ONE OF THESE.
YOU FIRST!
BAH!
krek
Y-YOU'RE SO DIS-TRUSTFUL...
THEY'RE ANTIBODY CAPSULES! THEY'LL WARD OFF INVADING NANO-MACHINES.
DON'T LEAVE HOME WITHOUT 'EM!
SO THERE'S A POSSIBILITY KETHERES MIGHT BE HOSTILE?
ECCH.
EVEN IF IT IS... WITH OUR HEROIC LINEUP, I DOUBT WE'LL FACE ANY REAL THREATS! ♡
LADDER IS NOT TO BE TRUSTED, I FEAR.
BUT LIKE THE ANCIENT CHINESE PROVERB SAYS...

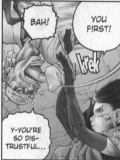

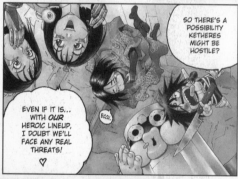

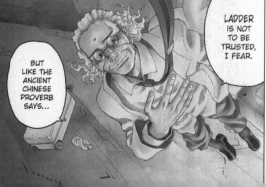

PHASE 13
The World's Zenith!

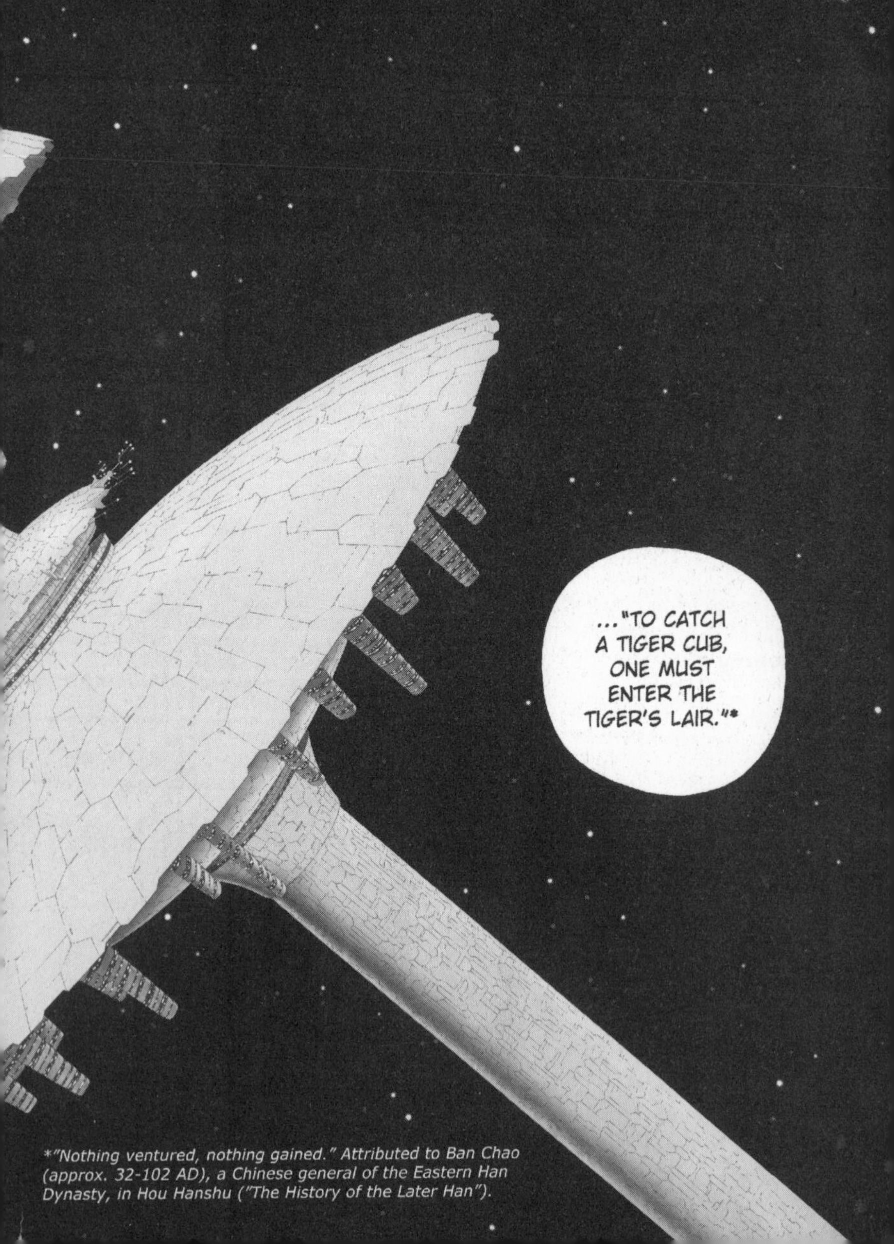
..."TO CATCH A TIGER CUB, ONE MUST ENTER THE TIGER'S LAIR."*

*"Nothing ventured, nothing gained." Attributed to Ban Chao (approx. 32-102 AD), a Chinese general of the Eastern Han Dynasty, in Hou Hanshu ("The History of the Later Han").

The Space City Ketheres

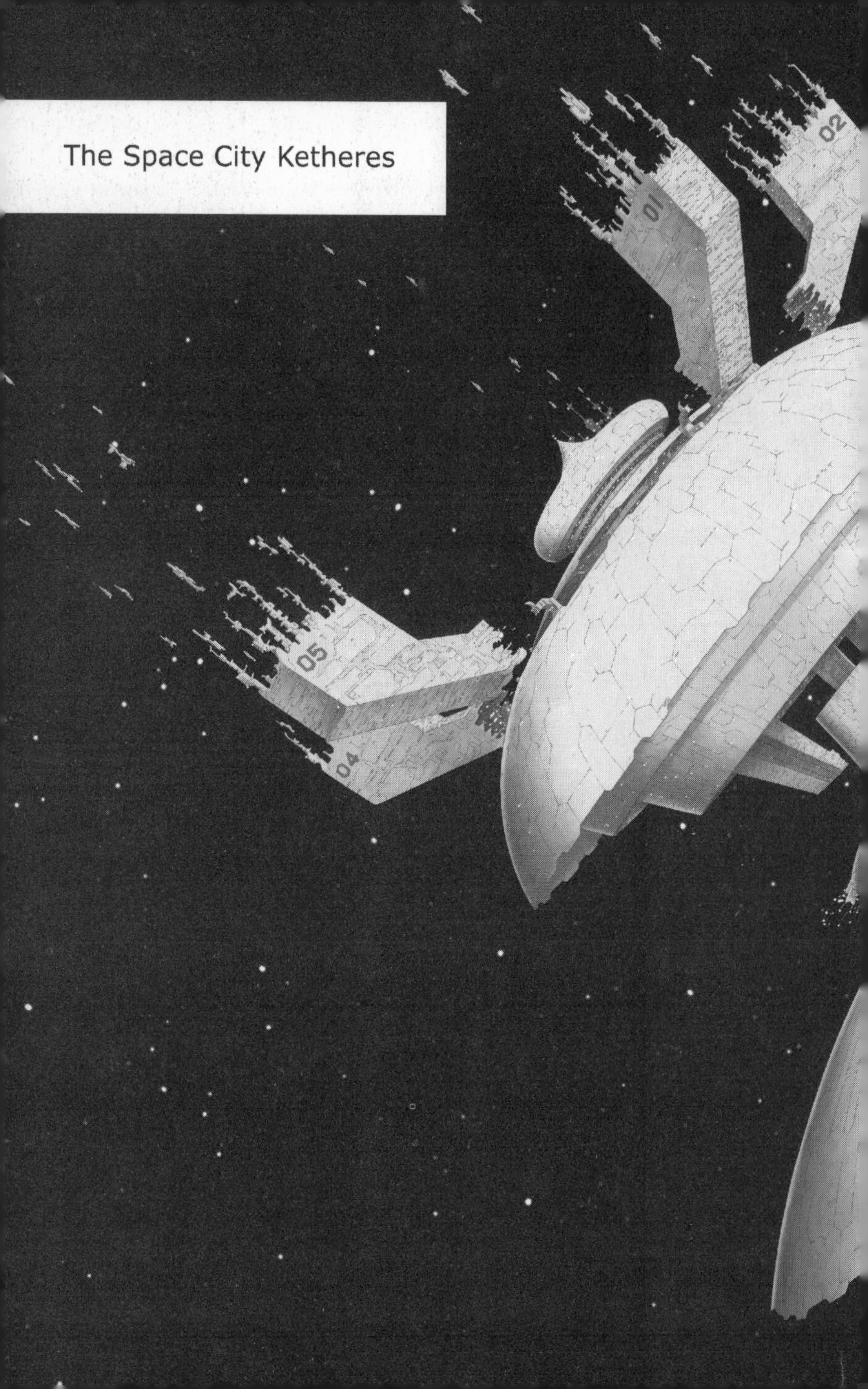
01
02
05
04

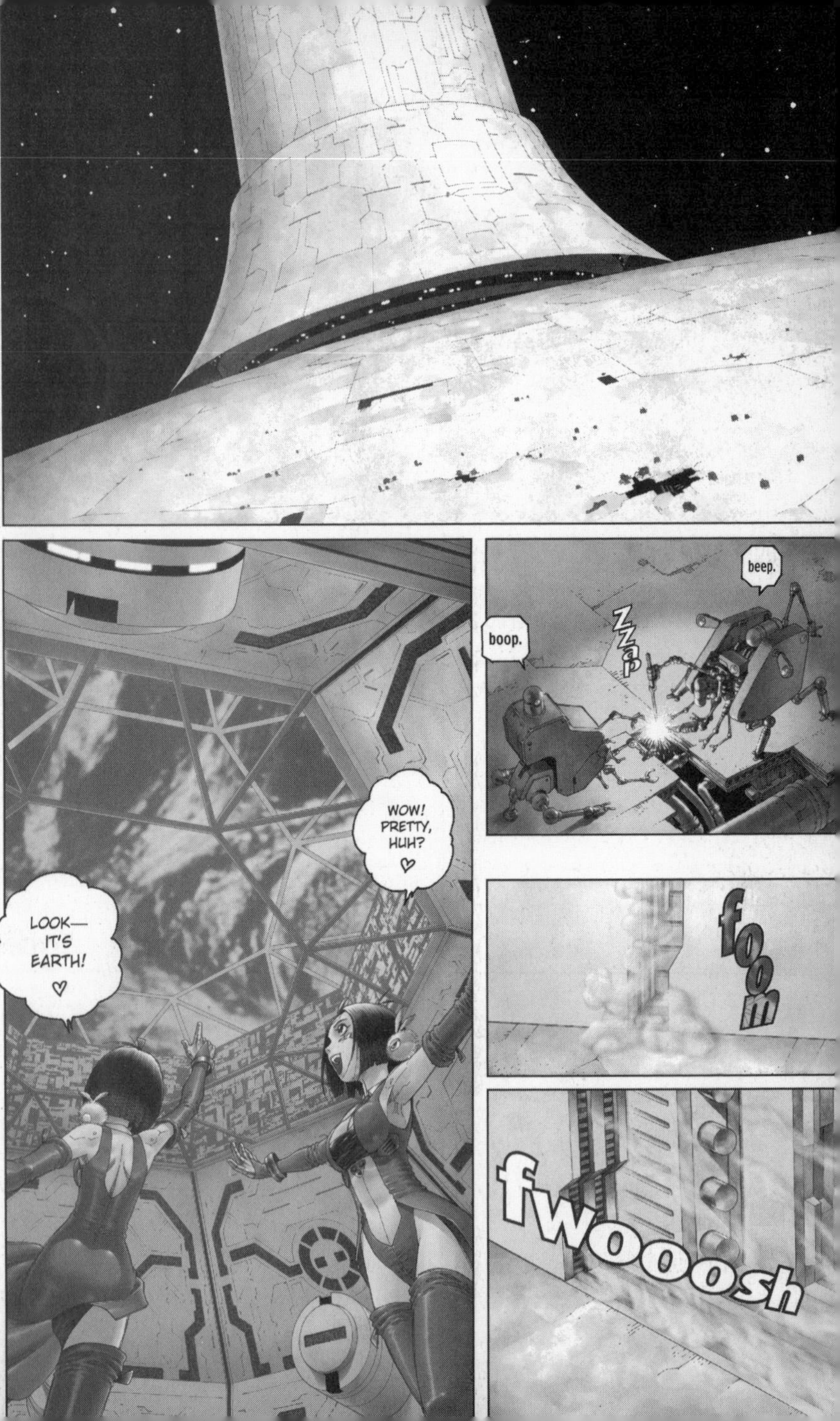

beep.
ZZap
boop.
foom
fwooosh
WOW! PRETTY, HUH? ♡
LOOK— IT'S EARTH! ♡

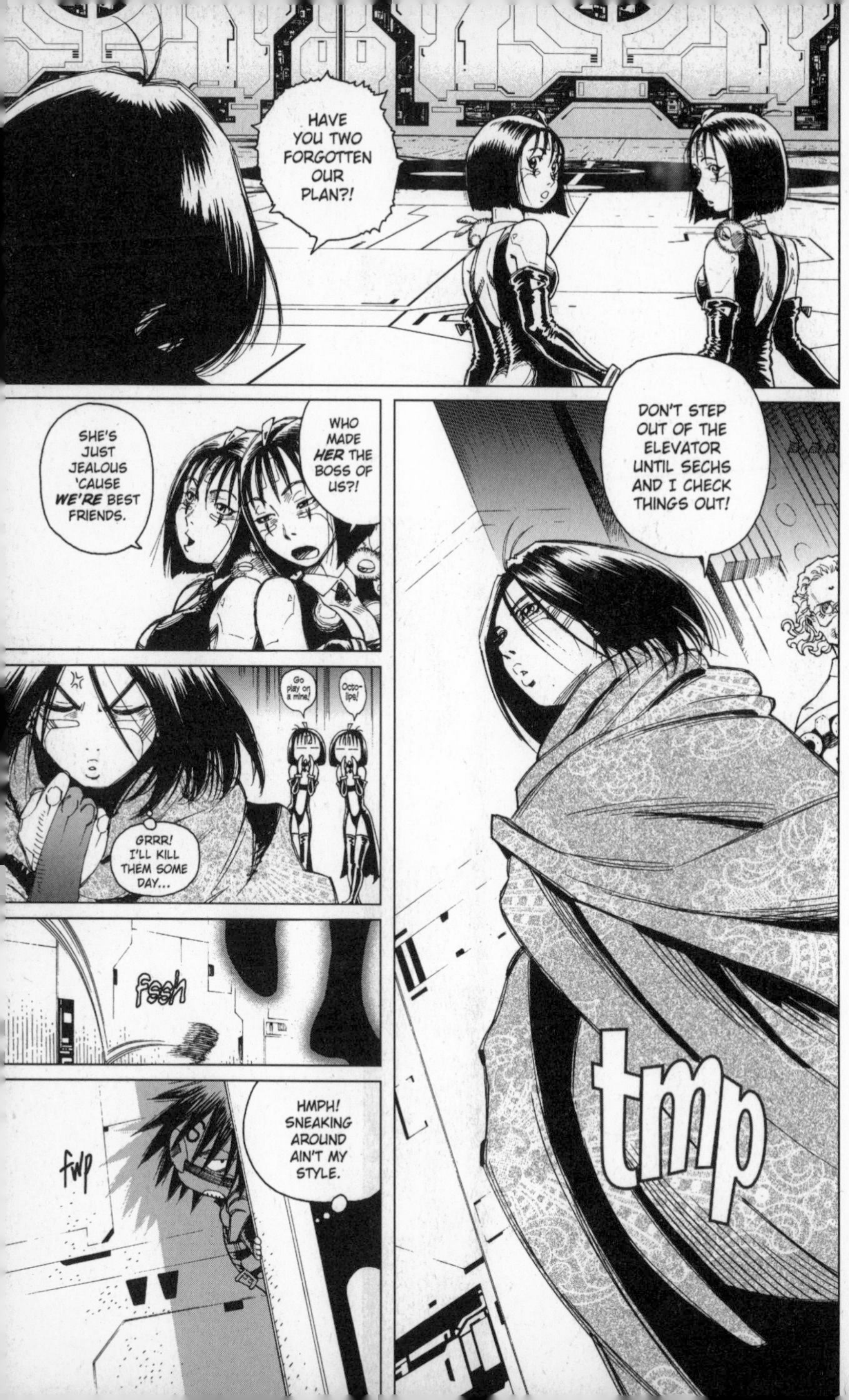
HAVE YOU TWO FORGOTTEN OUR PLAN?!
DON'T STEP OUT OF THE ELEVATOR UNTIL SECHS AND I CHECK THINGS OUT!
tmp
WHO MADE HER THE BOSS OF US?!
SHE'S JUST JEALOUS 'CAUSE WE'RE BEST FRIENDS.
Octo-lips!
Go play on a mine!
GRRR! I'LL KILL THEM SOME DAY...
fssh
HMPH! SNEAKING AROUND AIN'T MY STYLE.
fwp

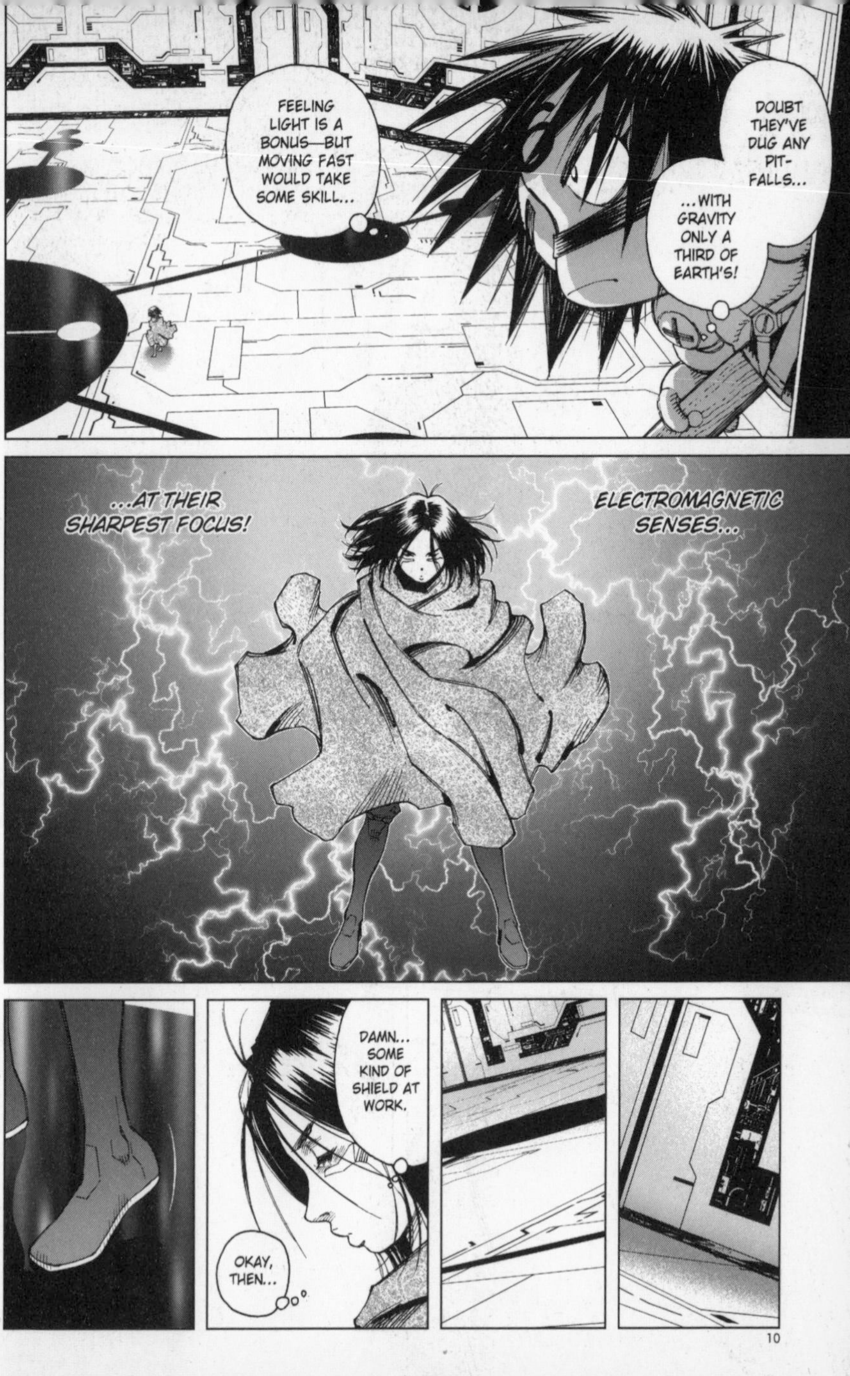
DOUBT THEY'VE DUG ANY PIT-FALLS...
...WITH GRAVITY ONLY A THIRD OF EARTH'S!
FEELING LIGHT IS A BONUS—BUT MOVING FAST WOULD TAKE SOME SKILL...
ELECTROMAGNETIC SENSES...
...AT THEIR SHARPEST FOCUS!
DAMN... SOME KIND OF SHIELD AT WORK.
OKAY, THEN...

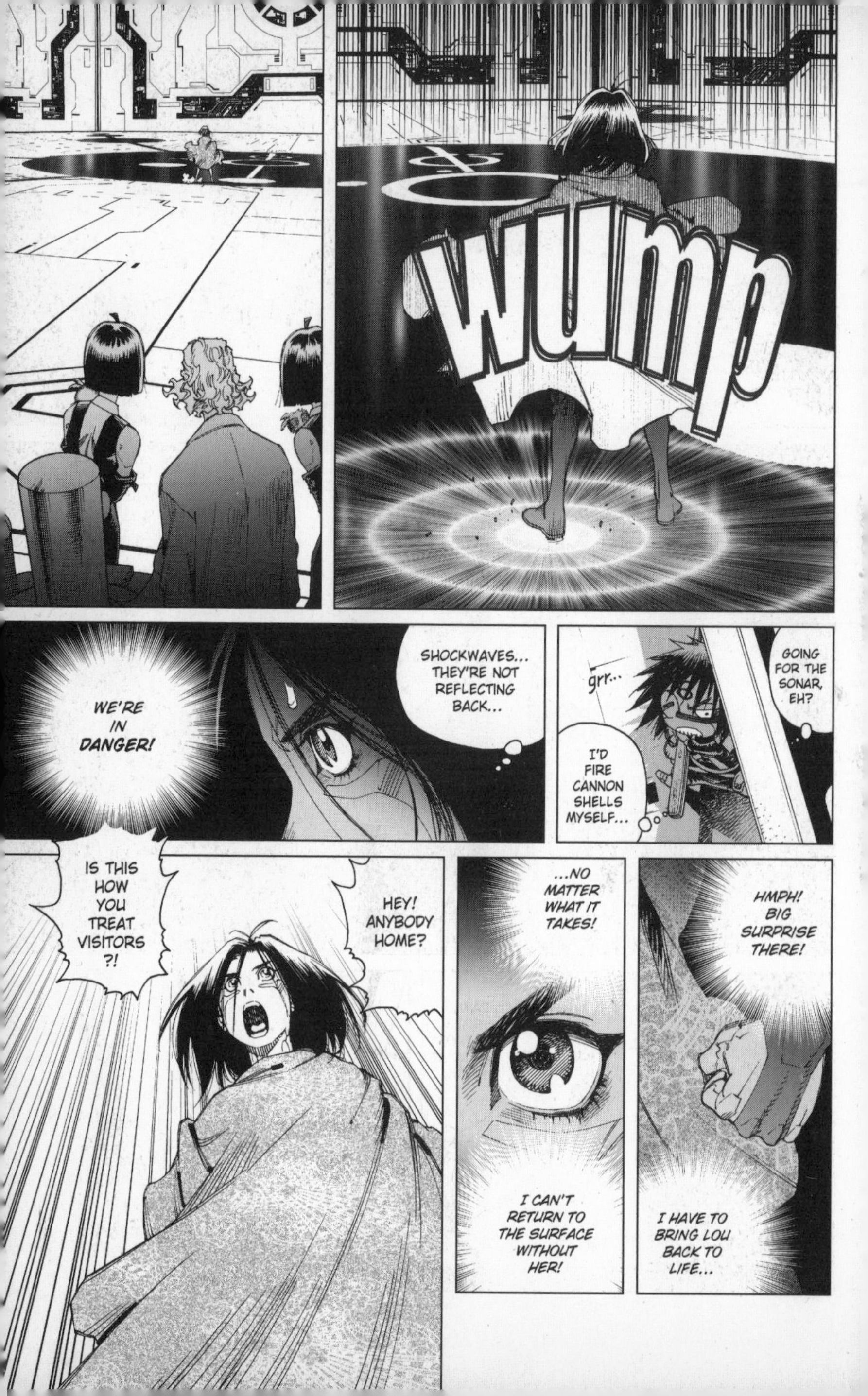
WUMP
GOING FOR THE SONAR, EH?
grr...
I'D FIRE CANNON SHELLS MYSELF...
SHOCKWAVES... THEY'RE NOT REFLECTING BACK...
WE'RE IN DANGER!
HMPH! BIG SURPRISE THERE!
I HAVE TO BRING LOU BACK TO LIFE...
...NO MATTER WHAT IT TAKES!
I CAN'T RETURN TO THE SURFACE WITHOUT HER!
HEY! ANYBODY HOME?
IS THIS HOW YOU TREAT VISITORS?!

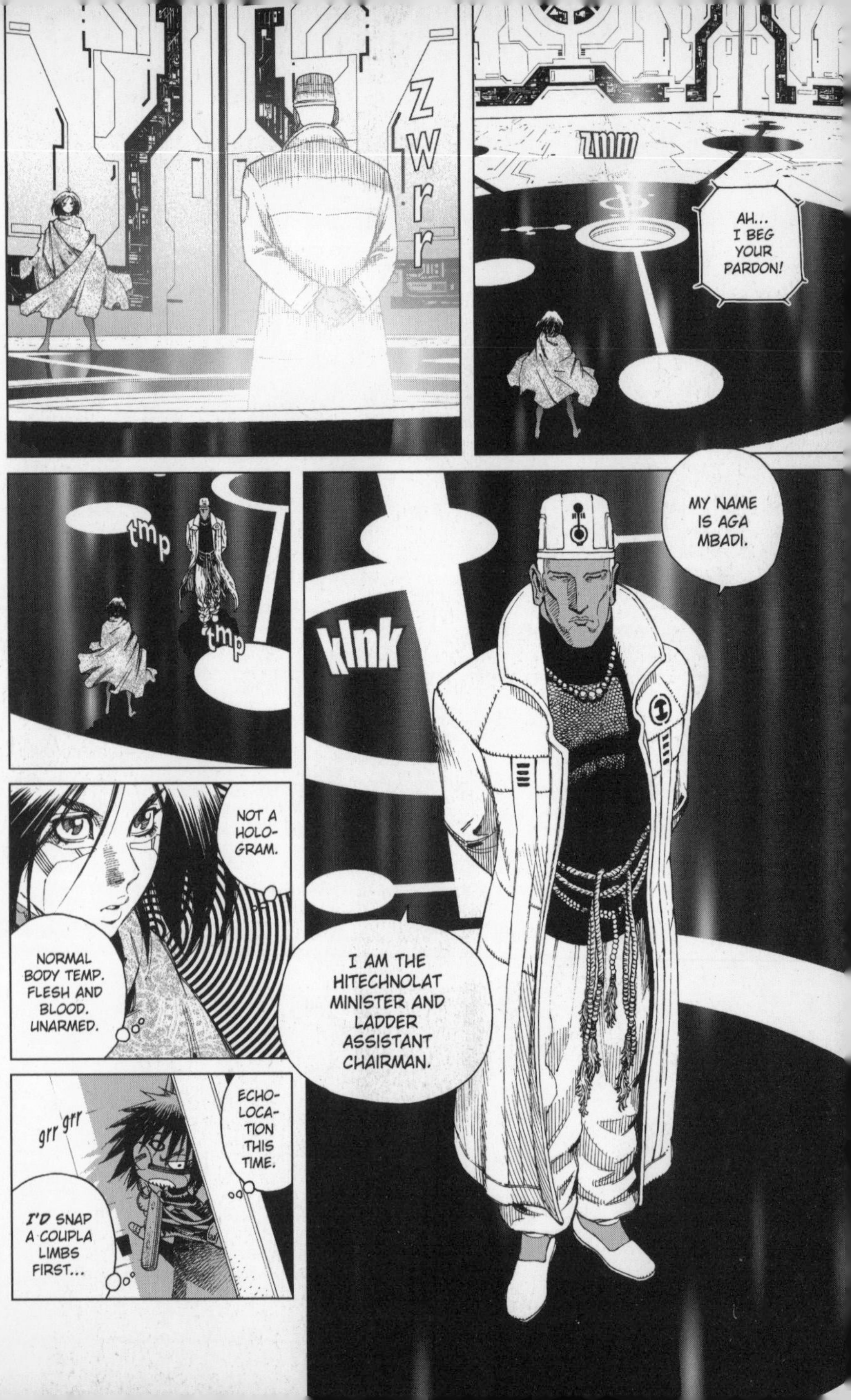
zmm
AH... I BEG YOUR PARDON!
zwrr
MY NAME IS AGA MBADI.
klink
I AM THE HITECHNOLAT MINISTER AND LADDER ASSISTANT CHAIRMAN.
tmp
tmp
NOT A HOLOGRAM.
NORMAL BODY TEMP. FLESH AND BLOOD. UNARMED.
ECHO-LOCA-TION THIS TIME.
grr grr
I'D SNAP A COUPLA LIMBS FIRST...

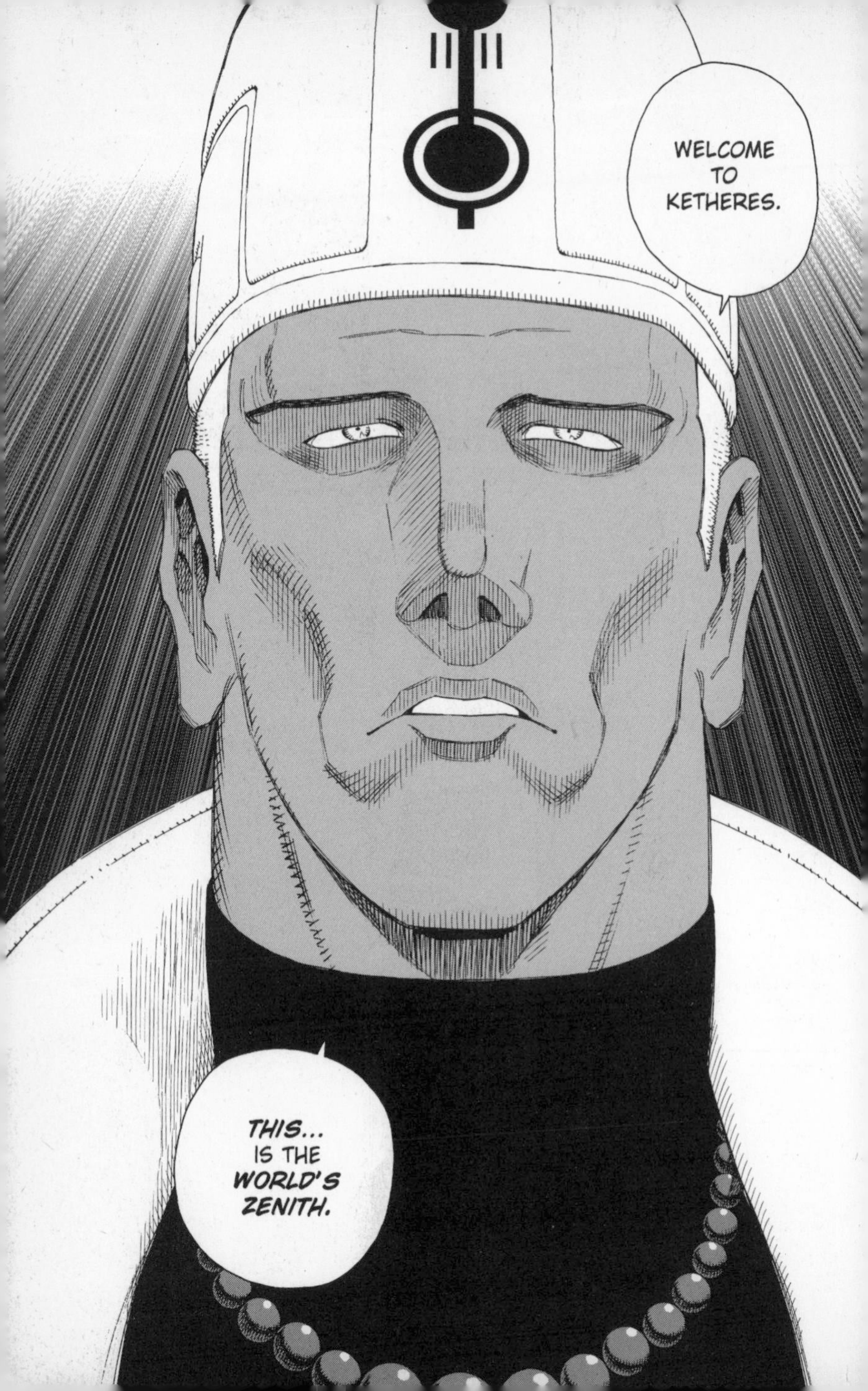
WELCOME TO KETHERES.
THIS... IS THE WORLD'S ZENITH.

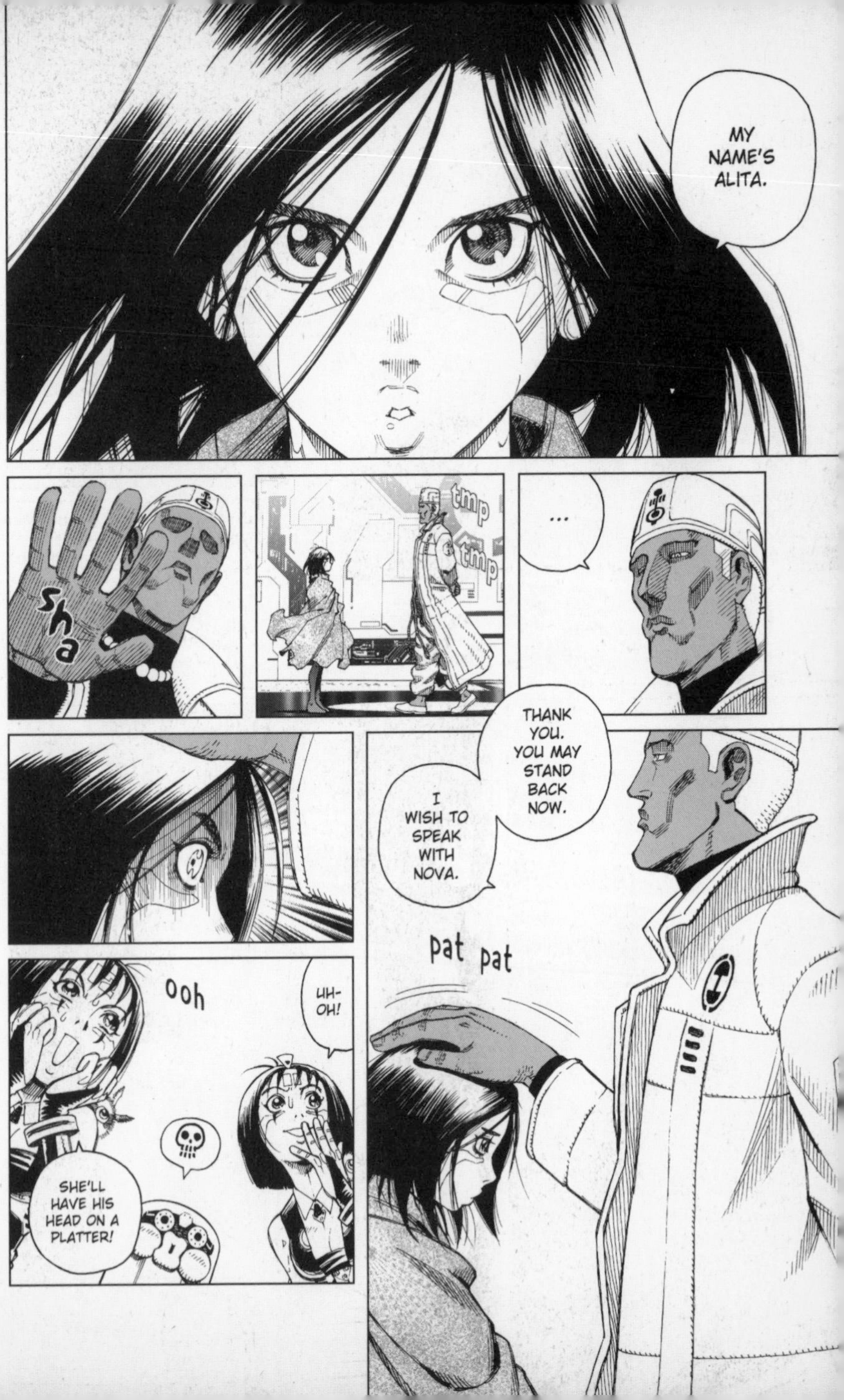
MY NAME'S ALITA.
...
tmp
tmp
sha
THANK YOU. YOU MAY STAND BACK NOW.
I WISH TO SPEAK WITH NOVA.
pat pat
UH-OH!
ooh
SHE'LL HAVE HIS HEAD ON A PLATTER!

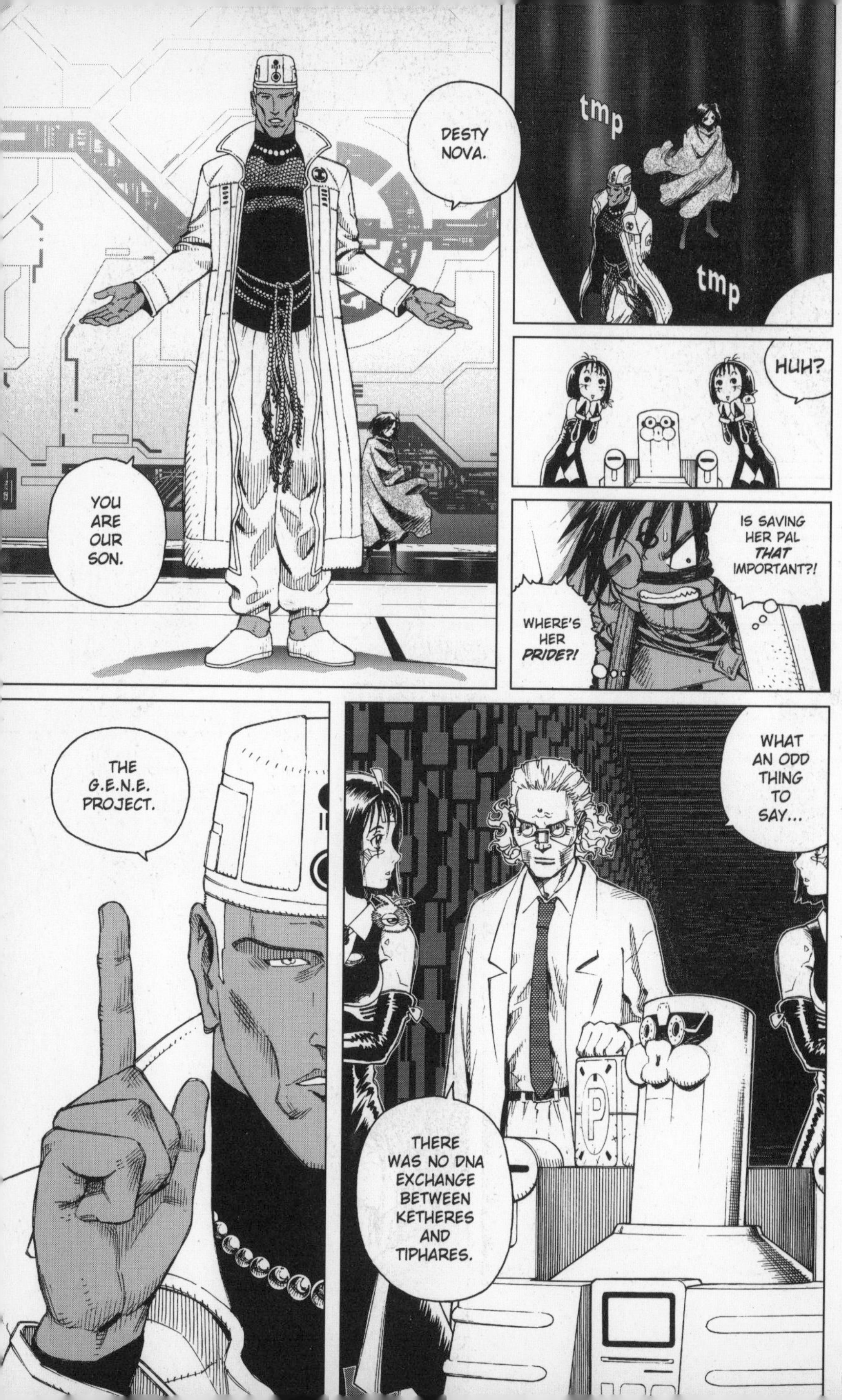
tmp
tmp
HUH?
IS SAVING HER PAL *THAT* IMPORTANT?!
WHERE'S HER *PRIDE?!*
DESTY NOVA.
YOU ARE OUR SON.
WHAT AN ODD THING TO SAY...
THERE WAS NO DNA EXCHANGE BETWEEN KETHERES AND TIPHARES.
THE G.E.N.E. PROJECT.

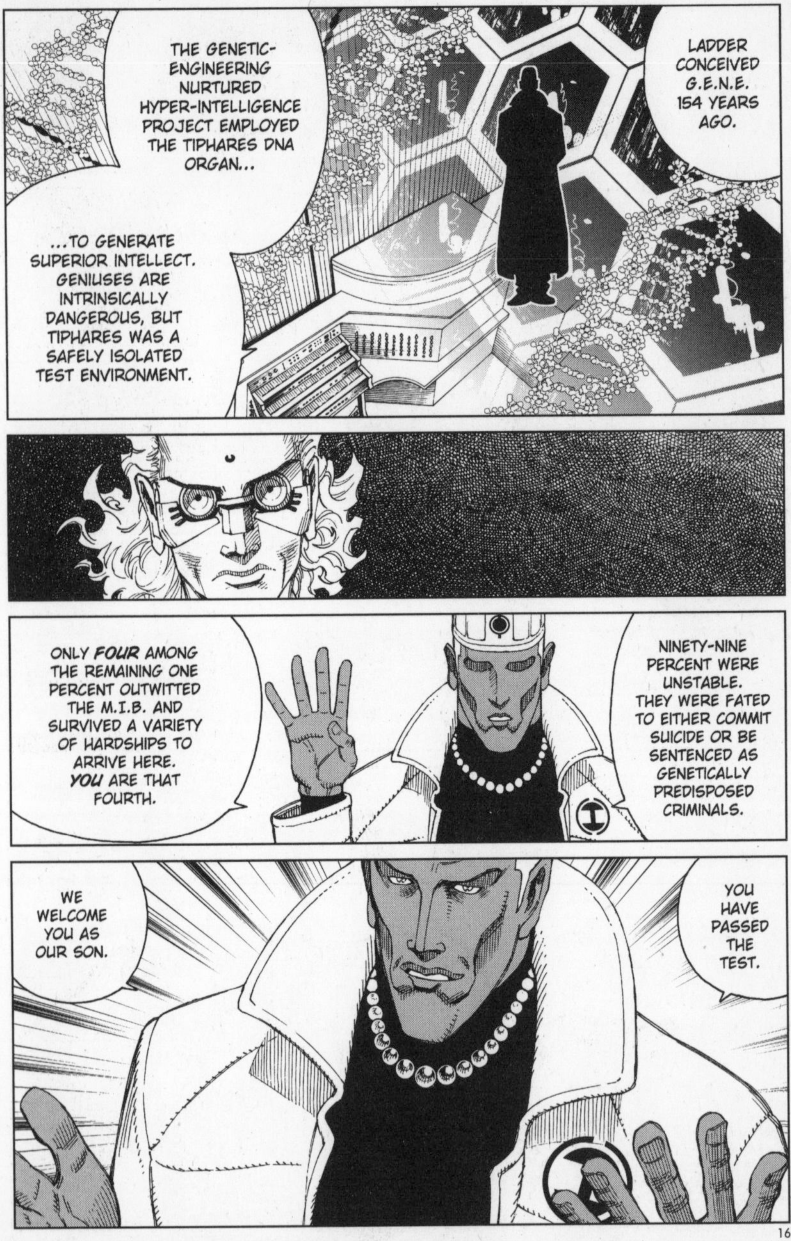
LADDER CONCEIVED G.E.N.E. 154 YEARS AGO.
THE GENETIC-ENGINEERING NURTURED HYPER-INTELLIGENCE PROJECT EMPLOYED THE TIPHARES DNA ORGAN...
...TO GENERATE SUPERIOR INTELLECT. GENIUSES ARE INTRINSICALLY DANGEROUS, BUT TIPHARES WAS A SAFELY ISOLATED TEST ENVIRONMENT.
NINETY-NINE PERCENT WERE UNSTABLE. THEY WERE FATED TO EITHER COMMIT SUICIDE OR BE SENTENCED AS GENETICALLY PREDISPOSED CRIMINALS.
ONLY FOUR AMONG THE REMAINING ONE PERCENT OUTWITTED THE M.I.B. AND SURVIVED A VARIETY OF HARDSHIPS TO ARRIVE HERE. YOU ARE THAT FOURTH.
YOU HAVE PASSED THE TEST.
WE WELCOME YOU AS OUR SON.

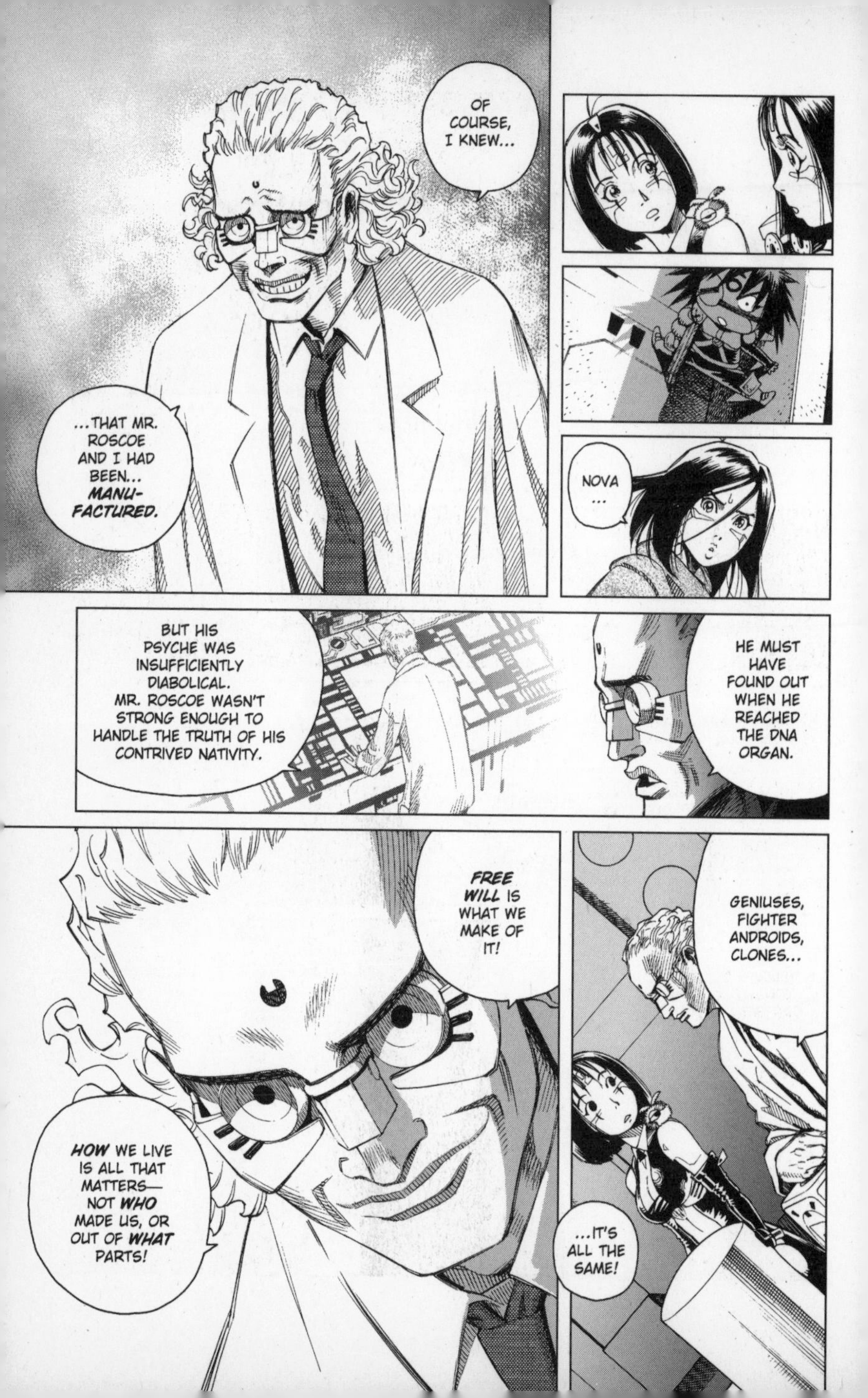
NOVA...
OF COURSE, I KNEW...
...THAT MR. ROSCOE AND I HAD BEEN... MANUFACTURED.
HE MUST HAVE FOUND OUT WHEN HE REACHED THE DNA ORGAN.
BUT HIS PSYCHE WAS INSUFFICIENTLY DIABOLICAL. MR. ROSCOE WASN'T STRONG ENOUGH TO HANDLE THE TRUTH OF HIS CONTRIVED NATIVITY.
GENIUSES, FIGHTER ANDROIDS, CLONES...
...IT'S ALL THE SAME!
FREE WILL IS WHAT WE MAKE OF IT!
HOW WE LIVE IS ALL THAT MATTERS— NOT WHO MADE US, OR OUT OF WHAT PARTS!

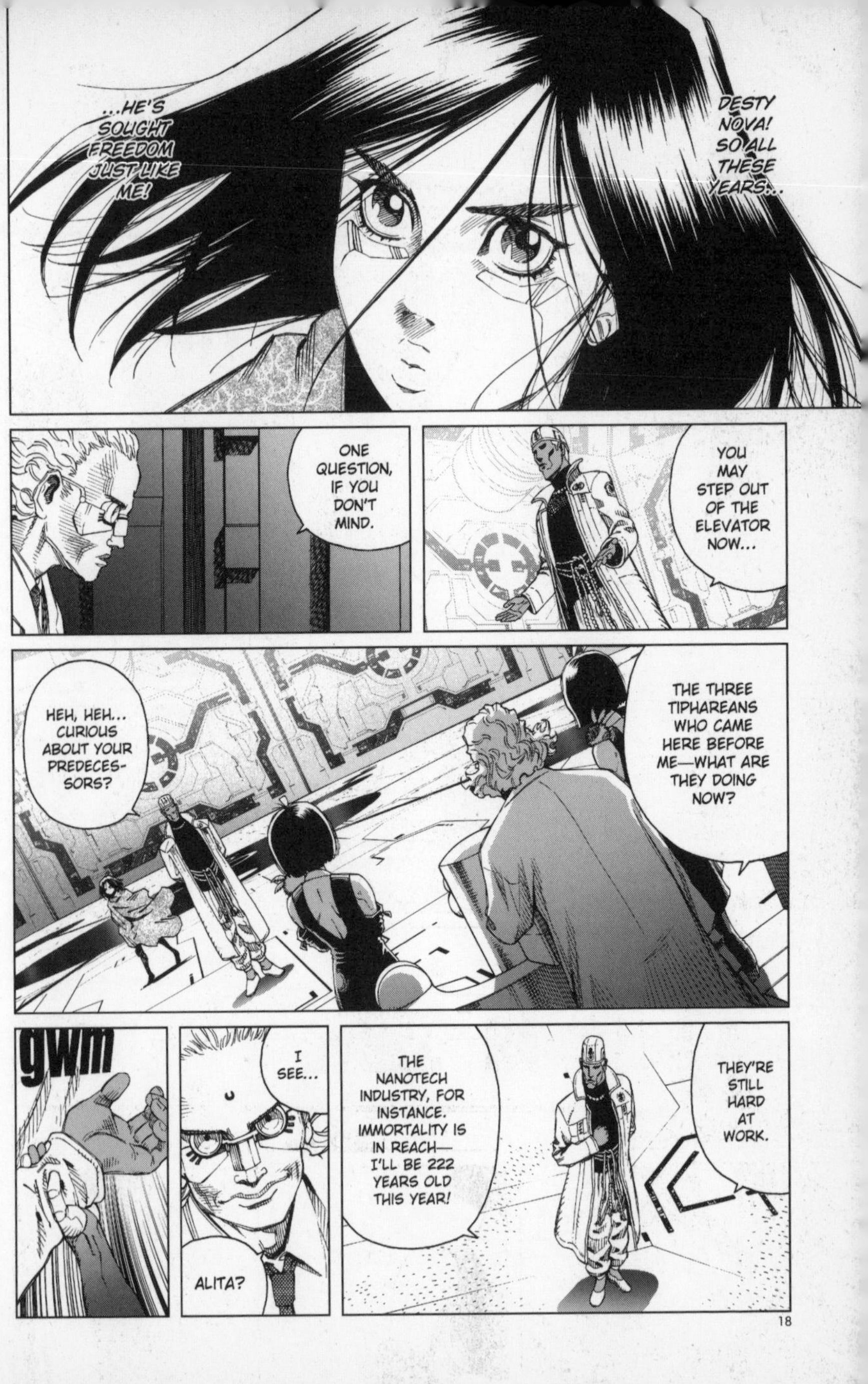
DESTY NOVA! SO ALL THESE YEARS...
...HE'S SOUGHT FREEDOM JUST LIKE ME!
YOU MAY STEP OUT OF THE ELEVATOR NOW...
ONE QUESTION, IF YOU DON'T MIND.
THE THREE TIPHAREANS WHO CAME HERE BEFORE ME—WHAT ARE THEY DOING NOW?
HEH, HEH... CURIOUS ABOUT YOUR PREDECES-SORS?
THEY'RE STILL HARD AT WORK.
THE NANOTECH INDUSTRY, FOR INSTANCE. IMMORTALITY IS IN REACH—I'LL BE 222 YEARS OLD THIS YEAR!
I SEE...
ALITA?
gwm

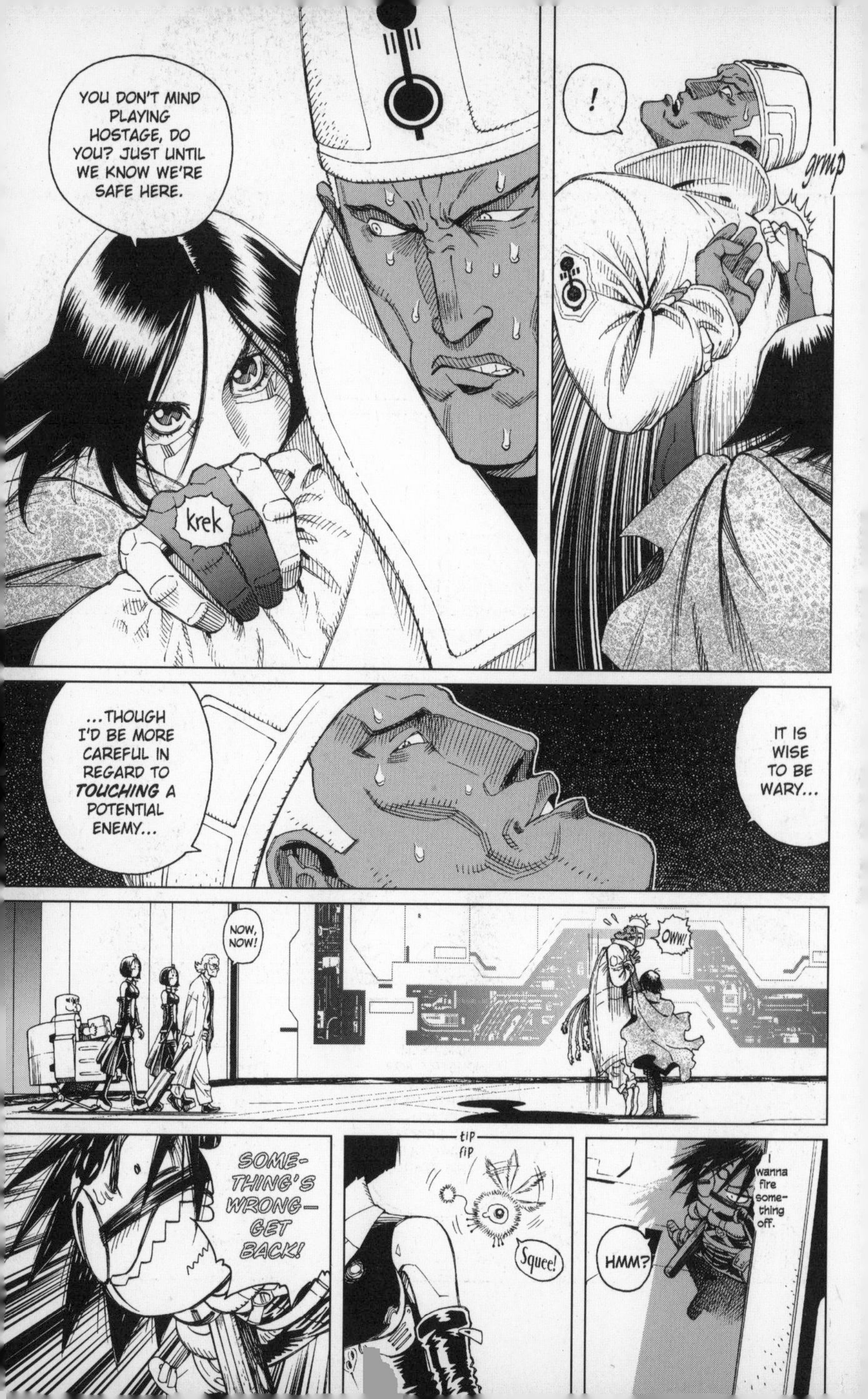
!
grmp
YOU DON'T MIND PLAYING HOSTAGE, DO YOU? JUST UNTIL WE KNOW WE'RE SAFE HERE.
krek
IT IS WISE TO BE WARY...
...THOUGH I'D BE MORE CAREFUL IN REGARD TO *TOUCHING* A POTENTIAL ENEMY...
OWW!
NOW, NOW!
I wanna fire some-thing off.
HMM?
tip tip
Squee!
SOME-THING'S WRONG— GET BACK!

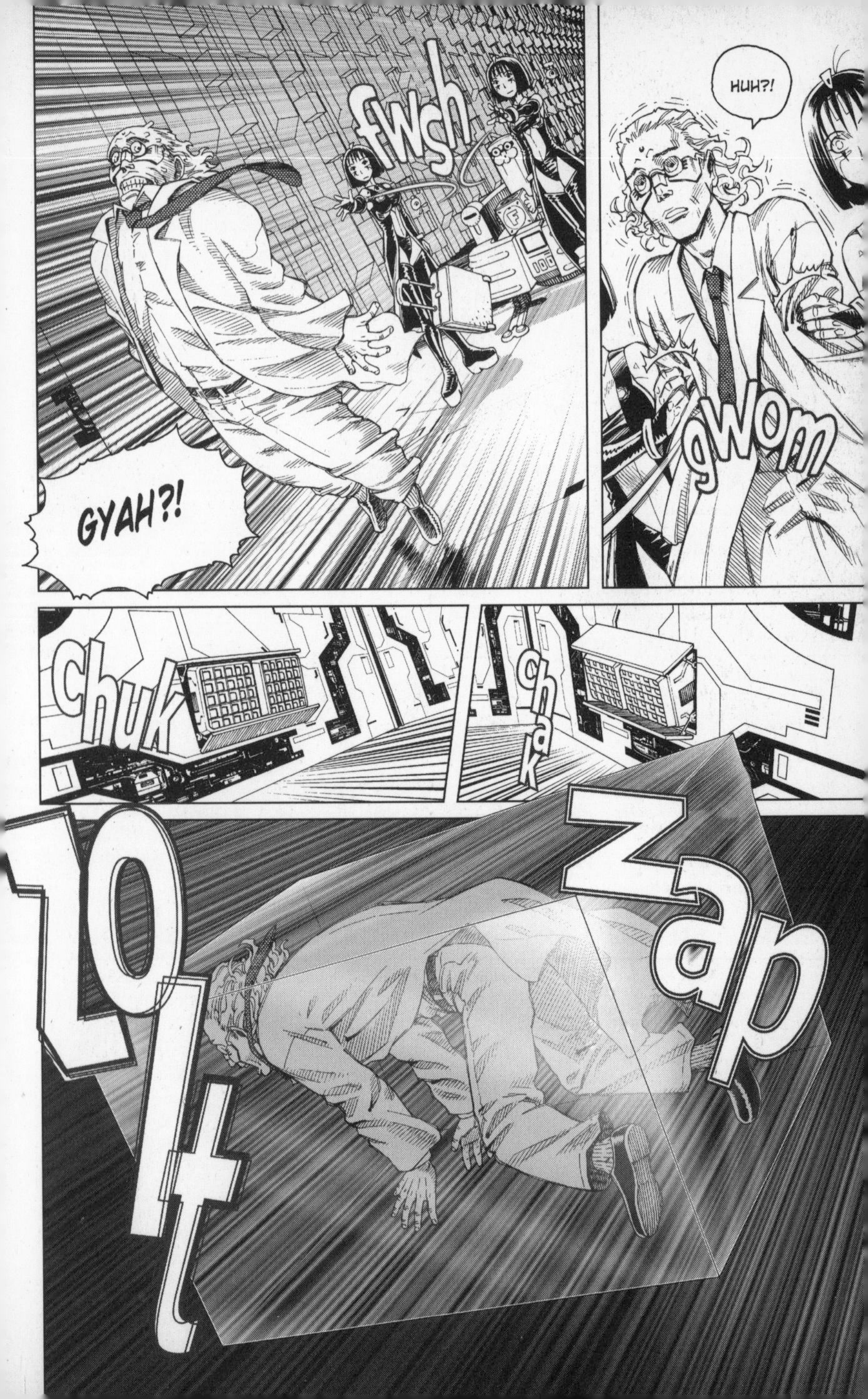
HUH?!
gwom
fwsh
GYAH?!
chak
Chuk
Zap

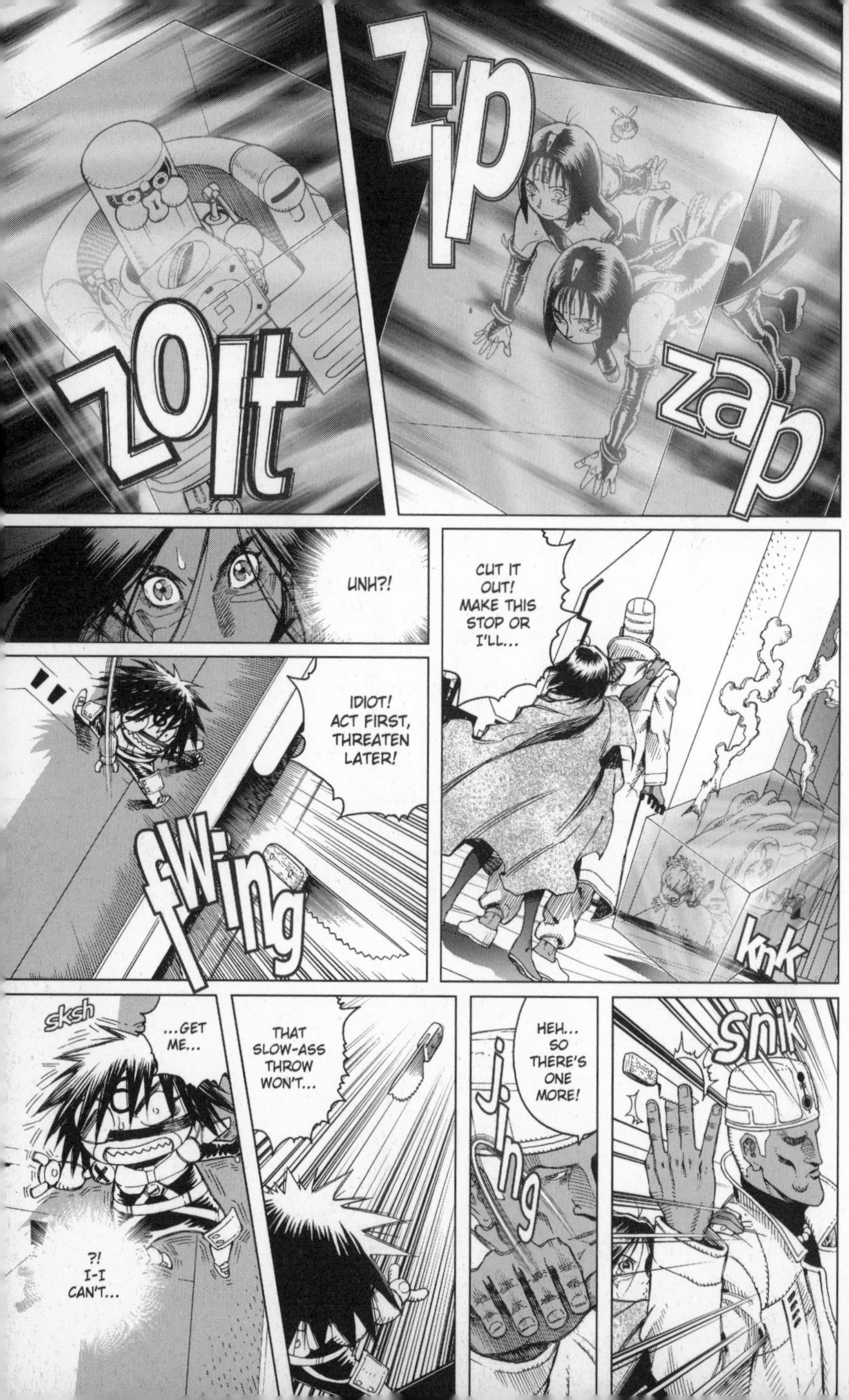
zip
zap
zolt
CUT IT OUT! MAKE THIS STOP OR I'LL...
knk
UNH?!
IDIOT! ACT FIRST, THREATEN LATER!
fwing
snik
HEH... SO THERE'S ONE MORE!
jing
THAT SLOW-ASS THROW WON'T...
sksh
...GET ME...
?! I-I CAN'T...

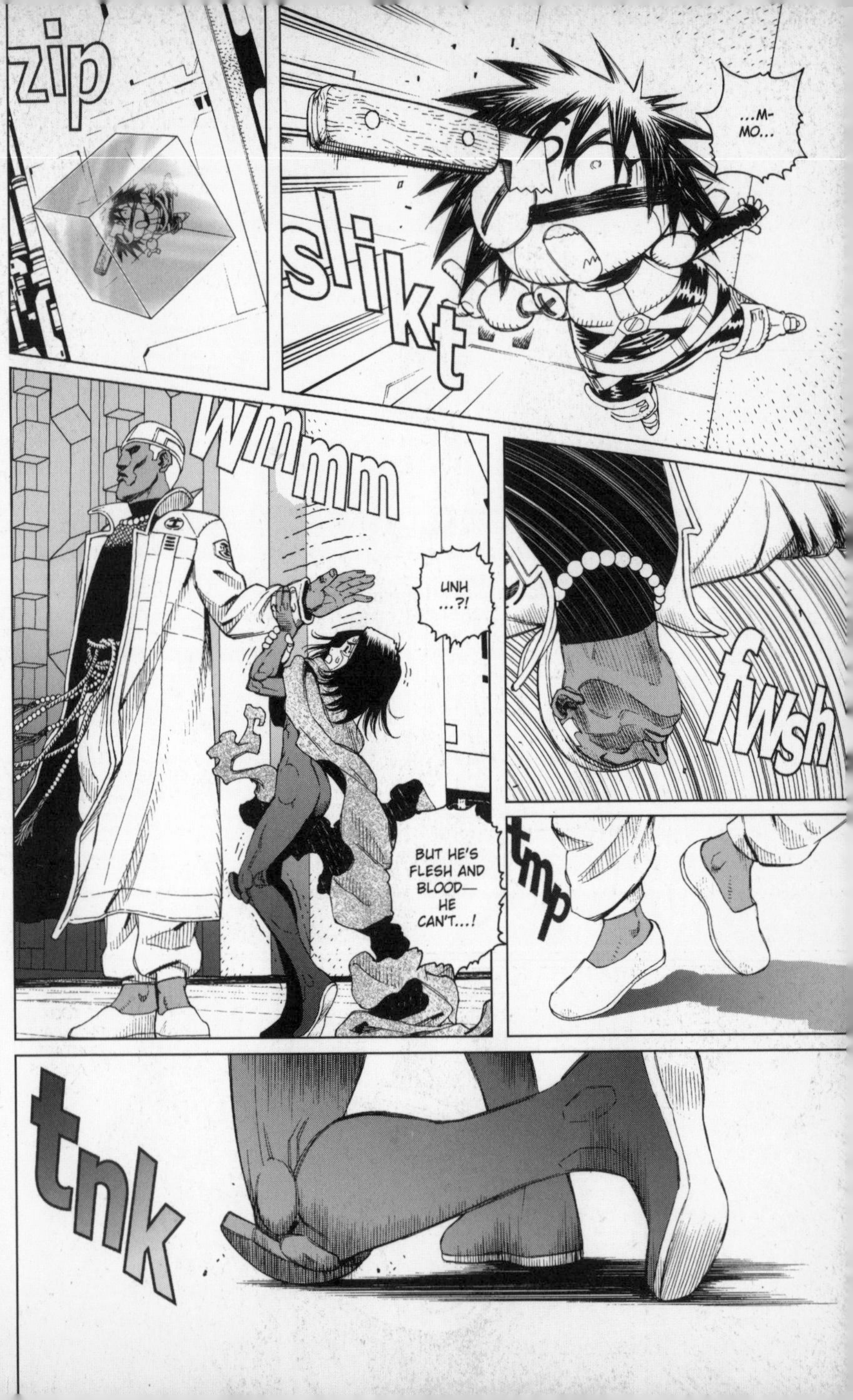
...M-
MO...
slikt
zip
fwsh
tmp
wmmm
UNH
...?!
BUT HE'S FLESH AND BLOOD— HE CAN'T...!
tnk

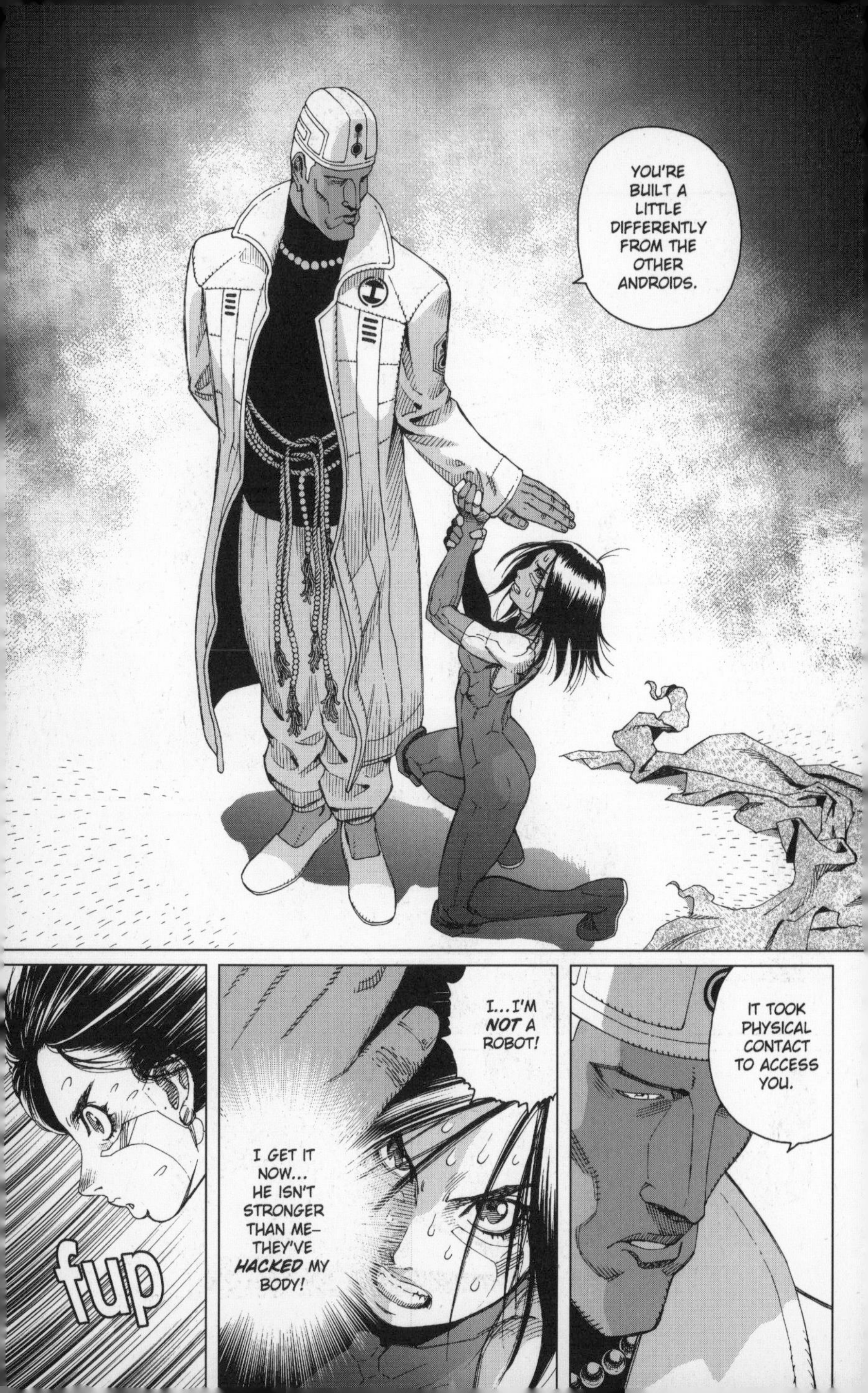
YOU'RE BUILT A LITTLE DIFFERENTLY FROM THE OTHER ANDROIDS.
IT TOOK PHYSICAL CONTACT TO ACCESS YOU.
I...I'M *NOT* A ROBOT!
I GET IT NOW... HE ISN'T STRONGER THAN ME– THEY'VE *HACKED* MY BODY!
fup

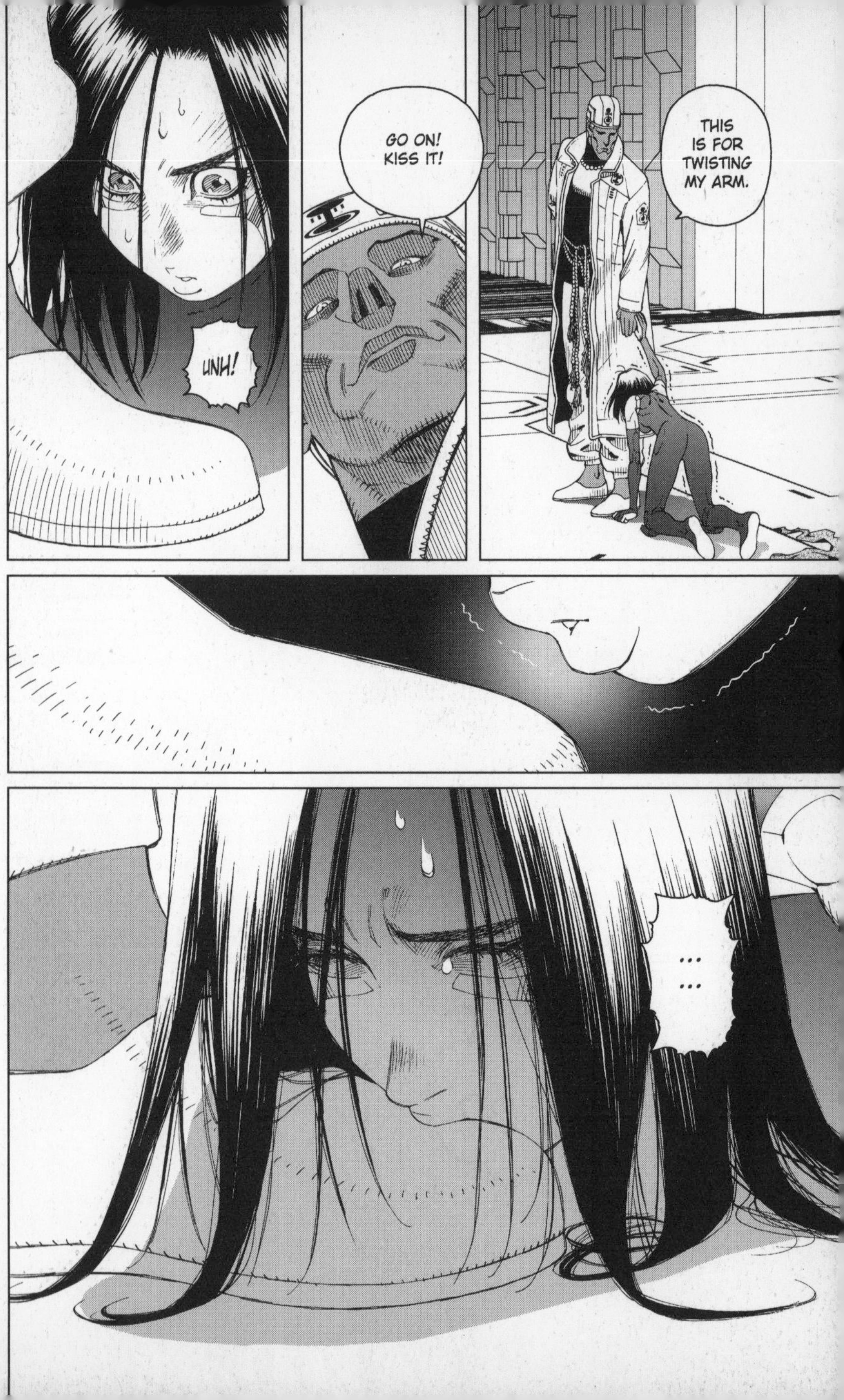
THIS IS FOR TWISTING MY ARM.
GO ON! KISS IT!
UNH!
... ...

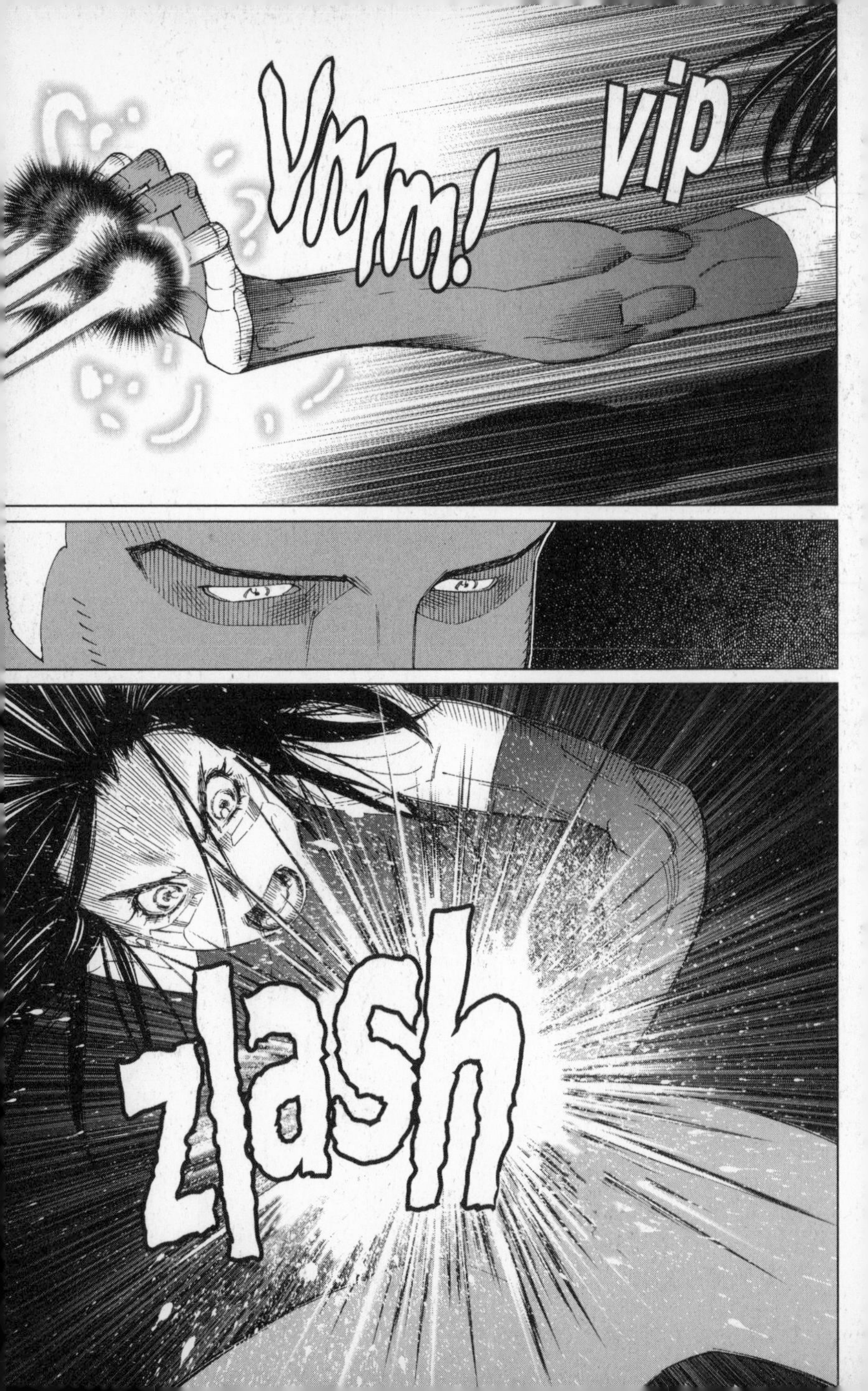

vip
Vmm!
zlash

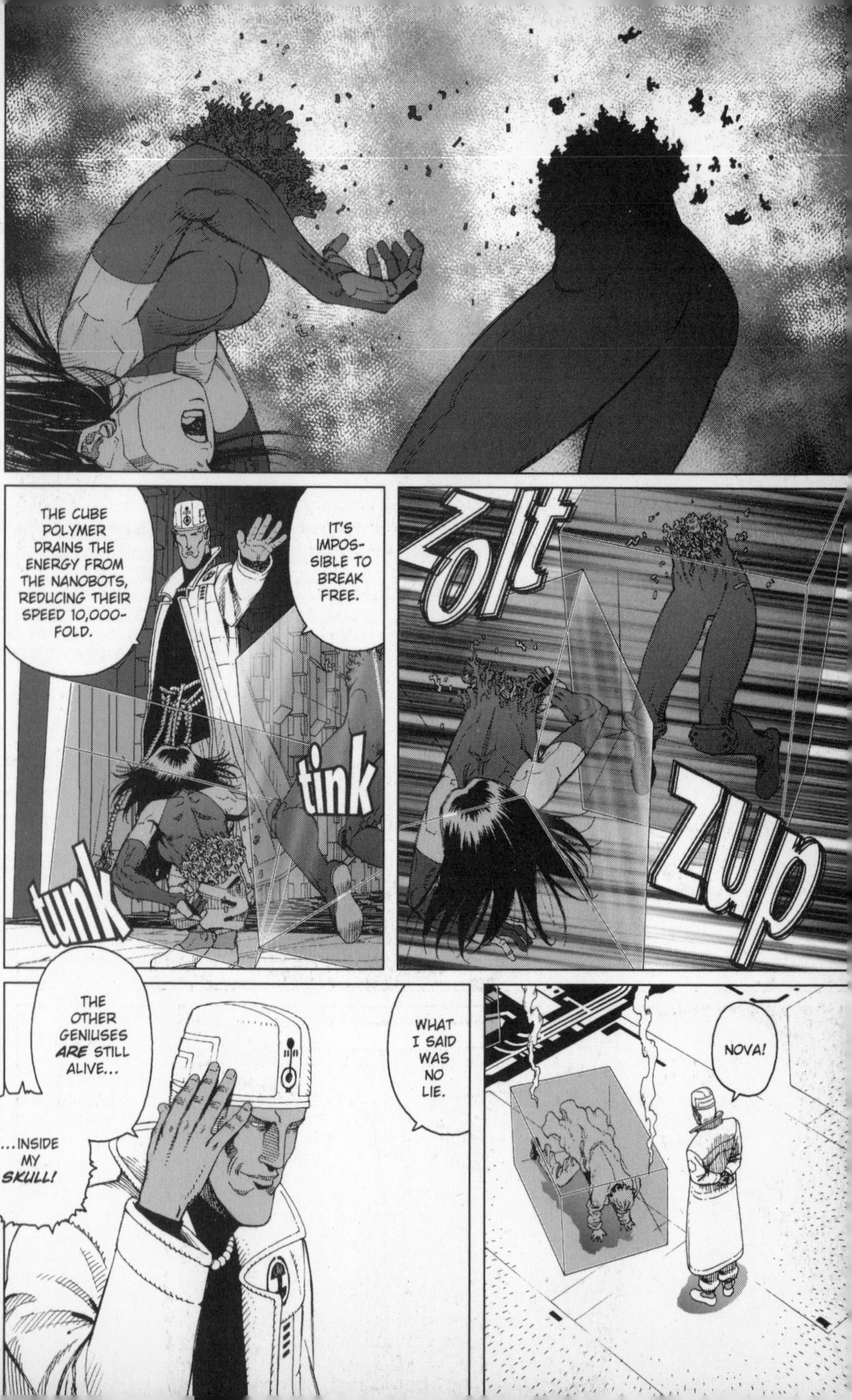
Zolt
ZUP
IT'S IMPOSSIBLE TO BREAK FREE.
THE CUBE POLYMER DRAINS THE ENERGY FROM THE NANOBOTS, REDUCING THEIR SPEED 10,000-FOLD.
tink
tunk
NOVA!
WHAT I SAID WAS NO LIE.
THE OTHER GENIUSES **ARE** STILL ALIVE...
...INSIDE MY **SKULL!**

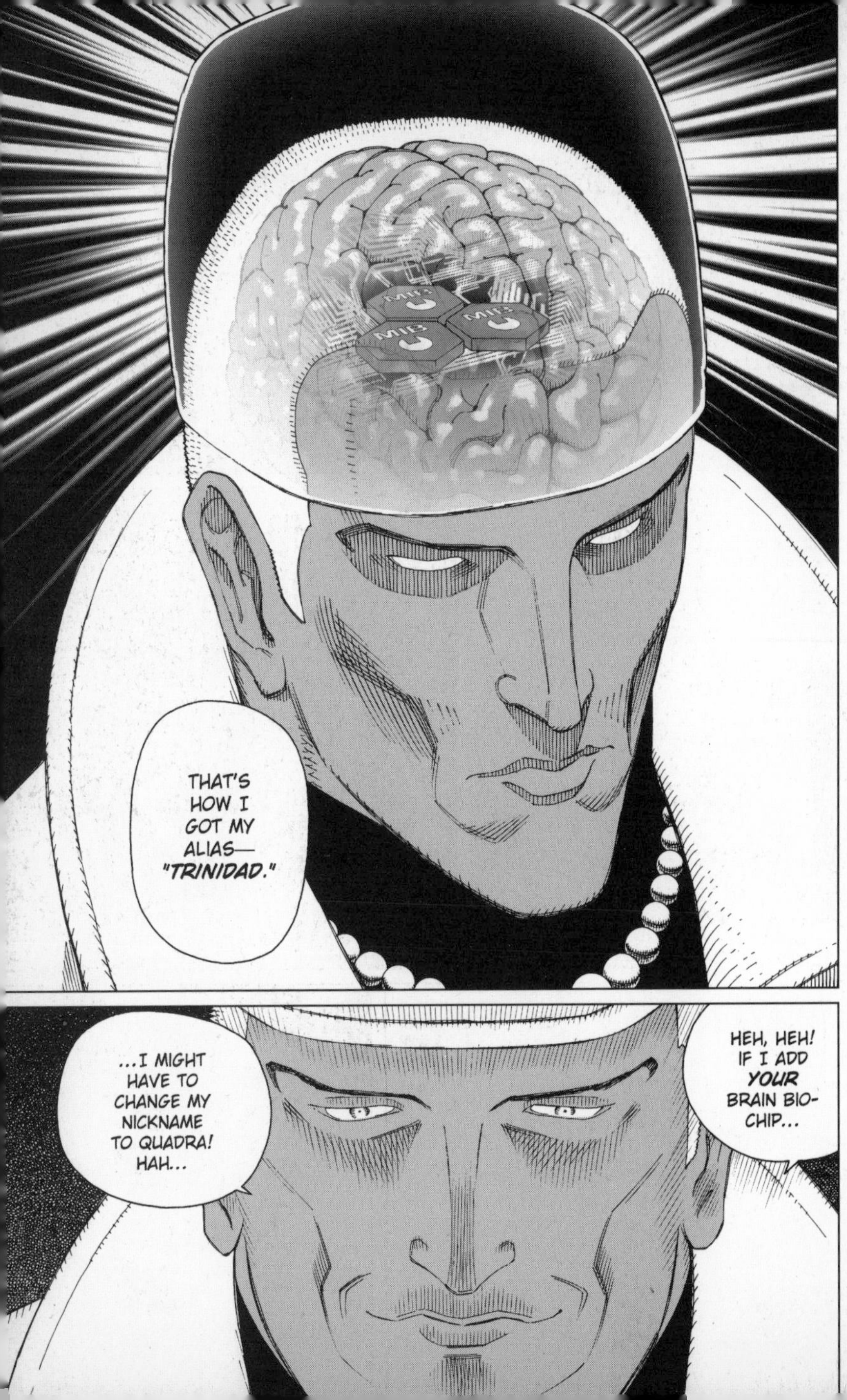
THAT'S HOW I GOT MY ALIAS— "*TRINIDAD.*"
HEH, HEH! IF I ADD *YOUR* BRAIN BIO-CHIP...
...I MIGHT HAVE TO CHANGE MY NICKNAME TO QUADRA! HAH...

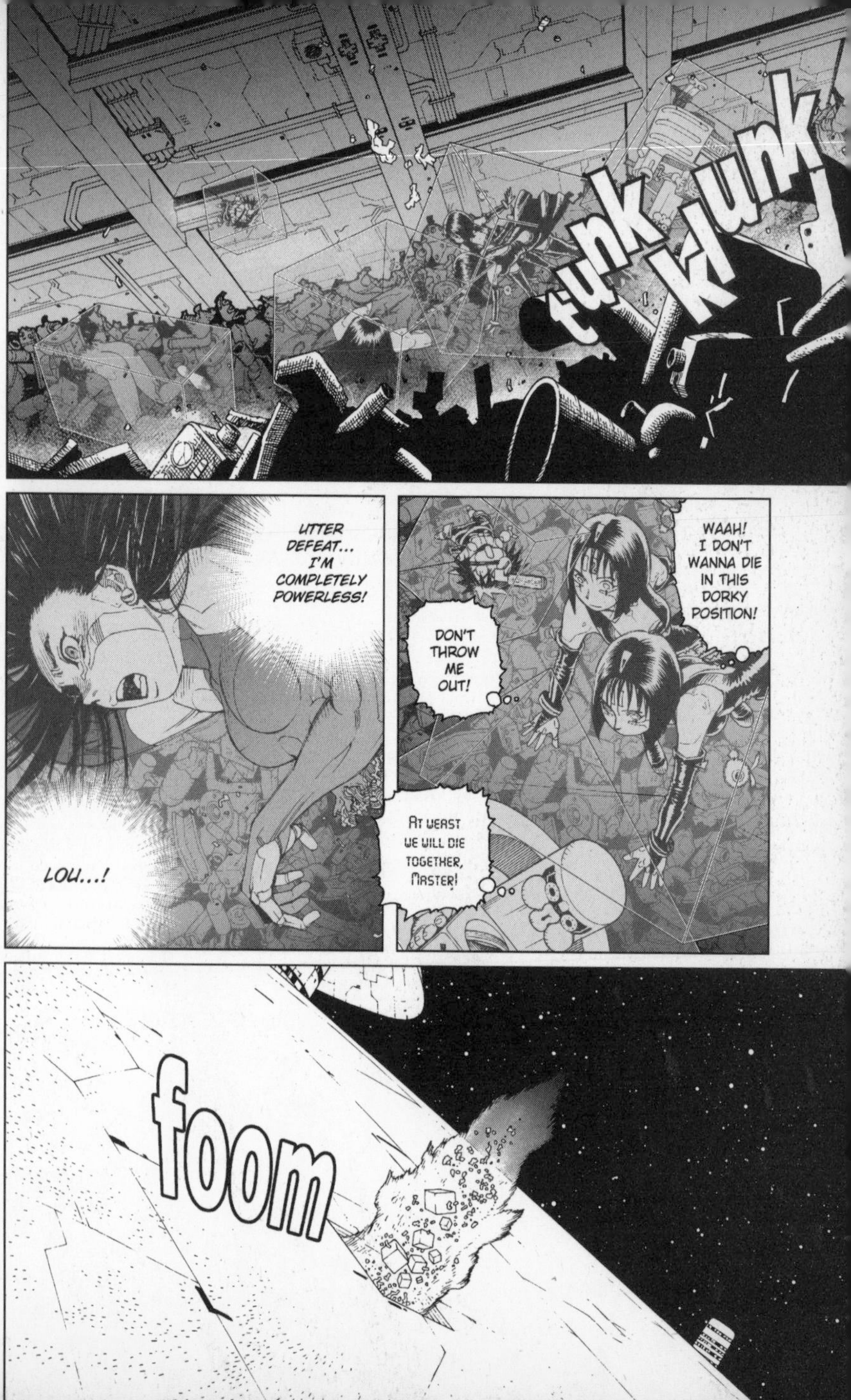
klunk
tunk
WAAH! I DON'T WANNA DIE IN THIS DORKY POSITION!
DON'T THROW ME OUT!
At weast we will die together, Master!
UTTER DEFEAT... I'M COMPLETELY POWERLESS!
LOU...!
foom

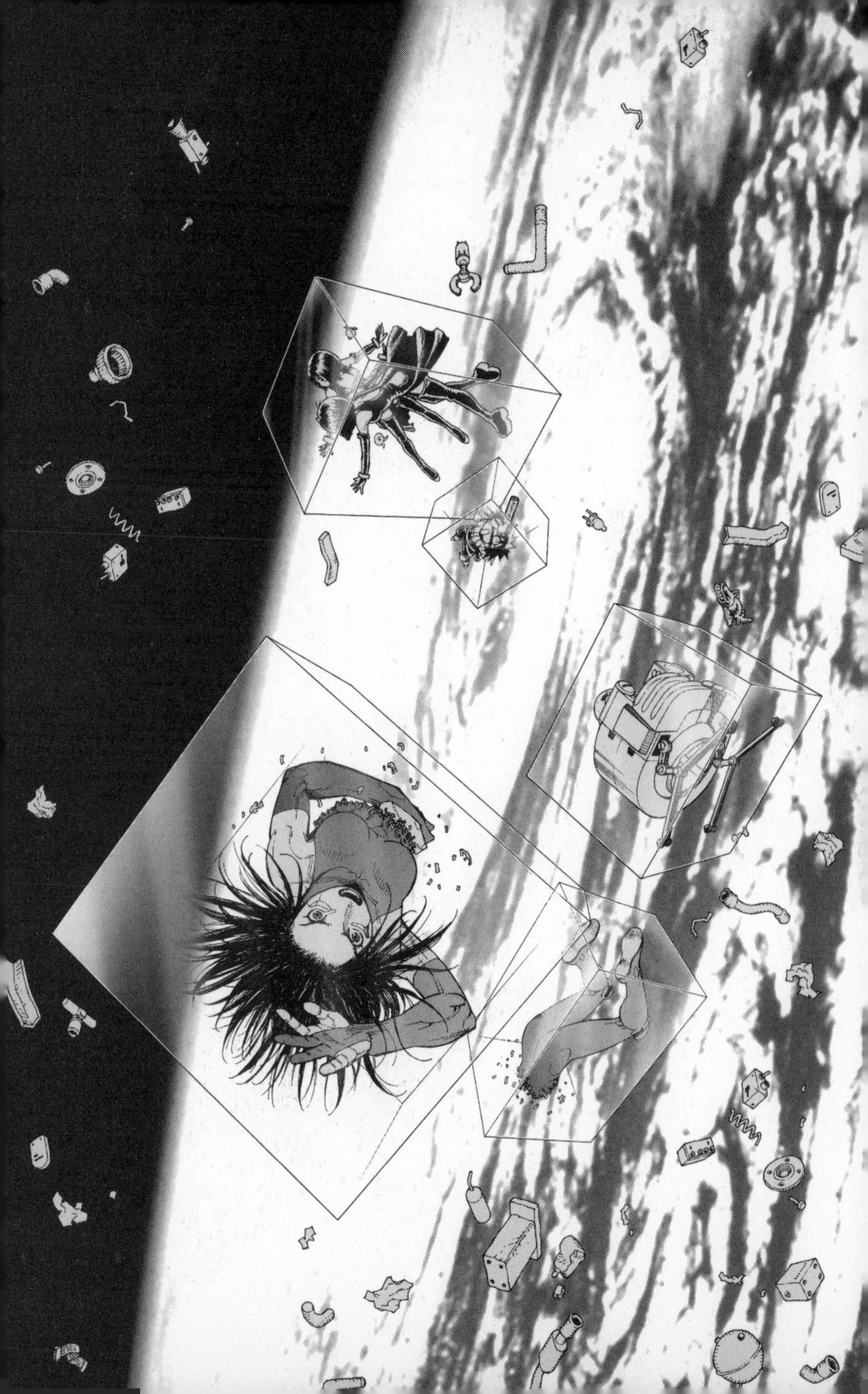

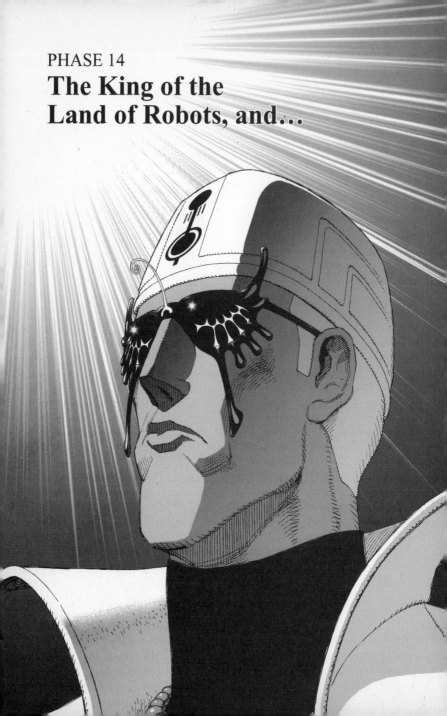

PHASE 14

The King of the Land of Robots, and...

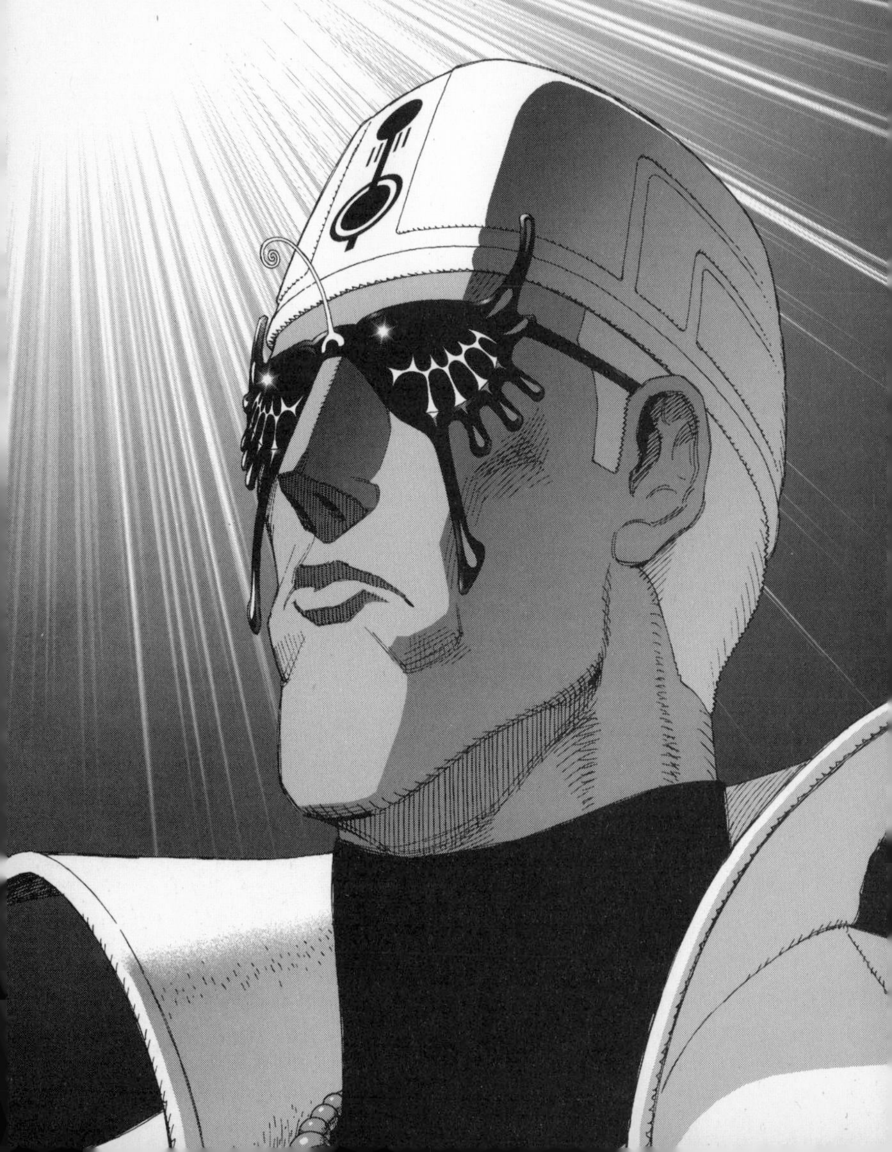

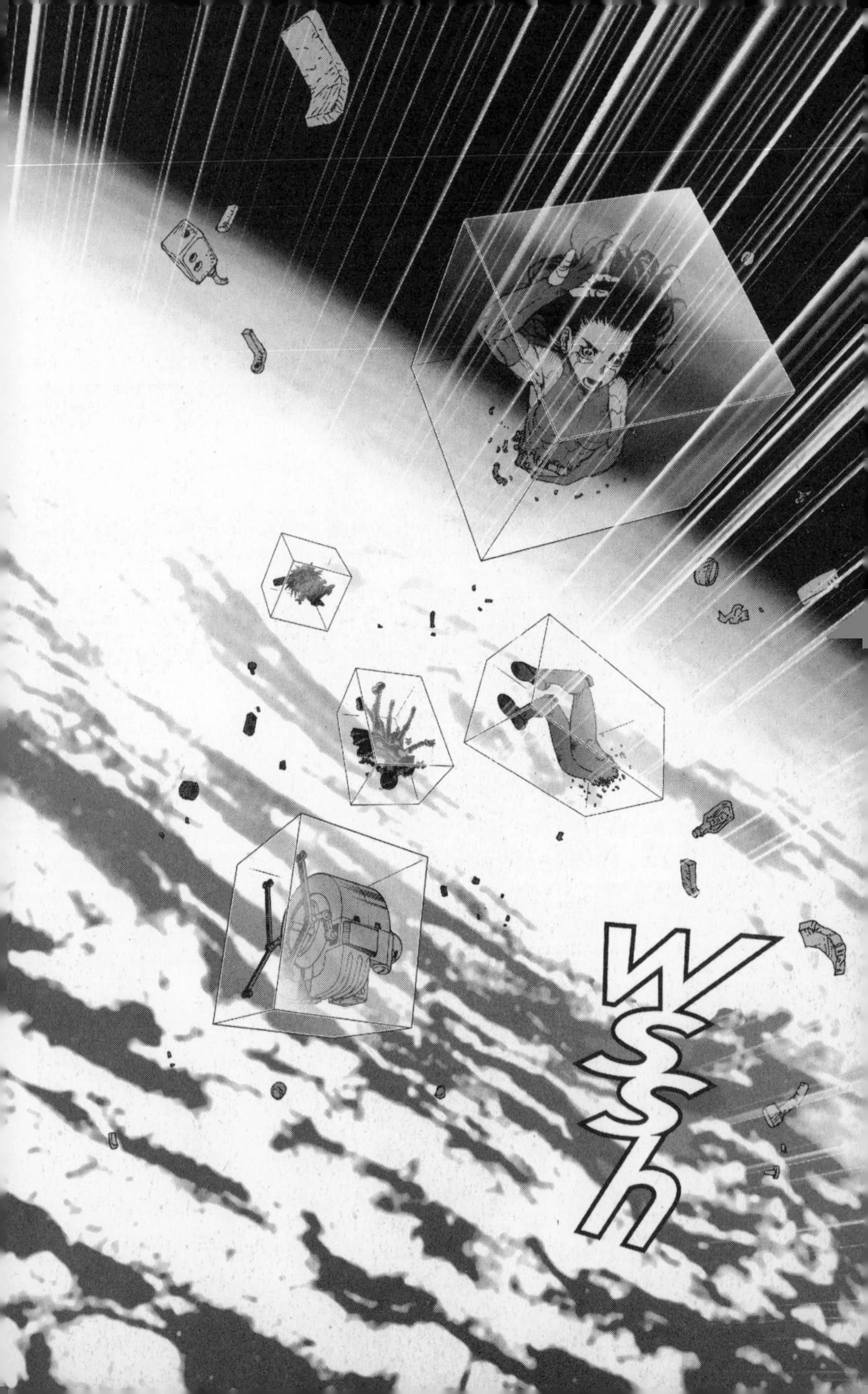
WSSH

DAMN! IT'S NO USE... I CAN'T EVEN PRODUCE PLASMA!

ATMOSPHERIC FRICTION WILL INCINERATE US! IF I CAN JUST—

...FAMILIAR SOMEHOW...

I... THIS FEELS...

WAIT!

fwsh

?!

tnk
bonk
klnk
YAY! ♡ WE'RE SAVED!
BUT BY FRIEND... OR FOE?

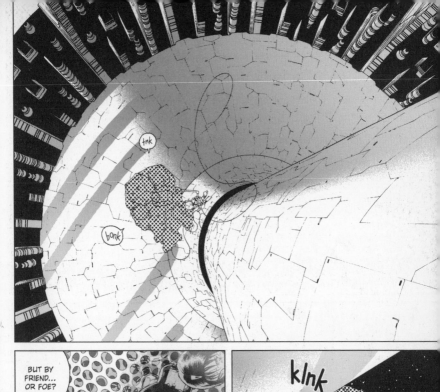

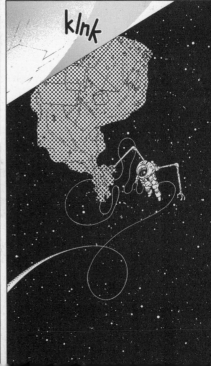

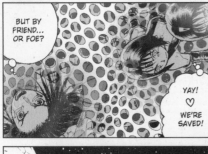

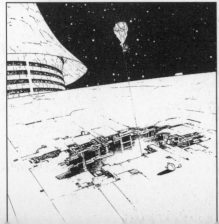

beep!
boop!
SCRAM! OUTTA MY WAY!
beeep!
fwshhh
bip
bip
bip
MOLE-CULAR-LOCK CODE MC 42.
CAN YOU MAKE A KEY, BOSS?
NO PROB'!
PIECE A' CAKE! ♪
baboop

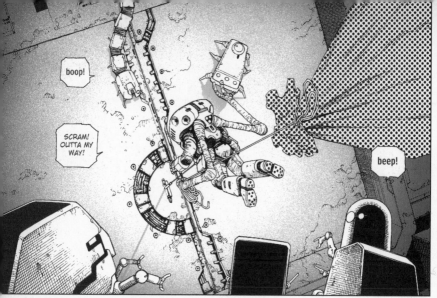

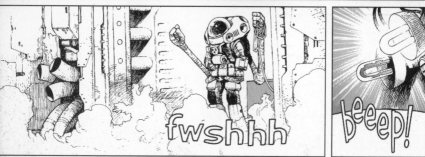

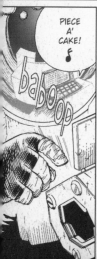

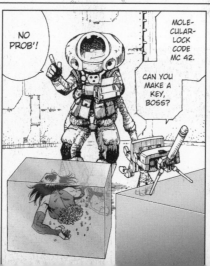

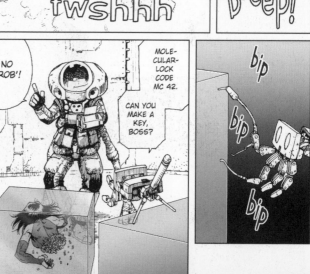

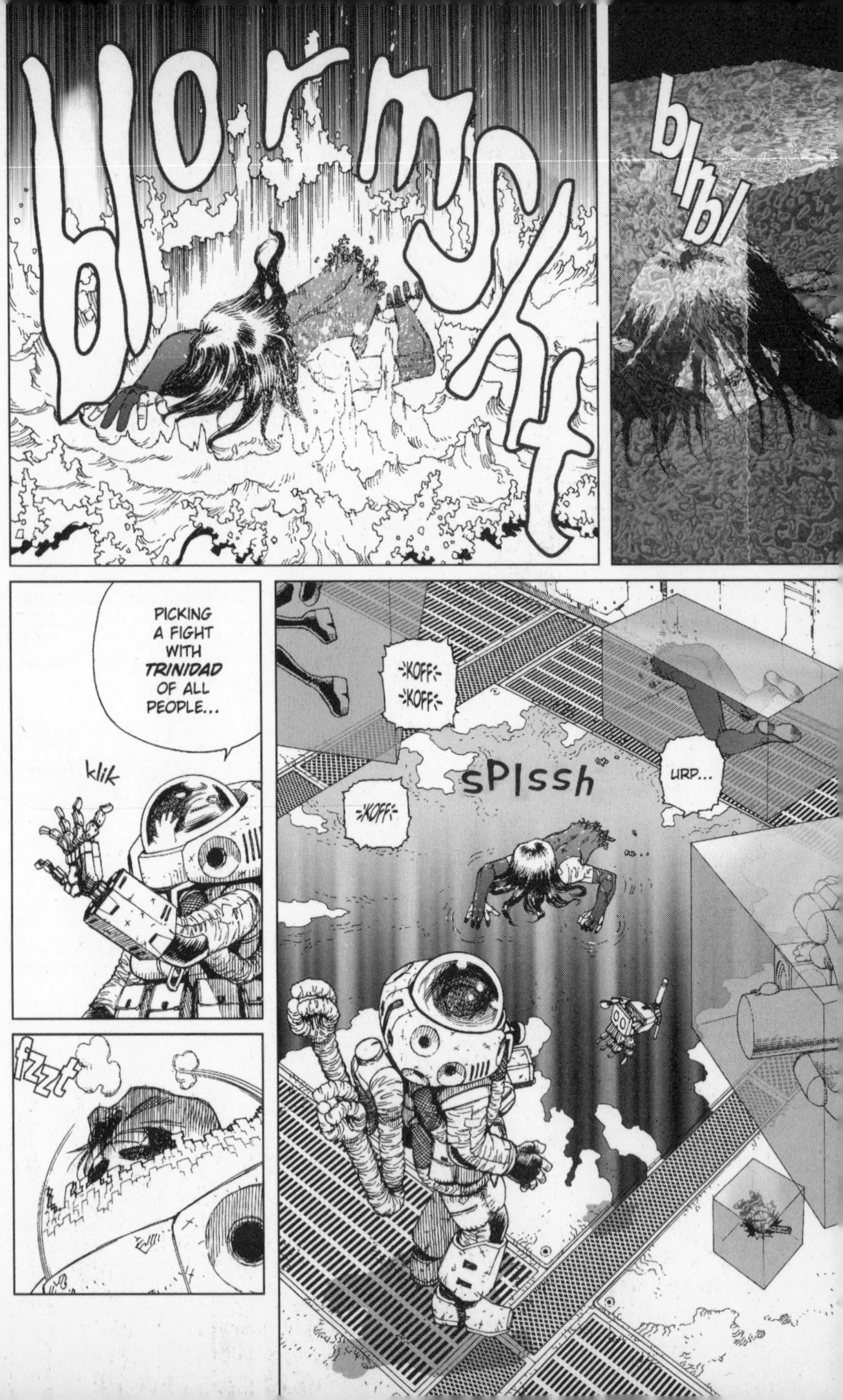
blrbl
blormsht
-KOFF- -KOFF-
URP...
sPlssh
-KOFF-
PICKING A FIGHT WITH *TRINIDAD* OF ALL PEOPLE...
klik
fzzt

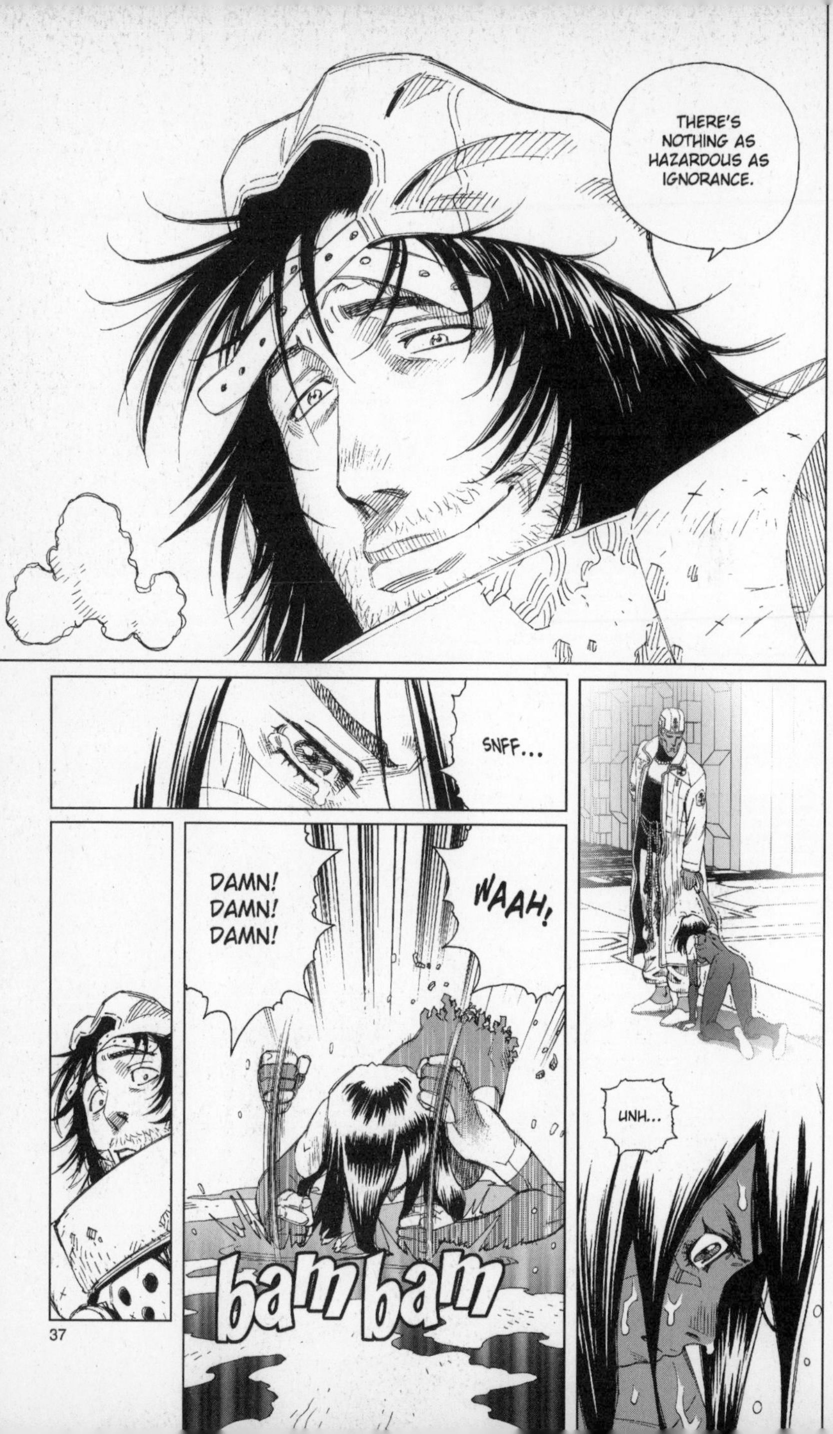
THERE'S NOTHING AS HAZARDOUS AS IGNORANCE.
SNFF...
UNH...
DAMN! DAMN! DAMN!
WAAH!
bam bam

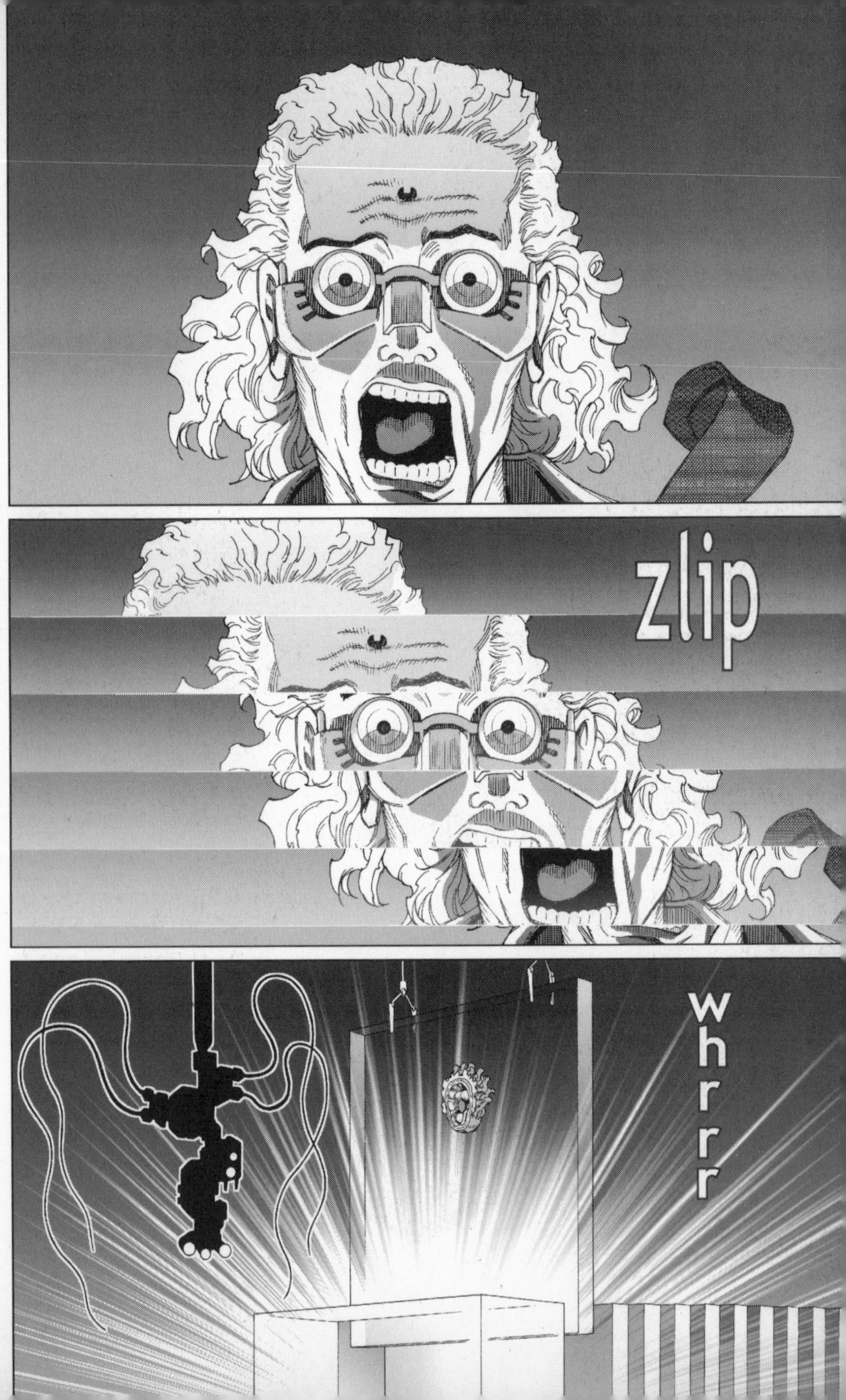
zlip
whrrr

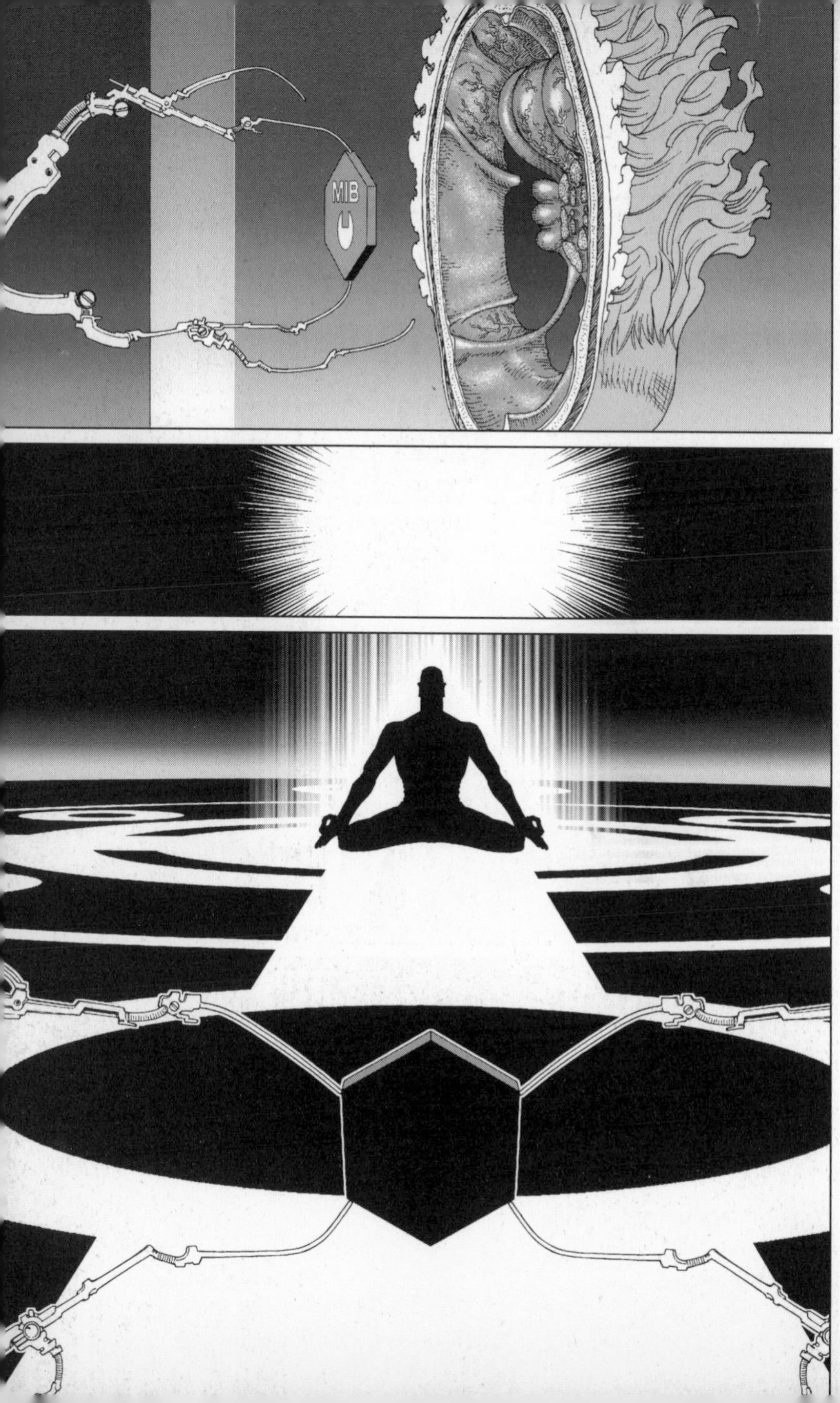
MIB

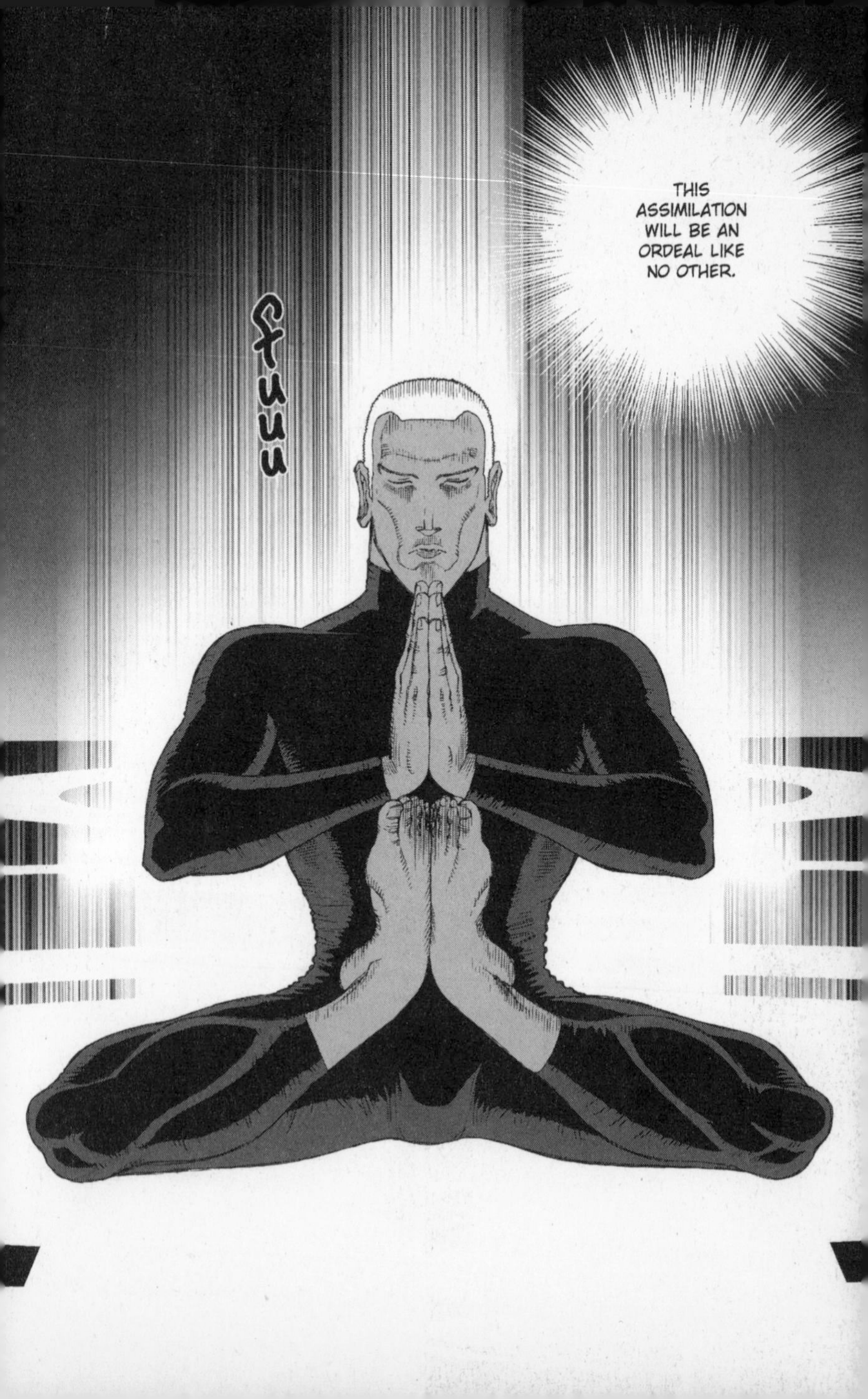
THIS ASSIMILATION WILL BE AN ORDEAL LIKE NO OTHER.
fuuu

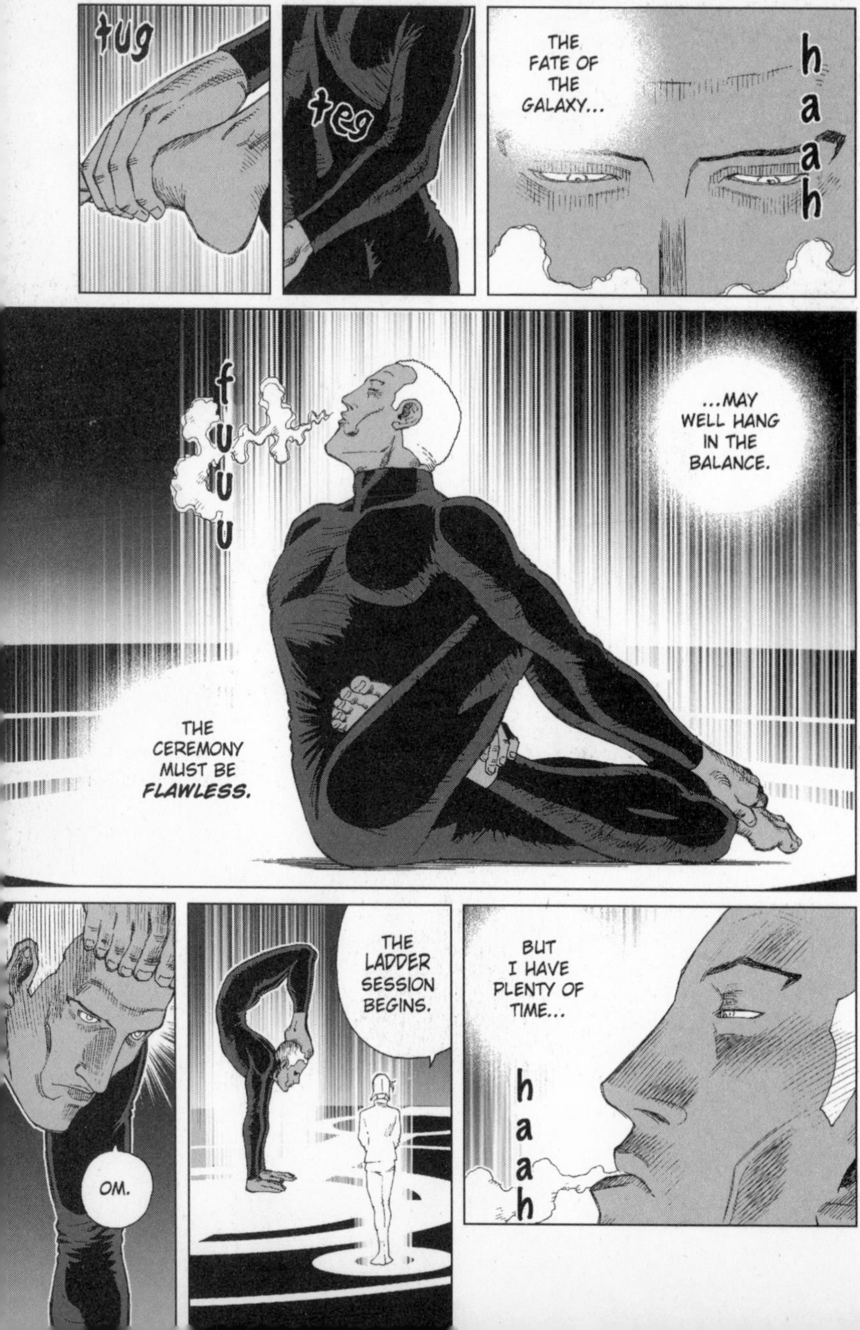
THE FATE OF THE GALAXY...
haah
teg
tug
...MAY WELL HANG IN THE BALANCE.
fuuuu
THE CEREMONY MUST BE *FLAWLESS.*
BUT I HAVE PLENTY OF TIME...
haah
THE LADDER SESSION BEGINS.
OM.

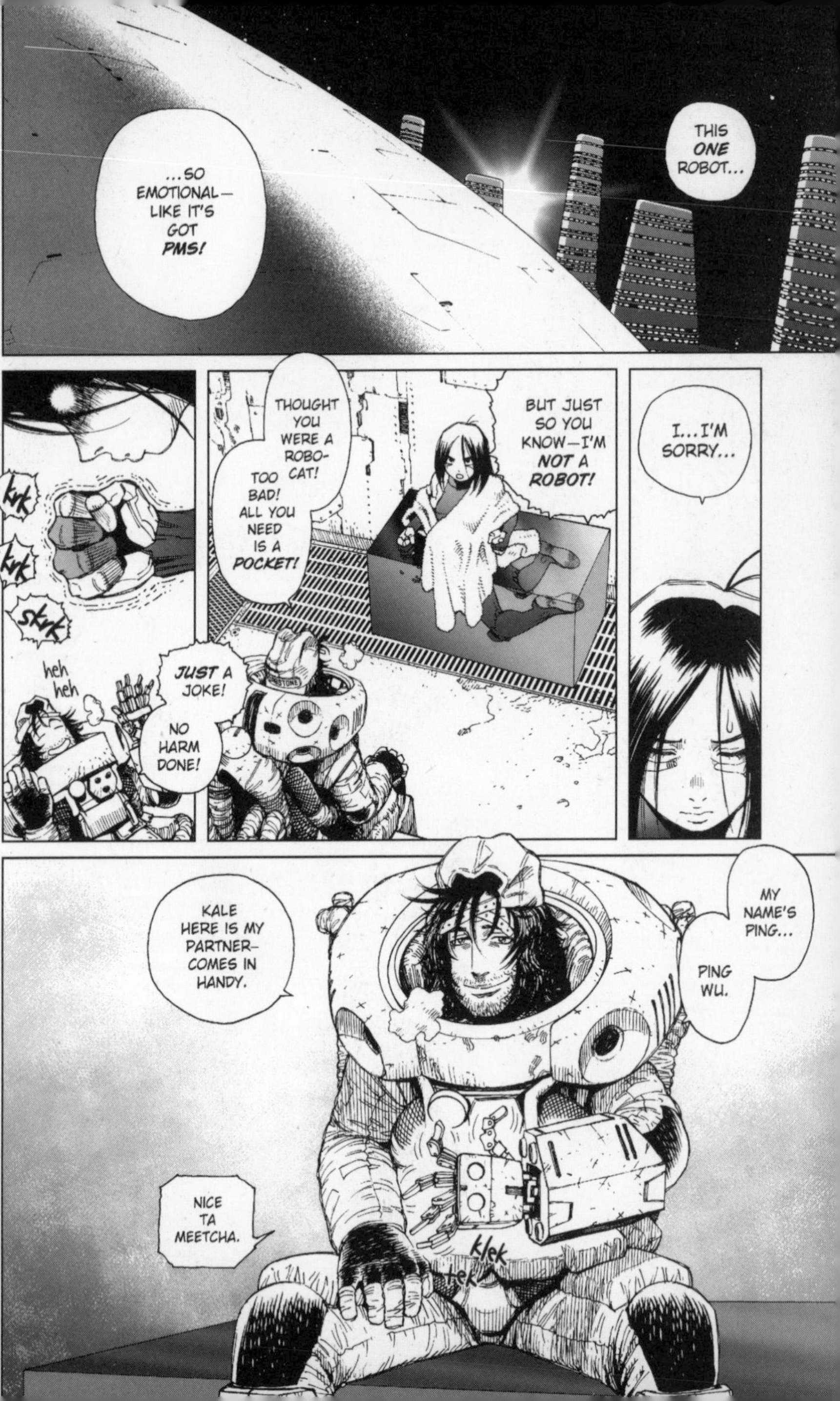
THIS ONE ROBOT...
...SO EMOTIONAL—LIKE IT'S GOT PMS!
I...I'M SORRY...
BUT JUST SO YOU KNOW—I'M NOT A ROBOT!
THOUGHT YOU WERE A ROBO-CAT!
TOO BAD! ALL YOU NEED IS A POCKET!
JUST A JOKE!
NO HARM DONE!
kyk
kyk
skrk
heh heh
MY NAME'S PING...
PING WU.
KALE HERE IS MY PARTNER-COMES IN HANDY.
NICE TA MEETCHA.
klek
tek

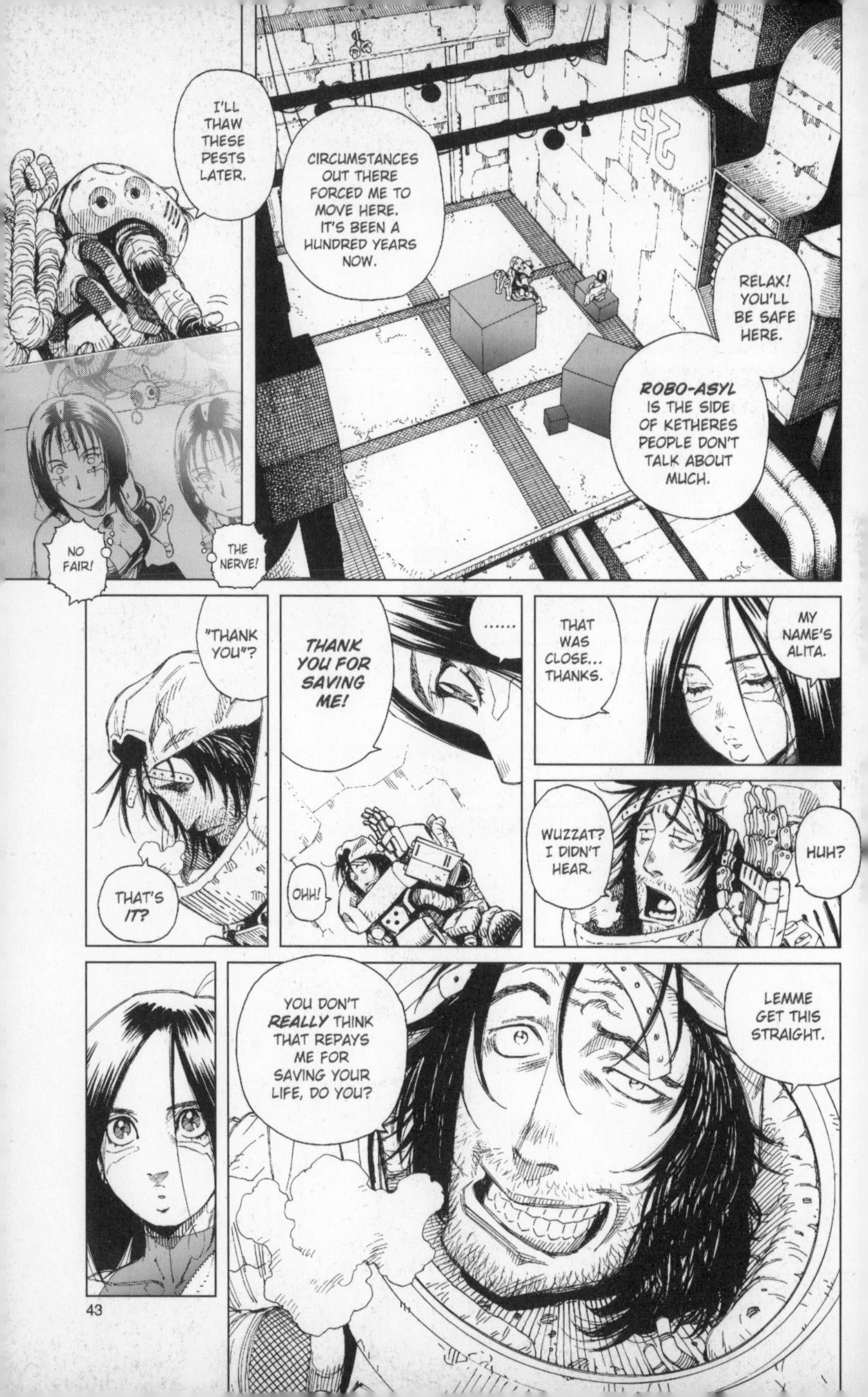
RELAX! YOU'LL BE SAFE HERE.
ROBO-ASYL IS THE SIDE OF KETHERES PEOPLE DON'T TALK ABOUT MUCH.
CIRCUMSTANCES OUT THERE FORCED ME TO MOVE HERE. IT'S BEEN A HUNDRED YEARS NOW.
I'LL THAW THESE PESTS LATER.
THE NERVE!
NO FAIR!
MY NAME'S ALITA.
THAT WAS CLOSE... THANKS.
HUH?
WUZZAT? I DIDN'T HEAR.
......
THANK YOU FOR SAVING ME!
OHH!
"THANK YOU"?
THAT'S *IT?*
LEMME GET THIS STRAIGHT.
YOU DON'T *REALLY* THINK THAT REPAYS ME FOR SAVING YOUR LIFE, DO YOU?

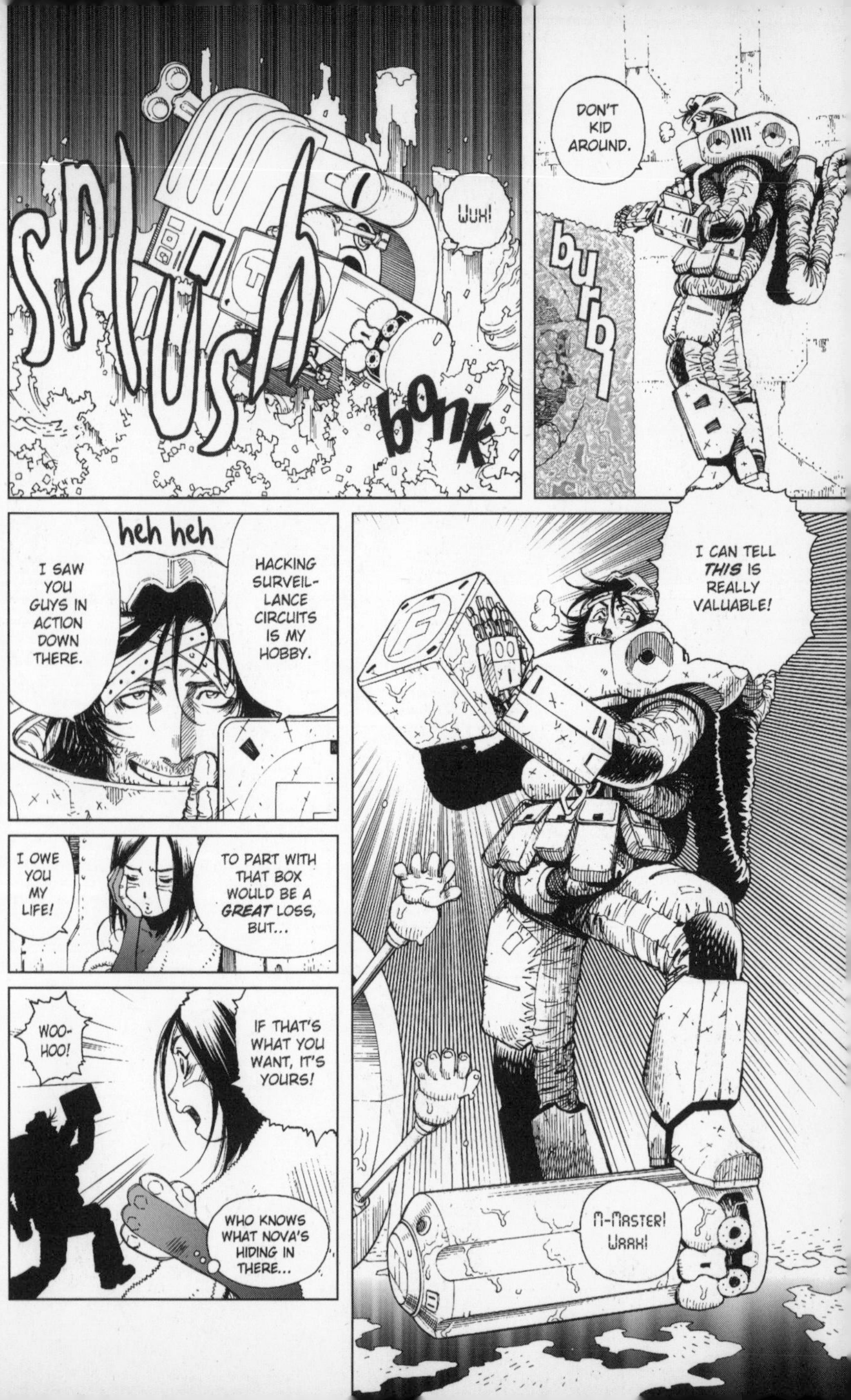
DON'T KID AROUND.
burp
WUH!
splush
bonk
I CAN TELL *THIS* IS REALLY VALUABLE!
M-MASTER! WAAH!
heh heh
HACKING SURVEIL-LANCE CIRCUITS IS MY HOBBY.
I SAW YOU GUYS IN ACTION DOWN THERE.
TO PART WITH THAT BOX WOULD BE A *GREAT* LOSS, BUT...
I OWE YOU MY LIFE!
IF THAT'S WHAT YOU WANT, IT'S YOURS!
WOO-HOO!
WHO KNOWS WHAT NOVA'S HIDING IN THERE...

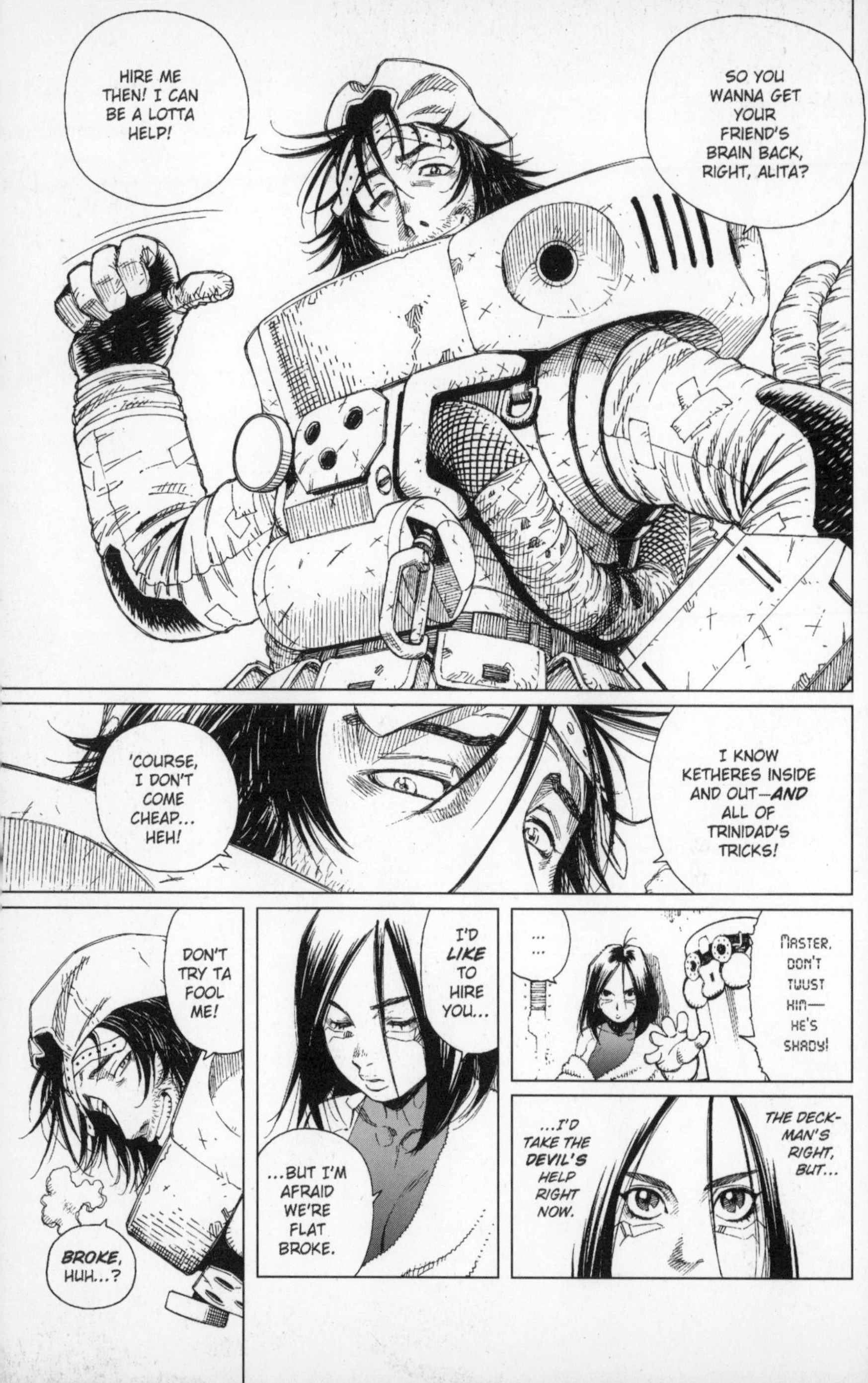
SO YOU WANNA GET YOUR FRIEND'S BRAIN BACK, RIGHT, ALITA?
HIRE ME THEN! I CAN BE A LOTTA HELP!
I KNOW KETHERES INSIDE AND OUT—*AND* ALL OF TRINIDAD'S TRICKS!
'COURSE, I DON'T COME CHEAP... HEH!
MASTER, DON'T TWUST HIM—HE'S SHADY!
... ...
THE DECK-MAN'S RIGHT, BUT...
...I'D TAKE THE *DEVIL'S* HELP RIGHT NOW.
I'D *LIKE* TO HIRE YOU...
...BUT I'M AFRAID WE'RE FLAT BROKE.
DON'T TRY TA FOOL ME!
BROKE, HUH...?

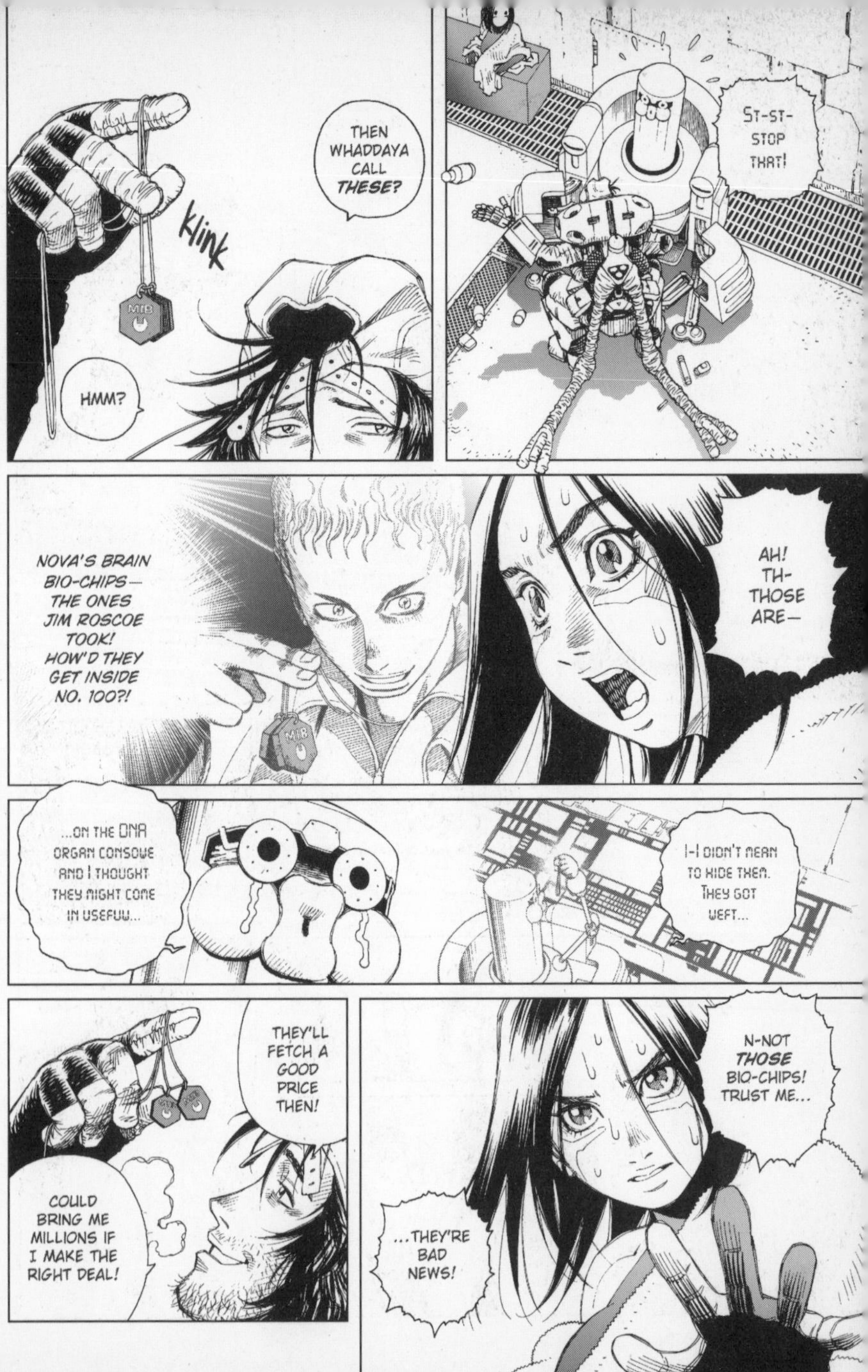
St-st-stop that!
Then whaddaya call *these?*
klink
Hmm?
Ah! Th-those are—
Nova's brain bio-chips— the ones Jim Roscoe took! How'd they get inside No. 100?!
I-I didn't mean to hide them. They got weft...
...on the DNA organ consowe and I thought they might come in usefuw...
N-not *those* bio-chips! Trust me...
...they're bad news!
They'll fetch a good price then!
Could bring me millions if I make the right deal!

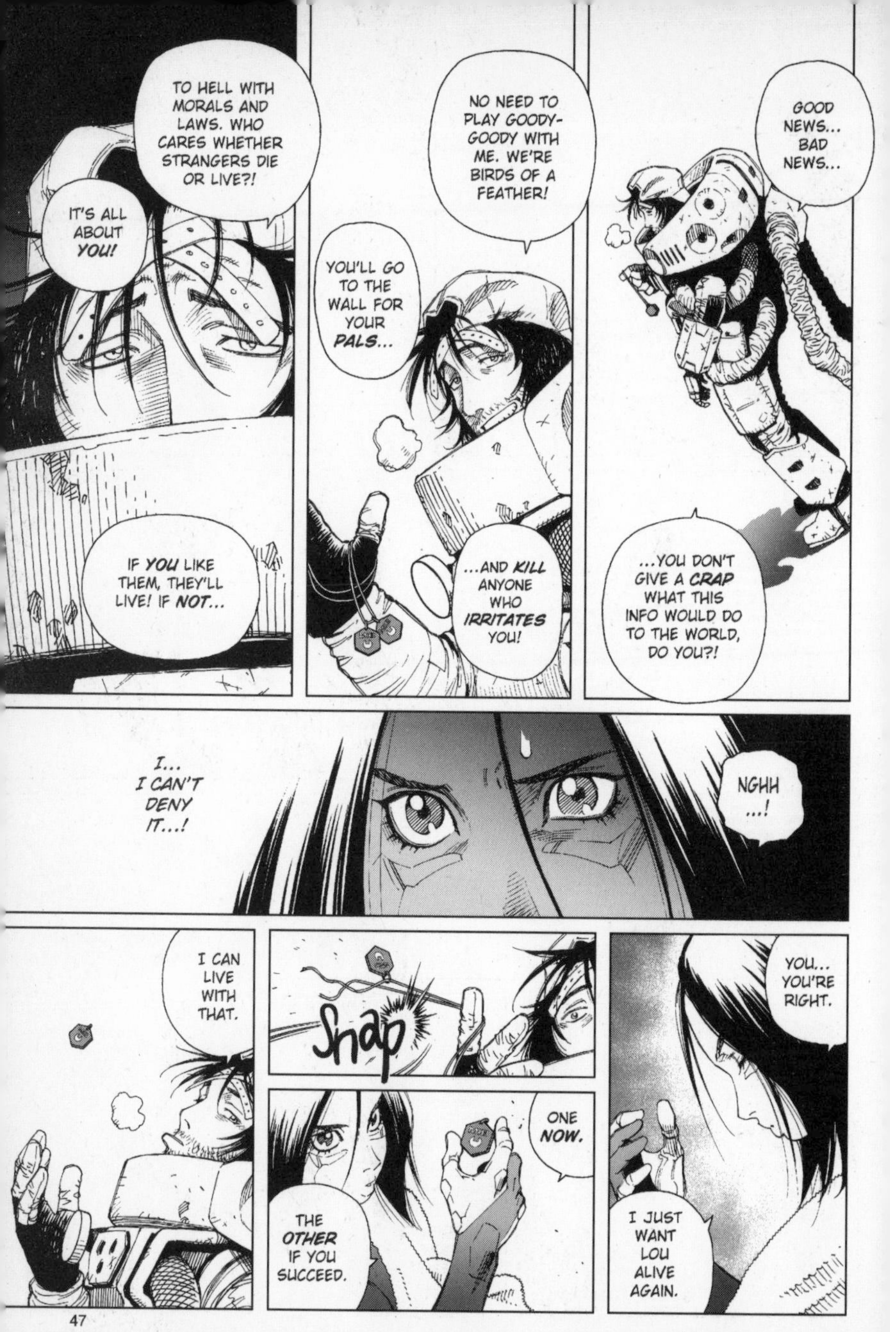
GOOD NEWS... BAD NEWS...
...YOU DON'T GIVE A CRAP WHAT THIS INFO WOULD DO TO THE WORLD, DO YOU?!
NO NEED TO PLAY GOODY-GOODY WITH ME. WE'RE BIRDS OF A FEATHER!
YOU'LL GO TO THE WALL FOR YOUR PALS...
...AND KILL ANYONE WHO IRRITATES YOU!
TO HELL WITH MORALS AND LAWS. WHO CARES WHETHER STRANGERS DIE OR LIVE?!
IT'S ALL ABOUT YOU!
IF YOU LIKE THEM, THEY'LL LIVE! IF NOT...
NGHH ...!
I... I CAN'T DENY IT...!
YOU... YOU'RE RIGHT.
I JUST WANT LOU ALIVE AGAIN.
Snap
ONE NOW.
THE OTHER IF YOU SUCCEED.
I CAN LIVE WITH THAT.

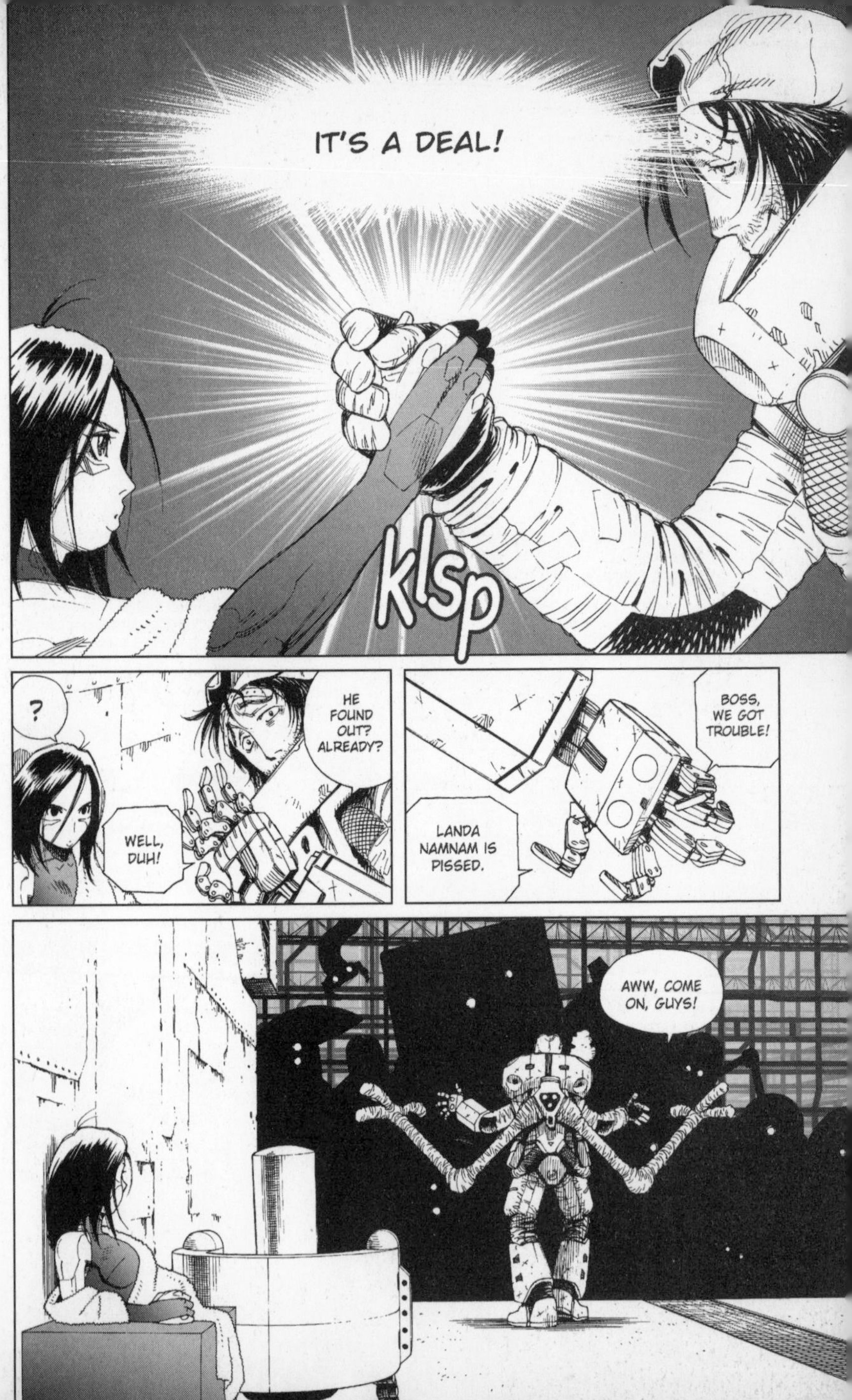
IT'S A DEAL!
klsp
BOSS, WE GOT TROUBLE!
LANDA NAMNAM IS PISSED.
HE FOUND OUT? ALREADY?
?
WELL, DUH!
AWW, COME ON, GUYS!

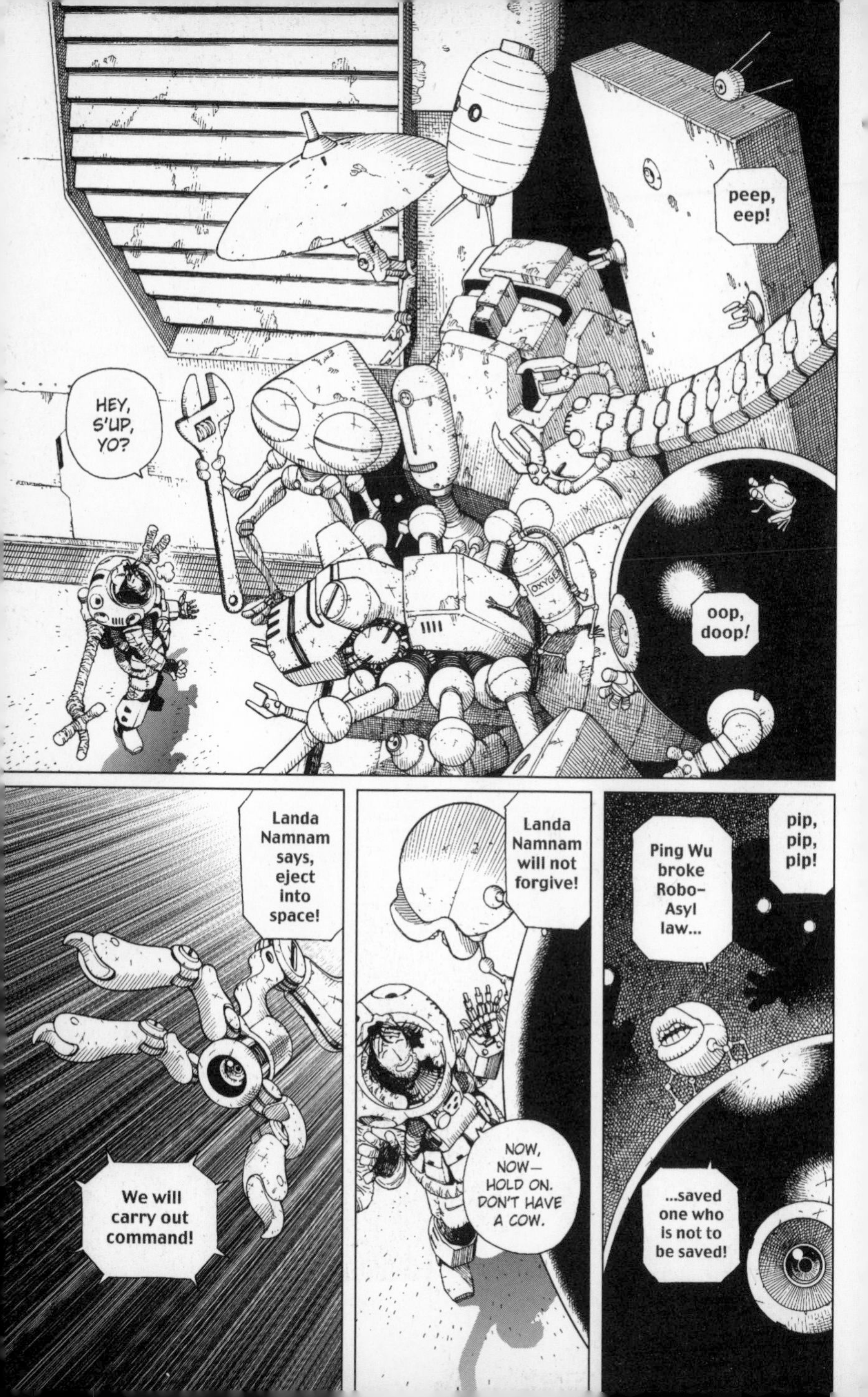
peep, eep!
oop, doop!
HEY, S'UP, YO?
pip, pip, pip!
Ping Wu broke Robo-Asyl law...
...saved one who is not to be saved!
Landa Namnam will not forgive!
NOW, NOW—HOLD ON. DON'T HAVE A COW.
Landa Namnam says, eject into space!
We will carry out command!

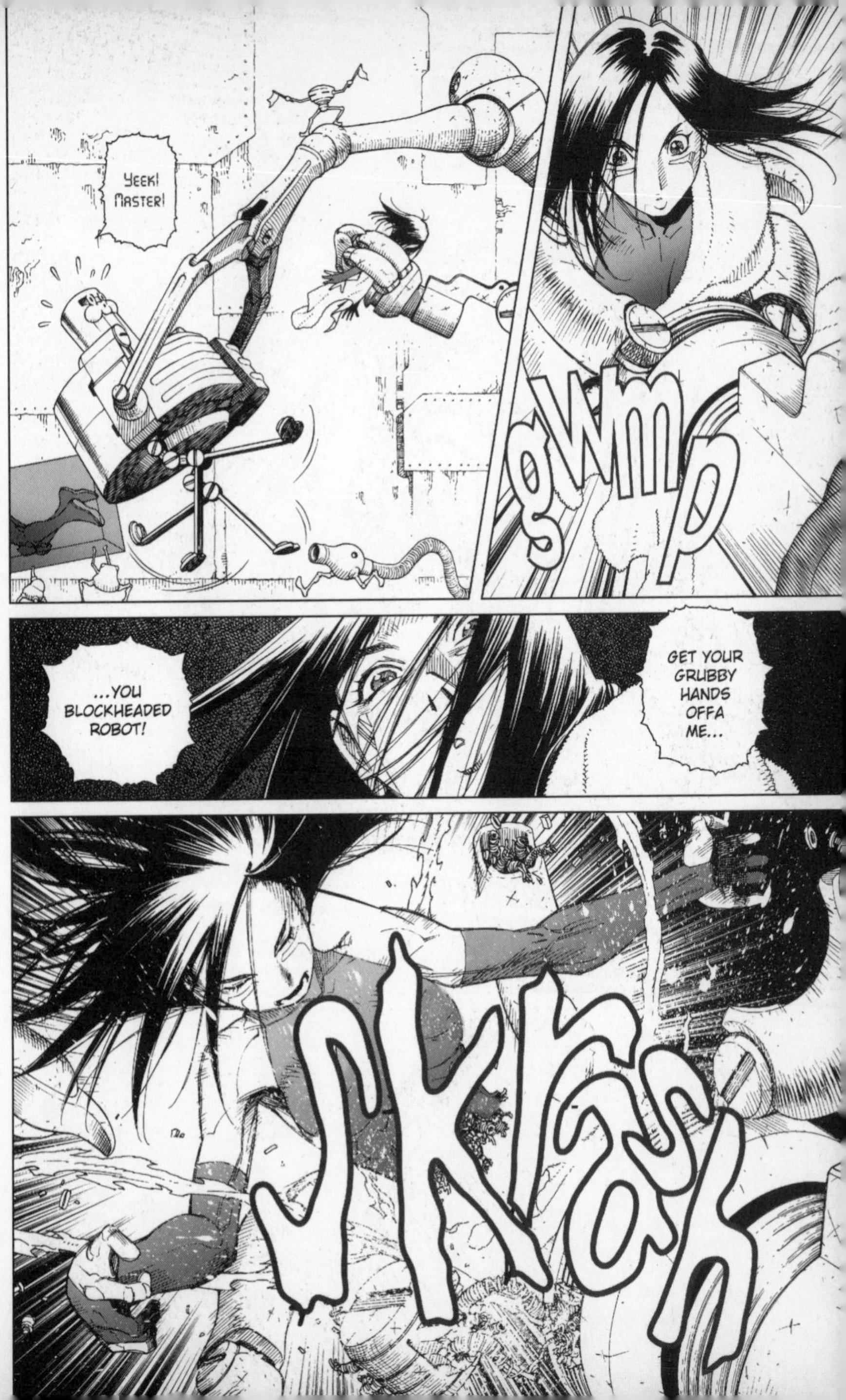
gwmp
YEEK! MASTER!
GET YOUR GRUBBY HANDS OFFA ME...
...YOU BLOCKHEADED ROBOT!
SKRASH

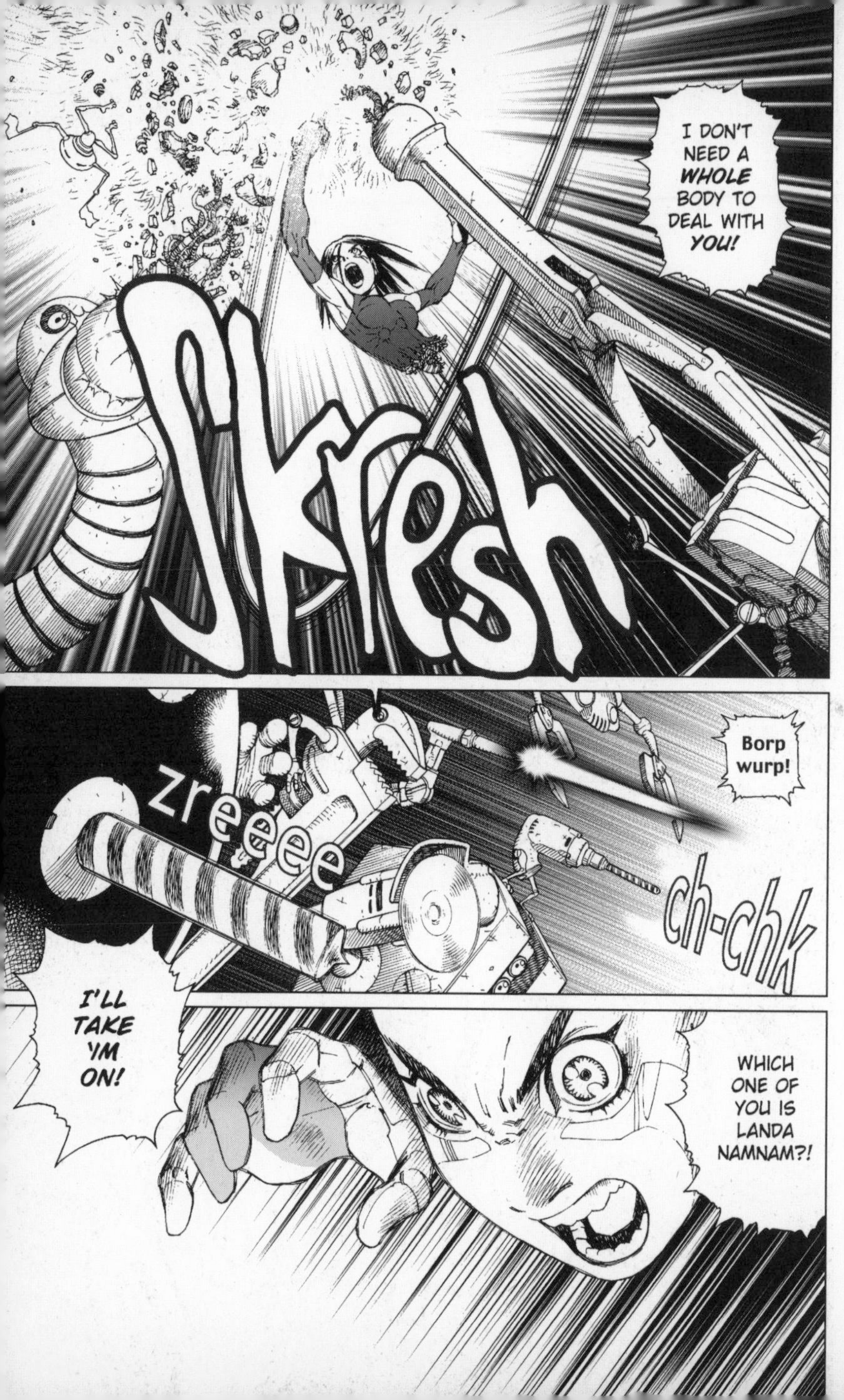
I DON'T NEED A *WHOLE* BODY TO DEAL WITH *YOU!*
Skresh
Borp wurp!
ch-chk
zreeeee
WHICH ONE OF YOU IS LANDA NAMNAM?!
I'LL TAKE 'IM ON!

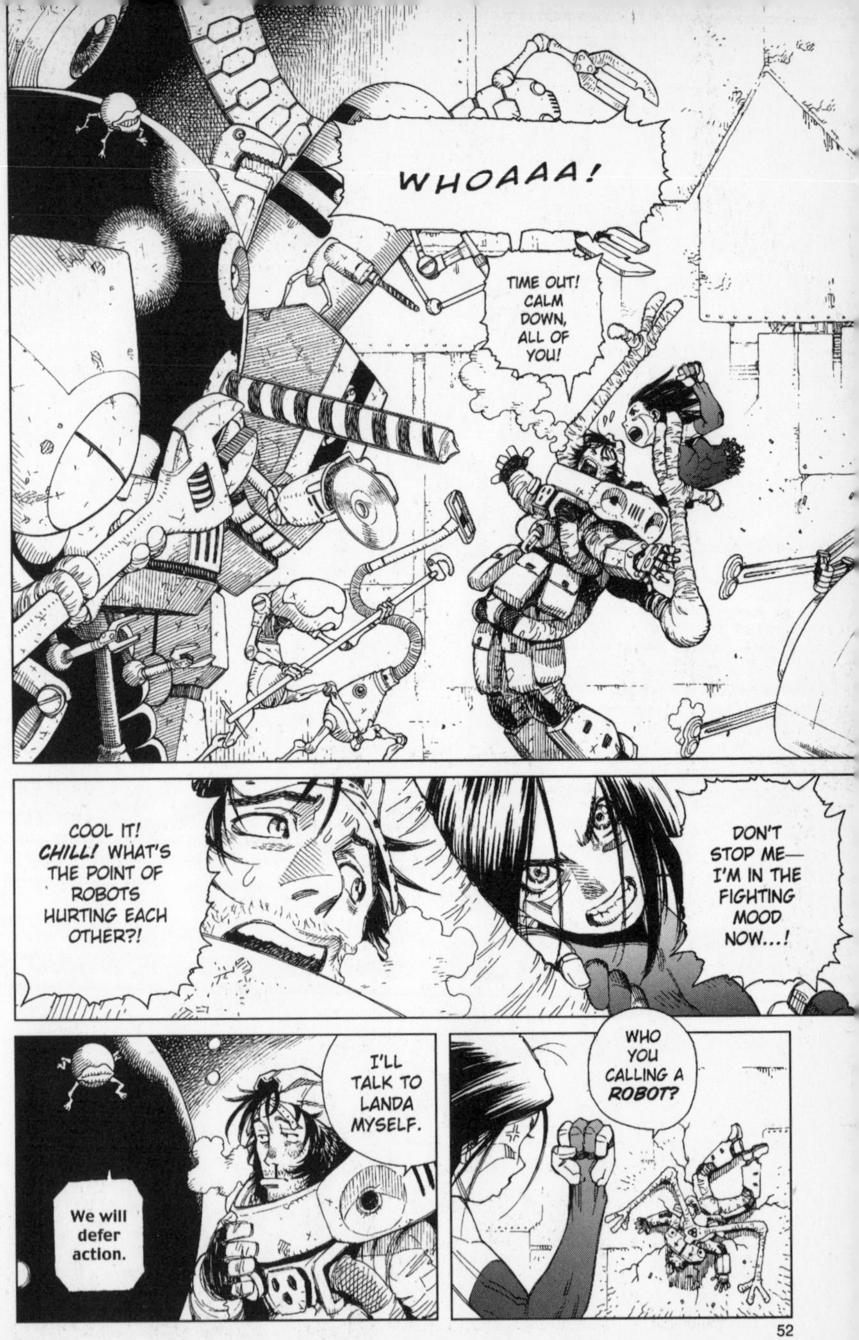
WHOAAA!
TIME OUT! CALM DOWN, ALL OF YOU!
DON'T STOP ME— I'M IN THE FIGHTING MOOD NOW...!
COOL IT! CHILL! WHAT'S THE POINT OF ROBOTS HURTING EACH OTHER?!
WHO YOU CALLING A ROBOT?
I'LL TALK TO LANDA MYSELF.
We will defer action.

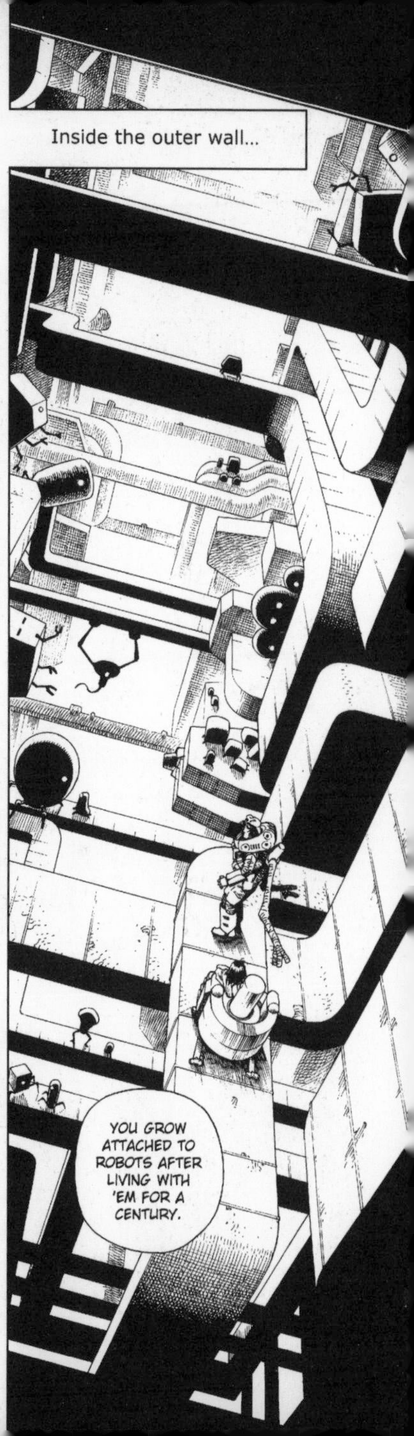
Inside the outer wall...
YOU GROW ATTACHED TO ROBOTS AFTER LIVING WITH 'EM FOR A CENTURY.

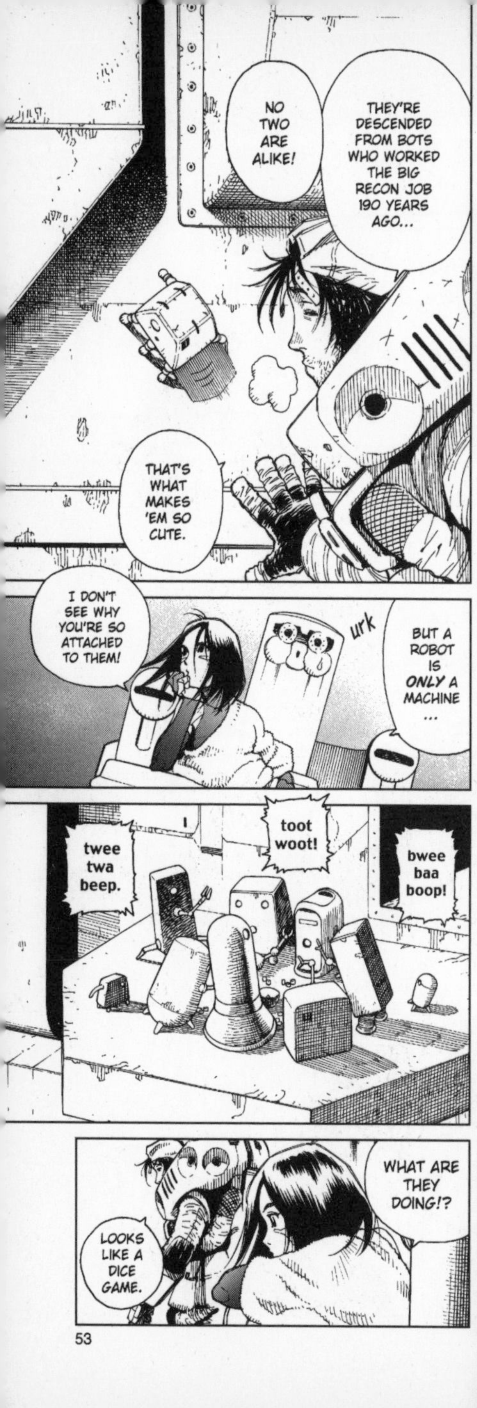
THEY'RE DESCENDED FROM BOTS WHO WORKED THE BIG RECON JOB 190 YEARS AGO...
NO TWO ARE ALIKE!
THAT'S WHAT MAKES 'EM SO CUTE.
BUT A ROBOT IS *ONLY* A MACHINE ...
urk
I DON'T SEE WHY YOU'RE SO ATTACHED TO THEM!
bwee baa boop!
toot woot!
twee twa beep.
WHAT ARE THEY DOING!?
LOOKS LIKE A DICE GAME.

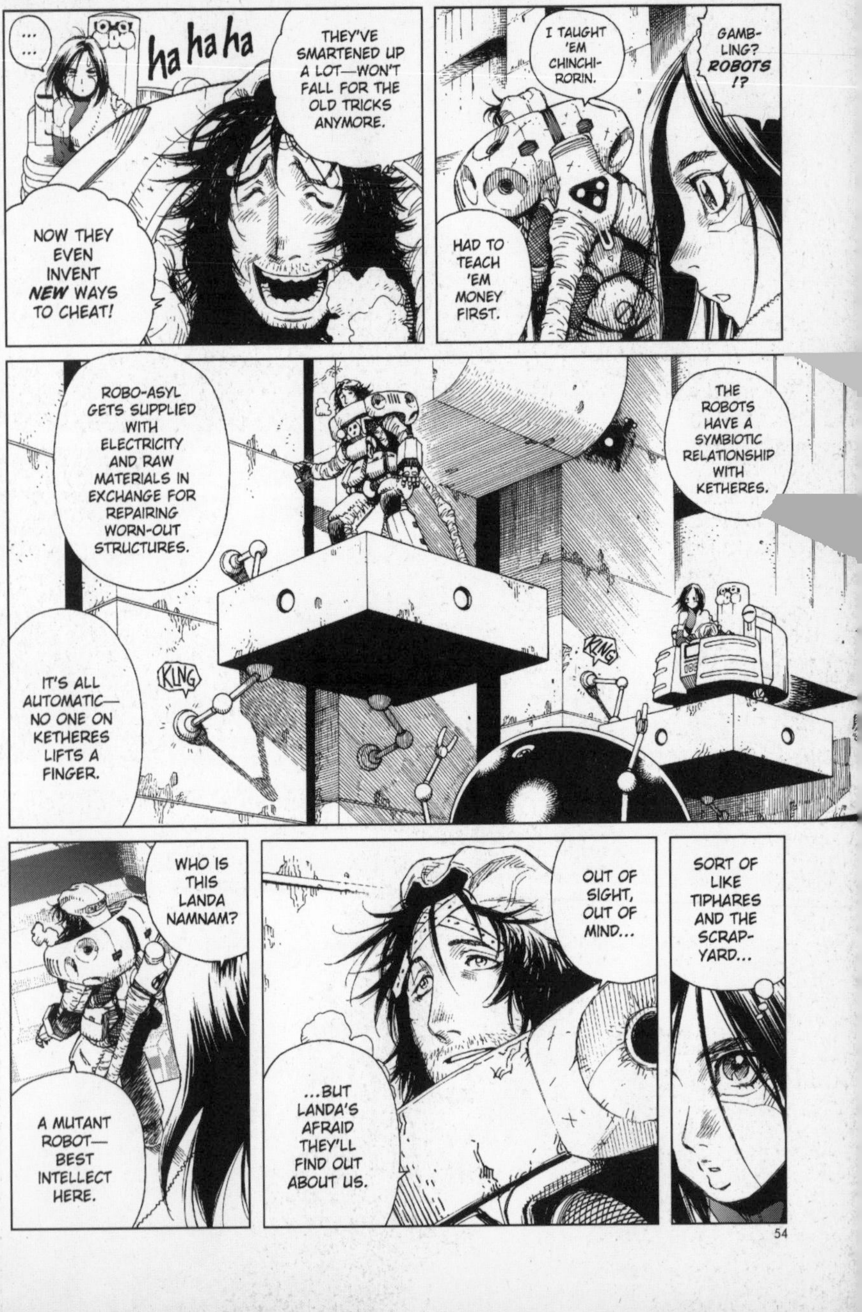
GAMBLING? ROBOTS!?
I TAUGHT 'EM CHINCHIRORIN.
HAD TO TEACH 'EM MONEY FIRST.
THEY'VE SMARTENED UP A LOT—WON'T FALL FOR THE OLD TRICKS ANYMORE.
ha ha ha
......
NOW THEY EVEN INVENT NEW WAYS TO CHEAT!
THE ROBOTS HAVE A SYMBIOTIC RELATIONSHIP WITH KETHERES.
KLING
ROBO-ASYL GETS SUPPLIED WITH ELECTRICITY AND RAW MATERIALS IN EXCHANGE FOR REPAIRING WORN-OUT STRUCTURES.
KLING
IT'S ALL AUTOMATIC—NO ONE ON KETHERES LIFTS A FINGER.
SORT OF LIKE TIPHARES AND THE SCRAPYARD...
OUT OF SIGHT, OUT OF MIND...
...BUT LANDA'S AFRAID THEY'LL FIND OUT ABOUT US.
WHO IS THIS LANDA NAMNAM?
A MUTANT ROBOT—BEST INTELLECT HERE.

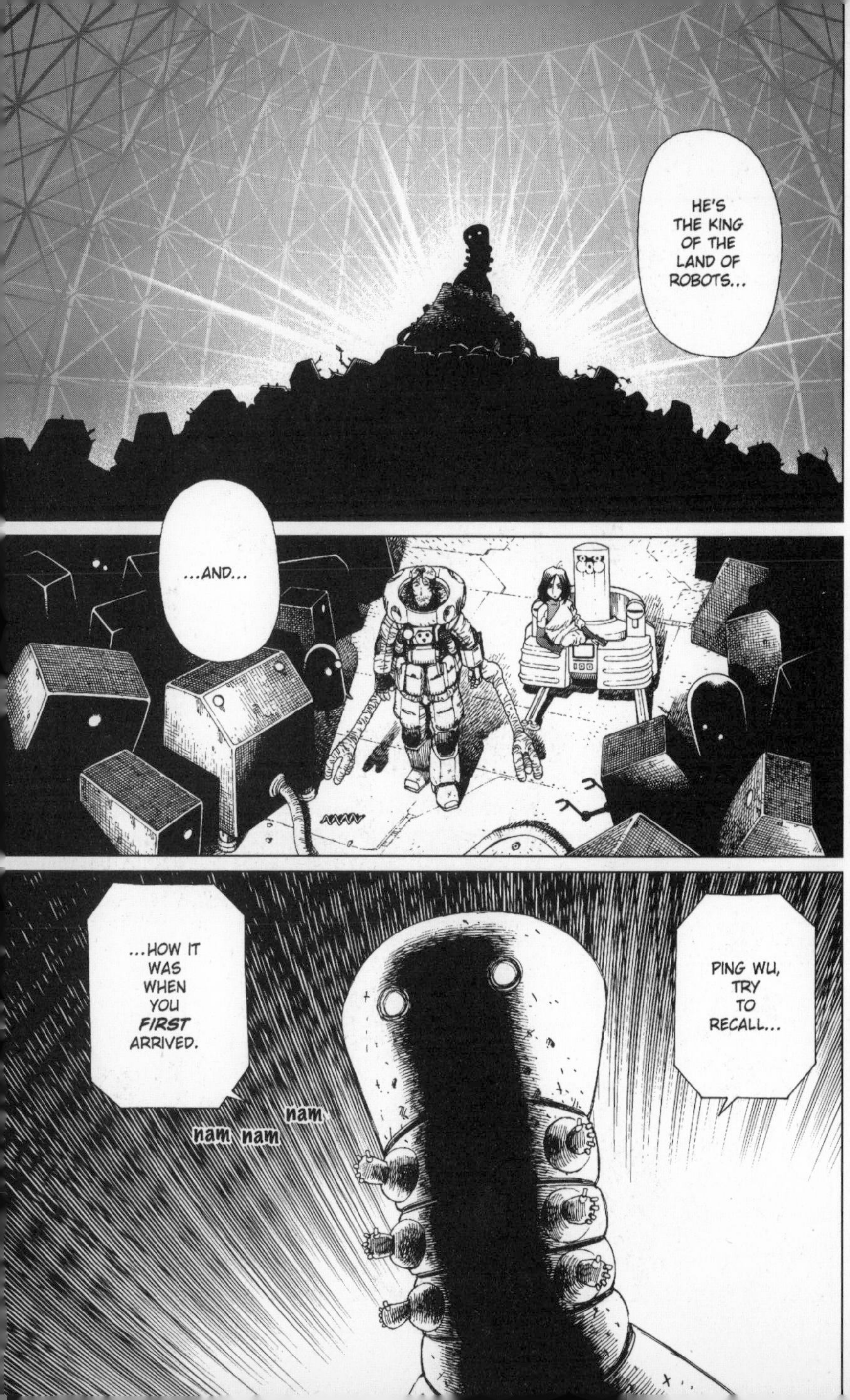
HE'S THE KING OF THE LAND OF ROBOTS...
...AND...
PING WU, TRY TO RECALL...
...HOW IT WAS WHEN YOU *FIRST* ARRIVED.
nam
nam nam

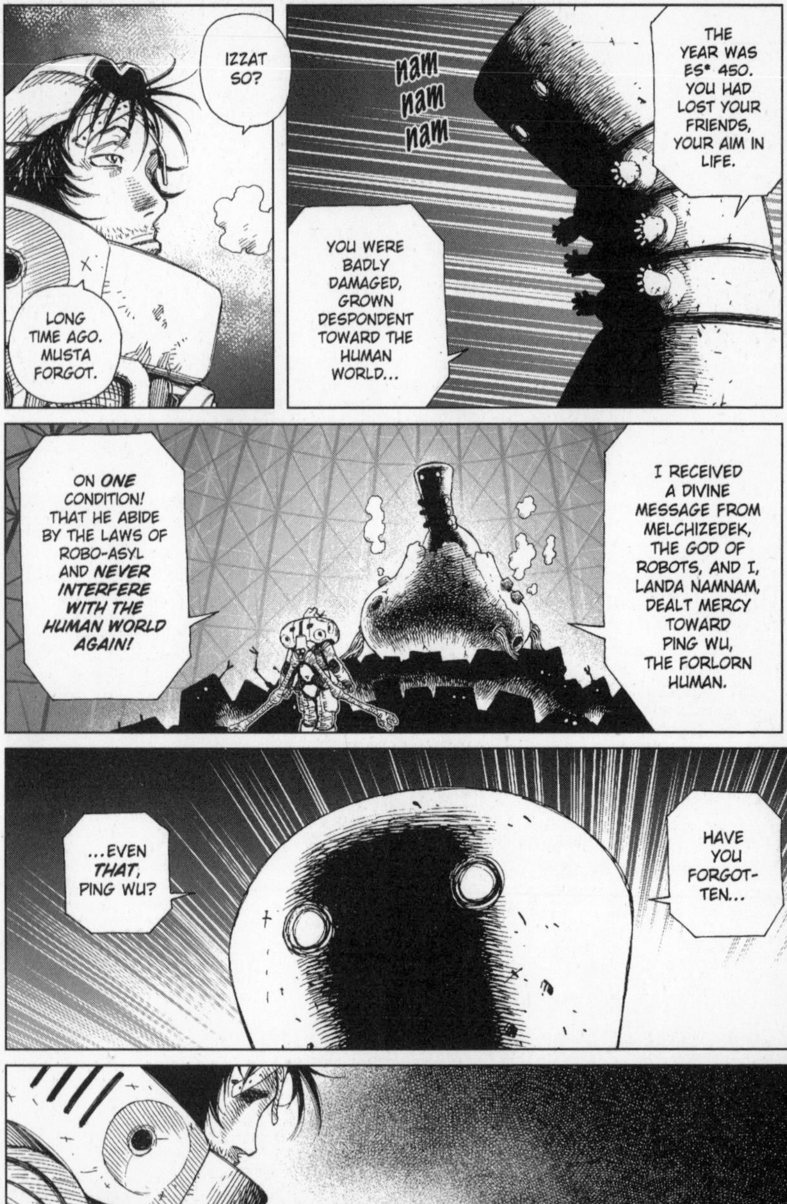
THE YEAR WAS ES* 450. YOU HAD LOST YOUR FRIENDS, YOUR AIM IN LIFE.
nam nam nam
YOU WERE BADLY DAMAGED, GROWN DESPONDENT TOWARD THE HUMAN WORLD...
IZZAT SO?
LONG TIME AGO. MUSTA FORGOT.
I RECEIVED A DIVINE MESSAGE FROM MELCHIZEDEK, THE GOD OF ROBOTS, AND I, LANDA NAMNAM, DEALT MERCY TOWARD PING WU, THE FORLORN HUMAN.
ON ONE CONDITION! THAT HE ABIDE BY THE LAWS OF ROBO-ASYL AND NEVER INTERFERE WITH THE HUMAN WORLD AGAIN!
HAVE YOU FORGOT-TEN...
...EVEN THAT, PING WU?

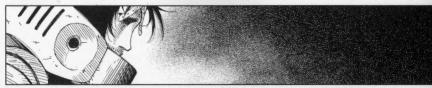

**ES (Era Sputnik): Standard dating system used in space. The year the first artificial satellite Sputnik was launched into space (1957) marks the first year. Based on the period of Earth's revolution around the sun.*

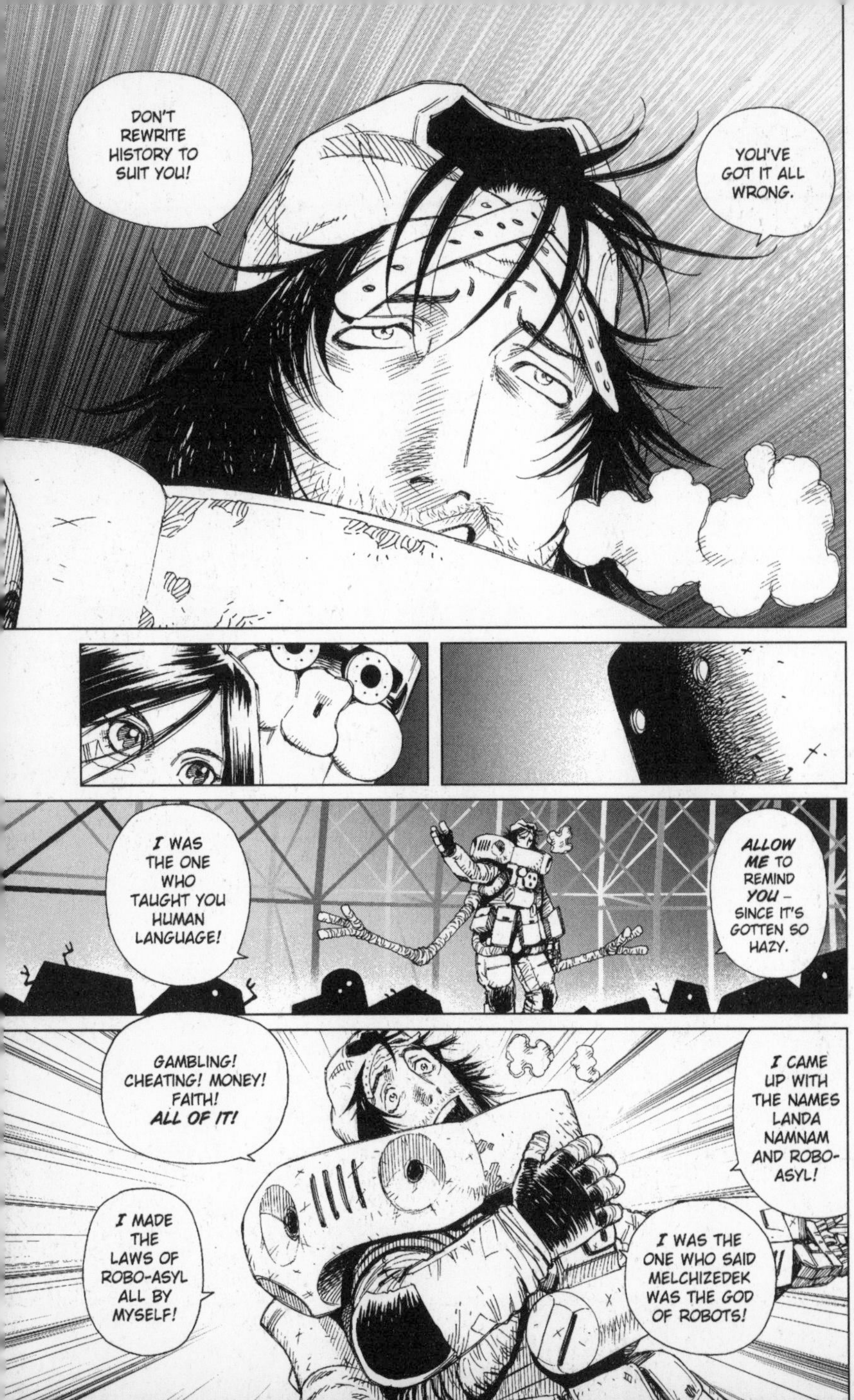
YOU'VE GOT IT ALL WRONG.
DON'T REWRITE HISTORY TO SUIT YOU!
ALLOW ME TO REMIND YOU – SINCE IT'S GOTTEN SO HAZY.
I WAS THE ONE WHO TAUGHT YOU HUMAN LANGUAGE!
I CAME UP WITH THE NAMES LANDA NAMNAM AND ROBO-ASYL!
GAMBLING! CHEATING! MONEY! FAITH! ALL OF IT!
I WAS THE ONE WHO SAID MELCHIZEDEK WAS THE GOD OF ROBOTS!
I MADE THE LAWS OF ROBO-ASYL ALL BY MYSELF!

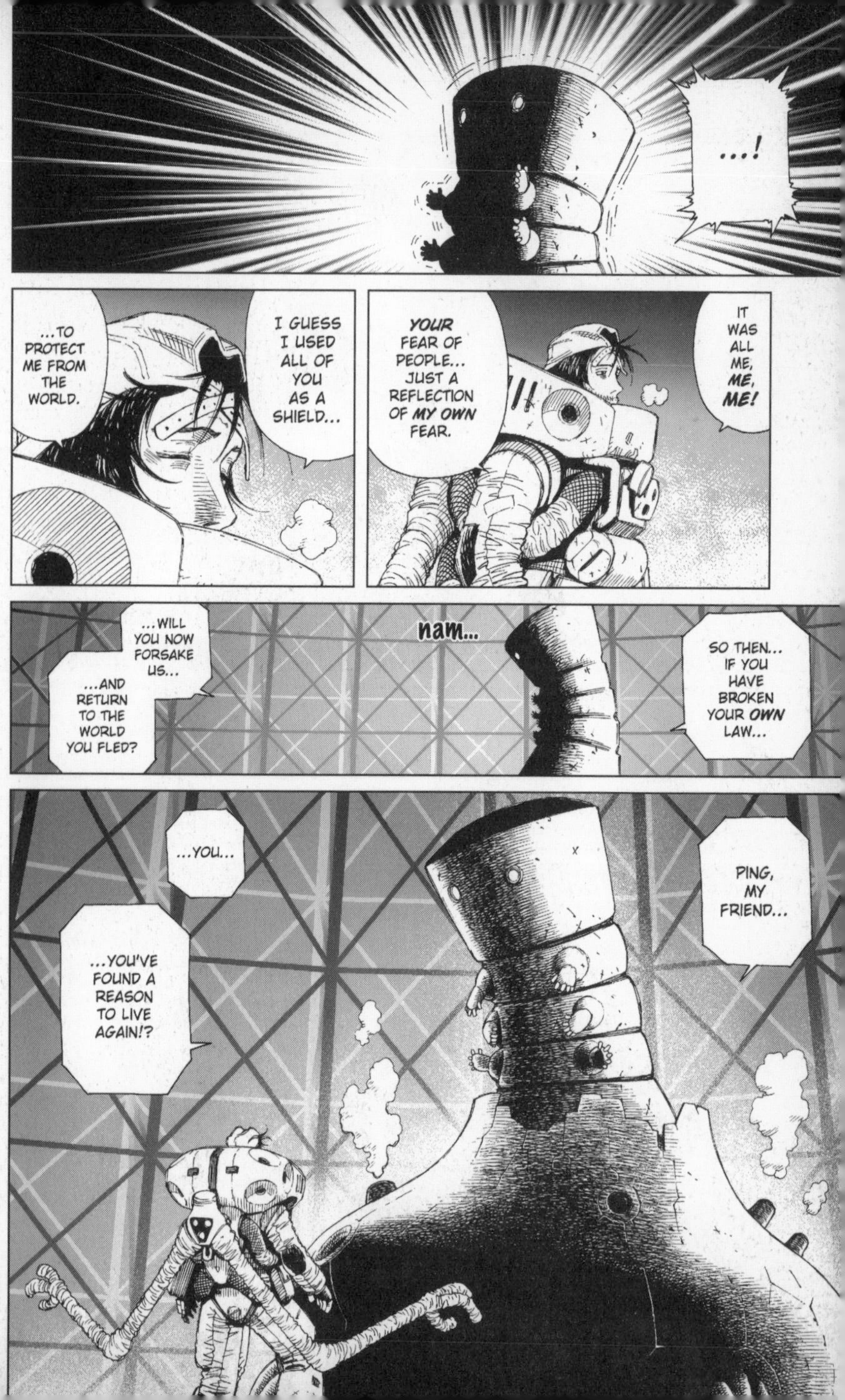
...!
IT WAS ALL ME, *ME, ME!*
YOUR FEAR OF PEOPLE... JUST A REFLECTION OF *MY OWN* FEAR.
I GUESS I USED ALL OF YOU AS A SHIELD...
...TO PROTECT ME FROM THE WORLD.
SO THEN... IF YOU HAVE BROKEN YOUR *OWN* LAW...
nam...
...WILL YOU NOW FORSAKE US...
...AND RETURN TO THE WORLD YOU FLED?
PING, MY FRIEND...
...YOU...
...YOU'VE FOUND A REASON TO LIVE AGAIN!?

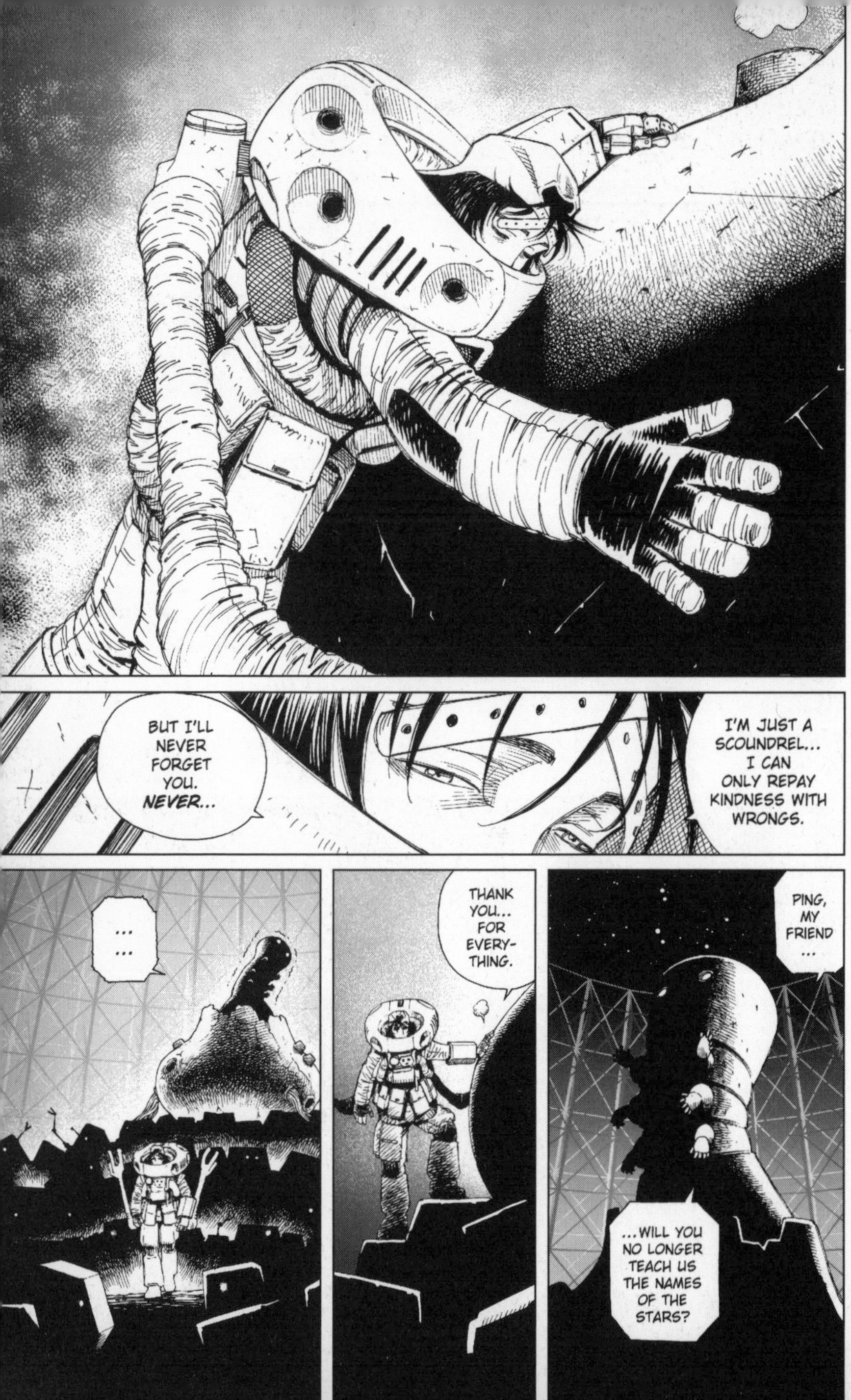
I'M JUST A SCOUNDREL... I CAN ONLY REPAY KINDNESS WITH WRONGS.
BUT I'LL NEVER FORGET YOU. *NEVER*...
PING, MY FRIEND ...
...WILL YOU NO LONGER TEACH US THE NAMES OF THE STARS?
THANK YOU... FOR EVERYTHING.
... ...

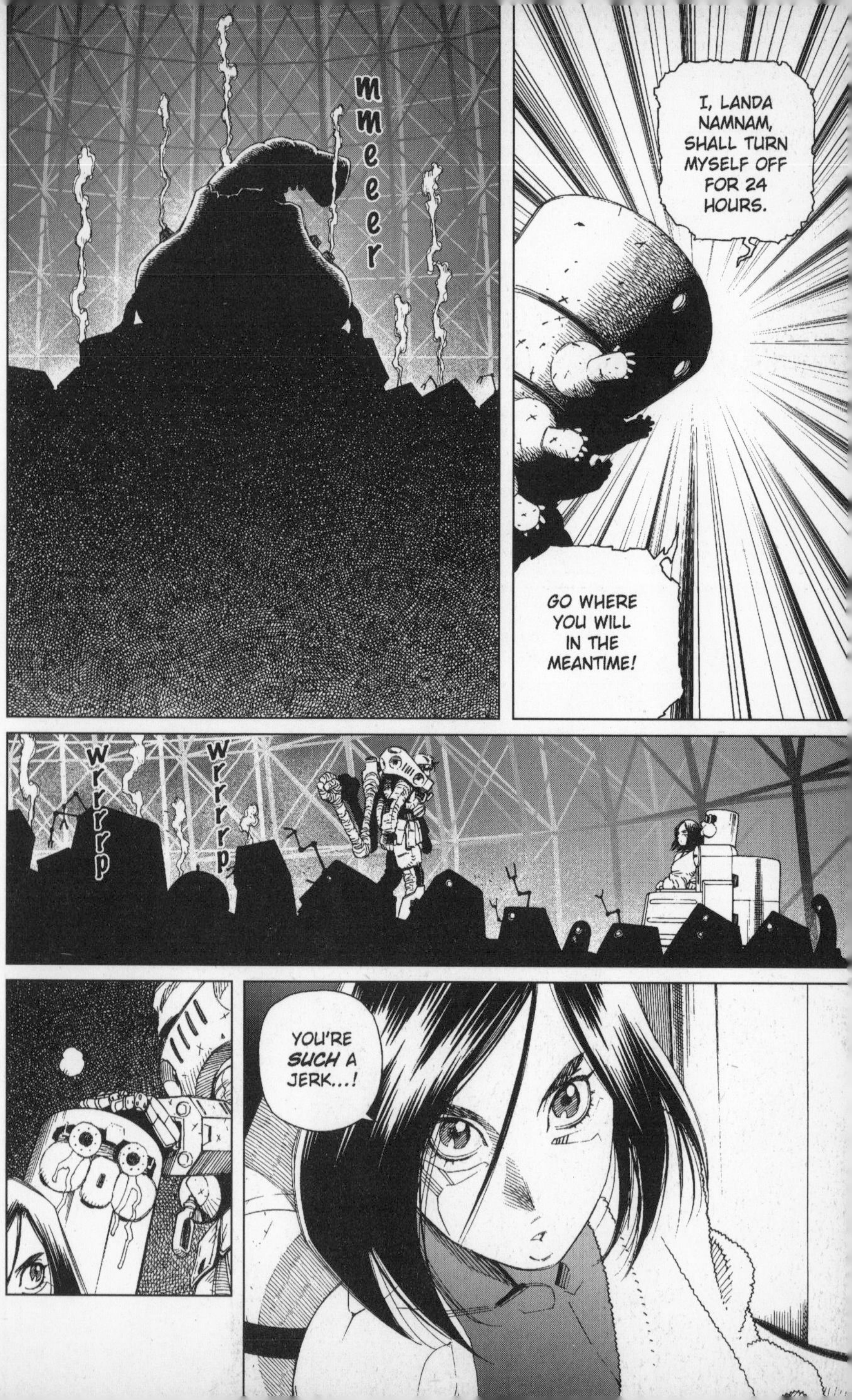
I, LANDA NAMNAM, SHALL TURN MYSELF OFF FOR 24 HOURS.
GO WHERE YOU WILL IN THE MEANTIME!
mmeeer
wrrrrp
wrrrrp
YOU'RE *SUCH* A JERK...!

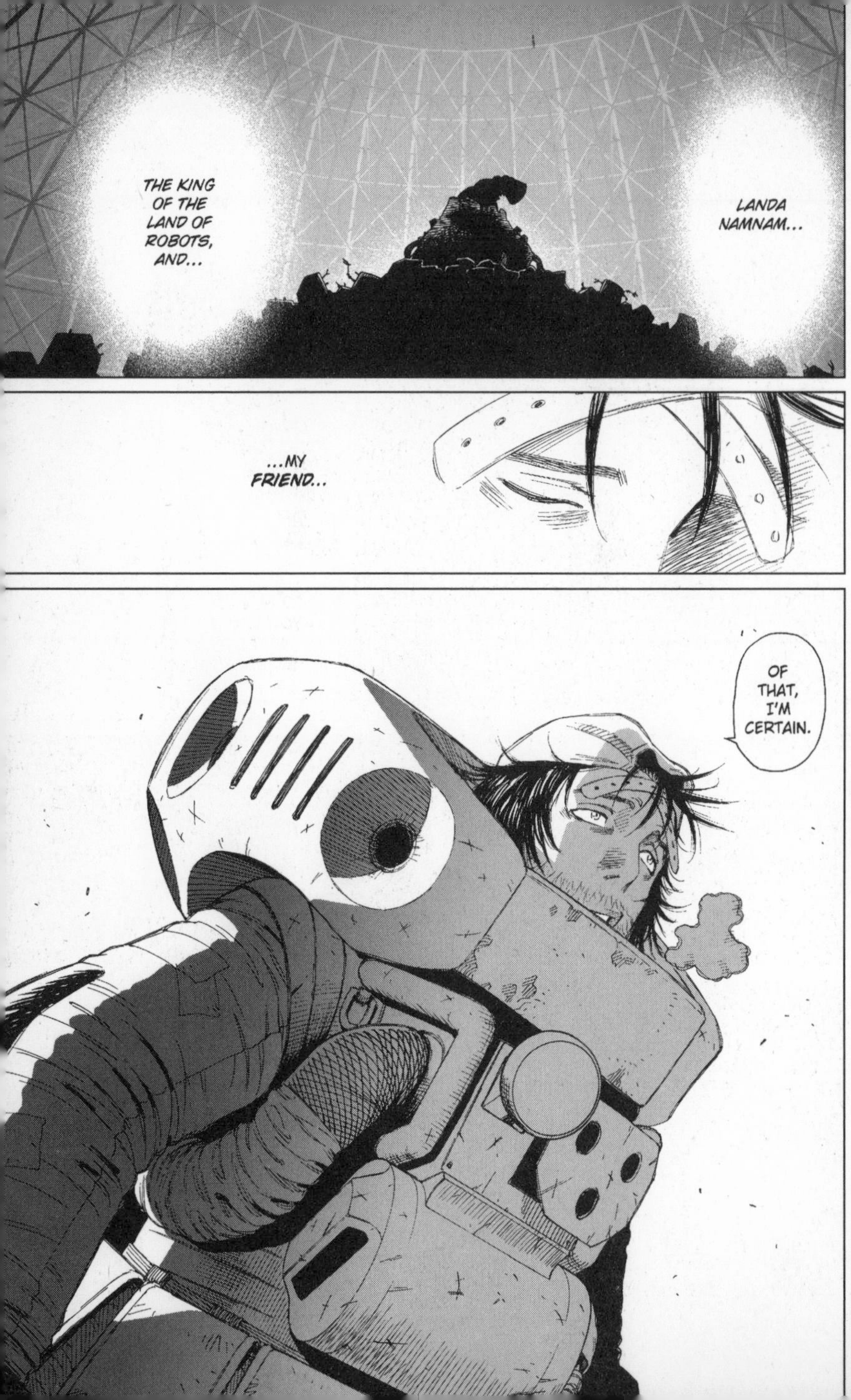
LANDA NAMNAM...
THE KING OF THE LAND OF ROBOTS, AND...
...MY FRIEND...
OF THAT, I'M CERTAIN.

PHASE 15

I'm Sure We'll Meet Again

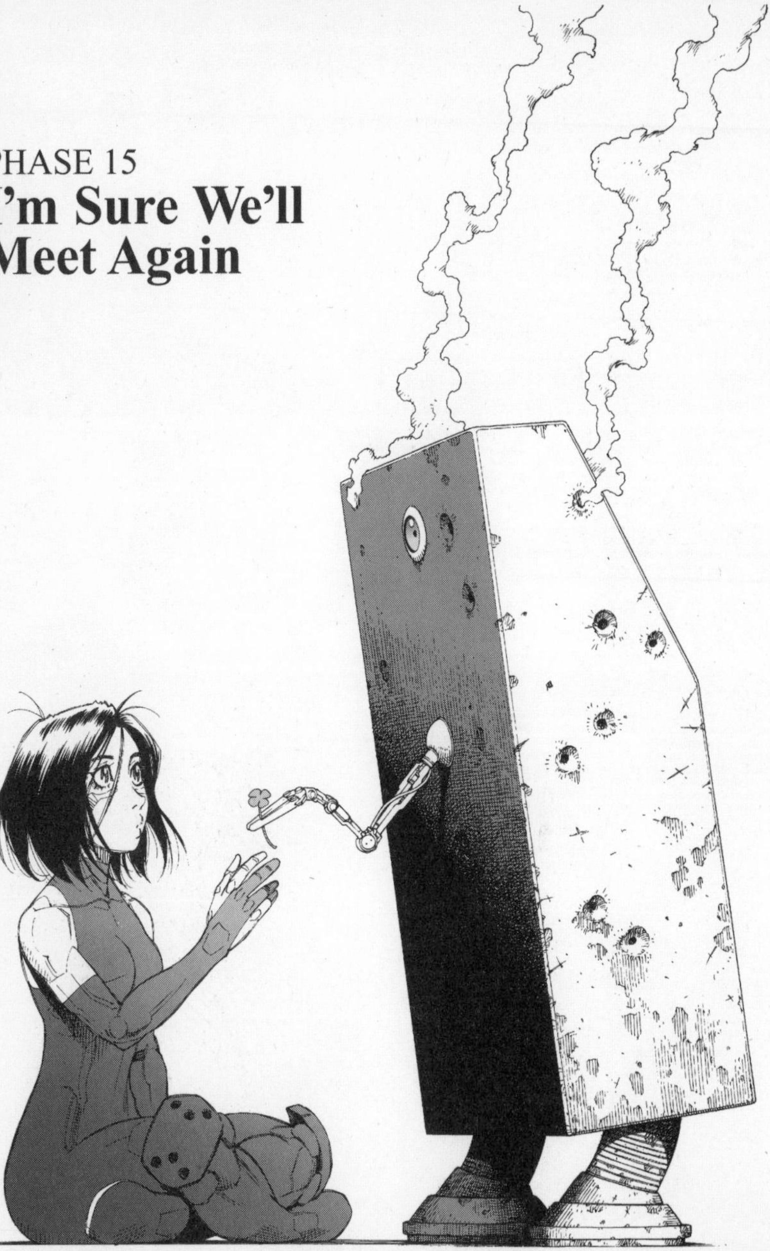

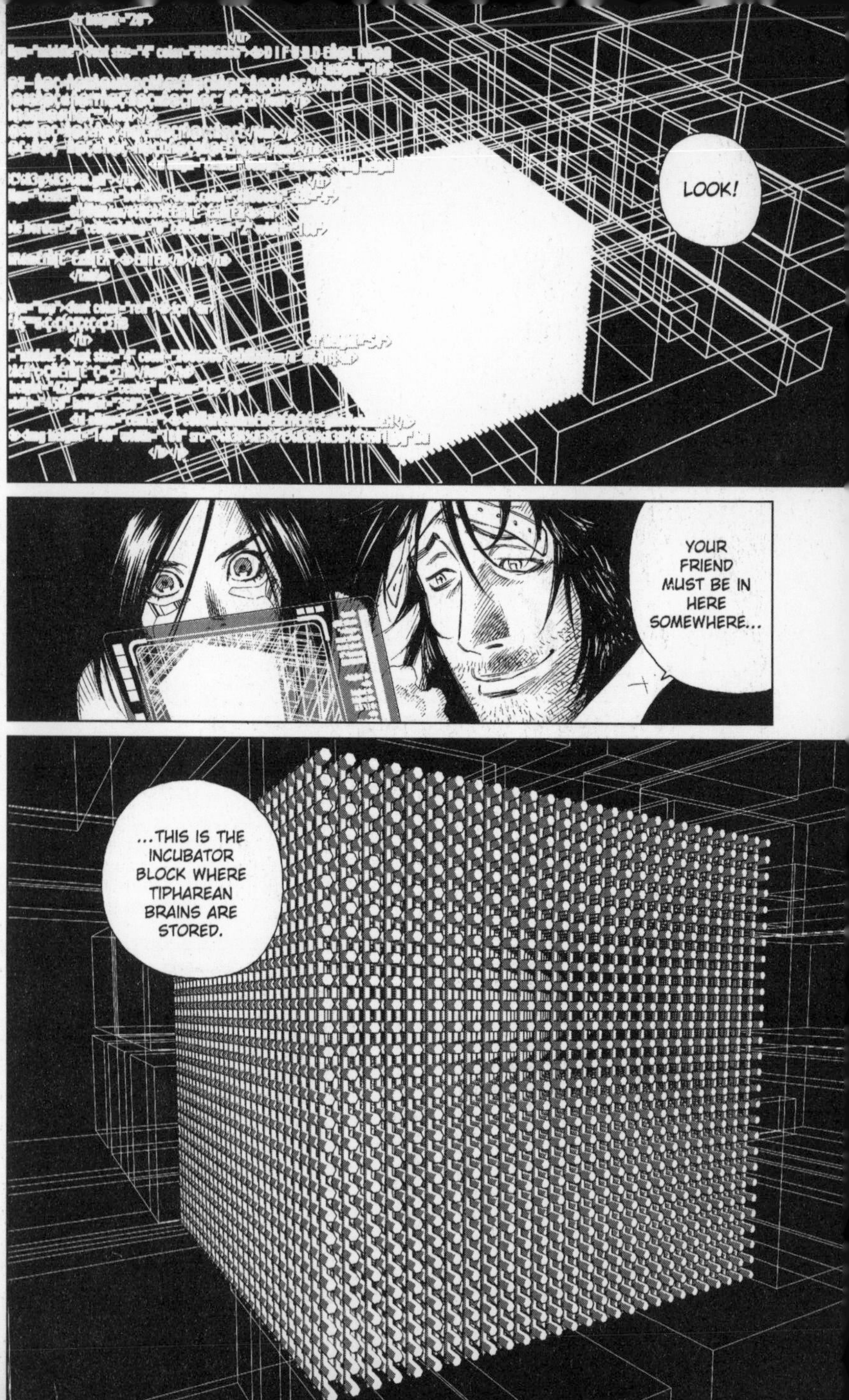
LOOK!
YOUR FRIEND MUST BE IN HERE SOMEWHERE...
...THIS IS THE INCUBATOR BLOCK WHERE TIPHAREAN BRAINS ARE STORED.

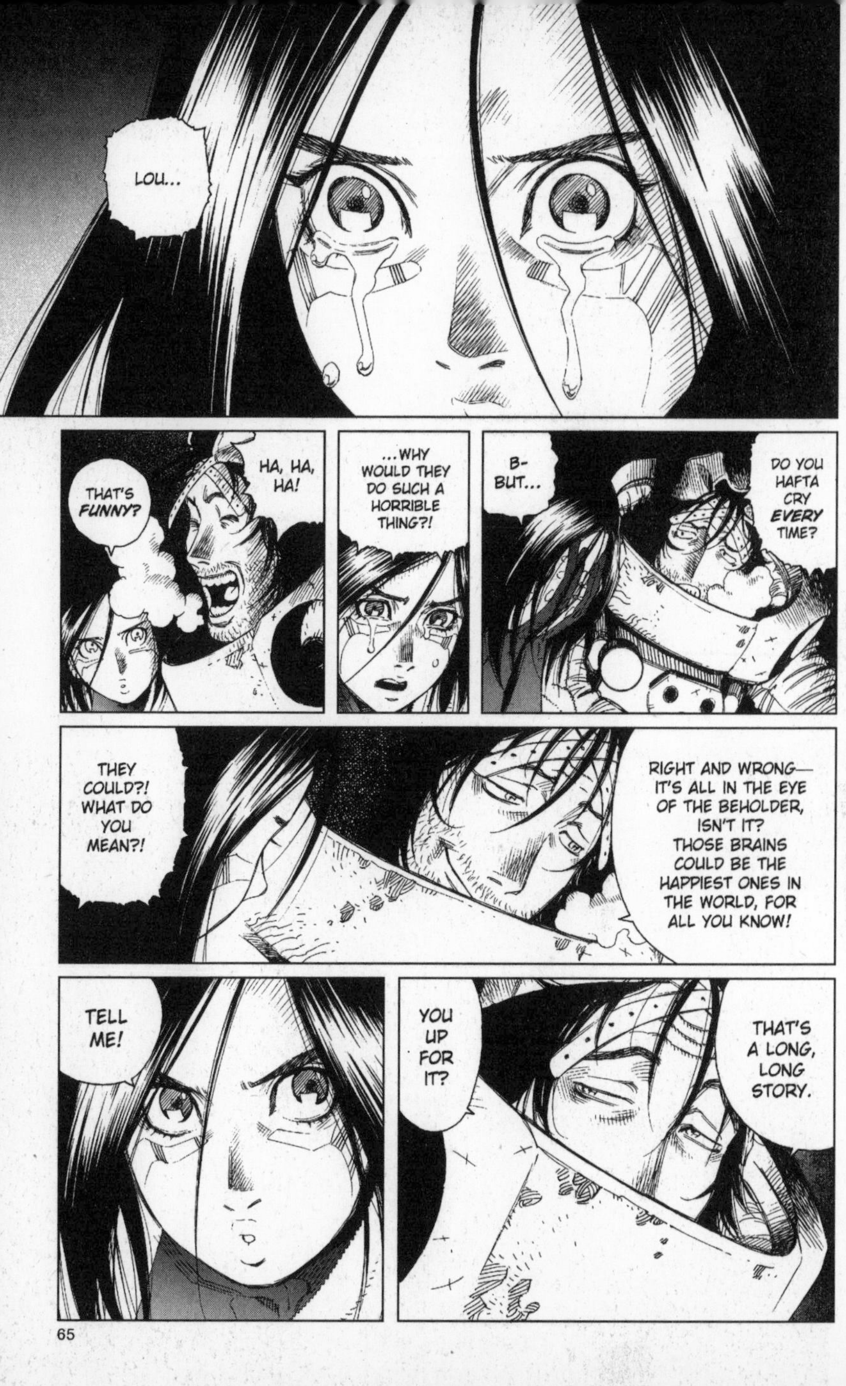
LOU...
DO YOU HAFTA CRY *EVERY* TIME?
B- BUT...
...WHY WOULD THEY DO SUCH A HORRIBLE THING?!
HA, HA, HA!
THAT'S *FUNNY?*
RIGHT AND WRONG— IT'S ALL IN THE EYE OF THE BEHOLDER, ISN'T IT? THOSE BRAINS COULD BE THE HAPPIEST ONES IN THE WORLD, FOR ALL YOU KNOW!
THEY COULD?! WHAT DO YOU MEAN?!
THAT'S A LONG, LONG STORY.
YOU UP FOR IT?
TELL ME!

EVEN THE ROBOTS OF ROBO-ASYL GET INTO FIGHTS AND DECEIVE EACH OTHER.

CRIME, SUICIDE, ADULTERY— SEEMS LIKE HUMAN NATURE, RIGHT?

BUT NOT IN KETHERES... NOT A *SINGLE* QUARREL IN A CENTURY! AND HOW?

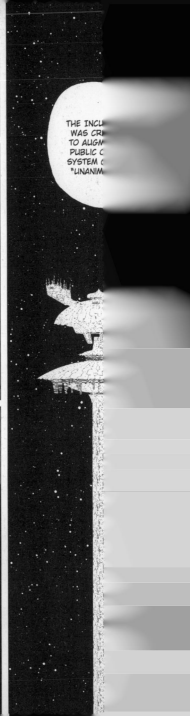

THE INCU... WAS CR... TO AUGM... PUBLIC O... SYSTEM O... "UNANIM...

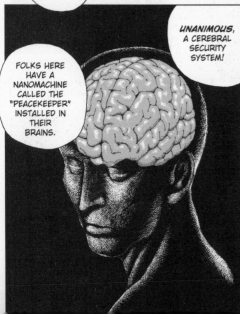

UNANIMOUS, A CEREBRAL SECURITY SYSTEM!

FOLKS HERE HAVE A NANOMACHINE CALLED THE "PEACEKEEPER" INSTALLED IN THEIR BRAINS.

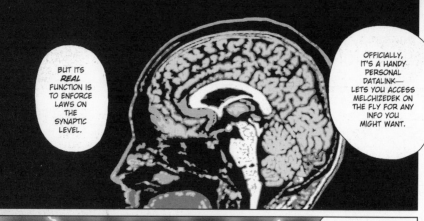

OFFICIALLY, IT'S A HANDY PERSONAL DATALINK— LETS YOU ACCESS MELCHIZEDEK ON THE FLY FOR ANY INFO YOU MIGHT WANT.
BUT ITS *REAL* FUNCTION IS TO ENFORCE LAWS ON THE SYNAPTIC LEVEL.
THE PEACEKEEPER SPIES ON ALL SYNAPTIC ACTIVITY. CRIMINAL INTENT MERITS A SHOCK TO THE BRAIN'S PAIN CENTER, GOOD BEHAVIOR A GENTLE JOLT TO THE PLEASURE CENTER.
IT'S SORT OF LIKE HAVING AN UN-BRIBABLE COP INSIDE YOUR HEAD SUPERVISING YOU FULL-TIME.
WITHIN A YEAR, YOU'RE PAVLOV'S DOG.
AND THE BEST PART? YOU NEVER REALIZE YOUR FREE WILL IS BEING CONTROLLED.
WHY ARE WE TALKING ABOUT THIS?
WHAT DOES IT HAVE TO DO WITH LOU?
HOLD YOUR HORSES ...
...YOU SEE, UNANIMOUS *SEEMED* PERFECT—BUT THERE WAS ONE FATAL FLAW.

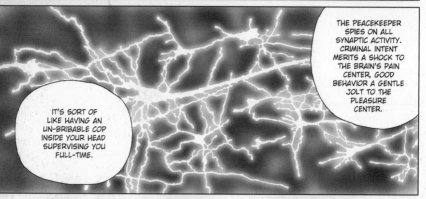

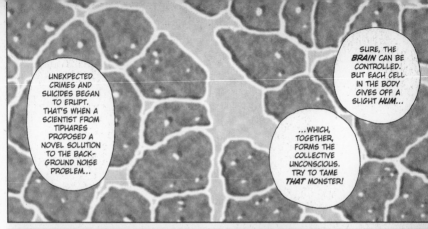

SURE, THE BRAIN CAN BE CONTROLLED. BUT EACH CELL IN THE BODY GIVES OFF A SLIGHT HUM...
...WHICH, TOGETHER, FORMS THE COLLECTIVE UNCONSCIOUS. TRY TO TAME THAT MONSTER!
UNEXPECTED CRIMES AND SUICIDES BEGAN TO ERUPT. THAT'S WHEN A SCIENTIST FROM TIPHARES PROPOSED A NOVEL SOLUTION TO THE BACK-GROUND NOISE PROBLEM...
...THE INCUBATOR! IT RECYCLED TIPHAREAN BRAINS PREVIOUSLY TOSSED AS WASTE BYPRODUCTS AND CONNECTED THEM INTO A COLLECTIVE DREAM WORLD...
...A VAST INNER FANTASY CALLED THE ARGO NAVIS!
DOUBT THEY EVEN KNOW THEY'RE DISEM-BODIED.
LOU! SO YOU'RE... DREAM-ING...
PEACEKEEPER FUNCTIONALITY IS SUSPENDED DURING SLEEP SO KETHERIANS CAN ACCESS THE ARGO NAVIS.
TIPHARES DUMPS ITS GARBAGE... KETHERES DUMPS ITS DREAMS.

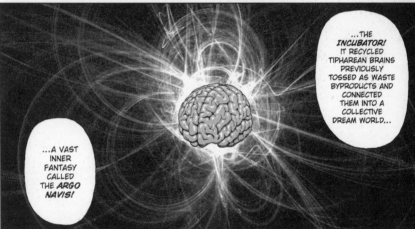

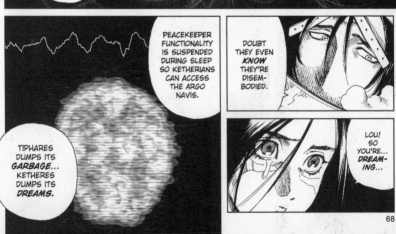

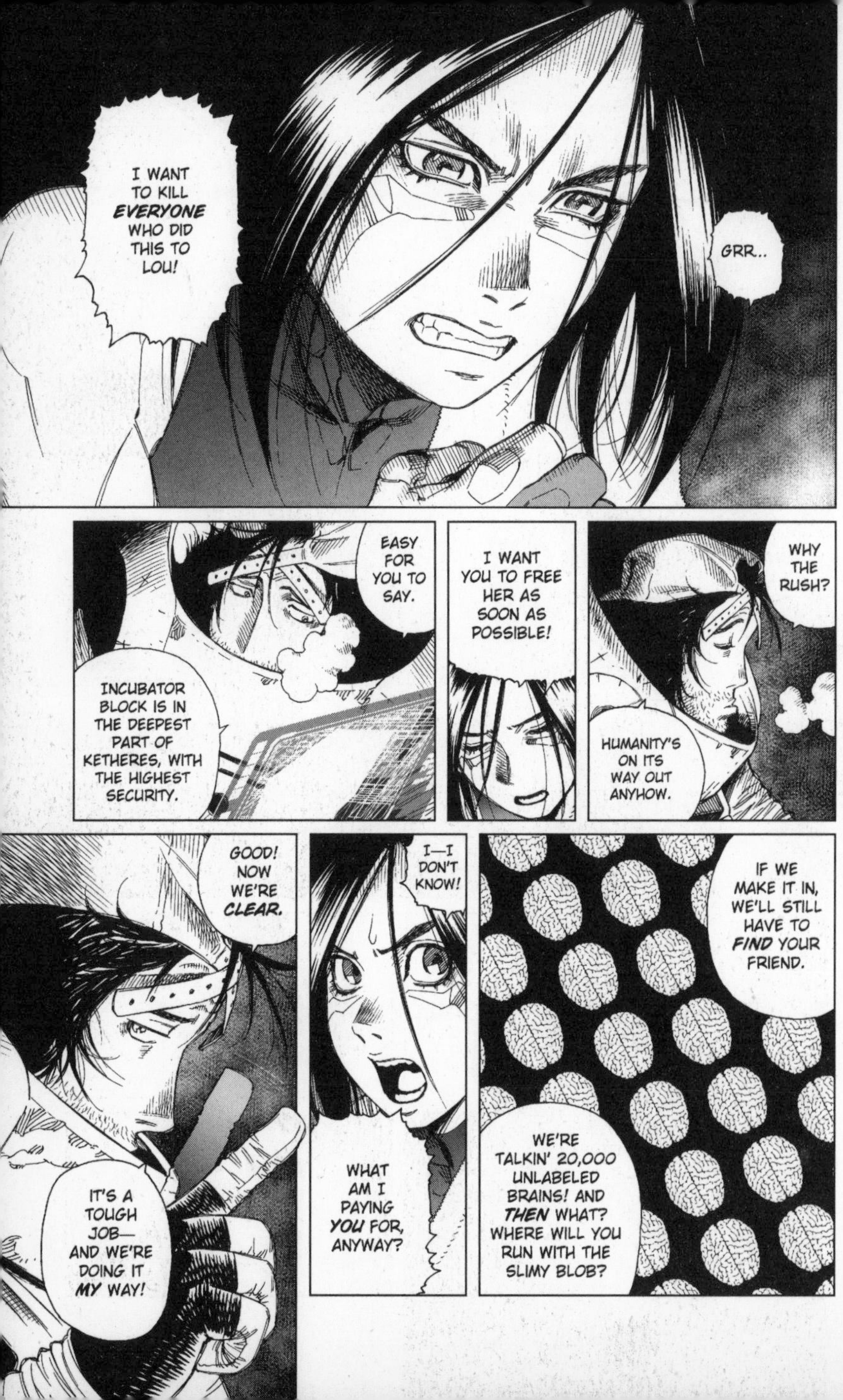
I WANT TO KILL *EVERYONE* WHO DID THIS TO LOU!
GRR..
WHY THE RUSH?
HUMANITY'S ON ITS WAY OUT ANYHOW.
I WANT YOU TO FREE HER AS SOON AS POSSIBLE!
EASY FOR YOU TO SAY.
INCUBATOR BLOCK IS IN THE DEEPEST PART OF KETHERES, WITH THE HIGHEST SECURITY.
IF WE MAKE IT IN, WE'LL STILL HAVE TO *FIND* YOUR FRIEND.
WE'RE TALKIN' 20,000 UNLABELED BRAINS! AND *THEN* WHAT? WHERE WILL YOU RUN WITH THE SLIMY BLOB?
I—I DON'T KNOW!
WHAT AM I PAYING *YOU* FOR, ANYWAY?
GOOD! NOW WE'RE *CLEAR.*
IT'S A TOUGH JOB— AND WE'RE DOING IT *MY* WAY!

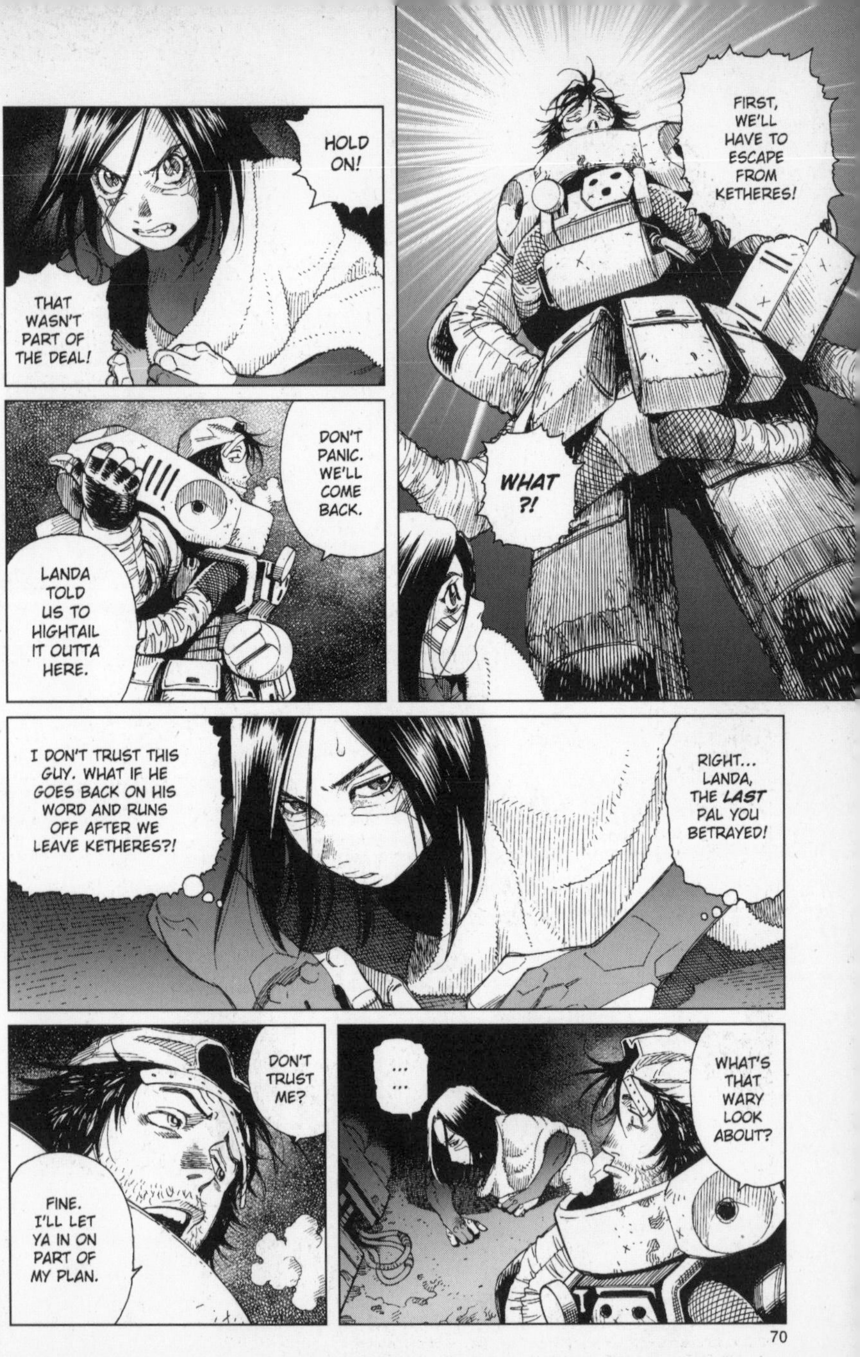
FIRST, WE'LL HAVE TO ESCAPE FROM KETHERES!
WHAT ?!
HOLD ON!
THAT WASN'T PART OF THE DEAL!
DON'T PANIC. WE'LL COME BACK.
LANDA TOLD US TO HIGHTAIL IT OUTTA HERE.
RIGHT... LANDA, THE LAST PAL YOU BETRAYED!
I DON'T TRUST THIS GUY. WHAT IF HE GOES BACK ON HIS WORD AND RUNS OFF AFTER WE LEAVE KETHERES?!
WHAT'S THAT WARY LOOK ABOUT?
... ...
DON'T TRUST ME?
FINE. I'LL LET YA IN ON PART OF MY PLAN.

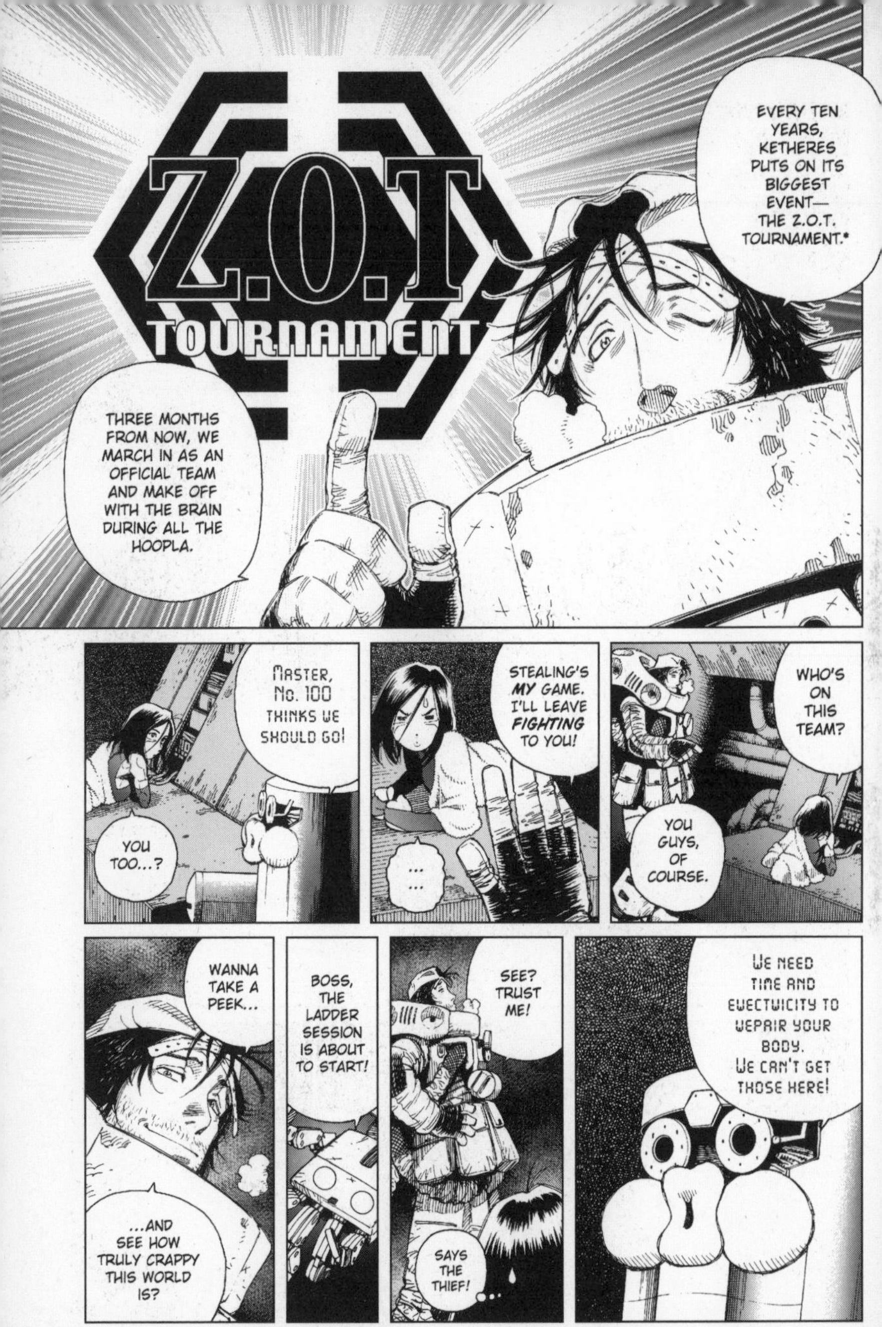
EVERY TEN YEARS, KETHERES PUTS ON ITS BIGGEST EVENT— THE Z.O.T. TOURNAMENT.*
Z.O.T
TOURNAMENT
THREE MONTHS FROM NOW, WE MARCH IN AS AN OFFICIAL TEAM AND MAKE OFF WITH THE BRAIN DURING ALL THE HOOPLA.
WHO'S ON THIS TEAM?
YOU GUYS, OF COURSE.
STEALING'S *MY* GAME. I'LL LEAVE *FIGHTING* TO YOU!
… …
MASTER, NO. 100 THINKS WE SHOULD GO!
YOU TOO...?
WE NEED TIME AND EWECTWICITY TO WEPAIR YOUR BODY. WE CAN'T GET THOSE HERE!
SEE? TRUST ME!
SAYS THE THIEF!
BOSS, THE LADDER SESSION IS ABOUT TO START!
WANNA TAKE A PEEK...
...AND SEE HOW TRULY CRAPPY THIS WORLD IS?

**Z.O.T. Tournament:* *Short for "Zenith of Things," it began as an experiment to see how robots would fare against trained soldiers.*

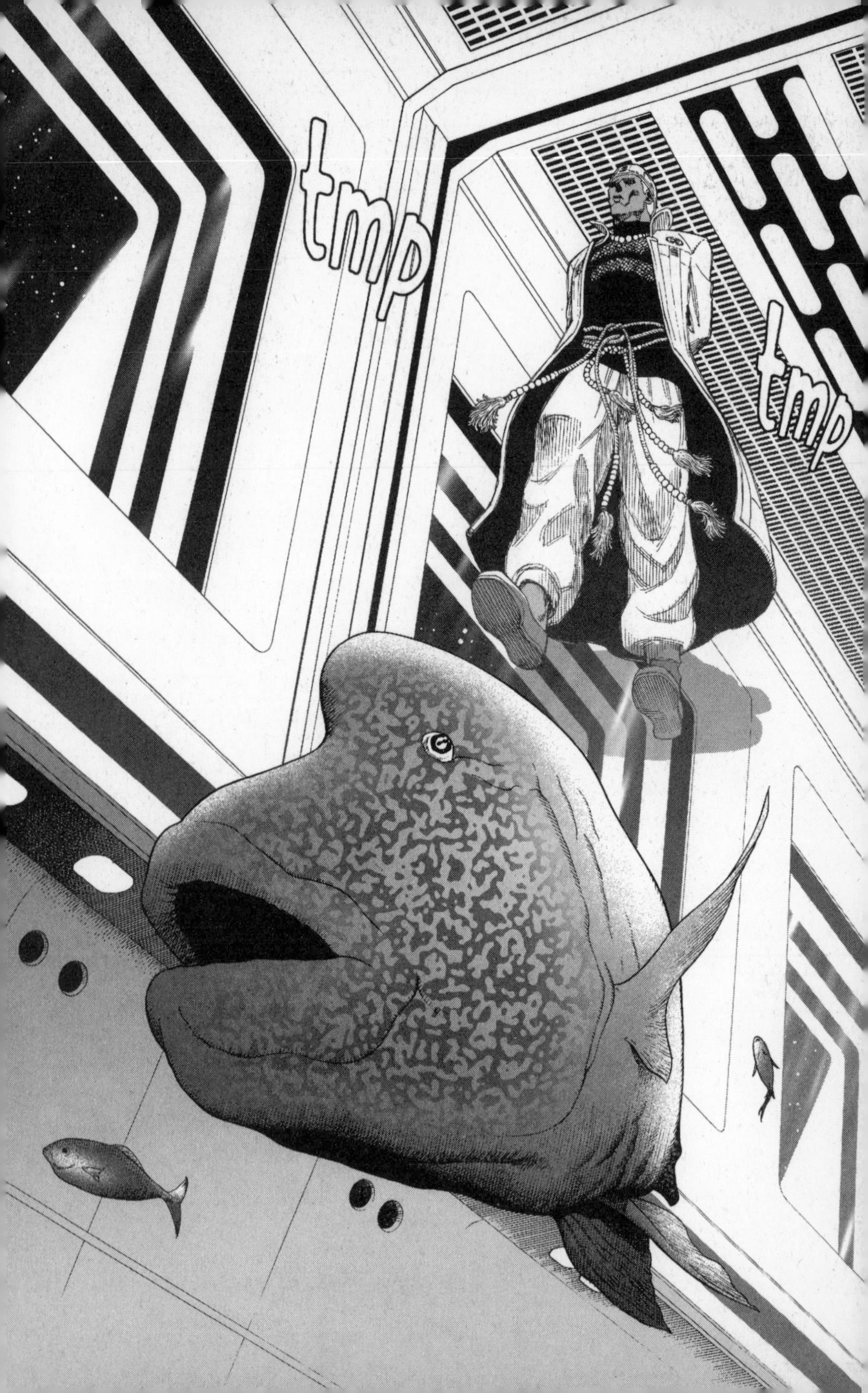
tmp
tmp

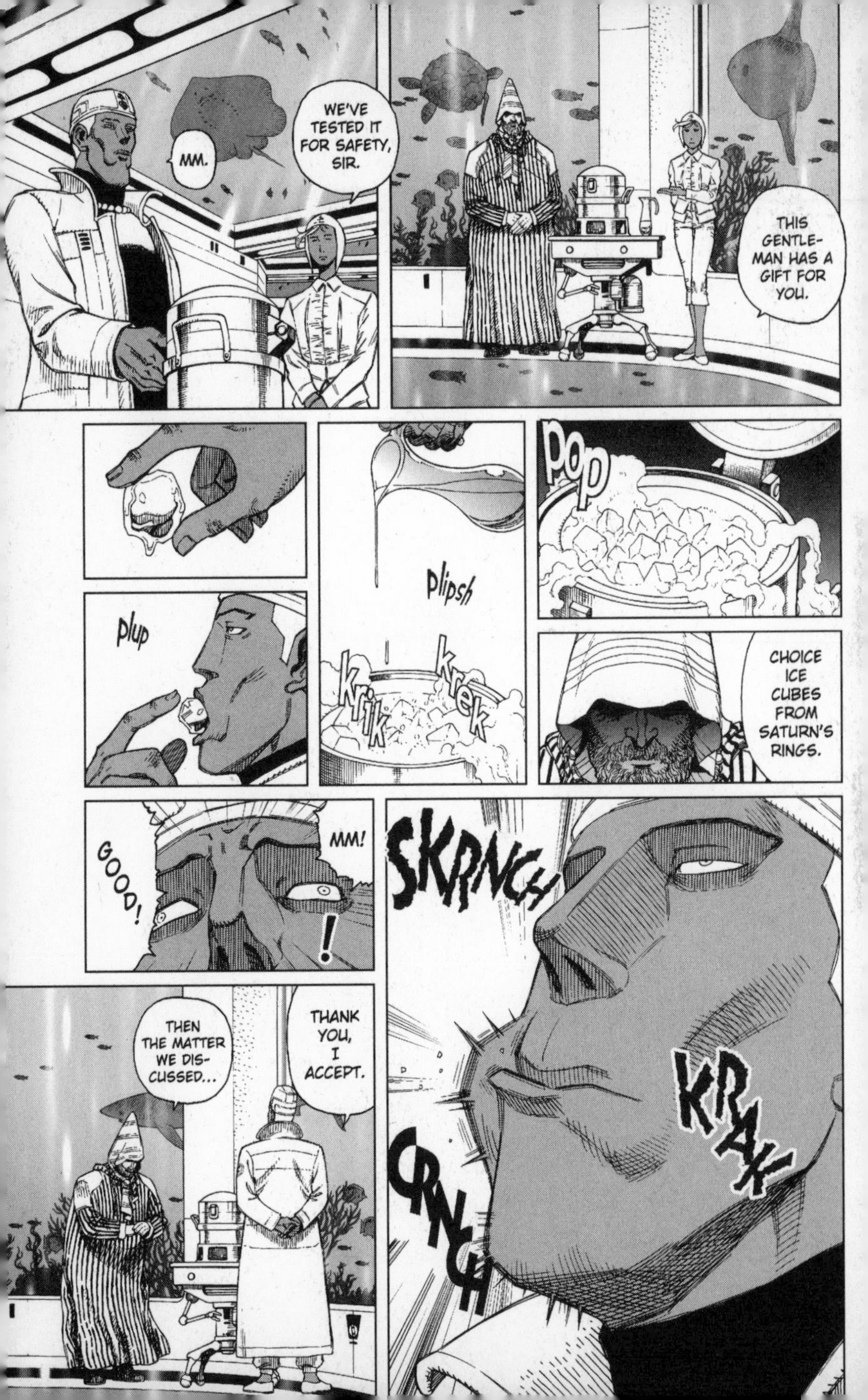
THIS GENTLEMAN HAS A GIFT FOR YOU.
WE'VE TESTED IT FOR SAFETY, SIR.
MM.
POP
CHOICE ICE CUBES FROM SATURN'S RINGS.
plipsh
krik
krek
plup
SKRNCH
KRAK
CRNCH
MM!
GOOD!
!
THANK YOU, I ACCEPT.
THEN THE MATTER WE DISCUSSED...

IN THE NAME OF PEACE FOR HUMANKIND...
...I HEREBY CONVENE THE 1355th SESSION OF LADDER, THE SOLAR SYSTEM TREATY MEDIATORY COUNCIL.

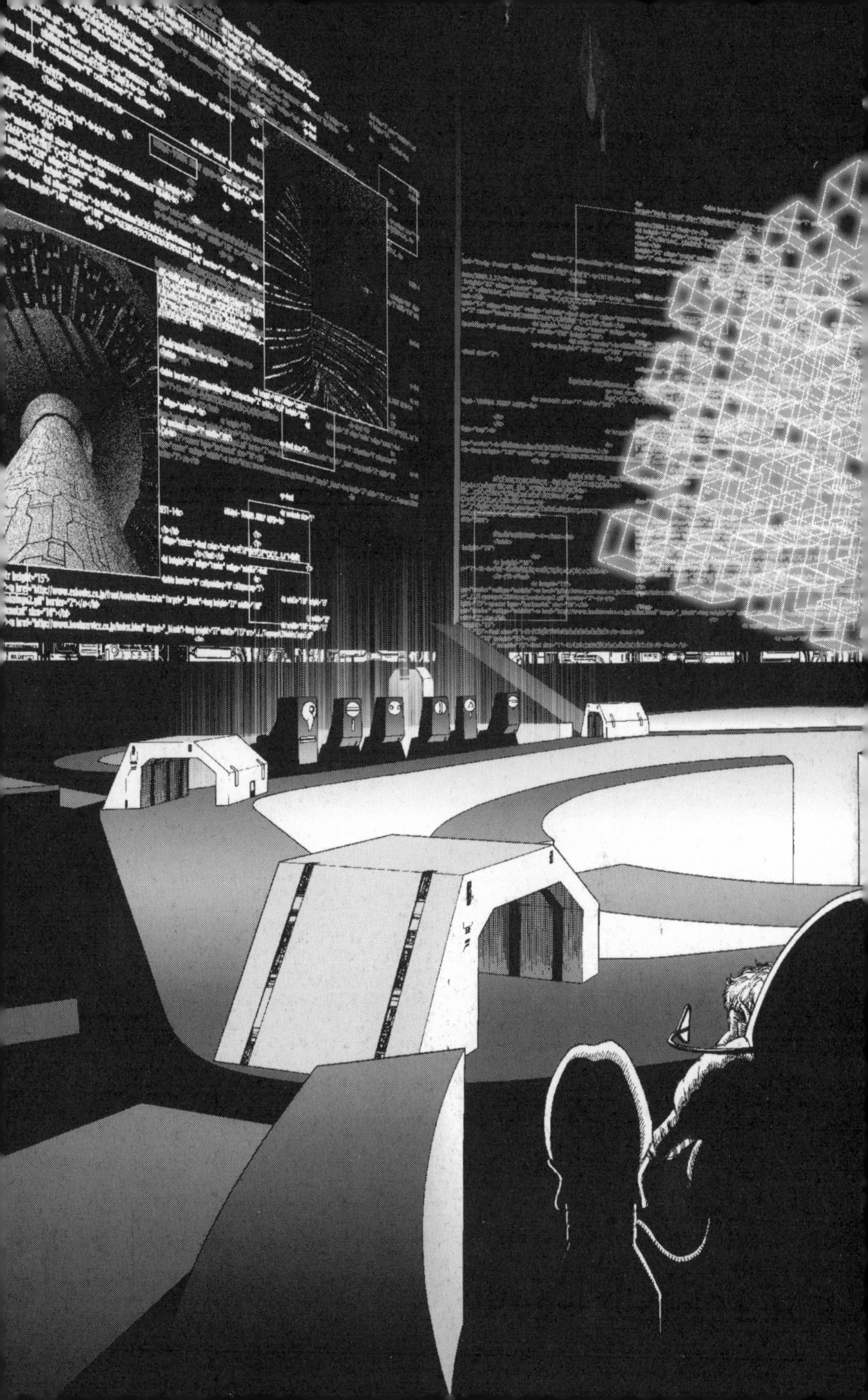

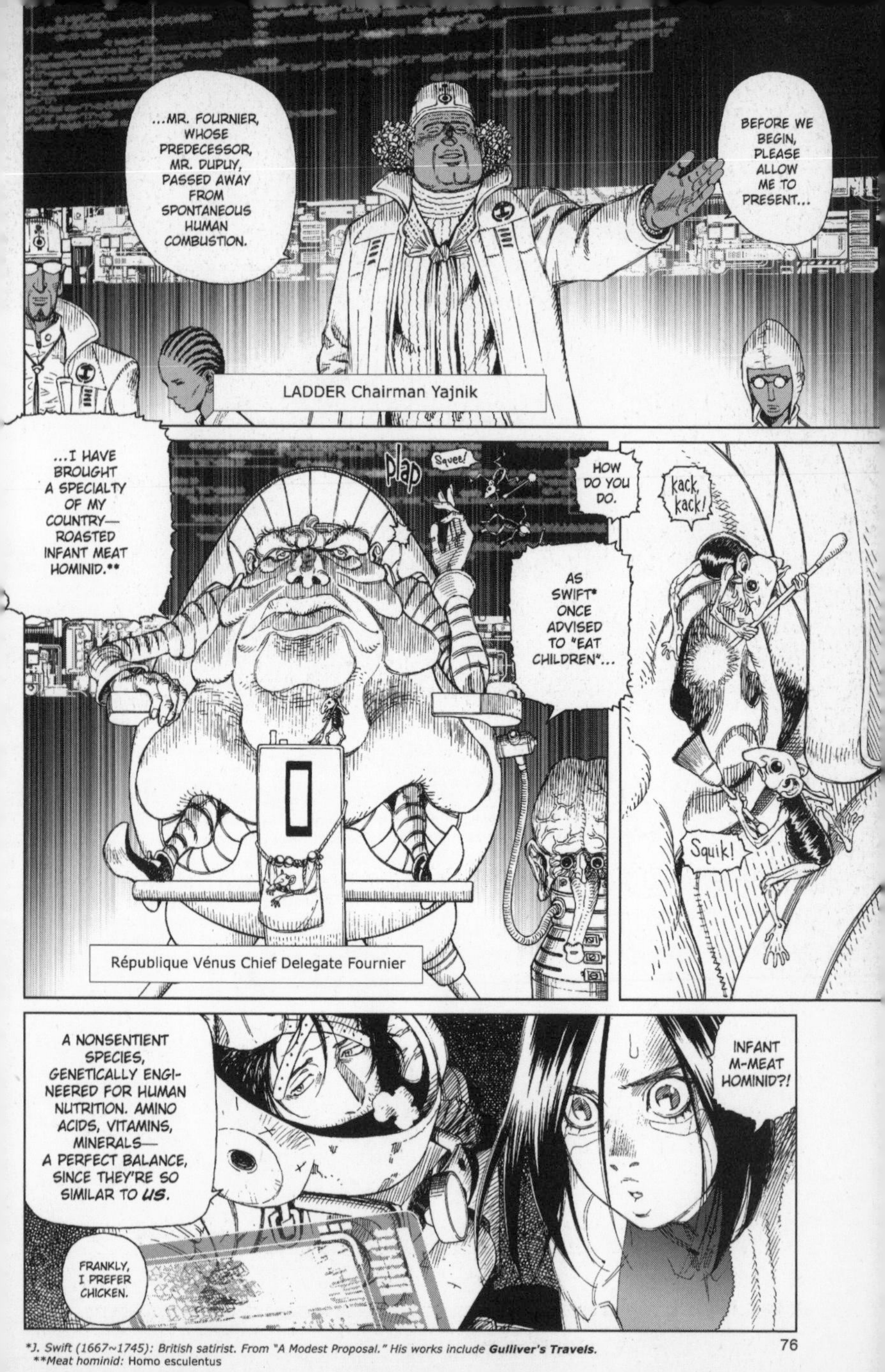
BEFORE WE BEGIN, PLEASE ALLOW ME TO PRESENT...
...MR. FOURNIER, WHOSE PREDECESSOR, MR. DUPUY, PASSED AWAY FROM SPONTANEOUS HUMAN COMBUSTION.
LADDER Chairman Yajnik
kack, kack!
Squik!
Squee!
plap
HOW DO YOU DO.
AS SWIFT* ONCE ADVISED TO "EAT CHILDREN"...
...I HAVE BROUGHT A SPECIALTY OF MY COUNTRY— ROASTED INFANT MEAT HOMINID.**
République Vénus Chief Delegate Fournier
INFANT M-MEAT HOMINID?!
A NONSENTIENT SPECIES, GENETICALLY ENGINEERED FOR HUMAN NUTRITION. AMINO ACIDS, VITAMINS, MINERALS— A PERFECT BALANCE, SINCE THEY'RE SO SIMILAR TO *US*.
FRANKLY, I PREFER CHICKEN.

J. Swift (1667~1745): British satirist. From "A Modest Proposal." His works include* ***Gulliver's Travels**.*
***Meat hominid:* Homo esculentus

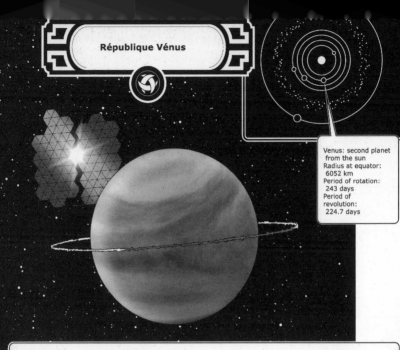

République Vénus

Venus: second planet from the sun
Radius at equator: 6052 km
Period of rotation: 243 days
Period of revolution: 224.7 days

ES 242: first Venusian space colony built in orbit.
ES 250: République Vénus, consisting of several colonial states, founded. Terraforming projects progress. Planet has mean surface temperature over 400°C, 90 mm Hg atmospheric pressure, and a sky covered by a dense cloud of sulfuric gas.
Construction of huge solar shield at the Lagrange point* cools atmosphere, with current surface temperatures of -50°C. Ownership of Enceladus,** the icy moon required for final stages of terraforming, in dispute with the Jupiter Union—thus terraforming only half finished.

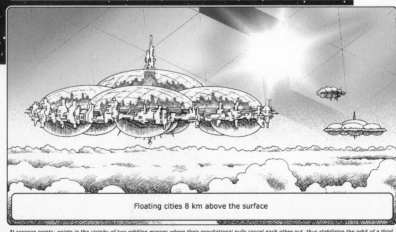

Floating cities 8 km above the surface

*Lagrange points: points in the vicinity of two orbiting masses where their gravitational pulls cancel each other out, thus stabilizing the orbit of a third mass. Theorem proven by the French mathematician Lagrange (1736~1813).
**Enceladus: Saturn's satellite II. Radius at equator: 251 km. Discovered in 1789 by Herschel, and named after a giant of Greek mythology.

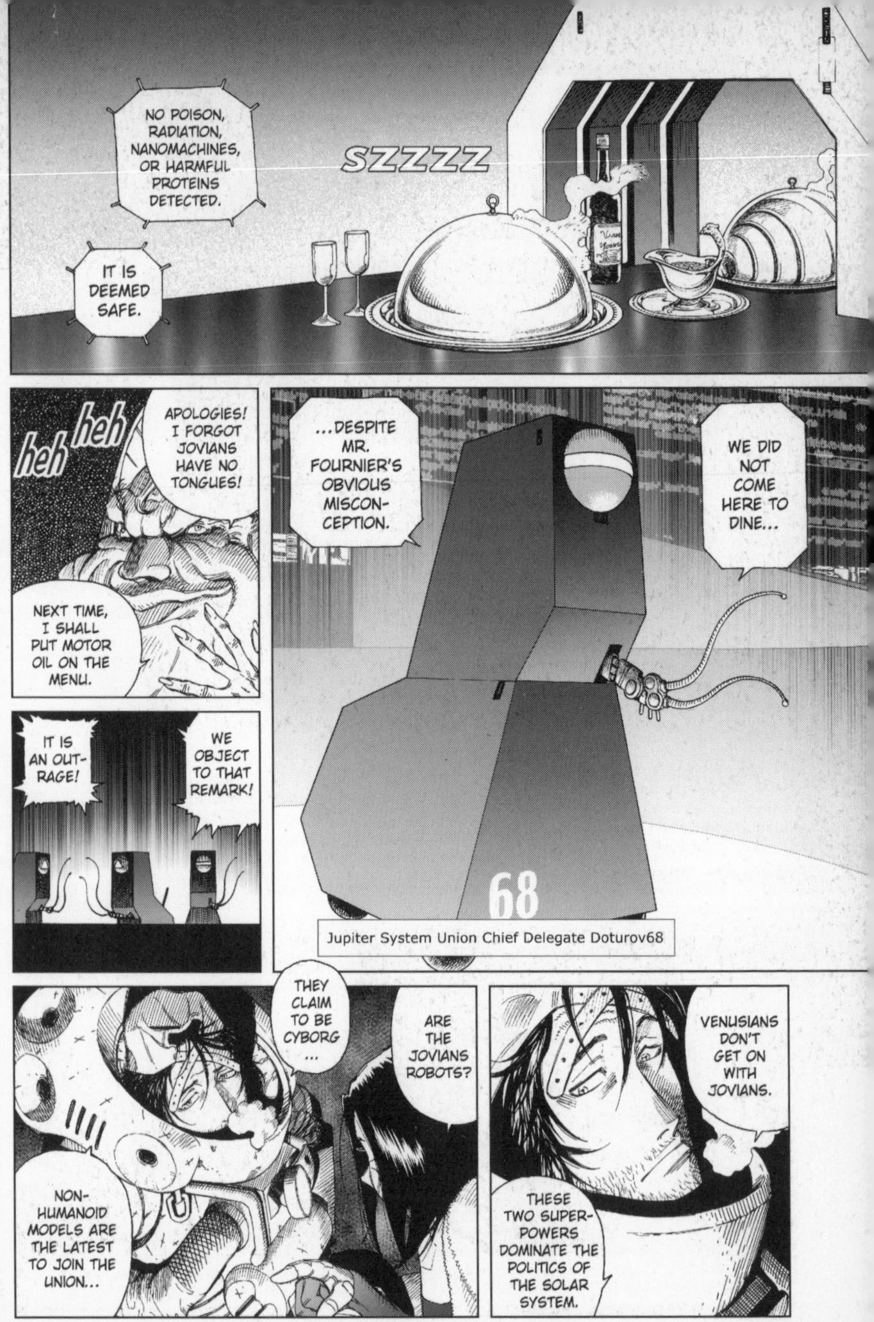

NO POISON, RADIATION, NANOMACHINES, OR HARMFUL PROTEINS DETECTED.
SZZZZ
IT IS DEEMED SAFE.
WE DID NOT COME HERE TO DINE...
...DESPITE MR. FOURNIER'S OBVIOUS MISCON-CEPTION.
68
Jupiter System Union Chief Delegate Doturov68
heh heh
APOLOGIES! I FORGOT JOVIANS HAVE NO TONGUES!
NEXT TIME, I SHALL PUT MOTOR OIL ON THE MENU.
WE OBJECT TO THAT REMARK!
IT IS AN OUT-RAGE!
VENUSIANS DON'T GET ON WITH JOVIANS.
THESE TWO SUPER-POWERS DOMINATE THE POLITICS OF THE SOLAR SYSTEM.
ARE THE JOVIANS ROBOTS?
THEY CLAIM TO BE CYBORG ...
NON-HUMANOID MODELS ARE THE LATEST TO JOIN THE UNION...

Jupiter System Union

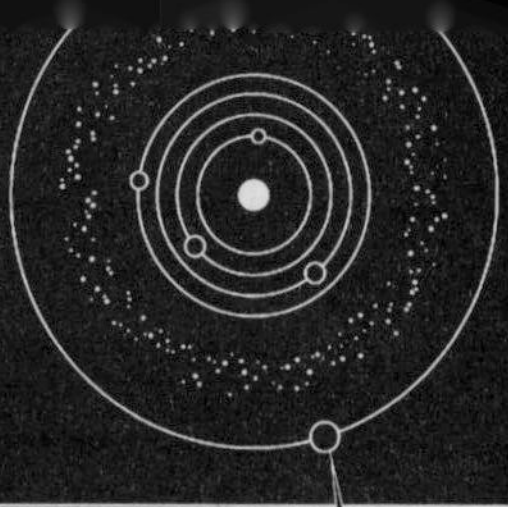

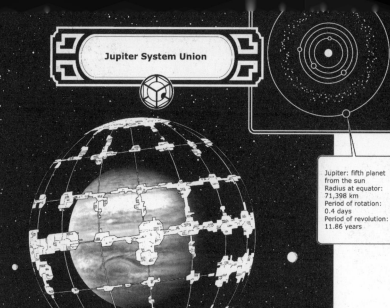

Jupiter: fifth planet from the sun
Radius at equator: 71,398 km
Period of rotation: 0.4 days
Period of revolution: 11.86 years

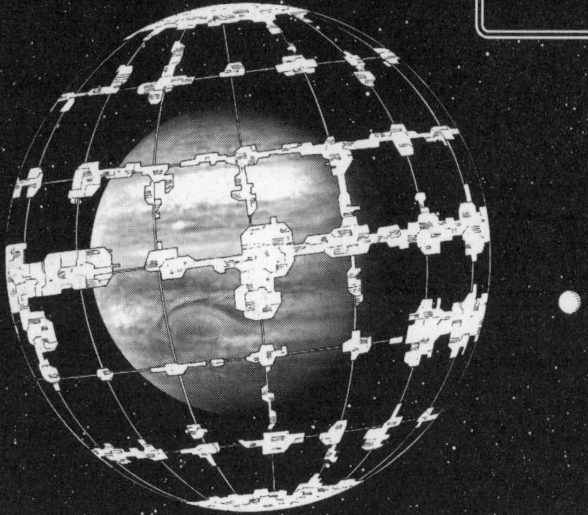

ES 263: The first colony is built on Ganymede, one of the Galilean satellites.*
ES 300: The Jupiter System Union declares independence, with colonies not only on the Galilean moons, but also on the Trojan asteroid clouds along Jupiter's orbital path. It maintains a healthy economy due to the wealth of mineral resources on the asteroids, and the abundance of the nuclear fusion fuel helium-3** in the Jovian atmosphere.
ES 316: Work begins on the "Toposphere Project," a giant shell to provide living space for Jupiter. Of the 16 original moons, all but three (Europa, Ganymede, and Callisto—each too urbanized to sacrifice) have been consumed to provide materials for the unfinished Toposphere. Jupiter and Venus both claim rights to Saturn's satellites and the asteroid belt to use as resources for their terraforming efforts.

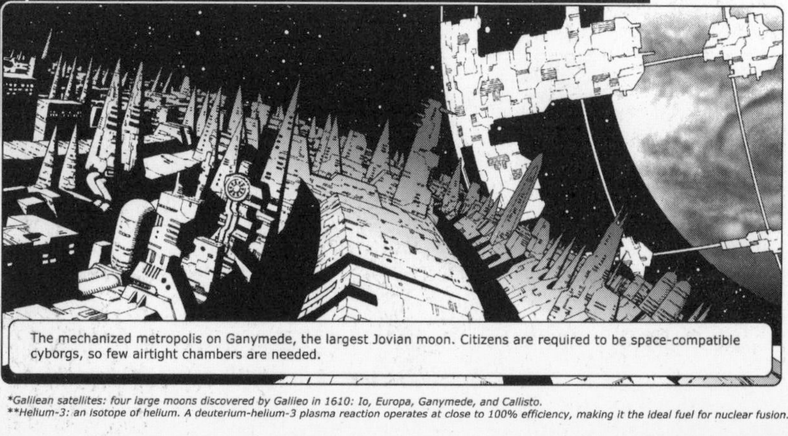

The mechanized metropolis on Ganymede, the largest Jovian moon. Citizens are required to be space-compatible cyborgs, so few airtight chambers are needed.

*Galilean satellites: four large moons discovered by Galileo in 1610: Io, Europa, Ganymede, and Callisto.
**Helium-3: an isotope of helium. A deuterium-helium-3 plasma reaction operates at close to 100% efficiency, making it the ideal fuel for nuclear fusion.

chmp
LET'S LEAVE THE BOORISH JOVIANS ASIDE...
krnch mnch
SURELY THE ALWAYS AMENABLE ORBITARIANS WOULDN'T REFUSE?
quake quake quake
UNHHHH...
tch twch tch
twtch vit vit tch
Federation Economics Minister Lawhear
Space City Binhar* Representative Meshach
Luna Colony Representative Pomponazzi
WHAT'S WRONG WITH *THEM?*
HEH, HEH! IT'S THAT DARN UNANIMOUS SYSTEM WORKING AGAINST THEM.
BAD ENOUGH BEING CAUGHT BETWEEN SUPERPOWERS, BUT WHEN THEY GET OVERT HARASSMENT LIKE THIS, THE EARTH REPS DON'T KNOW HOW TO HANDLE IT. TURNS THEM INTO BLITHERING IDIOTS.
FOR UNANIMOUS TO RUN SMOOTHLY, ***EVERYONE*** NEEDS TO HAVE THE PEACEKEEPER INSTALLED.

**Binhar: the Space City diametrically opposed to Ketheres pumps oxygen and seawater from the surface via the orbital elevator for export to the colonies. The corresponding surface gate city is Nezher.*

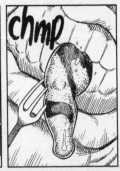

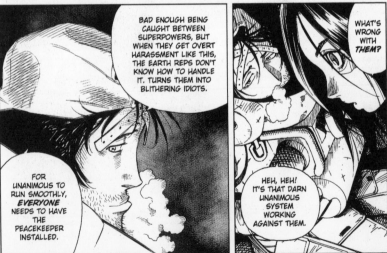

Earth Orbitary Federation

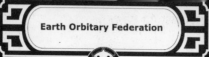

The Orbital Ring System
An orbital ring of two masses, wrapped in a tube and spinning in opposite directions, supports the diametrically opposed orbital elevators. The advantage of this structure is that the elevators can be constructed in places other than the equator, on any desired latitude and longitude.

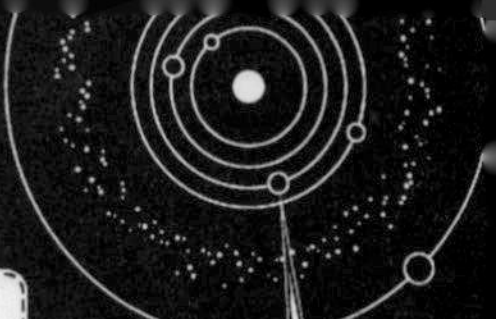

Earth: third planet from the sun
Radius at equator: 6378 km
Period of rotation: 0.997 days
Period of revolution: 365.26 days
Satellite: Luna
Radius at equator: 1738 km
Period of revolution: 27.32 days

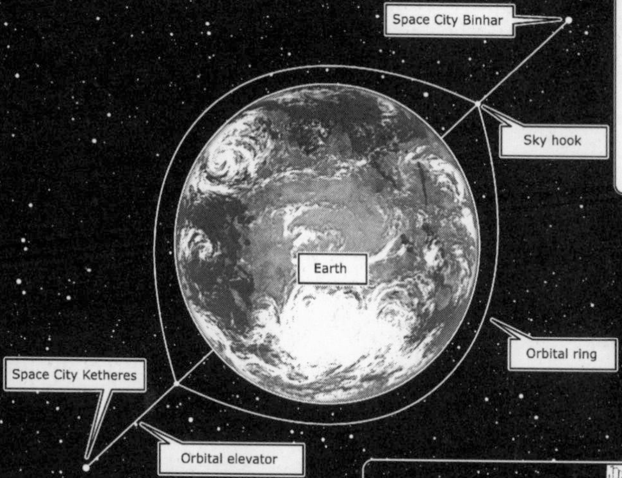

Space City Binhar
Sky hook
Earth
Orbital ring
Space City Ketheres
Orbital elevator

Earth: cradle of the human race.
ES 55: Geo Catastrophe—a giant meteor impact near Japan almost wipes out the entire population of the planet. Seventy years later, Melchizedek, an A.I. that managed to survive this extinction level event, implements the Rehabilitation Settlement Project, sending pioneers to other planets to dilute the danger of extinction.
ES 218: The orbital ring system "Jacob's Ladder" is complete. The settlement project shows steady progress, but Earth is forced to alter its role after the colonies declare independence.
ES 301: Earth and the lunar colonies declare the formation of the Earth Orbitary Federation.
ES 387: LADDER, the Solar System Treaty Mediatory Council, is founded on Space City Ketheres. Their unique history and political circumstances make the character of the Federation complex. Although weather patterns on the surface have been stable for two centuries, open redevelopment and transportation are still restricted by treaties.

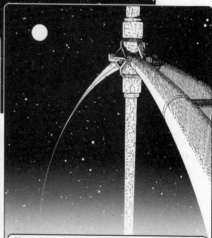

The **skyhook**, the link between the orbital elevator and the orbital ring. The orbital ring system has undergone many repairs, and its roles and functions have changed dramatically.

These planetary terraforming concepts were based on ideas of the British scientist Paul Birch.—Kishiro

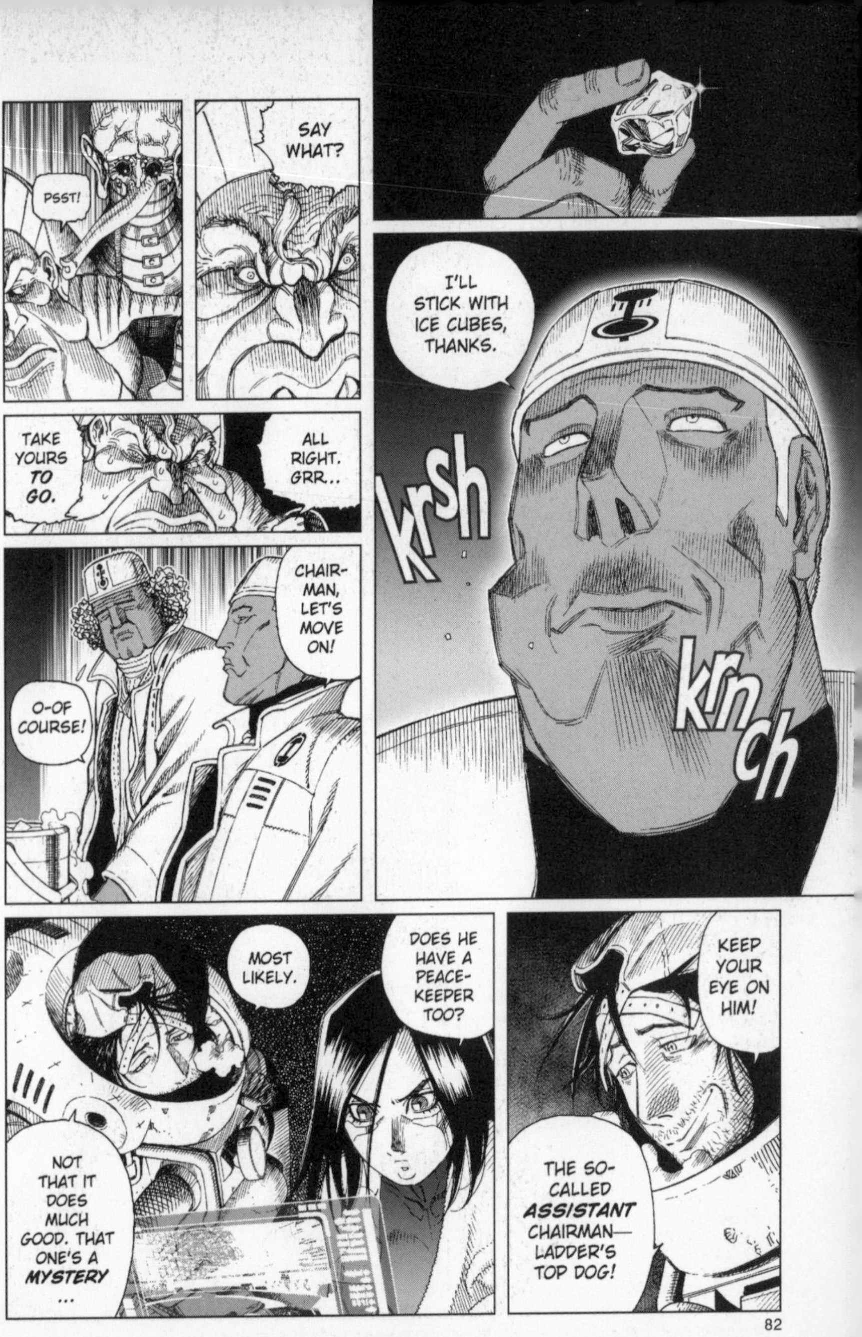
I'LL STICK WITH ICE CUBES, THANKS.
krsh
krnch
SAY WHAT?
PSST!
ALL RIGHT. GRR..
TAKE YOURS *TO GO.*
CHAIR-MAN, LET'S MOVE ON!
O-OF COURSE!
KEEP YOUR EYE ON HIM!
THE SO-CALLED ***ASSISTANT*** CHAIRMAN—LADDER'S TOP DOG!
DOES HE HAVE A PEACE-KEEPER TOO?
MOST LIKELY.
NOT THAT IT DOES MUCH GOOD. THAT ONE'S A ***MYSTERY*** ...

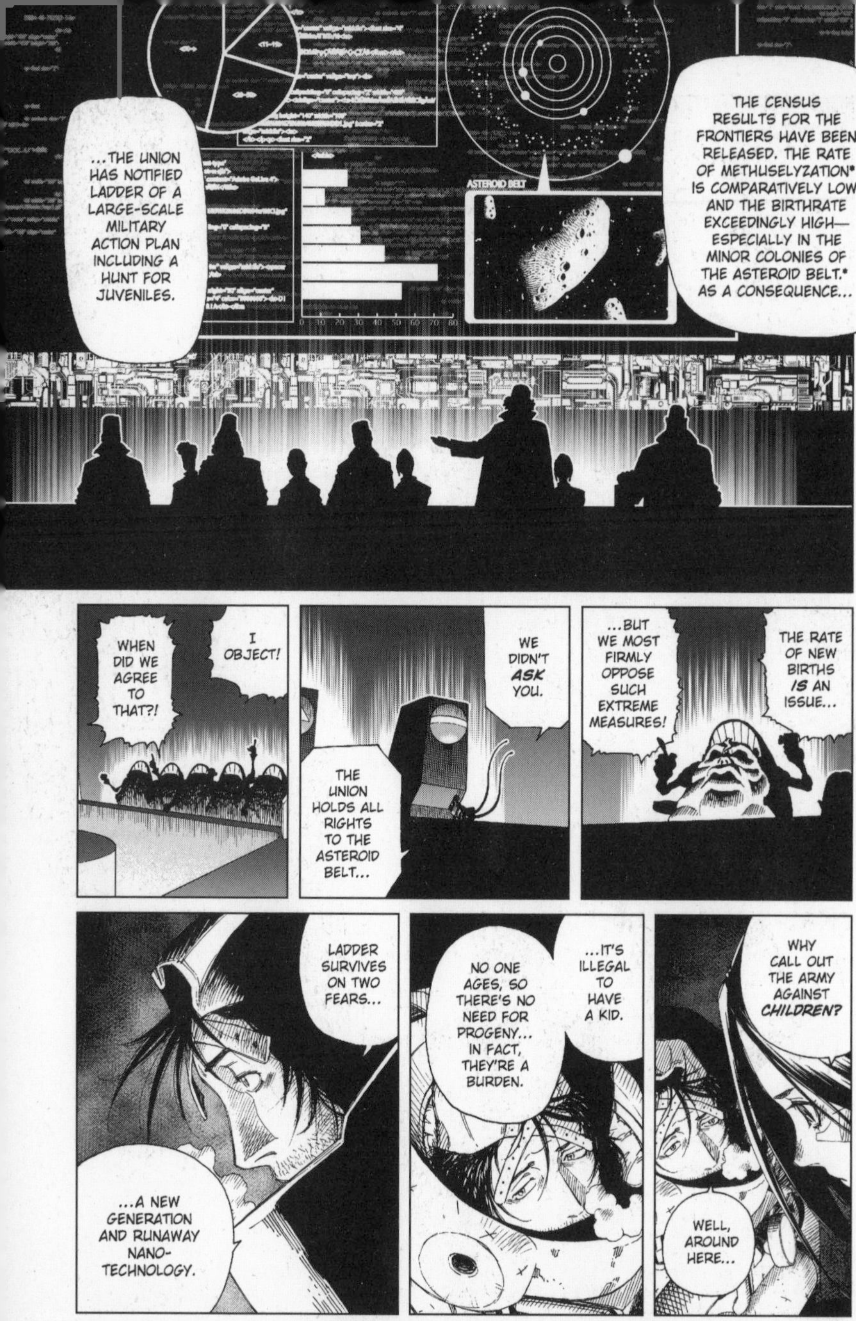
THE CENSUS RESULTS FOR THE FRONTIERS HAVE BEEN RELEASED. THE RATE OF METHUSELYZATION* IS COMPARATIVELY LOW, AND THE BIRTHRATE EXCEEDINGLY HIGH—ESPECIALLY IN THE MINOR COLONIES OF THE ASTEROID BELT.* AS A CONSEQUENCE...
ASTEROID BELT
...THE UNION HAS NOTIFIED LADDER OF A LARGE-SCALE MILITARY ACTION PLAN INCLUDING A HUNT FOR JUVENILES.
THE RATE OF NEW BIRTHS *IS* AN ISSUE...
...BUT WE MOST FIRMLY OPPOSE SUCH EXTREME MEASURES!
WE DIDN'T ***ASK*** YOU.
THE UNION HOLDS ALL RIGHTS TO THE ASTEROID BELT...
I OBJECT!
WHEN DID WE AGREE TO THAT?!
WHY CALL OUT THE ARMY AGAINST ***CHILDREN?***
WELL, AROUND HERE...
...IT'S ILLEGAL TO HAVE A KID.
NO ONE AGES, SO THERE'S NO NEED FOR PROGENY... IN FACT, THEY'RE A BURDEN.
LADDER SURVIVES ON TWO FEARS...
...A NEW GENERATION AND RUNAWAY NANO-TECHNOLOGY.

**Methuselyzation: halting the aging process by installing personal nanomachines in the body, thus making immortality a reality. Methuselah, a figure in the Bible's Book of Genesis, is purported to have lived 969 years.*
***Asteroid belt: a donut-shaped region between the orbits of Mars and Jupiter in which most asteroids are found.*

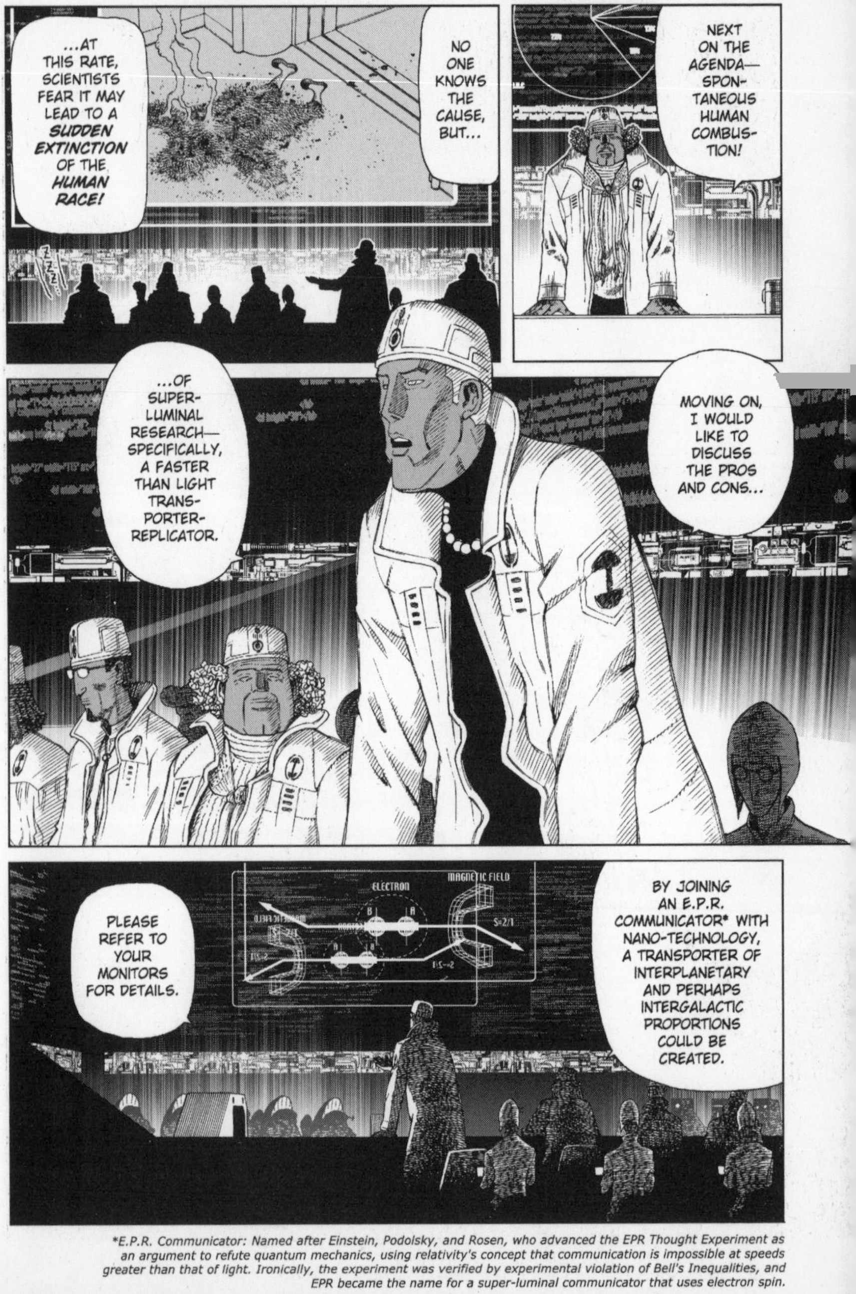
NEXT ON THE AGENDA— SPONTANEOUS HUMAN COMBUSTION!
NO ONE KNOWS THE CAUSE, BUT...
...AT THIS RATE, SCIENTISTS FEAR IT MAY LEAD TO A SUDDEN EXTINCTION OF THE HUMAN RACE!
ZZZ
MOVING ON, I WOULD LIKE TO DISCUSS THE PROS AND CONS...
...OF SUPER-LUMINAL RESEARCH— SPECIFICALLY, A FASTER THAN LIGHT TRANSPORTER-REPLICATOR.
BY JOINING AN E.P.R. COMMUNICATOR* WITH NANO-TECHNOLOGY, A TRANSPORTER OF INTERPLANETARY AND PERHAPS INTERGALACTIC PROPORTIONS COULD BE CREATED.
MAGNETIC FIELD
ELECTRON
PLEASE REFER TO YOUR MONITORS FOR DETAILS.

*E.P.R. Communicator: Named after Einstein, Podolsky, and Rosen, who advanced the EPR Thought Experiment as an argument to refute quantum mechanics, using relativity's concept that communication is impossible at speeds greater than that of light. Ironically, the experiment was verified by experimental violation of Bell's Inequalities, and EPR became the name for a super-luminal communicator that uses electron spin.

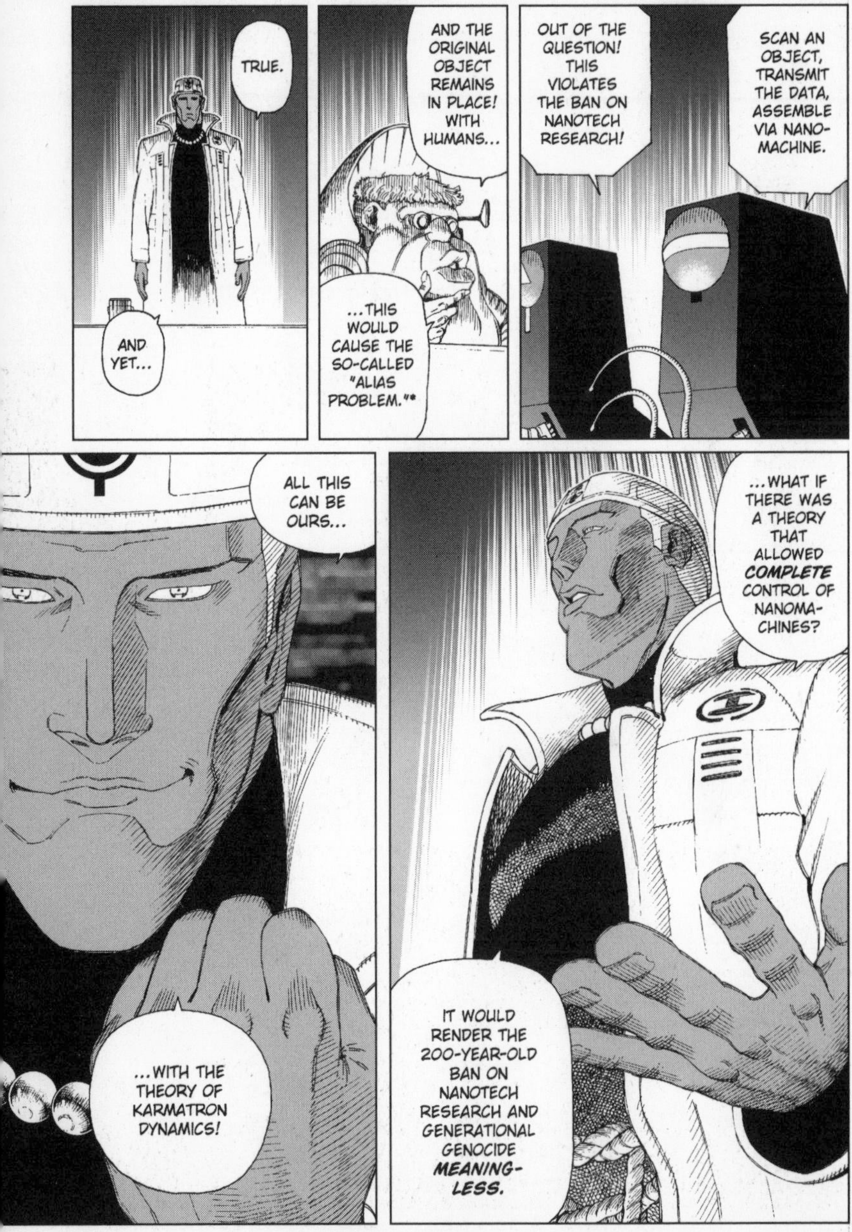
SCAN AN OBJECT, TRANSMIT THE DATA, ASSEMBLE VIA NANO-MACHINE.
OUT OF THE QUESTION! THIS VIOLATES THE BAN ON NANOTECH RESEARCH!
AND THE ORIGINAL OBJECT REMAINS IN PLACE! WITH HUMANS...
...THIS WOULD CAUSE THE SO-CALLED "ALIAS PROBLEM."*
TRUE.
AND YET...
...WHAT IF THERE WAS A THEORY THAT ALLOWED ***COMPLETE*** CONTROL OF NANOMA-CHINES?
IT WOULD RENDER THE 200-YEAR-OLD BAN ON NANOTECH RESEARCH AND GENERATIONAL GENOCIDE ***MEANING-LESS.***
ALL THIS CAN BE OURS...
...WITH THE THEORY OF KARMATRON DYNAMICS!

**Alias Problem: when two people with the same memories, personalities, and bodies exist at the same time in the same society.*

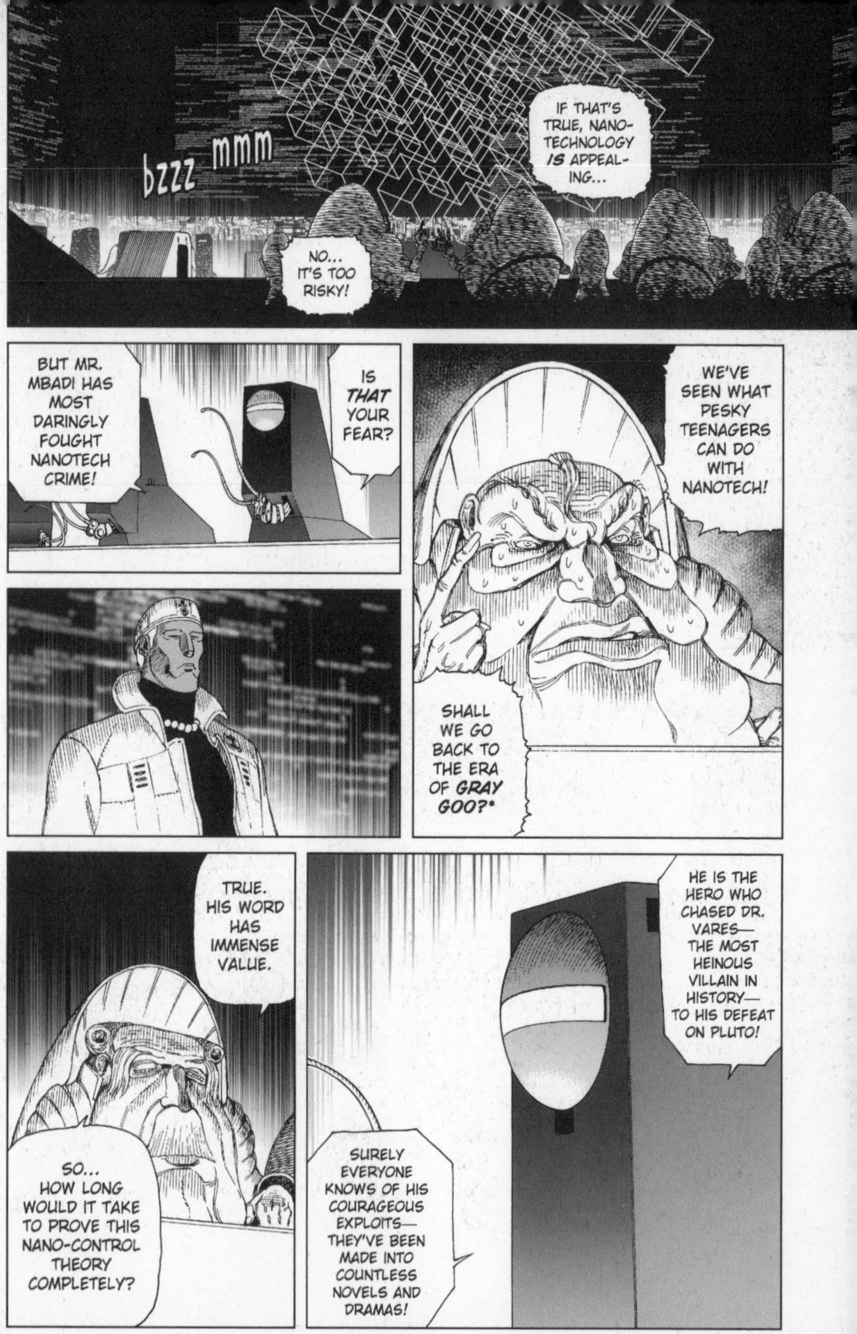
IF THAT'S TRUE, NANO-TECHNOLOGY *IS* APPEAL-ING...
bzzz mmm
NO... IT'S TOO RISKY!
WE'VE SEEN WHAT PESKY TEENAGERS CAN DO WITH NANOTECH!
SHALL WE GO BACK TO THE ERA OF *GRAY GOO?**
IS *THAT* YOUR FEAR?
BUT MR. MBADI HAS MOST DARINGLY FOUGHT NANOTECH CRIME!
HE IS THE HERO WHO CHASED DR. VARES— THE MOST HEINOUS VILLAIN IN HISTORY— TO HIS DEFEAT ON PLUTO!
SURELY EVERYONE KNOWS OF HIS COURAGEOUS EXPLOITS— THEY'VE BEEN MADE INTO COUNTLESS NOVELS AND DRAMAS!
TRUE. HIS WORD HAS IMMENSE VALUE.
SO... HOW LONG WOULD IT TAKE TO PROVE THIS NANO-CONTROL THEORY COMPLETELY?

**Gray goo: jargon for a disaster brought about by self-replicating nanomachines running amuck.*

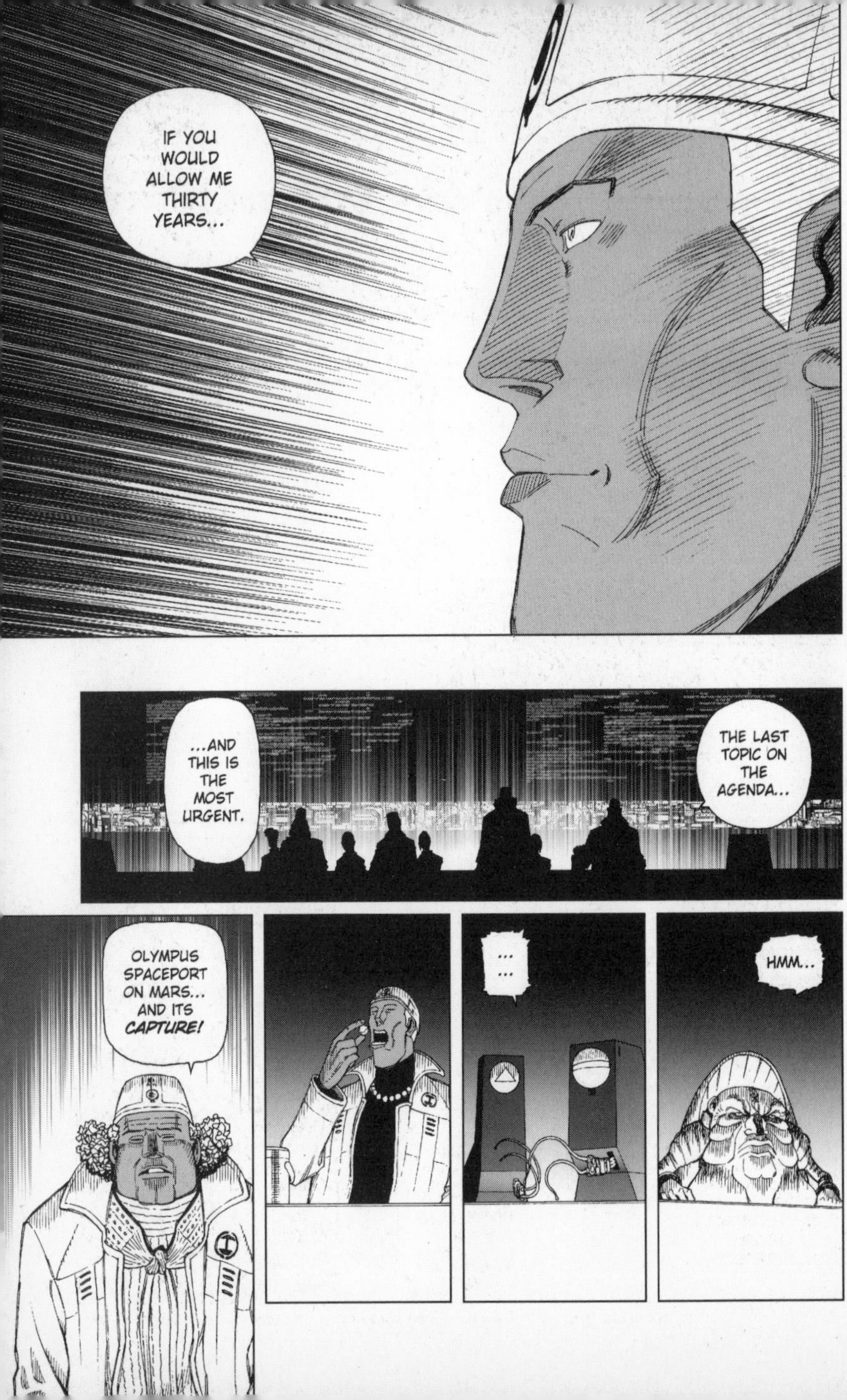
IF YOU WOULD ALLOW ME THIRTY YEARS...
THE LAST TOPIC ON THE AGENDA...
...AND THIS IS THE MOST URGENT.
HMM...
......
OLYMPUS SPACEPORT ON MARS... AND ITS *CAPTURE!*

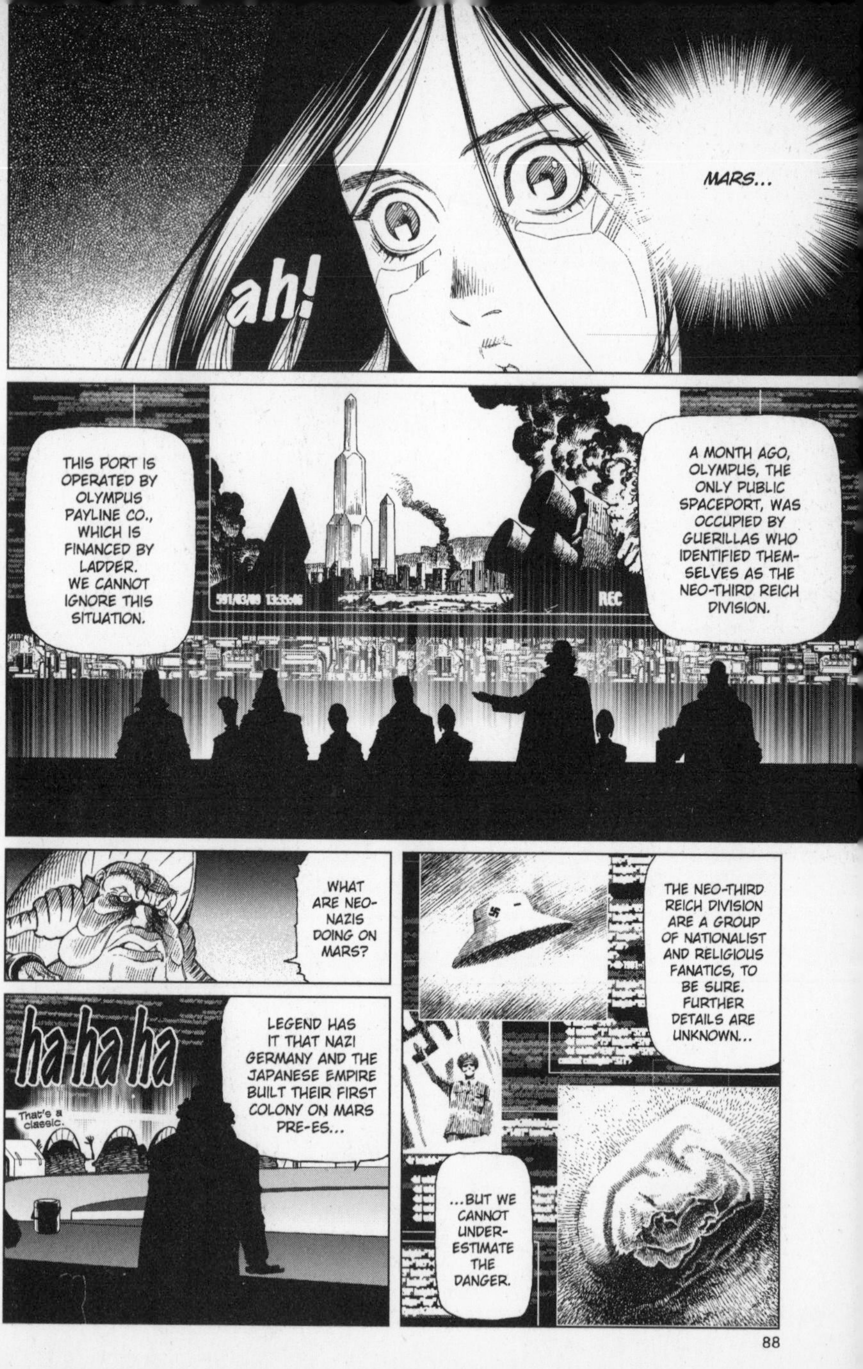

MARS...
ah!
A MONTH AGO, OLYMPUS, THE ONLY PUBLIC SPACEPORT, WAS OCCUPIED BY GUERILLAS WHO IDENTIFIED THEMSELVES AS THE NEO-THIRD REICH DIVISION.
REC
591/03/09 13:35:06
THIS PORT IS OPERATED BY OLYMPUS PAYLINE CO., WHICH IS FINANCED BY LADDER. WE CANNOT IGNORE THIS SITUATION.
THE NEO-THIRD REICH DIVISION ARE A GROUP OF NATIONALIST AND RELIGIOUS FANATICS, TO BE SURE. FURTHER DETAILS ARE UNKNOWN...
...BUT WE CANNOT UNDERESTIMATE THE DANGER.
WHAT ARE NEO-NAZIS DOING ON MARS?
LEGEND HAS IT THAT NAZI GERMANY AND THE JAPANESE EMPIRE BUILT THEIR FIRST COLONY ON MARS PRE-ES...
ha ha ha
That's a classic.

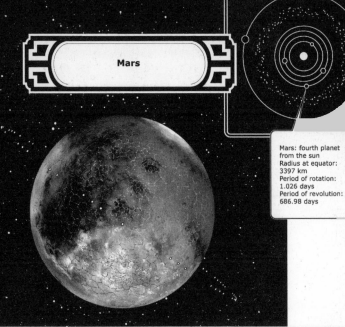

Mars

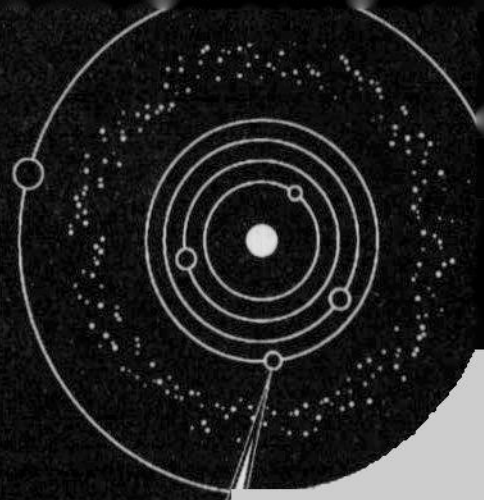

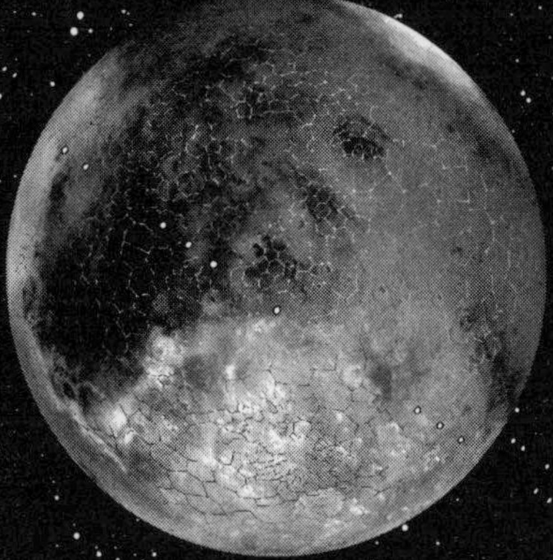

Mars: fourth planet from the sun
Radius at equator: 3397 km
Period of rotation: 1.026 days
Period of revolution: 686.98 days

A planet with the oldest history of settlers. The first emigration to Mars occurred by ES 53. After the Geo Catastrophe, construction of a full-scale colony began in ES 235, but ease of emigration and a comparatively hospitable environment led to oversettling—and a prolonged civil war. The planet remains divided to this day.
Making space access difficult, more than 80% of the surface is covered by a canopy that is self-repaired by nanomachines. Squabbles erupt over control of orbiting mirror satellites that supplement the insufficient sunlight, but the atmosphere is breathable.
Four roughly divided groups currently vy for supremacy:
MRH (Mars Republik Heer): Mars Republic Army: funded by République Vénus to unify Mars and make it join the République.
**MFB (Mars Front der Befreien): funded by the Jupiter Union to unify Mars and make it join the Union.
Mars Kingdom Parliament: LADDER-spearheaded attempt at constitutional monarchy.
Neo Third Reich Division: an emergent group calling itself the "Last Battalion" that aims to unify Mars, resurrect the Third Reich, and conquer the entire galaxy.

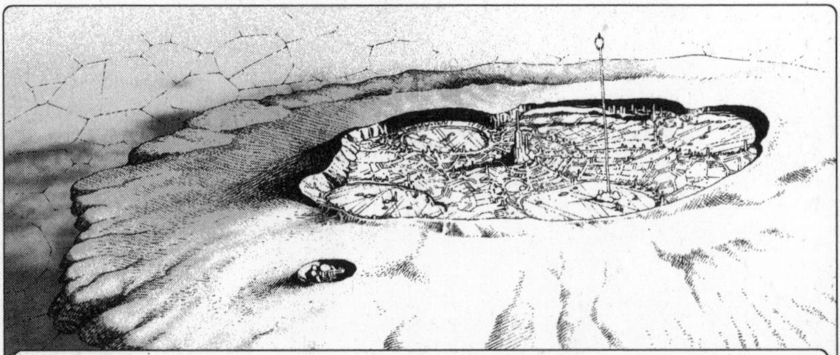

Olympus Spaceport, built in a caldera on Olympus Mons, largest mountain on Mars.

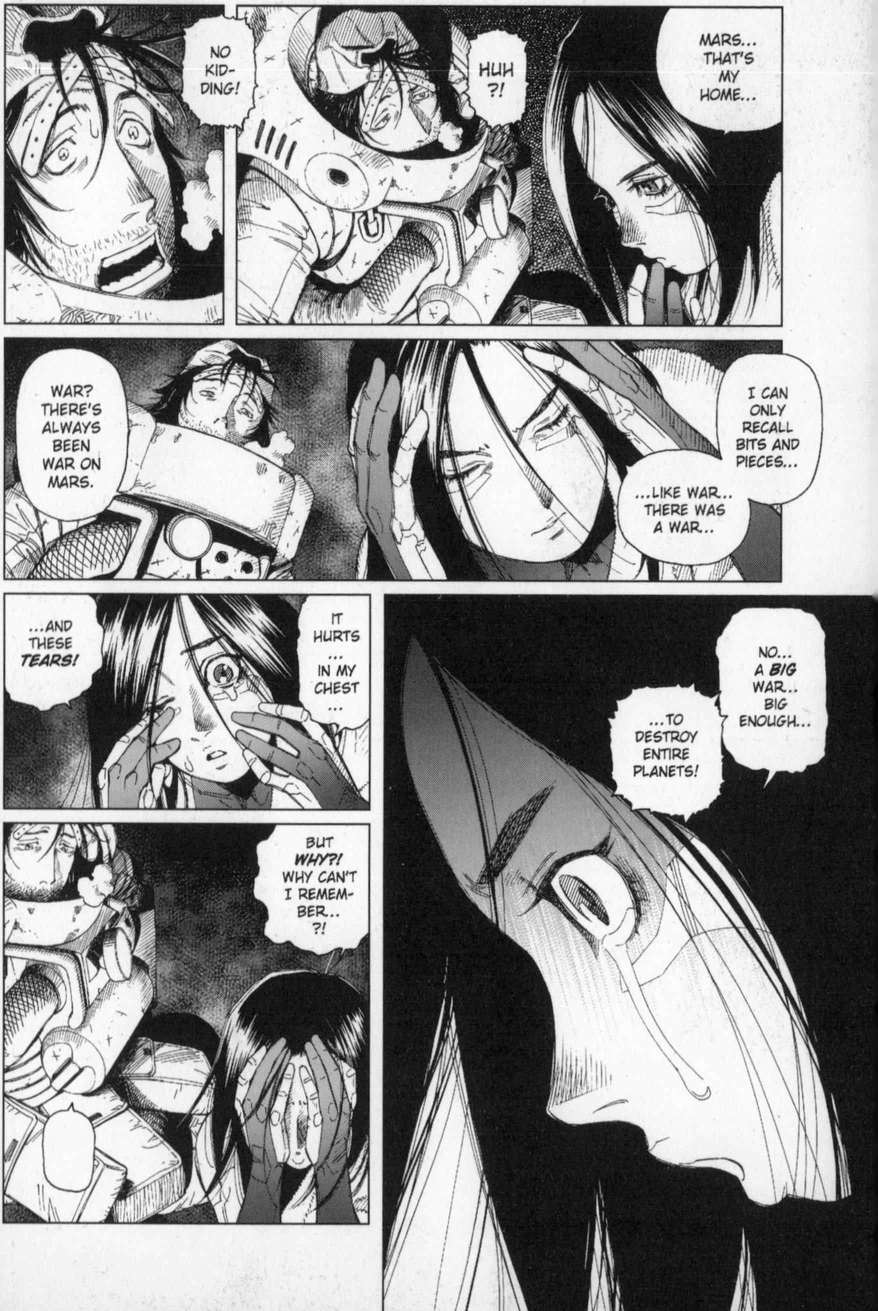
MARS... THAT'S MY HOME...
HUH ?!
NO KID-DING!
I CAN ONLY RECALL BITS AND PIECES...
...LIKE WAR... THERE WAS A WAR...
WAR? THERE'S ALWAYS BEEN WAR ON MARS.
NO... A BIG WAR.. BIG ENOUGH...
...TO DESTROY ENTIRE PLANETS!
IT HURTS ... IN MY CHEST ...
...AND THESE TEARS!
BUT WHY?! WHY CAN'T I REMEM-BER.. ?!

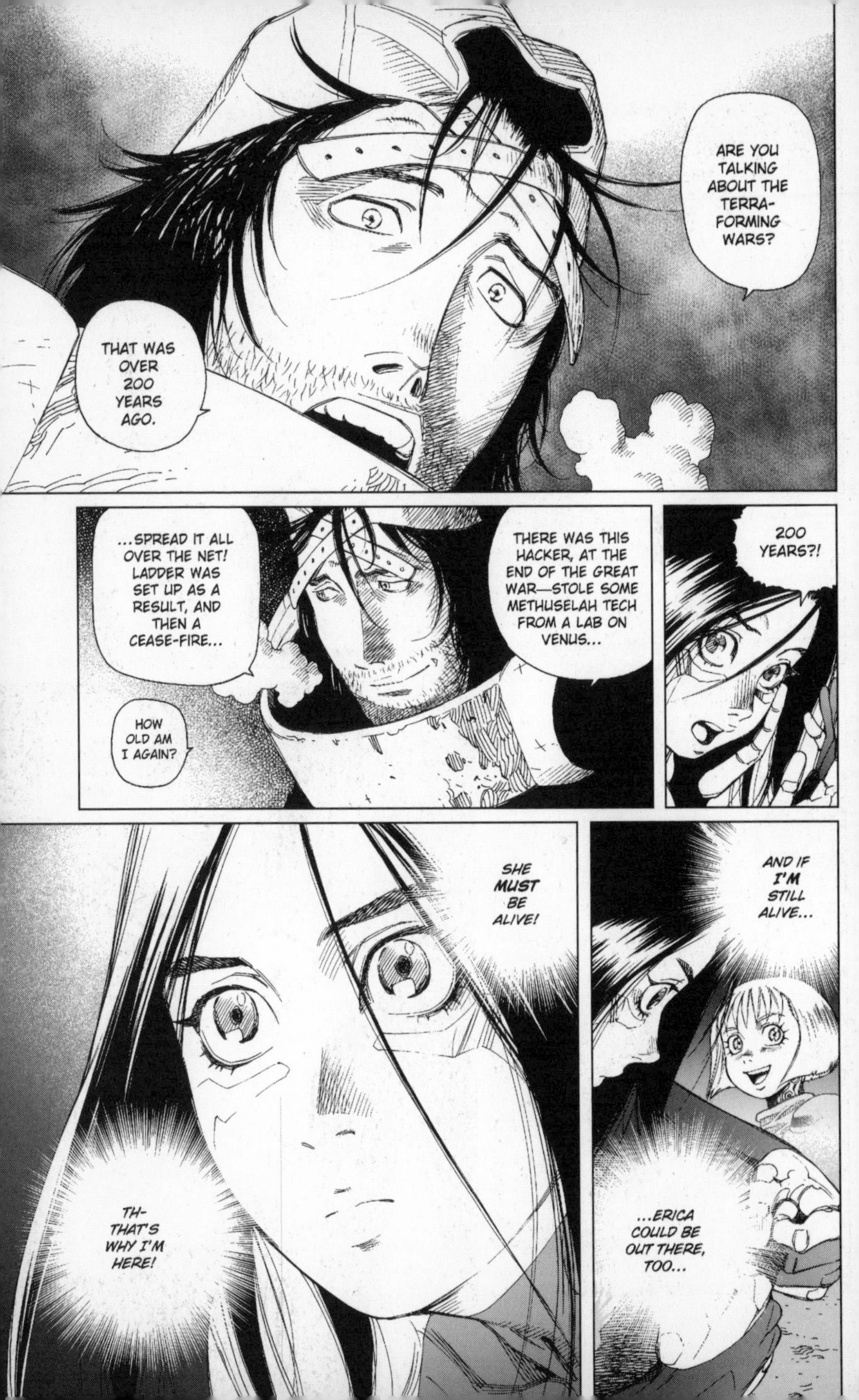
ARE YOU TALKING ABOUT THE TERRA-FORMING WARS?
THAT WAS OVER 200 YEARS AGO.
200 YEARS?!
THERE WAS THIS HACKER, AT THE END OF THE GREAT WAR—STOLE SOME METHUSELAH TECH FROM A LAB ON VENUS...
...SPREAD IT ALL OVER THE NET! LADDER WAS SET UP AS A RESULT, AND THEN A CEASE-FIRE...
HOW OLD AM I AGAIN?
AND IF I'M STILL ALIVE...
...ERICA COULD BE OUT THERE, TOO...
SHE MUST BE ALIVE!
TH- THAT'S WHY I'M HERE!

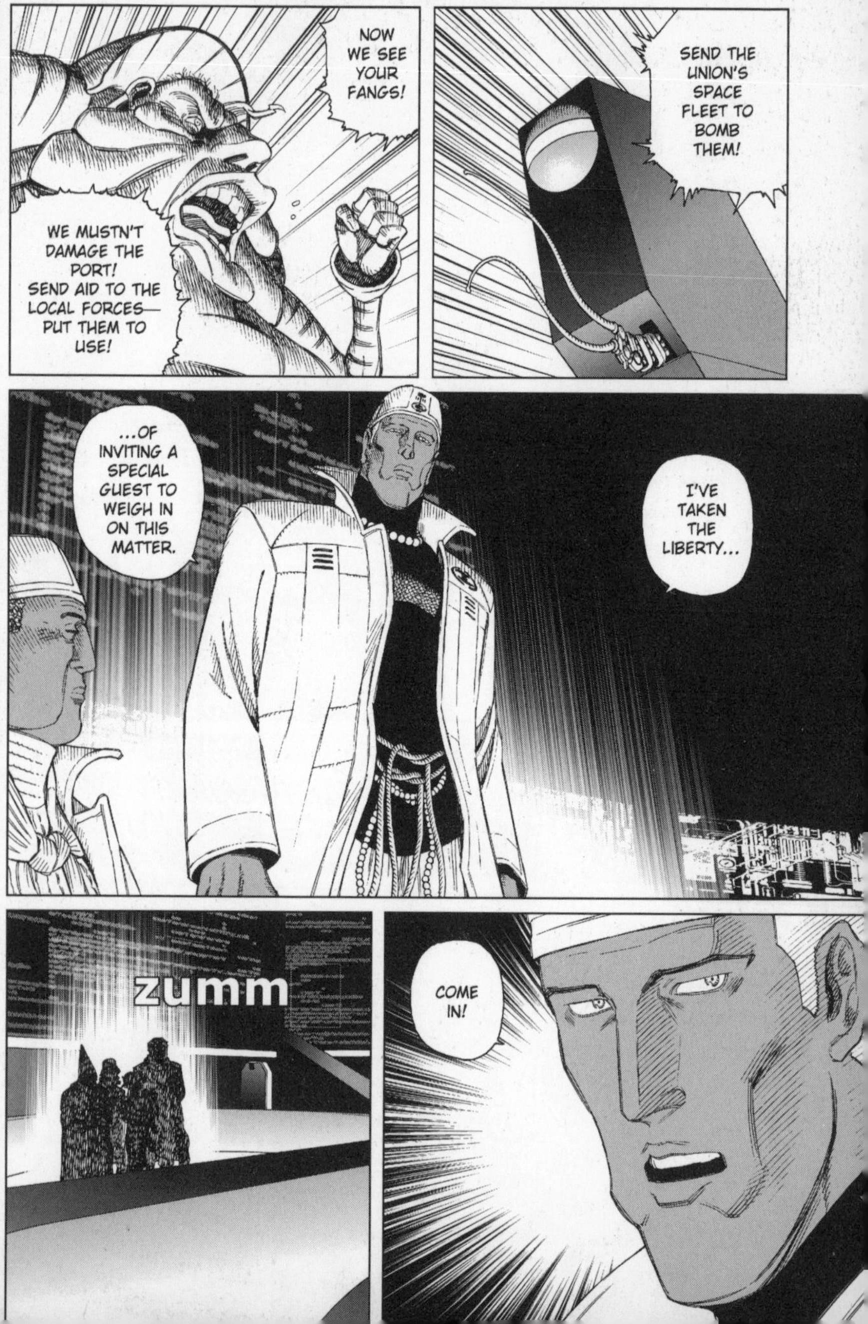
SEND THE UNION'S SPACE FLEET TO BOMB THEM!
NOW WE SEE YOUR FANGS!
WE MUSTN'T DAMAGE THE PORT! SEND AID TO THE LOCAL FORCES—PUT THEM TO USE!
I'VE TAKEN THE LIBERTY...
...OF INVITING A SPECIAL GUEST TO WEIGH IN ON THIS MATTER.
COME IN!
zumm

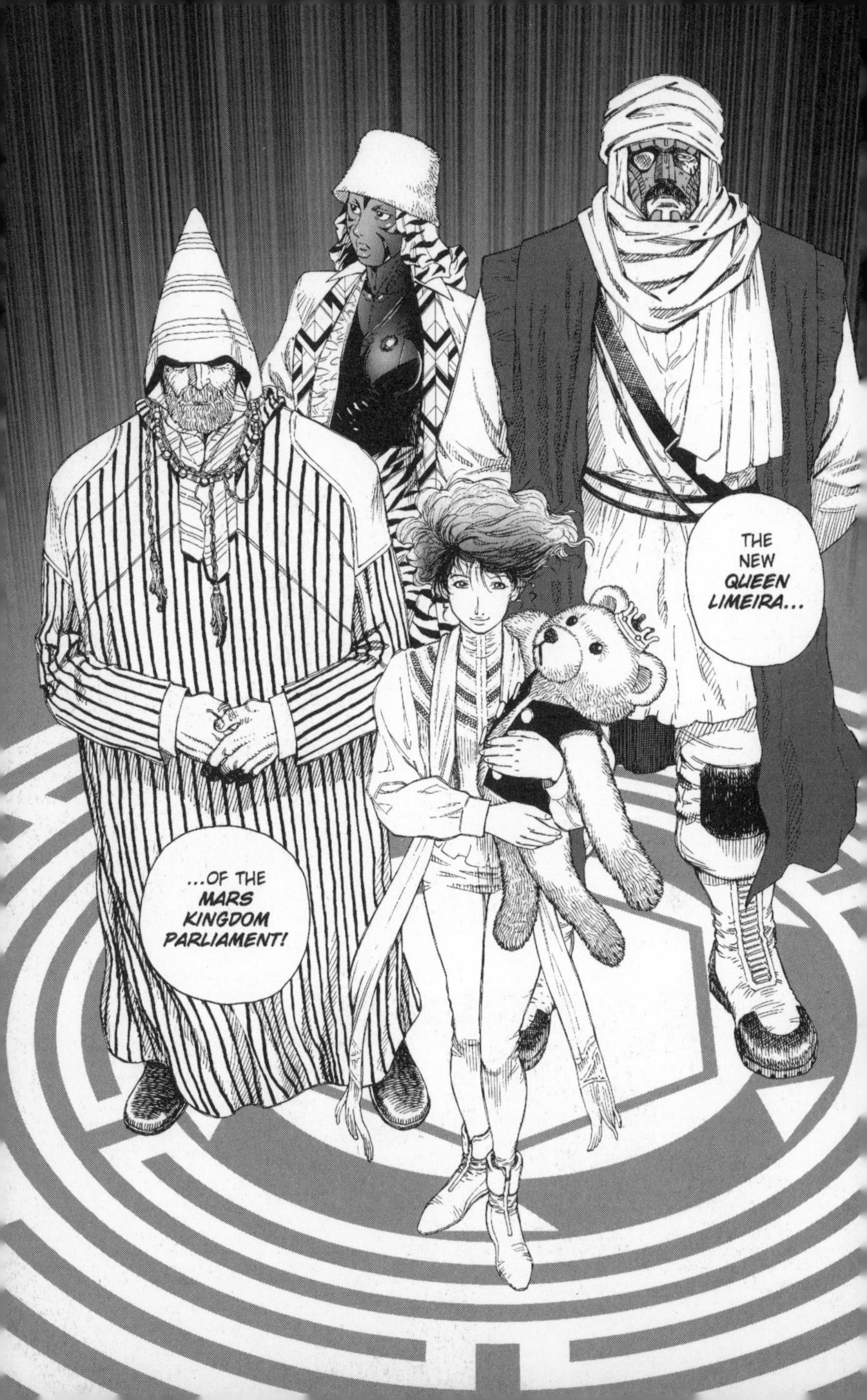
THE NEW QUEEN LIMEIRA...
...OF THE MARS KINGDOM PARLIAMENT!

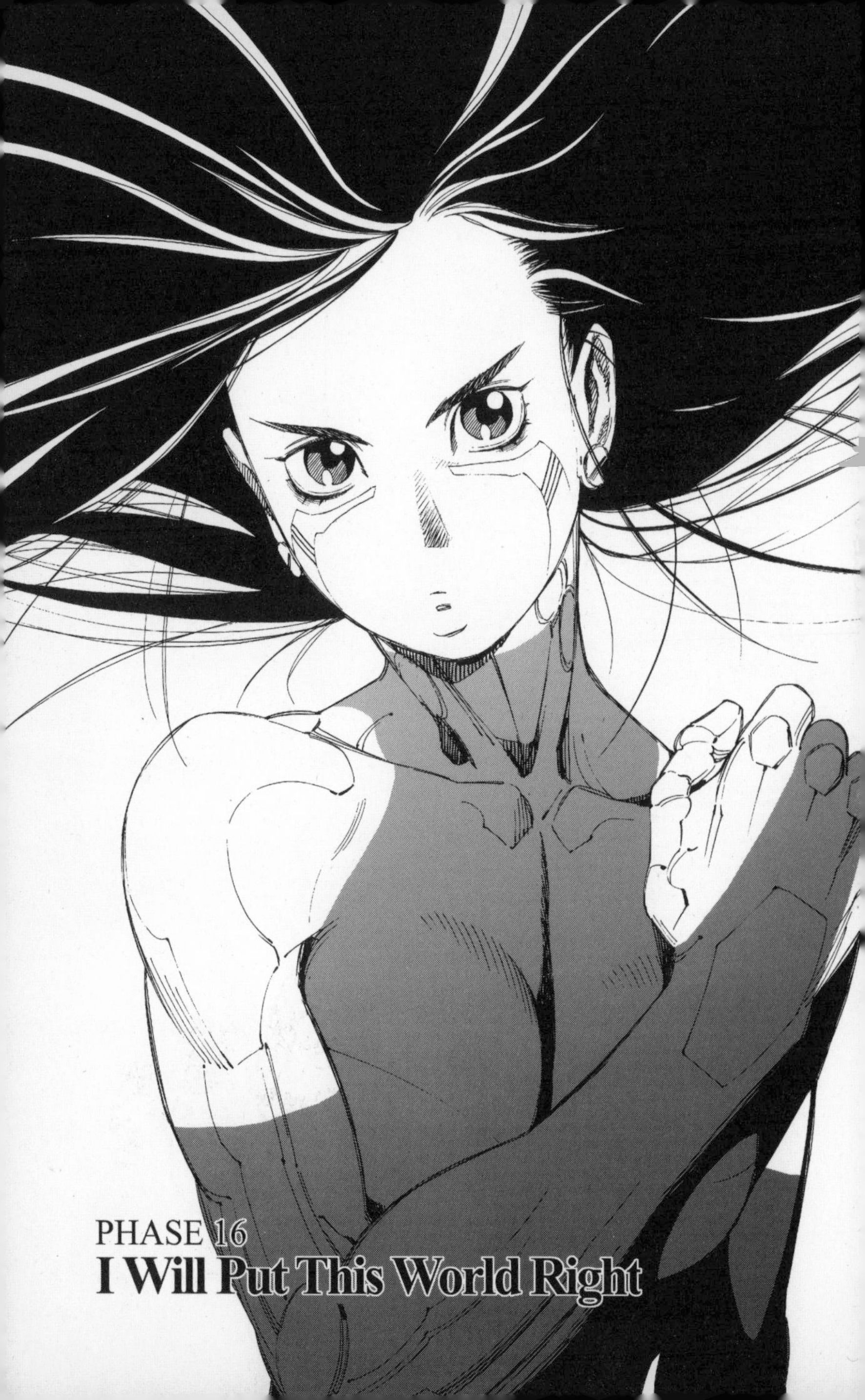

PHASE 16
I Will Put This World Right

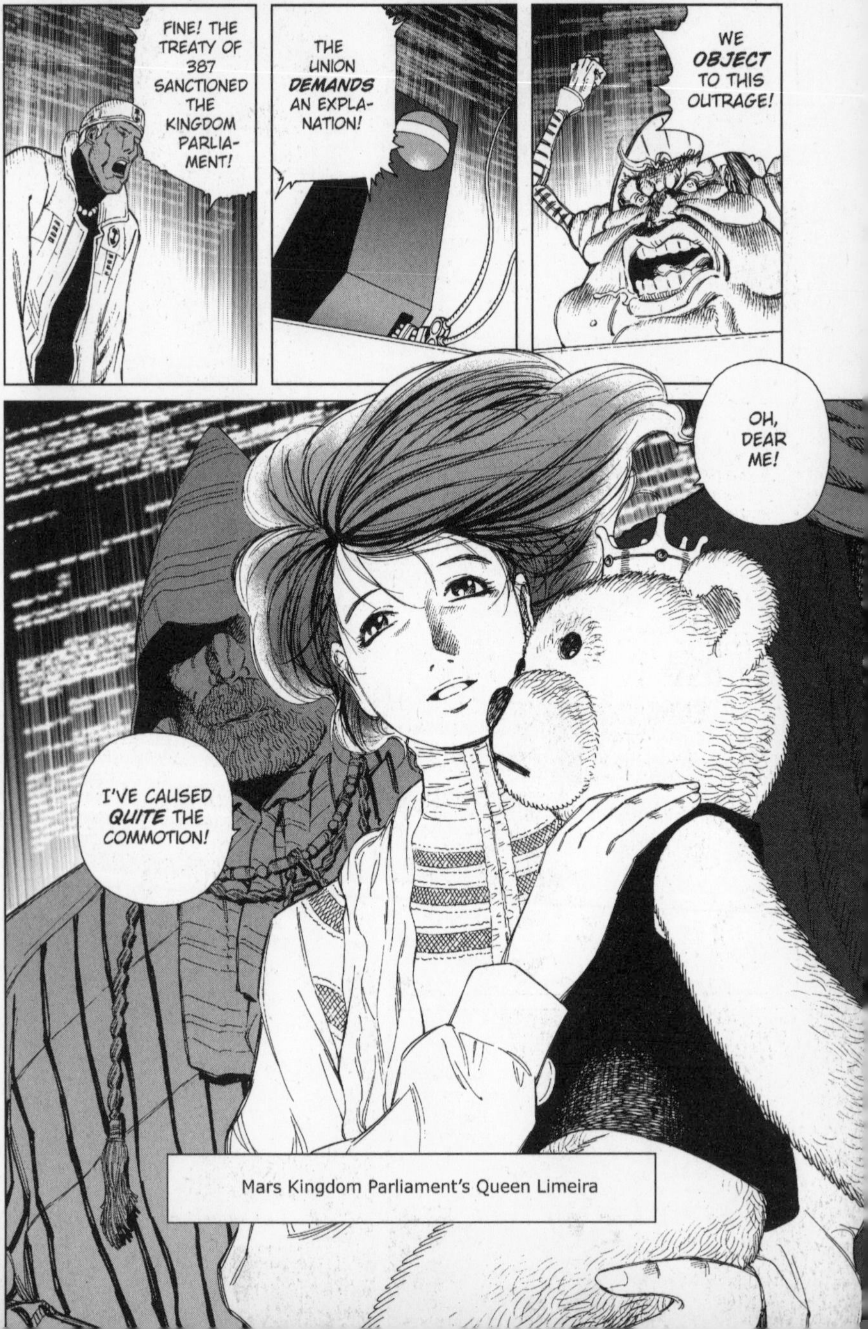
WE OBJECT TO THIS OUTRAGE!
THE UNION DEMANDS AN EXPLANATION!
FINE! THE TREATY OF 387 SANCTIONED THE KINGDOM PARLIAMENT!
OH, DEAR ME!
I'VE CAUSED QUITE THE COMMOTION!
Mars Kingdom Parliament's Queen Limeira

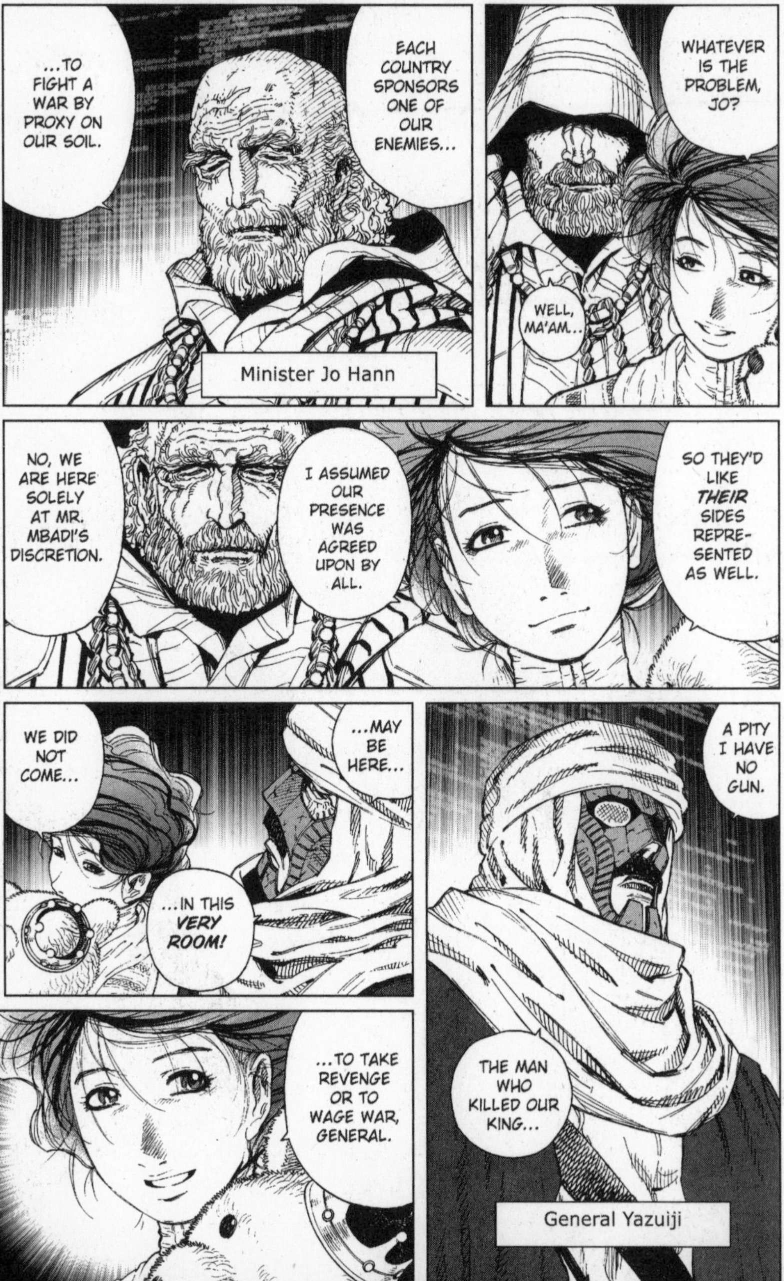
WHATEVER IS THE PROBLEM, JO?
WELL, MA'AM...
EACH COUNTRY SPONSORS ONE OF OUR ENEMIES...
...TO FIGHT A WAR BY PROXY ON OUR SOIL.
Minister Jo Hann
SO THEY'D LIKE *THEIR* SIDES REPRESENTED AS WELL.
I ASSUMED OUR PRESENCE WAS AGREED UPON BY ALL.
NO, WE ARE HERE SOLELY AT MR. MBADI'S DISCRETION.
A PITY I HAVE NO GUN.
THE MAN WHO KILLED OUR KING...
General Yazuiji
...MAY BE HERE...
WE DID NOT COME...
...IN THIS *VERY ROOM!*
...TO TAKE REVENGE OR TO WAGE WAR, GENERAL.

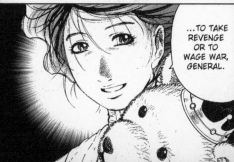

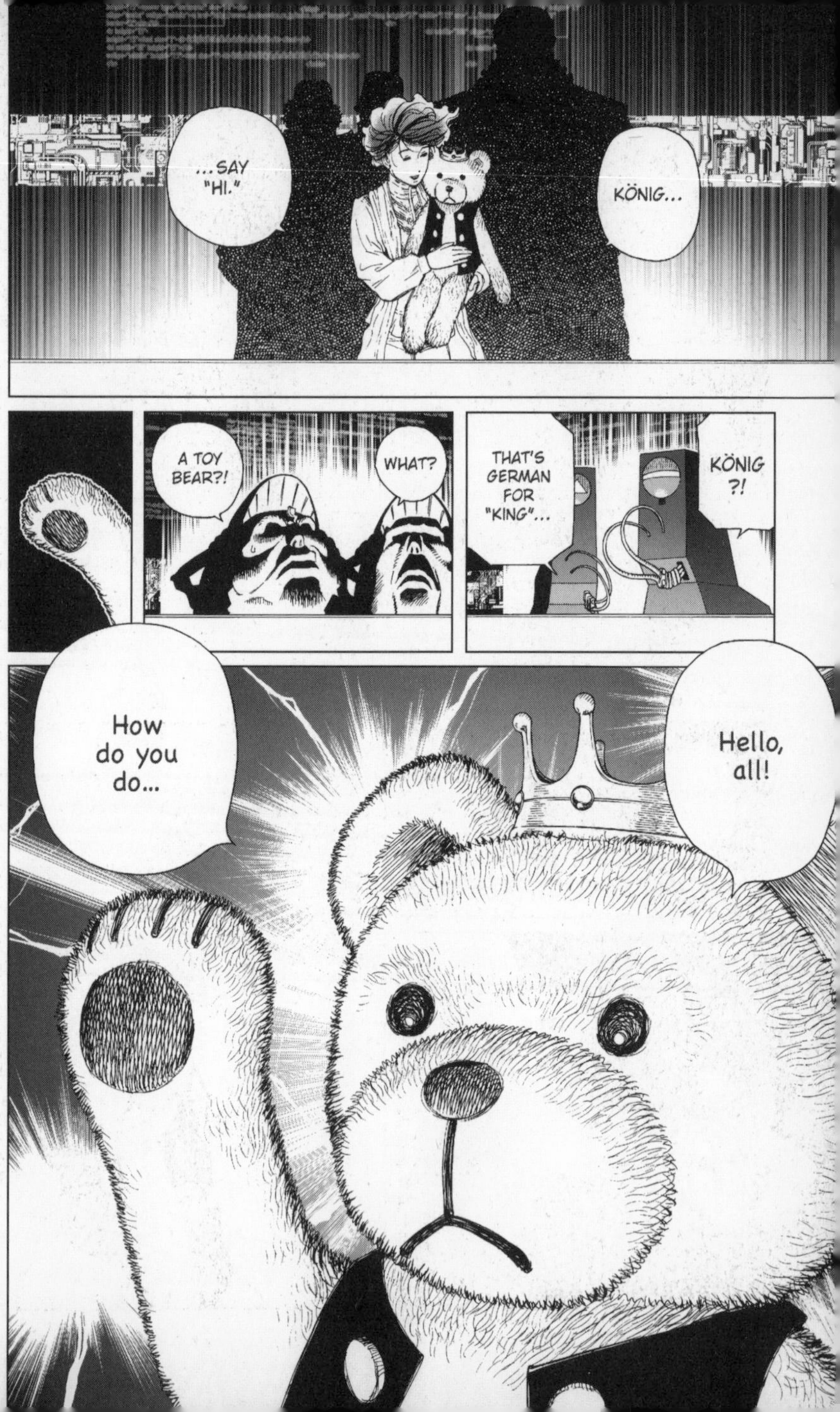
KÖNIG...
...SAY "HI."
KÖNIG ?!
THAT'S GERMAN FOR "KING"...
WHAT?
A TOY BEAR?!
Hello, all!
How do you do...

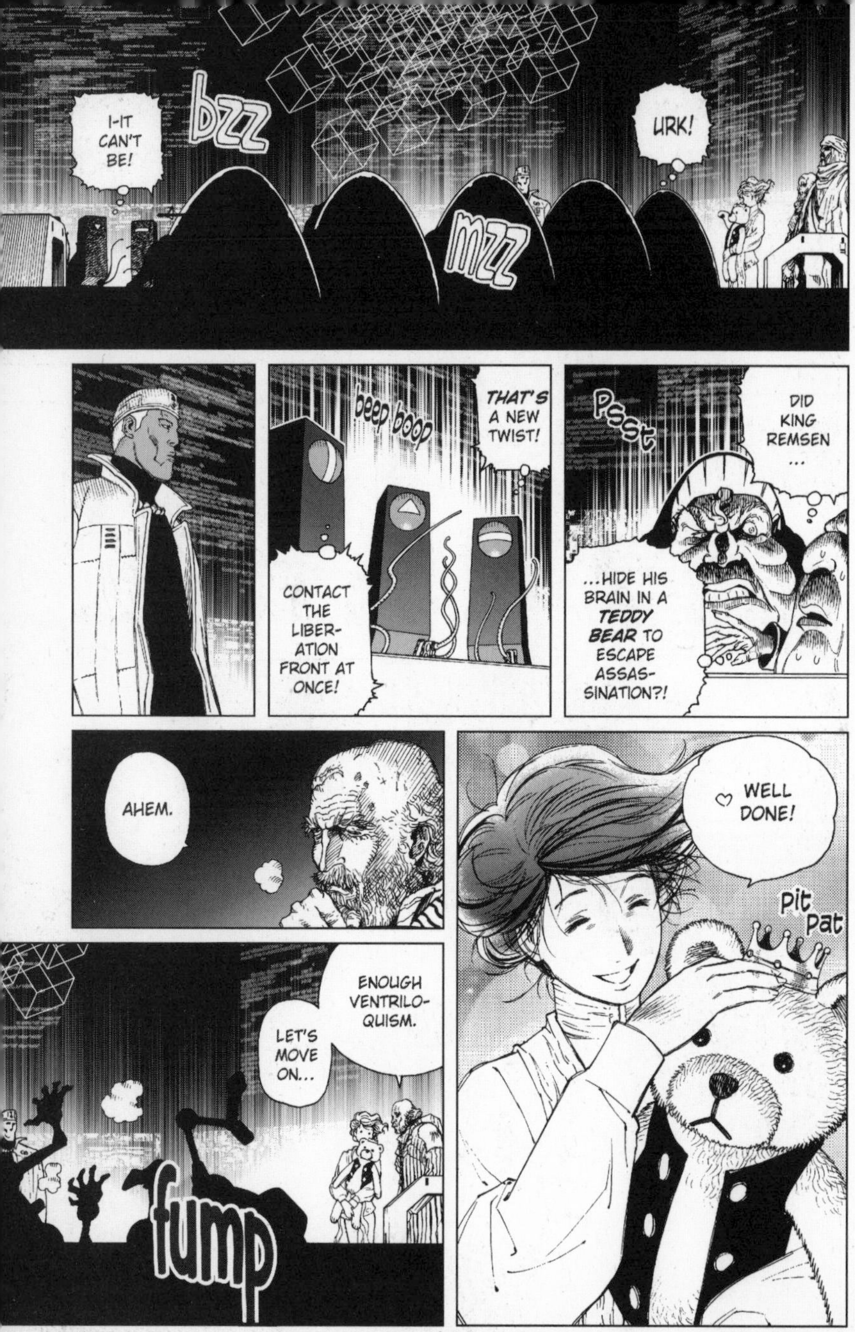
URK!
bzz
I-IT CAN'T BE!
mzz
DID KING REMSEN ...
Psst
...HIDE HIS BRAIN IN A **TEDDY BEAR** TO ESCAPE ASSAS-SINATION?!
THAT'S A NEW TWIST!
beep boop
CONTACT THE LIBER-ATION FRONT AT ONCE!
♡ WELL DONE!
pit pat
AHEM.
ENOUGH VENTRILO-QUISM.
LET'S MOVE ON...
fump

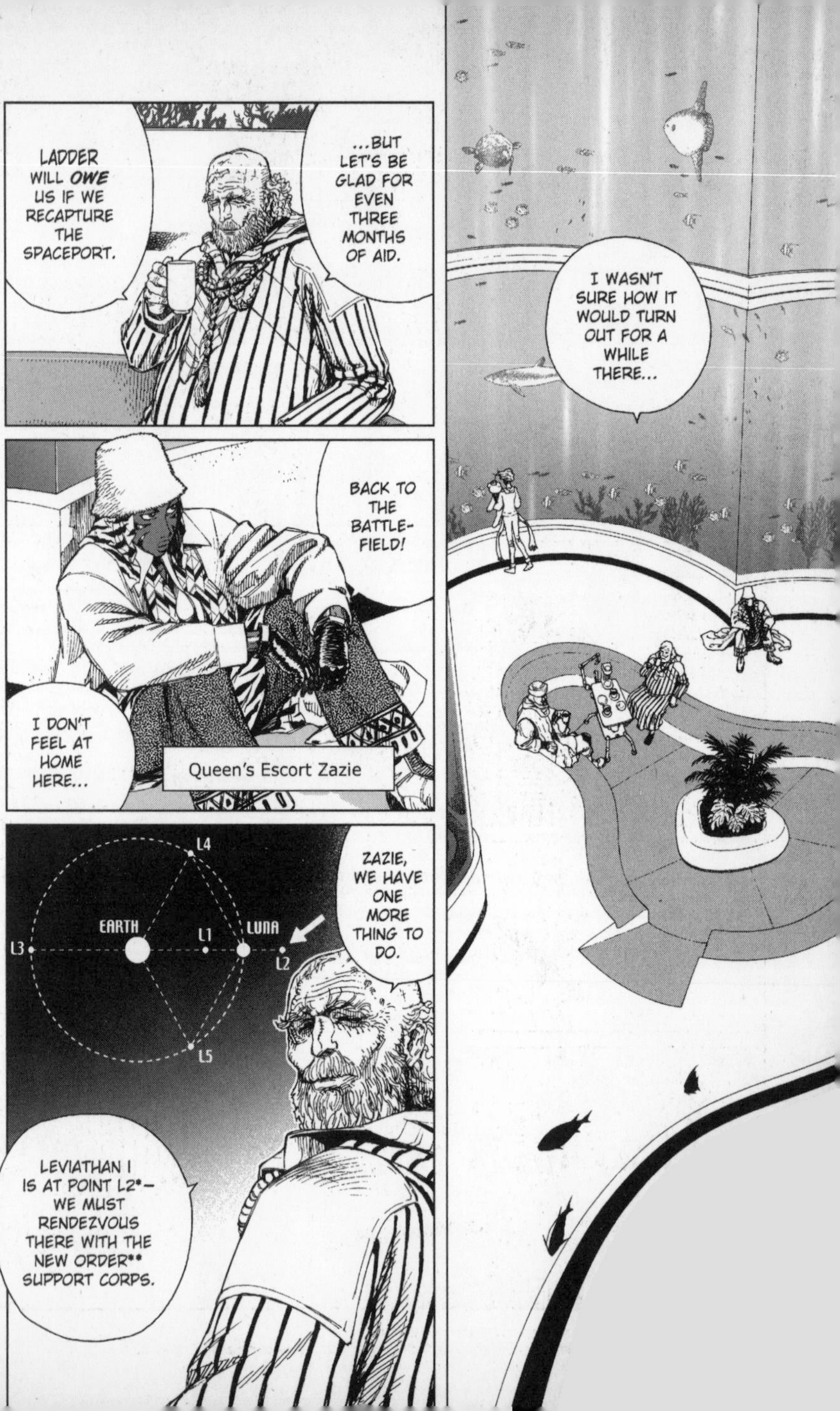
I WASN'T SURE HOW IT WOULD TURN OUT FOR A WHILE THERE...
...BUT LET'S BE GLAD FOR EVEN THREE MONTHS OF AID.
LADDER WILL *OWE* US IF WE RECAPTURE THE SPACEPORT.
BACK TO THE BATTLE-FIELD!
I DON'T FEEL AT HOME HERE...
Queen's Escort Zazie
ZAZIE, WE HAVE ONE MORE THING TO DO.
L4
EARTH
L1
LUNA
L3
L2
L5
LEVIATHAN I IS AT POINT L2*— WE MUST RENDEZVOUS THERE WITH THE NEW ORDER** SUPPORT CORPS.

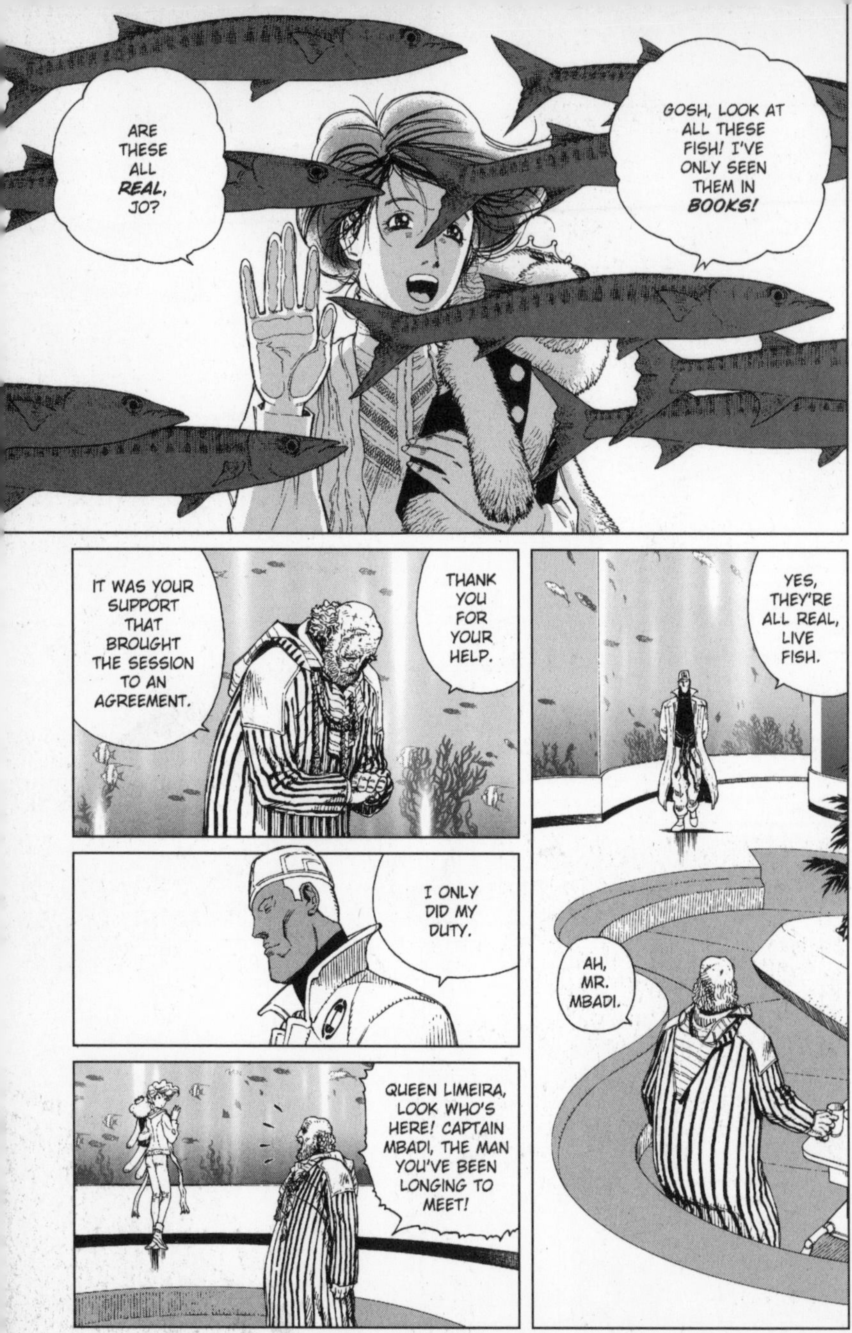
GOSH, LOOK AT ALL THESE FISH! I'VE ONLY SEEN THEM IN BOOKS!
ARE THESE ALL REAL, JO?
YES, THEY'RE ALL REAL, LIVE FISH.
AH, MR. MBADI.
THANK YOU FOR YOUR HELP.
IT WAS YOUR SUPPORT THAT BROUGHT THE SESSION TO AN AGREEMENT.
I ONLY DID MY DUTY.
QUEEN LIMEIRA, LOOK WHO'S HERE! CAPTAIN MBADI, THE MAN YOU'VE BEEN LONGING TO MEET!

*Point L2: one of the five Lagrange points in the lunar system.

**NEW ORDER: LADDER's interplanetary keepers of the peace, under the command of Aga Mbadi.

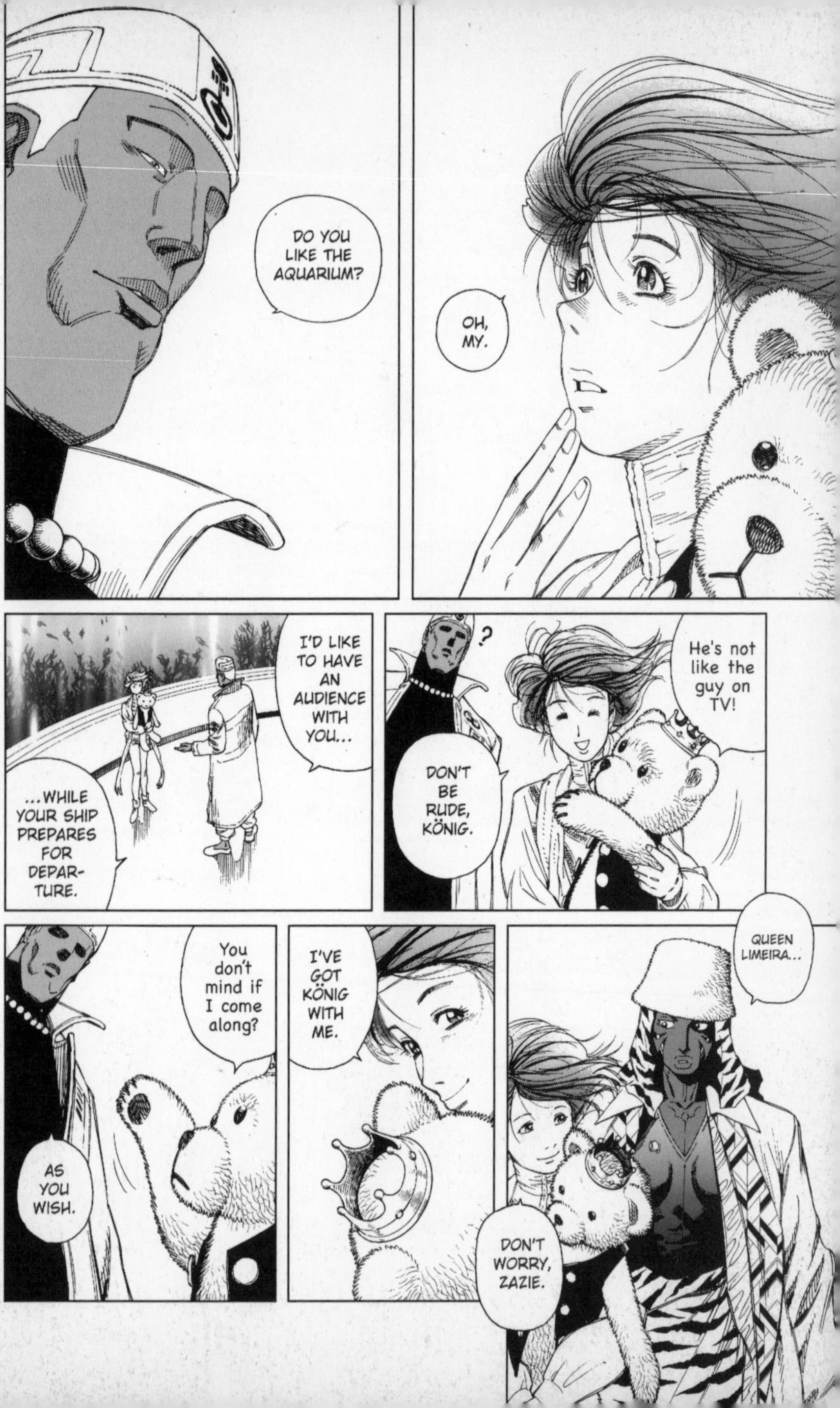
OH, MY.
DO YOU LIKE THE AQUARIUM?
He's not like the guy on TV!
?
DON'T BE RUDE, KÖNIG.
I'D LIKE TO HAVE AN AUDIENCE WITH YOU...
...WHILE YOUR SHIP PREPARES FOR DEPAR-TURE.
QUEEN LIMEIRA...
DON'T WORRY, ZAZIE.
I'VE GOT KÖNIG WITH ME.
You don't mind if I come along?
AS YOU WISH.

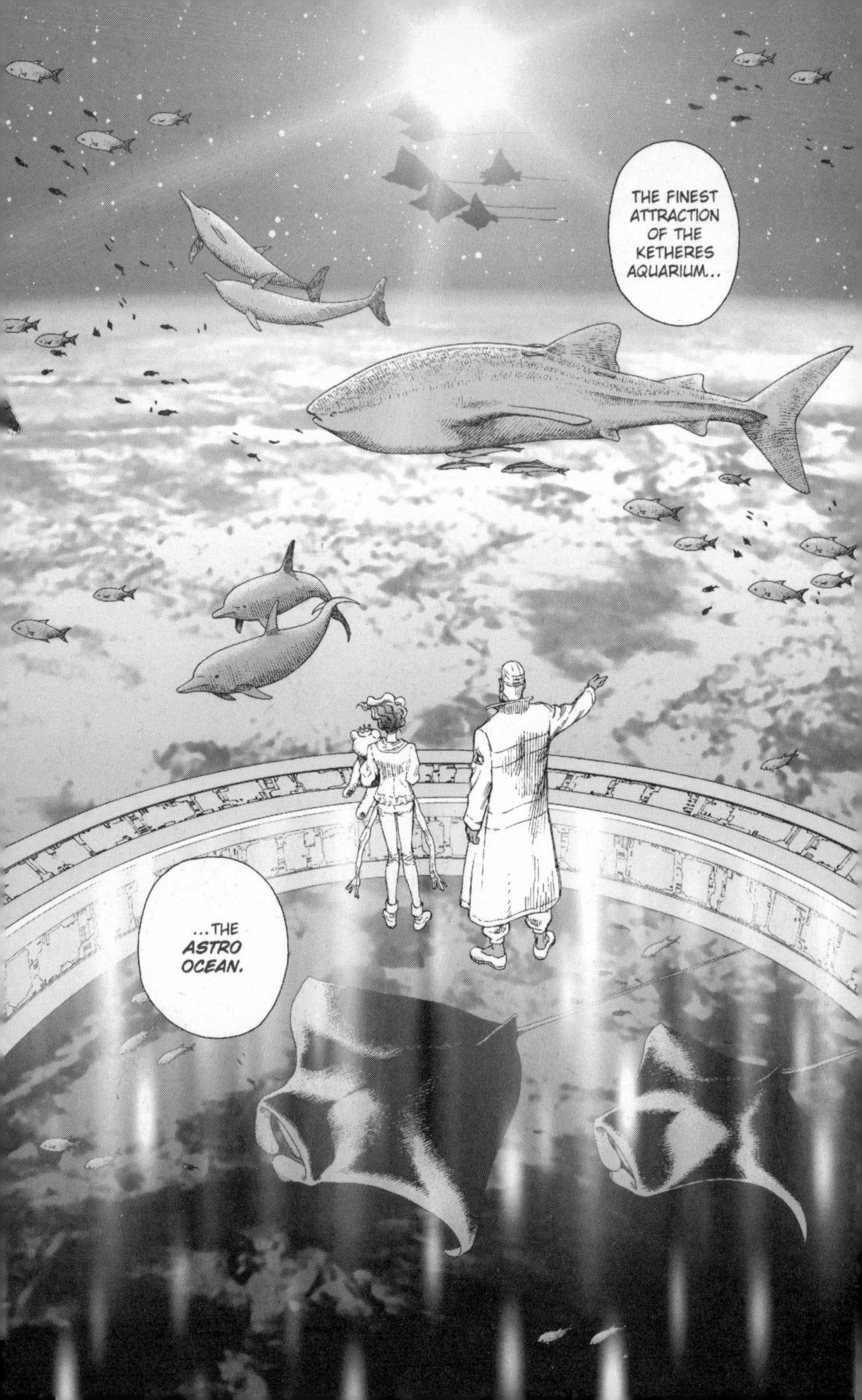
THE FINEST ATTRACTION OF THE KETHERES AQUARIUM...
...THE *ASTRO OCEAN.*

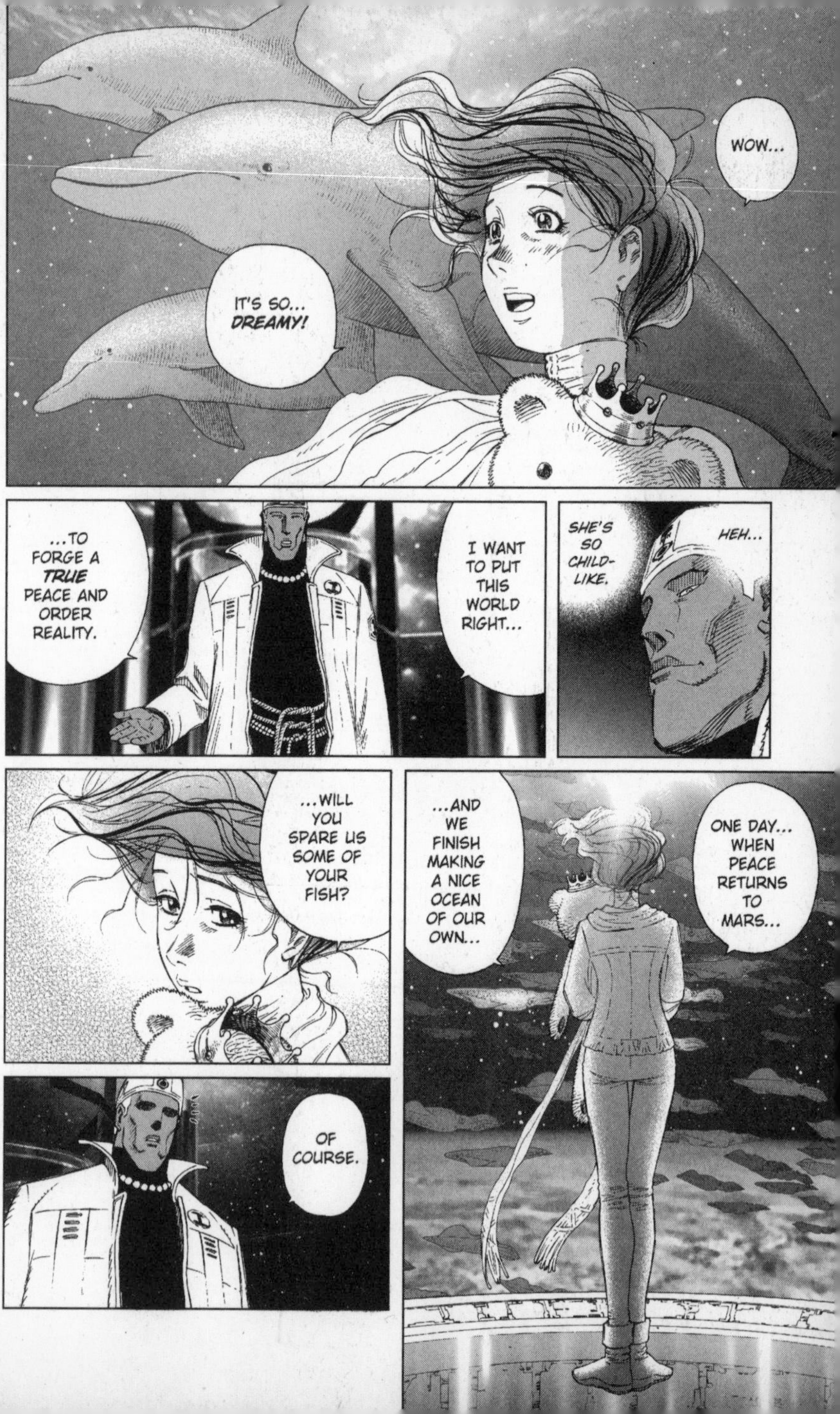
WOW...
IT'S SO... **DREAMY!**
HEH...
SHE'S SO CHILD-LIKE.
I WANT TO PUT THIS WORLD RIGHT...
...TO FORGE A **TRUE** PEACE AND ORDER REALITY.
ONE DAY... WHEN PEACE RETURNS TO MARS...
...AND WE FINISH MAKING A NICE OCEAN OF OUR OWN...
...WILL YOU SPARE US SOME OF YOUR FISH?
OF COURSE.

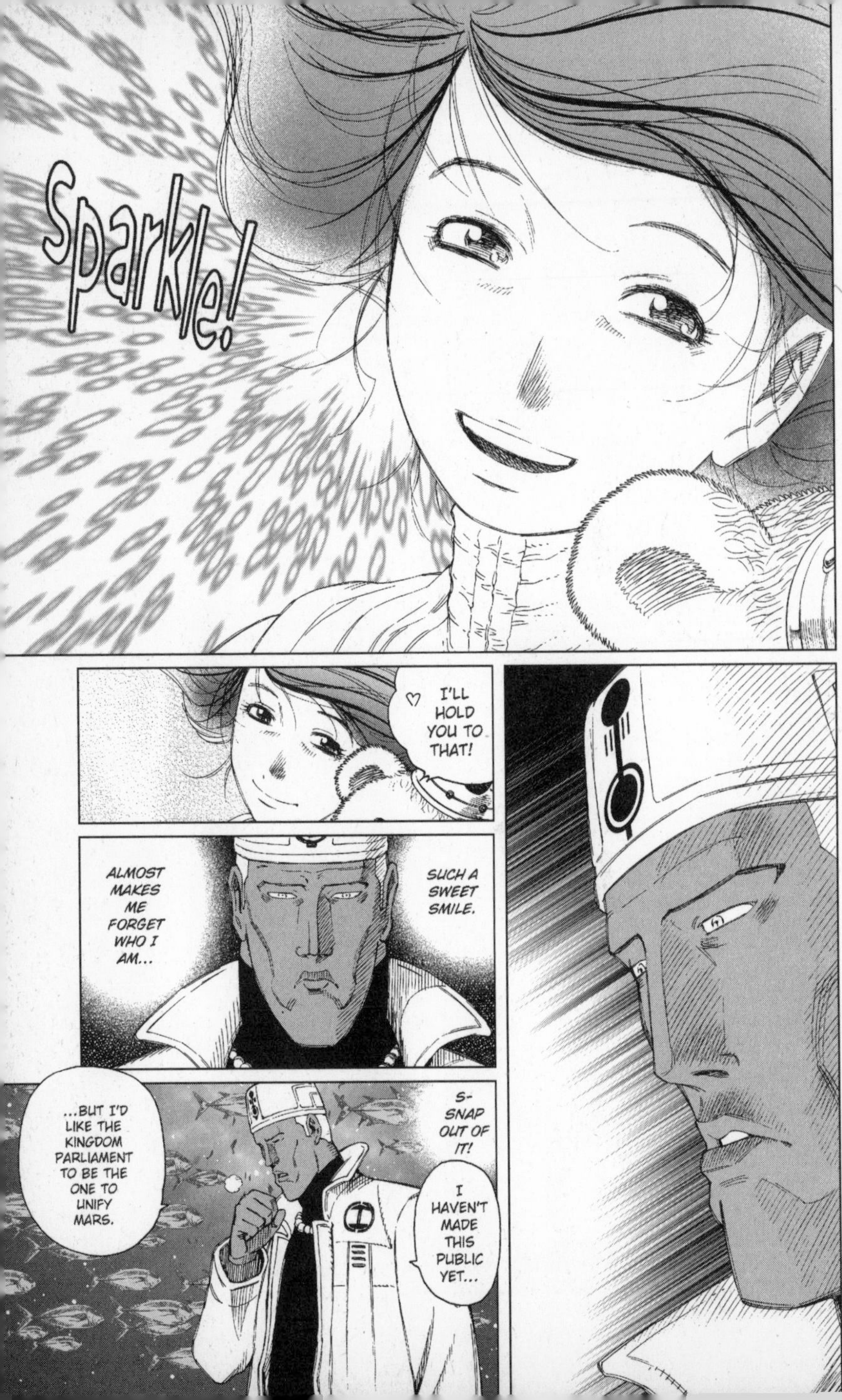
Sparkle!
♡ I'LL HOLD YOU TO THAT!
SUCH A SWEET SMILE.
ALMOST MAKES ME FORGET WHO I AM...
S-SNAP OUT OF IT!
I HAVEN'T MADE THIS PUBLIC YET...
...BUT I'D LIKE THE KINGDOM PARLIAMENT TO BE THE ONE TO UNIFY MARS.

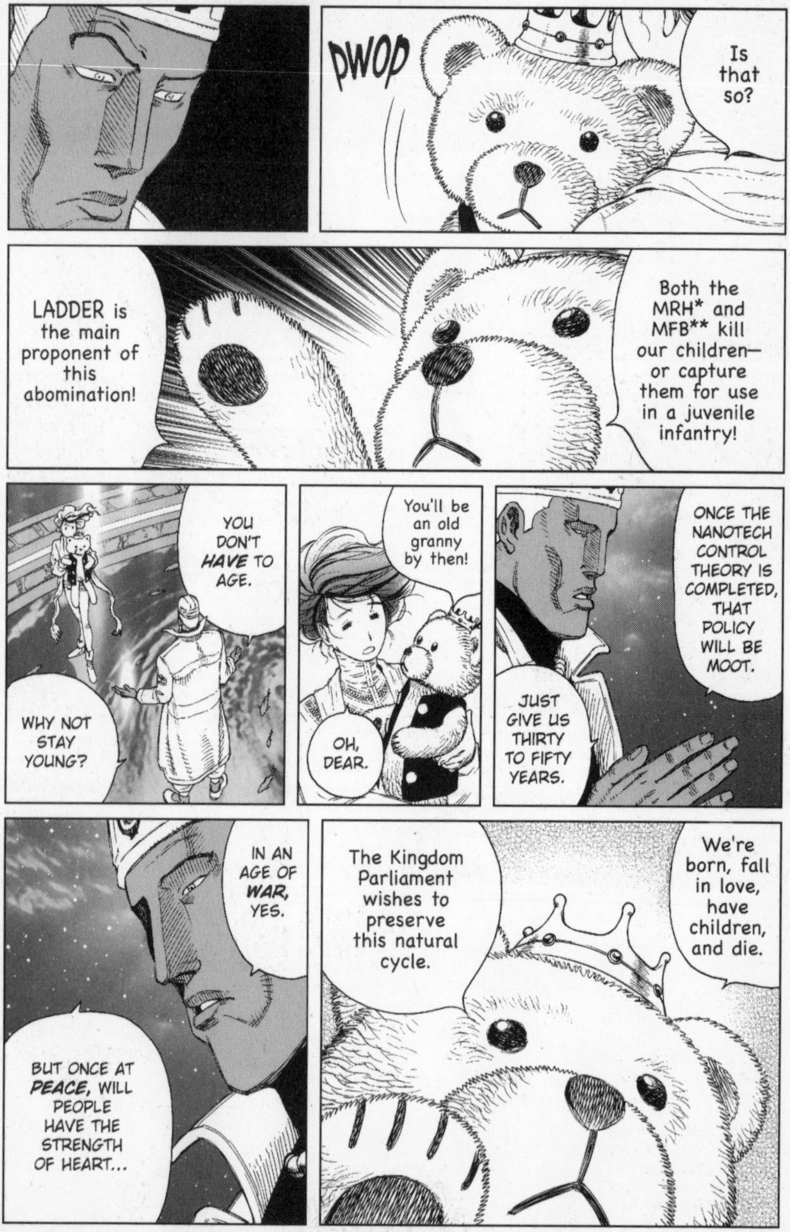
PWOP
Is that so?
Both the MRH* and MFB** kill our children— or capture them for use in a juvenile infantry!
LADDER is the main proponent of this abomination!
ONCE THE NANOTECH CONTROL THEORY IS COMPLETED, THAT POLICY WILL BE MOOT.
JUST GIVE US THIRTY TO FIFTY YEARS.
You'll be an old granny by then!
OH, DEAR.
YOU DON'T *HAVE* TO AGE.
WHY NOT STAY YOUNG?
We're born, fall in love, have children, and die.
The Kingdom Parliament wishes to preserve this natural cycle.
IN AN AGE OF *WAR*, YES.
BUT ONCE AT *PEACE*, WILL PEOPLE HAVE THE STRENGTH OF HEART...

**MRH (Mars Republik Heer): Mars Republic Army*
***MFB (Mars Front der Befreien): Mars Liberation Front*

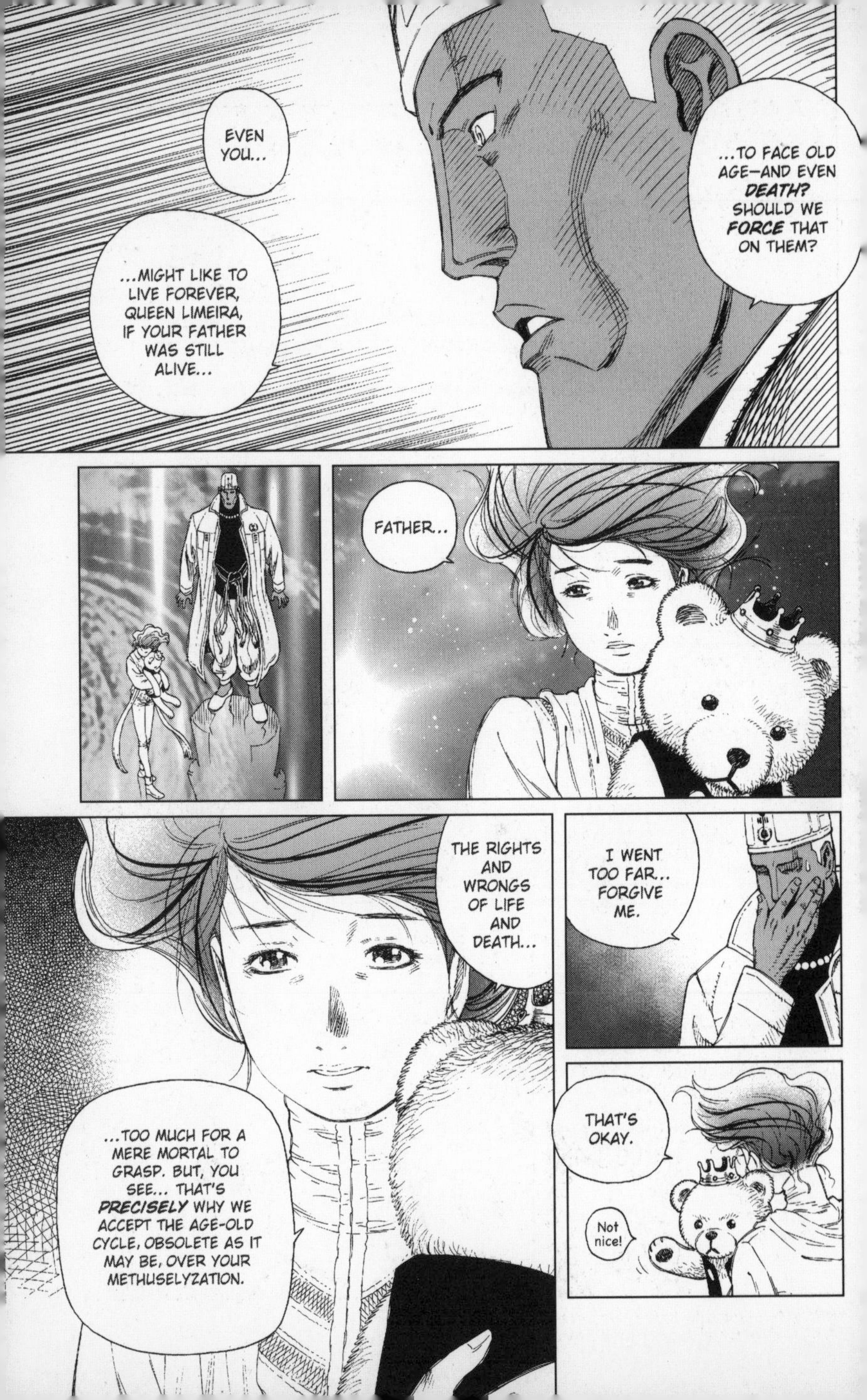
...TO FACE OLD AGE—AND EVEN ***DEATH?*** SHOULD WE ***FORCE*** THAT ON THEM?
EVEN YOU...
...MIGHT LIKE TO LIVE FOREVER, QUEEN LIMEIRA, IF YOUR FATHER WAS STILL ALIVE...
FATHER...
I WENT TOO FAR... FORGIVE ME.
THAT'S OKAY.
Not nice!
THE RIGHTS AND WRONGS OF LIFE AND DEATH...
...TOO MUCH FOR A MERE MORTAL TO GRASP. BUT, YOU SEE... THAT'S ***PRECISELY*** WHY WE ACCEPT THE AGE-OLD CYCLE, OBSOLETE AS IT MAY BE, OVER YOUR METHUSELYZATION.

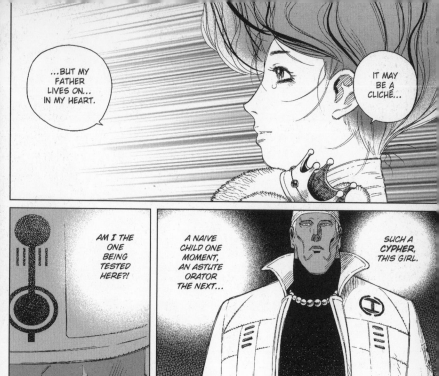

IT MAY BE A CLICHÉ...
...BUT MY FATHER LIVES ON... IN MY HEART.
SUCH A CYPHER, THIS GIRL.
A NAIVE CHILD ONE MOMENT, AN ASTUTE ORATOR THE NEXT...
AM I THE ONE BEING TESTED HERE?!
VIP
"DEATH MAY COME, BUT MY AMBITIONS WILL LIVE ON!
... ...
... ...
THAT'S A QUOTE FROM "SPACE MBADI!"
HUH ?!

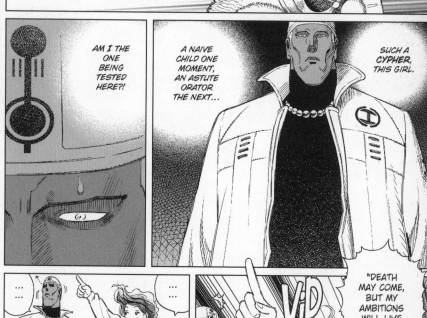

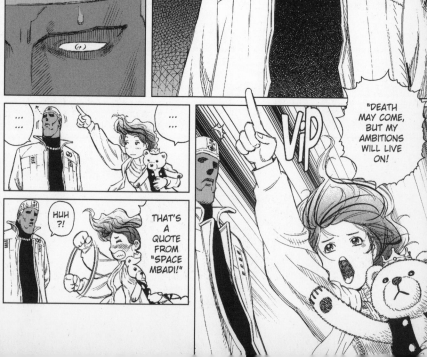

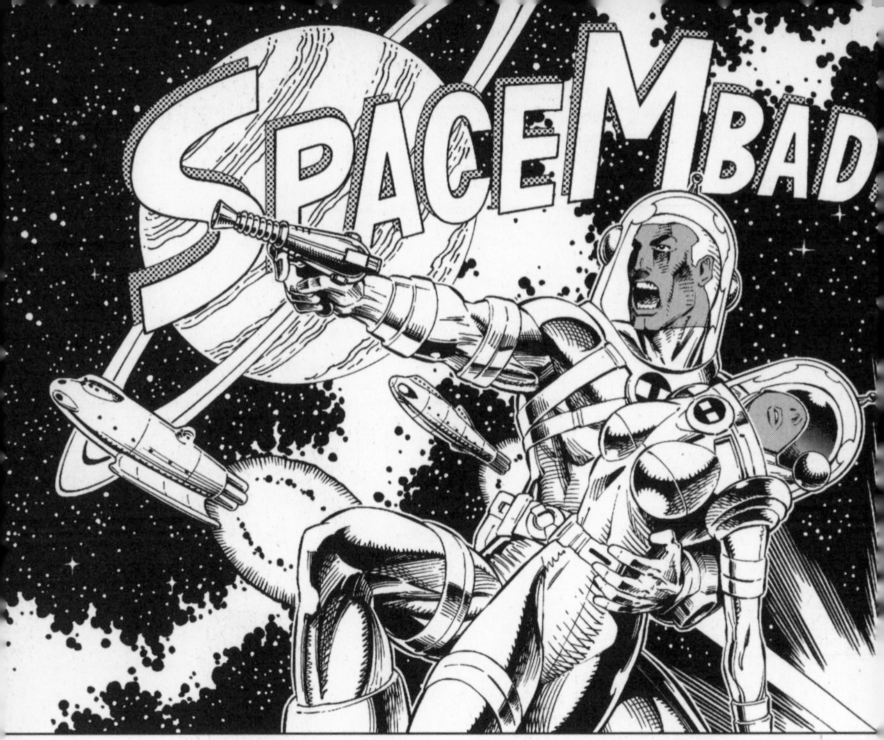
SPACE MBAD

TV series "Space Mbadi"
Produced by Vesta Studios. 156 episodes (and a dozen TV specials) of this epic adventure aired between ES 543 and 556. Based on the 25-volume series "**Space Hero Mbadi**," by bestselling novelist (and Ceres resident) Oleg Zaccagni, the action-packed drama follows ORDER, the interplanetary investigative team, from its creation to its demise.

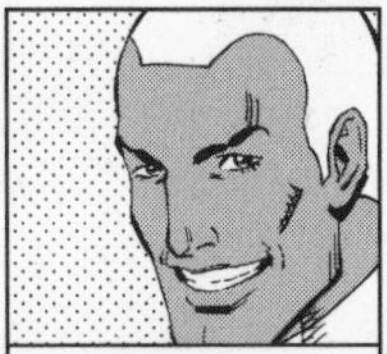

Captain Mbadi
Roy Nars

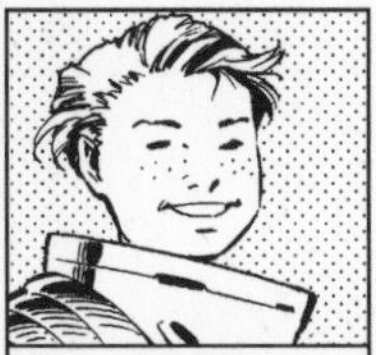

Revelle
W. Conant

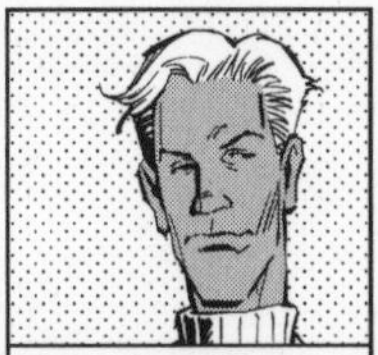

1st Officer Chandler
V. Manabendra

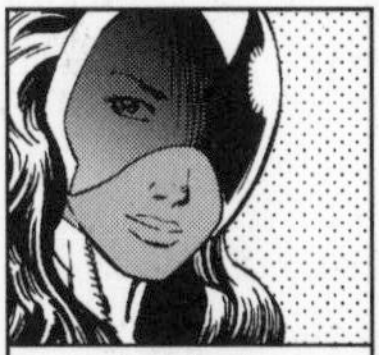

Lakshmi
N. Tripathi

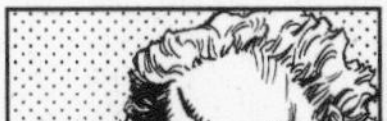

Dr. Maurois
J. Cugnot

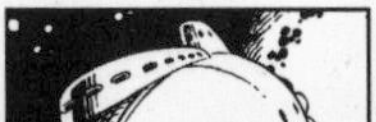

Yakovlev 44
(voice of) A. Volgin

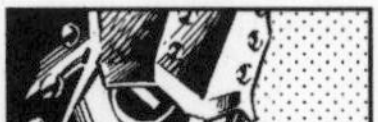

Martian Warrior Menzel
G. Helder

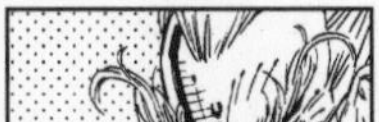

Dr. Vares
K. T. Conrad

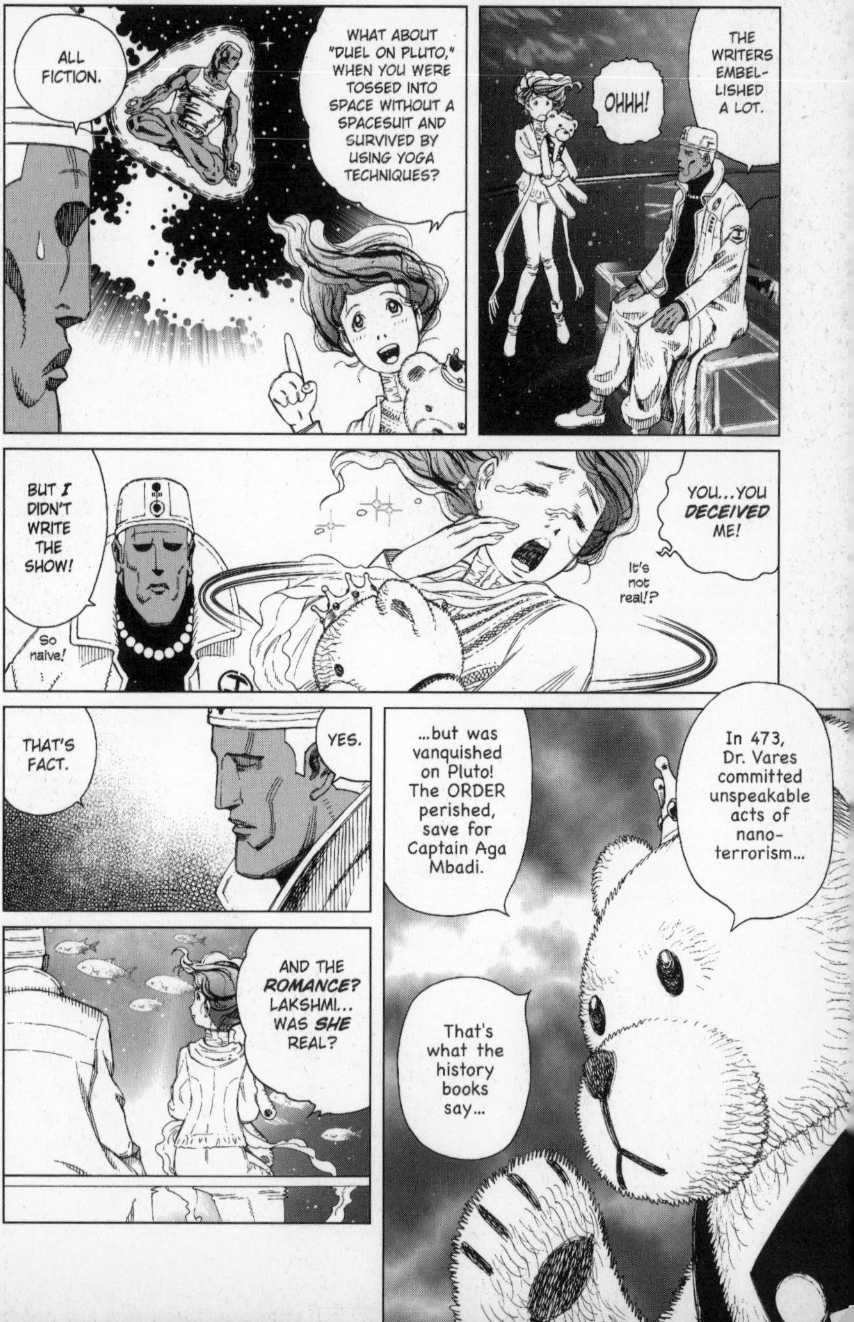
THE WRITERS EMBEL-LISHED A LOT.
OHHH!
WHAT ABOUT "DUEL ON PLUTO," WHEN YOU WERE TOSSED INTO SPACE WITHOUT A SPACESUIT AND SURVIVED BY USING YOGA TECHNIQUES?
ALL FICTION.
YOU...YOU DECEIVED ME!
It's not real!?
BUT I DIDN'T WRITE THE SHOW!
So naive!
In 473, Dr. Vares committed unspeakable acts of nano-terrorism...
...but was vanquished on Pluto! The ORDER perished, save for Captain Aga Mbadi.
That's what the history books say...
YES.
THAT'S FACT.
AND THE ROMANCE? LAKSHMI... WAS SHE REAL?

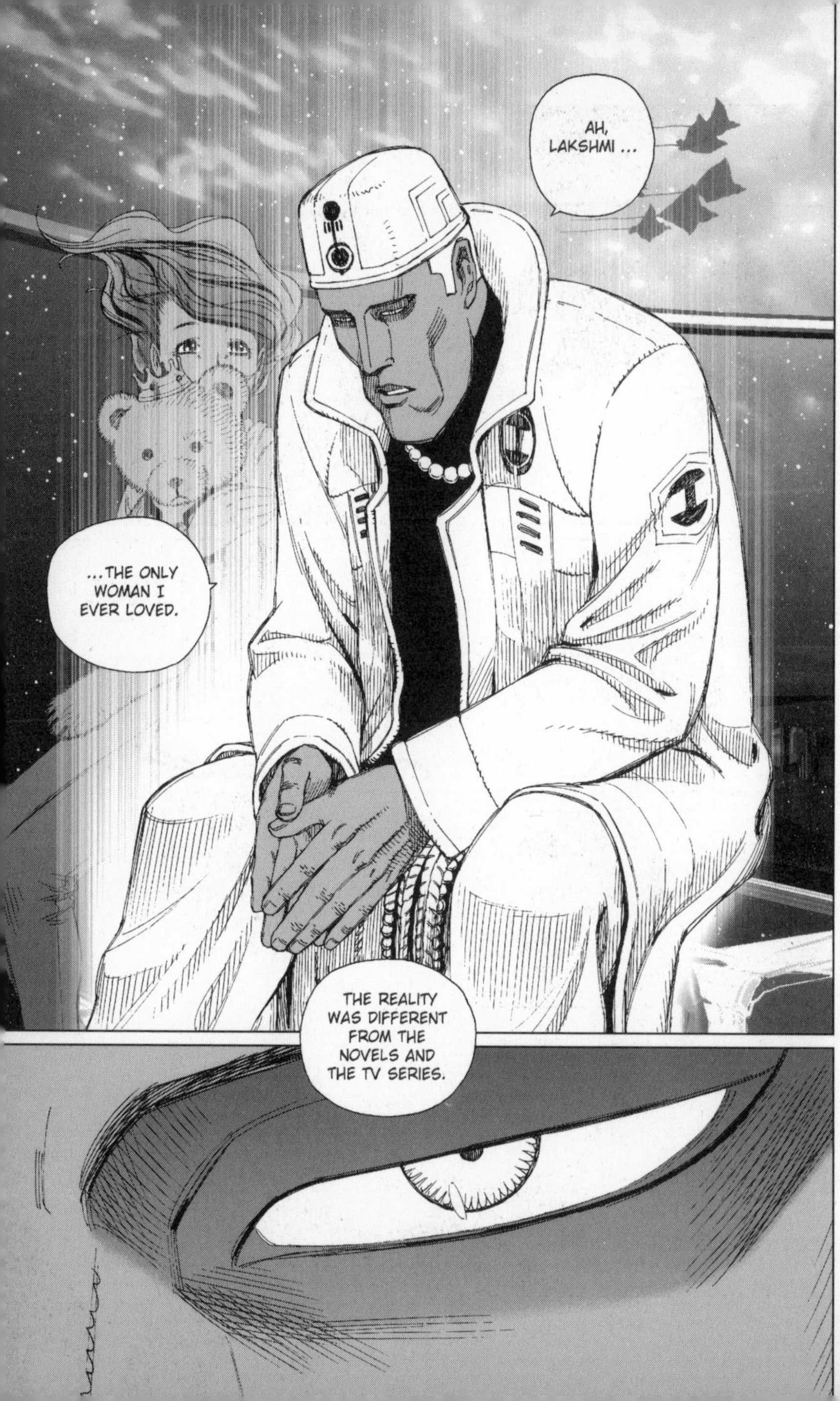
AH, LAKSHMI ...
...THE ONLY WOMAN I EVER LOVED.
THE REALITY WAS DIFFERENT FROM THE NOVELS AND THE TV SERIES.

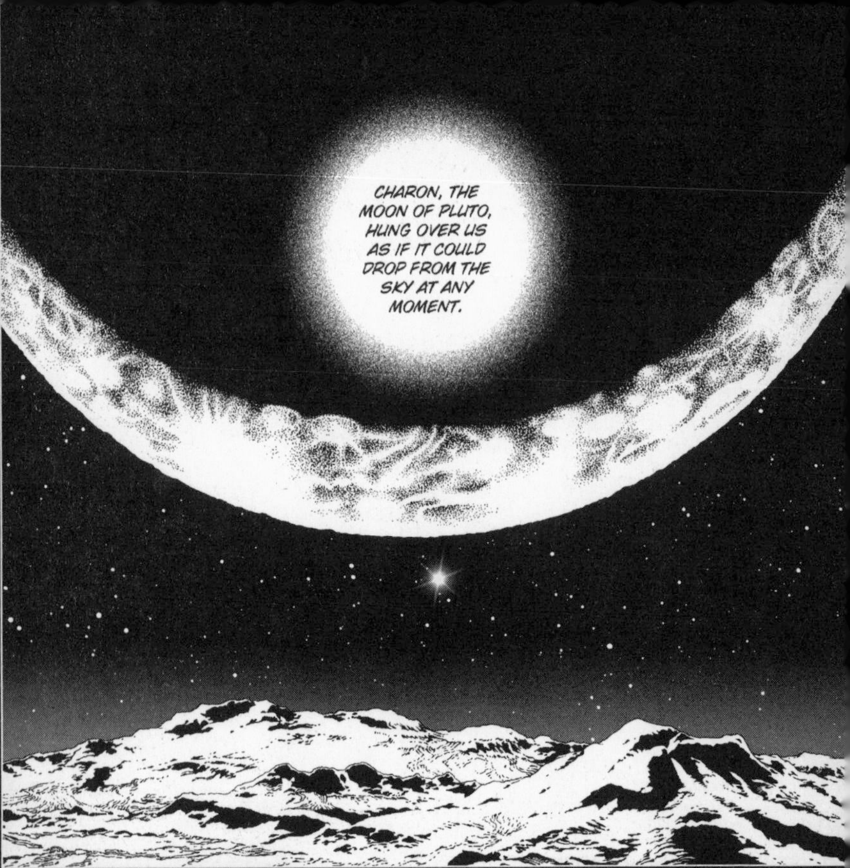
CHARON, THE MOON OF PLUTO, HUNG OVER US AS IF IT COULD DROP FROM THE SKY AT ANY MOMENT.
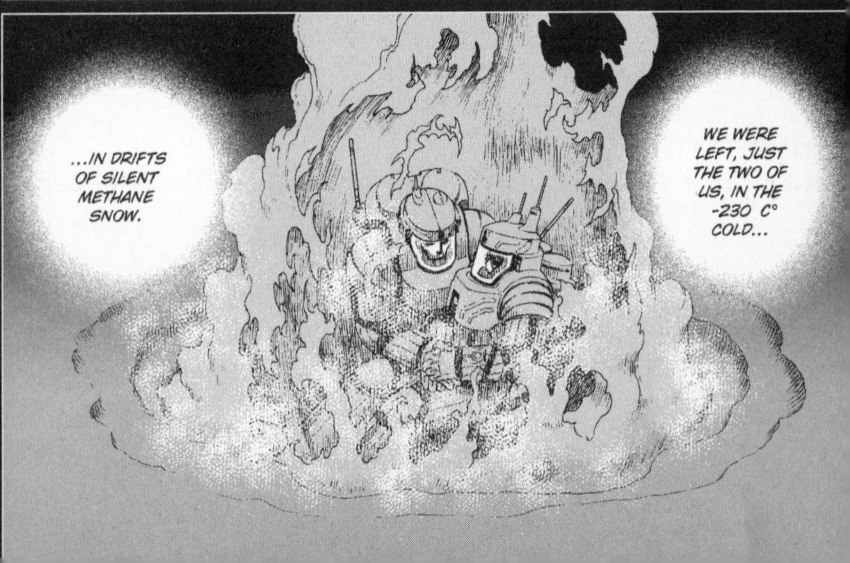
WE WERE LEFT, JUST THE TWO OF US, IN THE -230 C° COLD...
...IN DRIFTS OF SILENT METHANE SNOW.

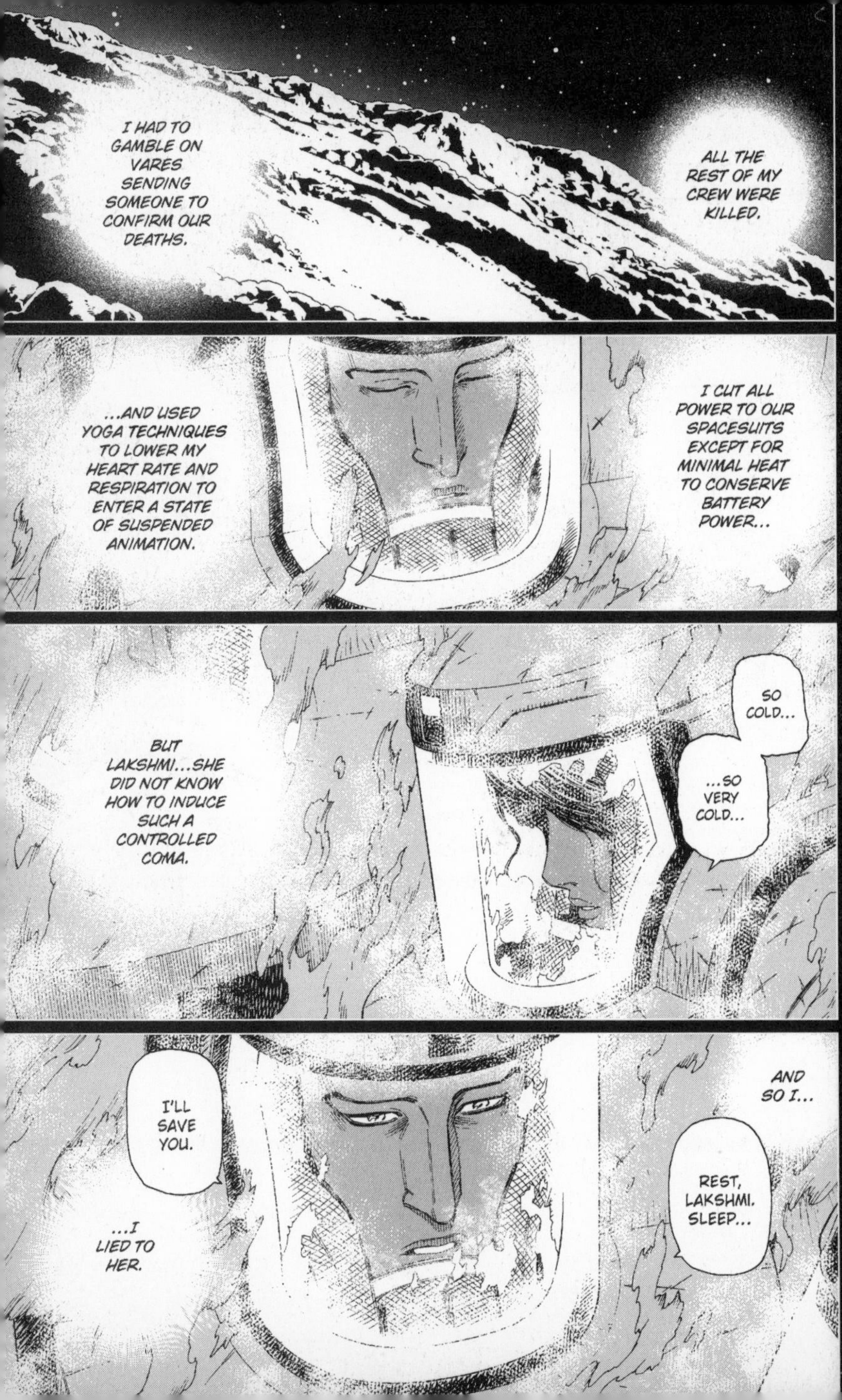

ALL THE REST OF MY CREW WERE KILLED.
I HAD TO GAMBLE ON VARES SENDING SOMEONE TO CONFIRM OUR DEATHS.
I CUT ALL POWER TO OUR SPACESUITS EXCEPT FOR MINIMAL HEAT TO CONSERVE BATTERY POWER...
...AND USED YOGA TECHNIQUES TO LOWER MY HEART RATE AND RESPIRATION TO ENTER A STATE OF SUSPENDED ANIMATION.
SO COLD...
...SO VERY COLD...
BUT LAKSHMI...SHE DID NOT KNOW HOW TO INDUCE SUCH A CONTROLLED COMA.
AND SO I...
REST, LAKSHMI. SLEEP...
I'LL SAVE YOU.
...I LIED TO HER.

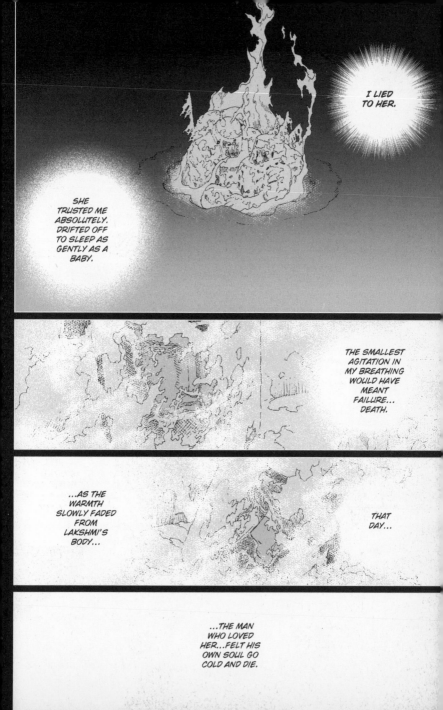

I LIED TO HER.

SHE TRUSTED ME ABSOLUTELY. DRIFTED OFF TO SLEEP AS GENTLY AS A BABY.

THE SMALLEST AGITATION IN MY BREATHING WOULD HAVE MEANT FAILURE... DEATH.

...AS THE WARMTH SLOWLY FADED FROM LAKSHMI'S BODY...

THAT DAY...

...THE MAN WHO LOVED HER...FELT HIS OWN SOUL GO COLD AND DIE.

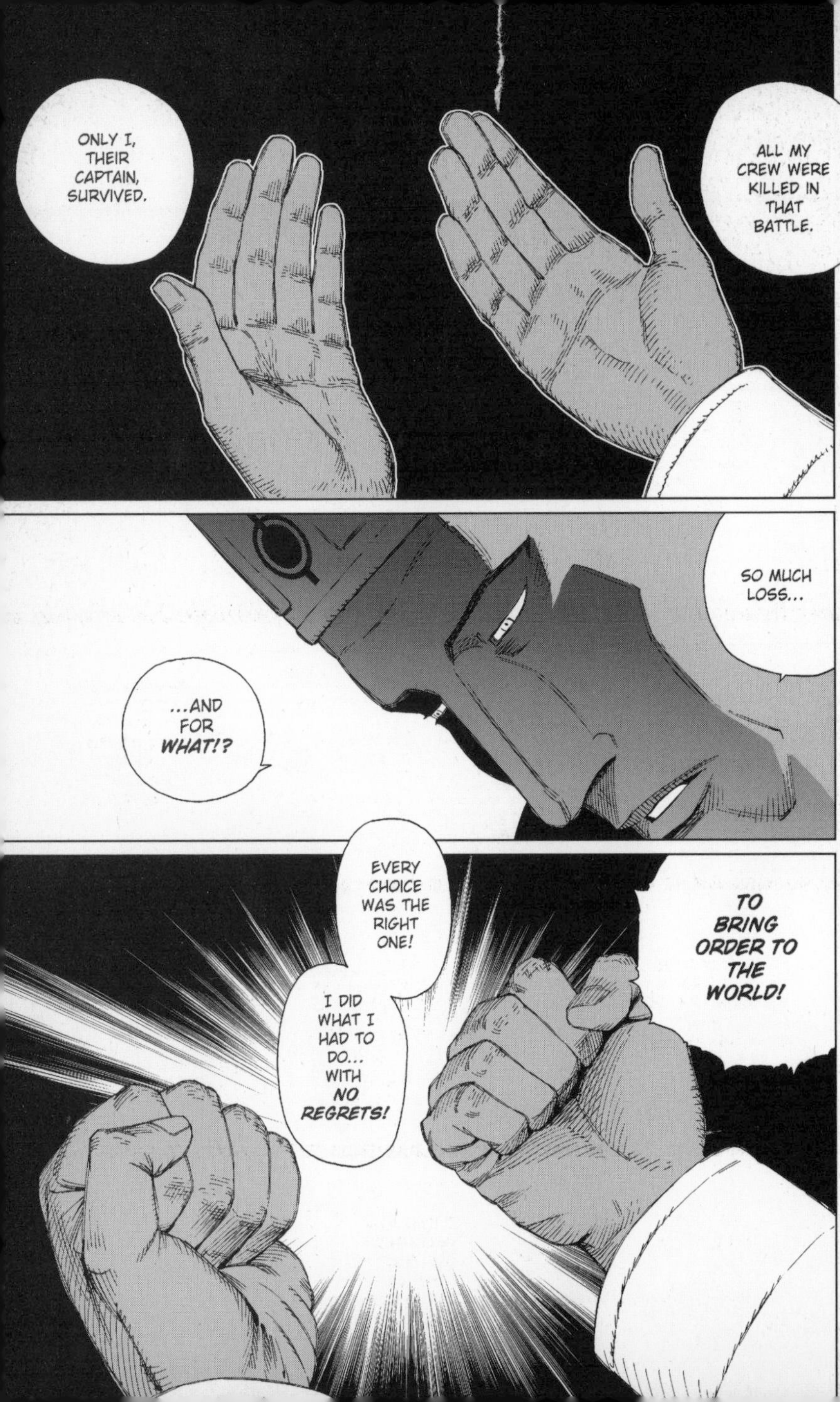
ALL MY CREW WERE KILLED IN THAT BATTLE.
ONLY I, THEIR CAPTAIN, SURVIVED.
SO MUCH LOSS...
...AND FOR *WHAT!?*
TO BRING ORDER TO THE WORLD!
EVERY CHOICE WAS THE RIGHT ONE!
I DID WHAT I HAD TO DO... WITH *NO REGRETS!*

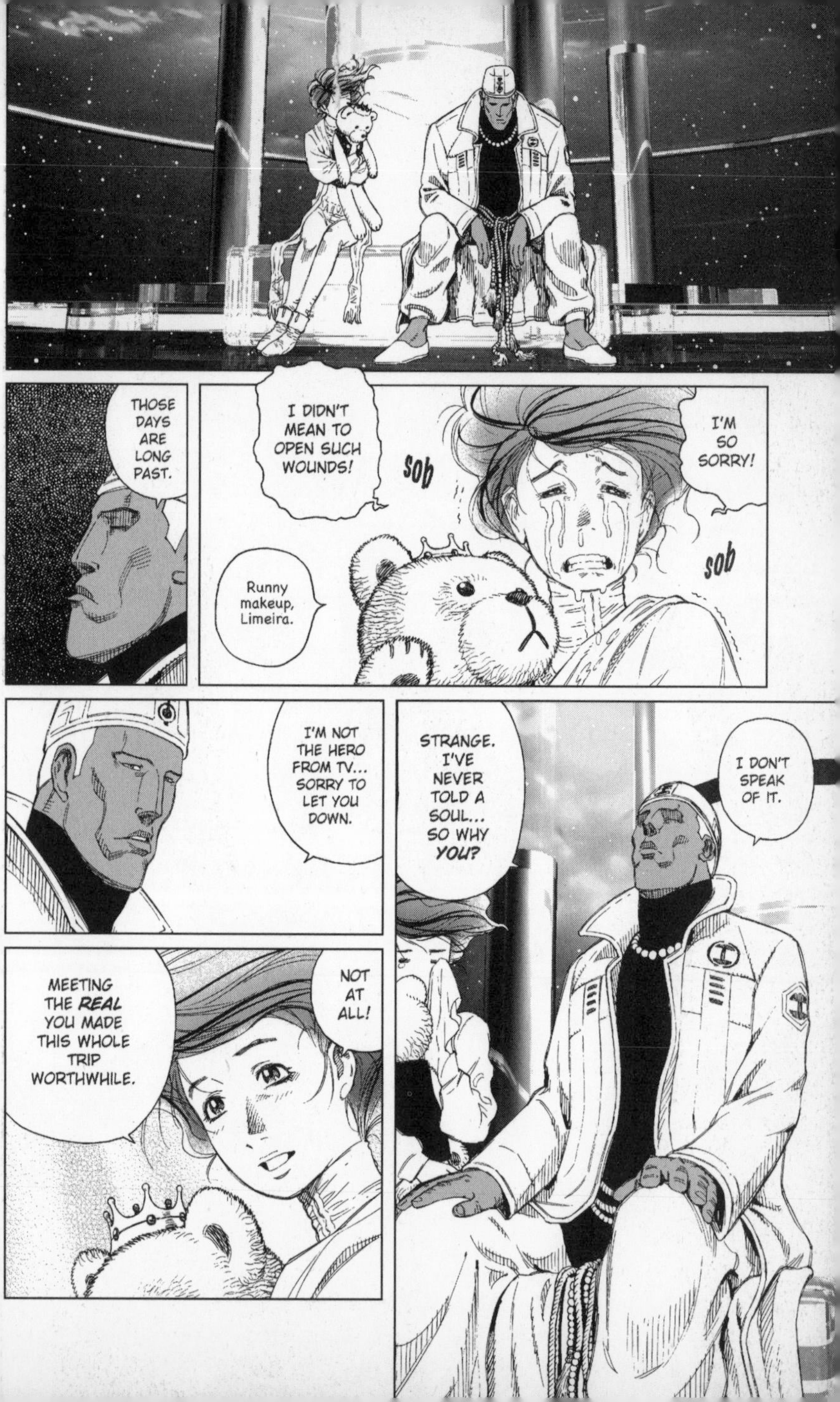
I'M SO SORRY!
I DIDN'T MEAN TO OPEN SUCH WOUNDS!
sob
sob
Runny makeup, Limeira.
THOSE DAYS ARE LONG PAST.
I DON'T SPEAK OF IT.
STRANGE. I'VE NEVER TOLD A SOUL... SO WHY *YOU?*
I'M NOT THE HERO FROM TV... SORRY TO LET YOU DOWN.
NOT AT ALL!
MEETING THE *REAL* YOU MADE THIS WHOLE TRIP WORTHWHILE.

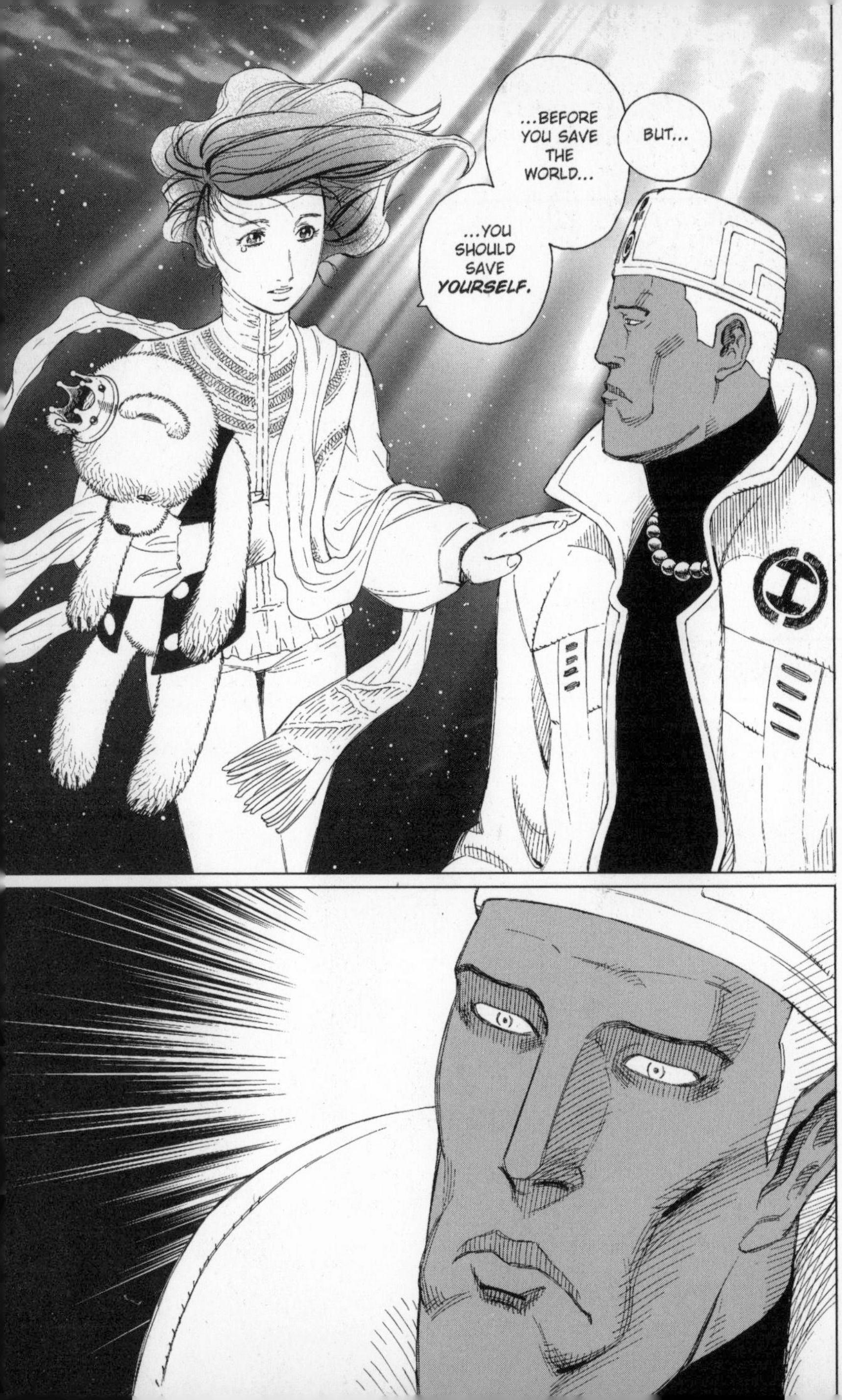
BUT...
...BEFORE YOU SAVE THE WORLD...
...YOU SHOULD SAVE ***YOURSELF.***

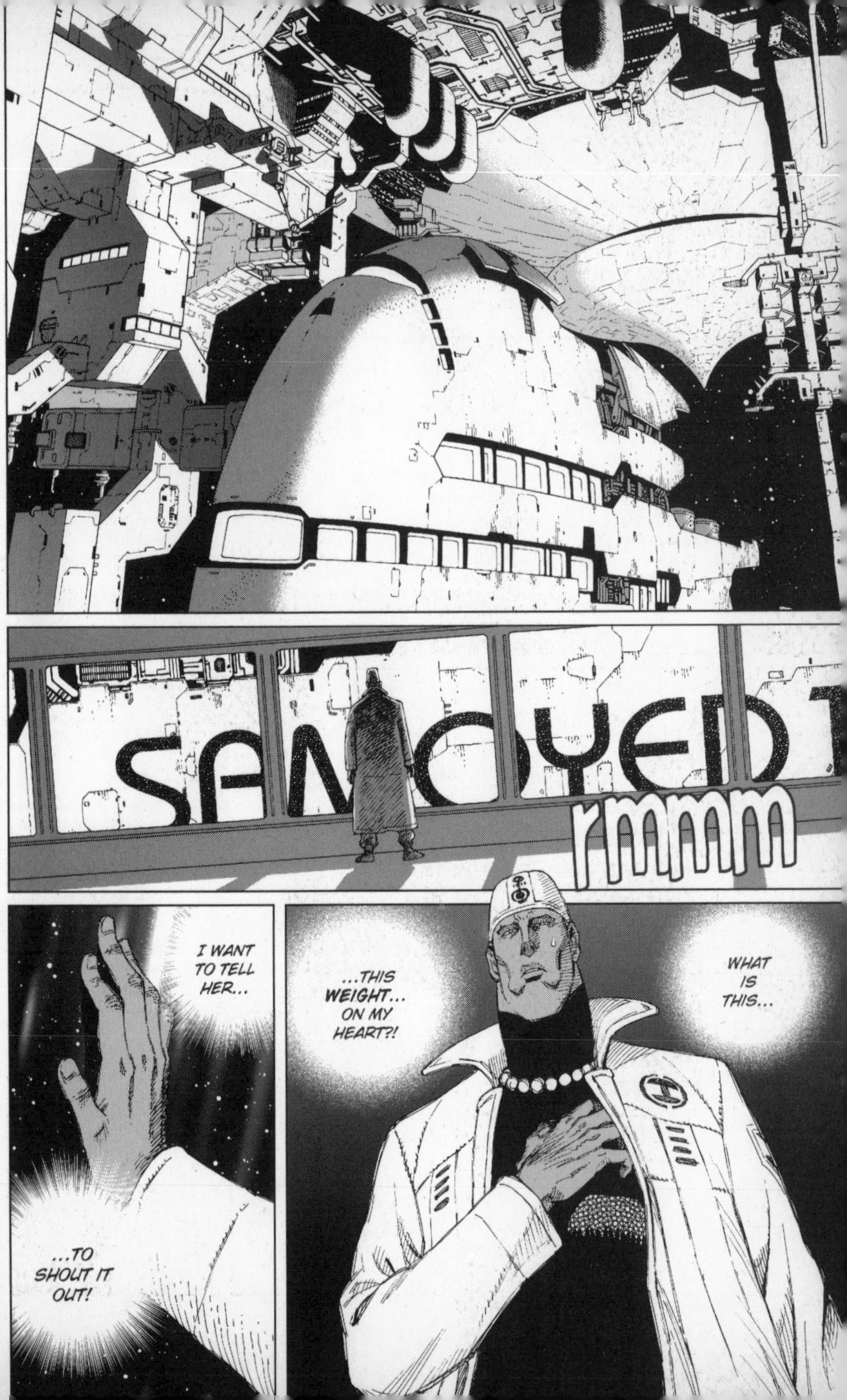
rmmmm
WHAT IS THIS...
...THIS WEIGHT... ON MY HEART?!
I WANT TO TELL HER...
...TO SHOUT IT OUT!

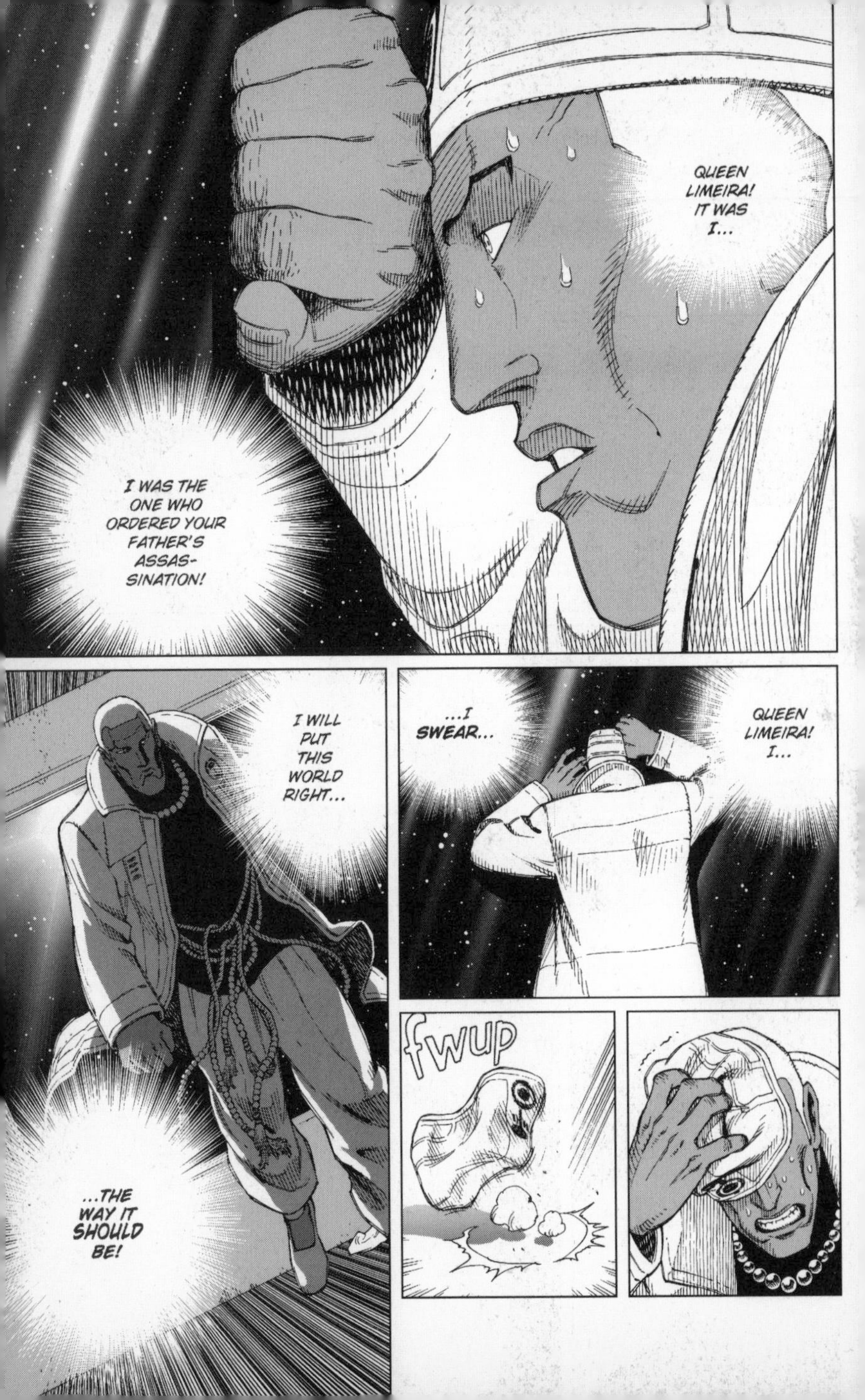
QUEEN LIMEIRA! IT WAS I...
I WAS THE ONE WHO ORDERED YOUR FATHER'S ASSAS-SINATION!
QUEEN LIMEIRA! I...
...I SWEAR...
fwup
I WILL PUT THIS WORLD RIGHT...
...THE WAY IT SHOULD BE!

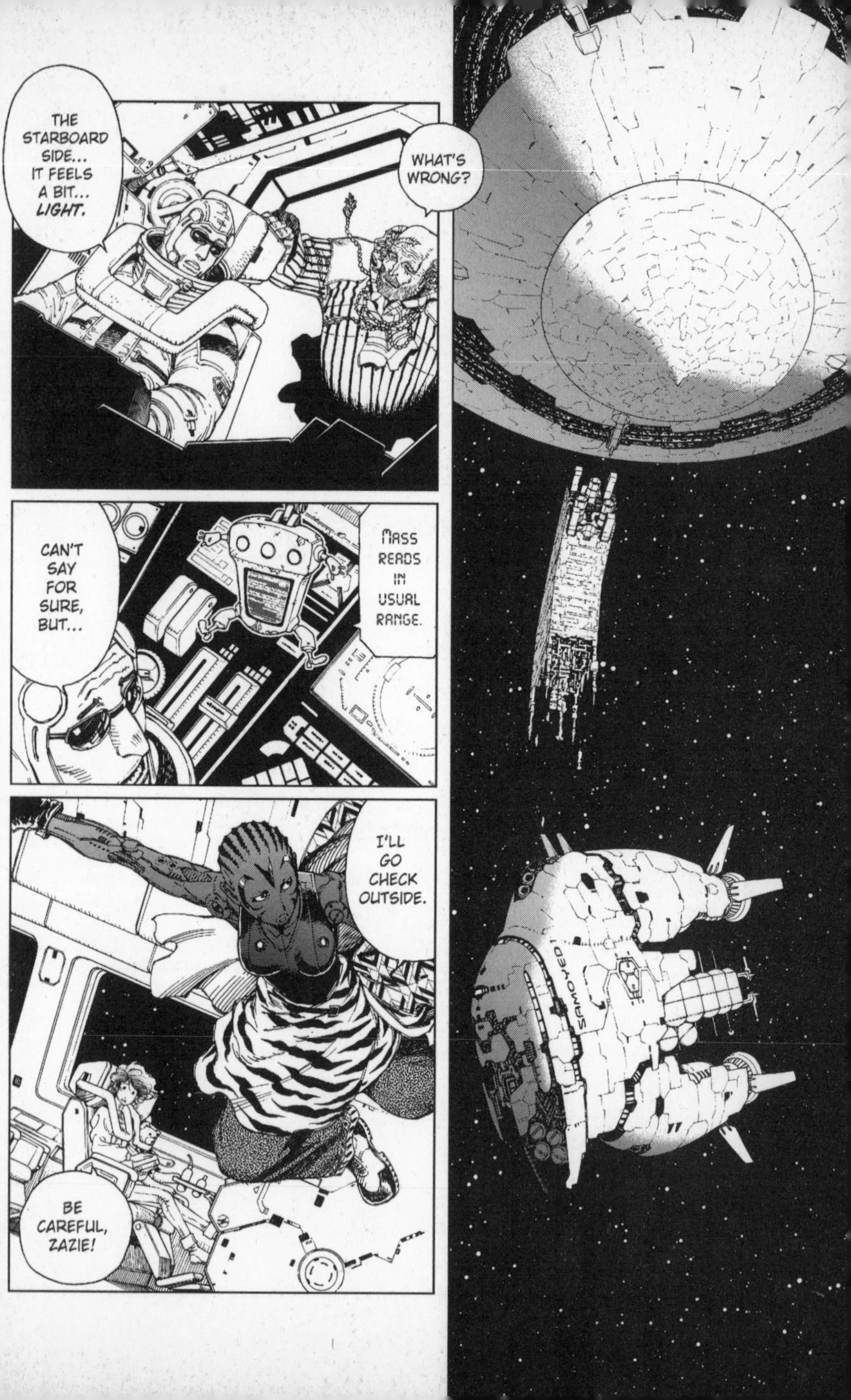
SAMOYED
WHAT'S WRONG?
THE STARBOARD SIDE... IT FEELS A BIT... *LIGHT.*
MASS READS IN USUAL RANGE.
CAN'T SAY FOR SURE, BUT...
I'LL GO CHECK OUTSIDE.
BE CAREFUL, ZAZIE!

SOMEONE'S COMING TO CHECK ON THINGS.

UH-OH.

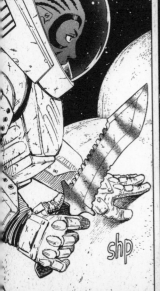

shp

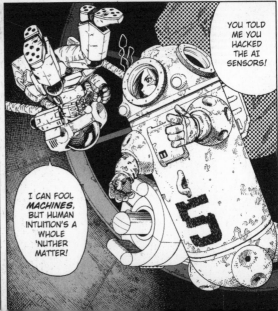

YOU TOLD ME YOU HACKED THE AI SENSORS!

I CAN FOOL *MACHINES*, BUT HUMAN INTUITION'S A WHOLE 'NUTHER MATTER!

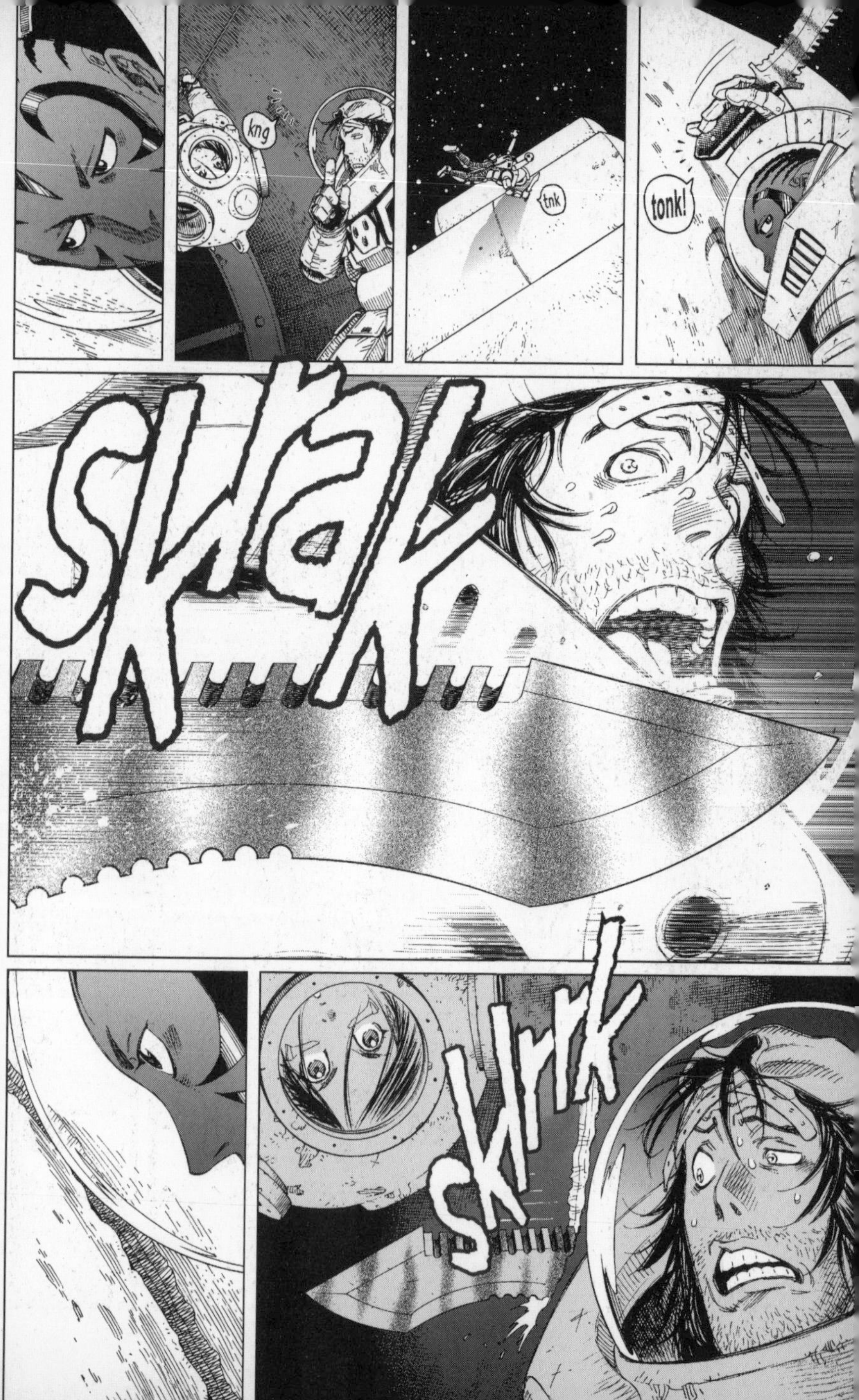
tonk!
tnk
kng
SKRAK
SKRRK

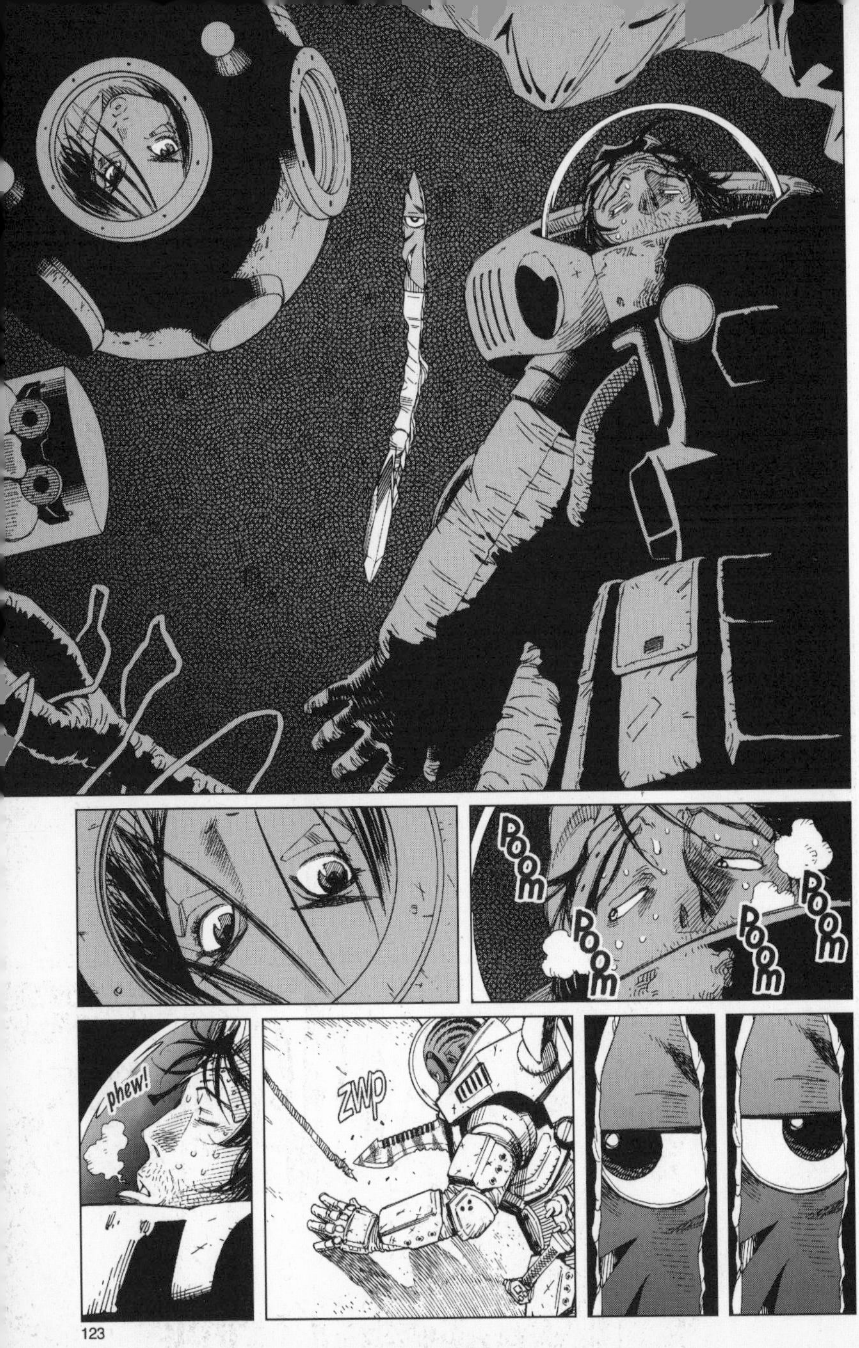
Poom
Poom
Poom
Poom
zwp
phew!

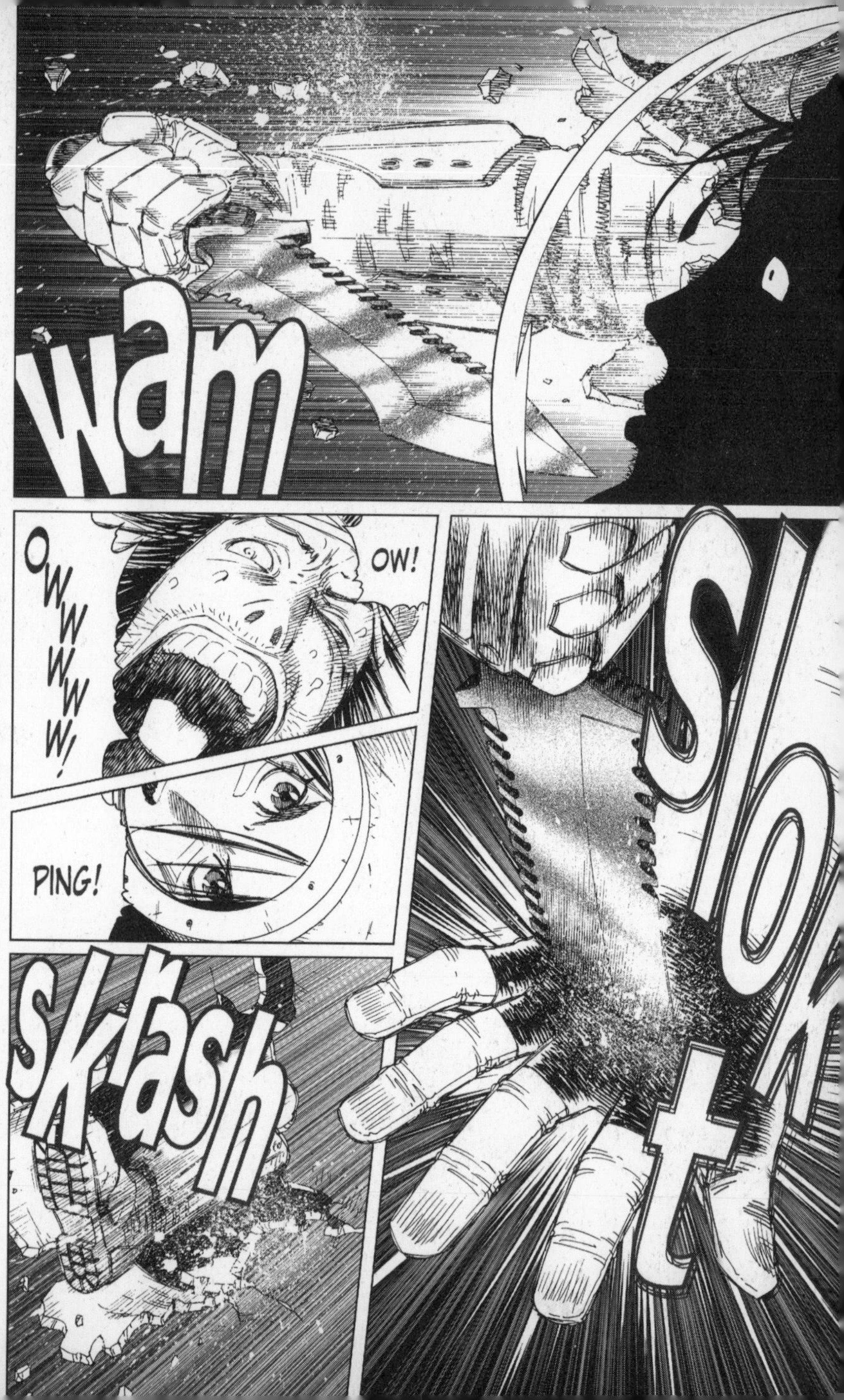
WAM
OW!
OWWWWWW!
PING!
SKLASH

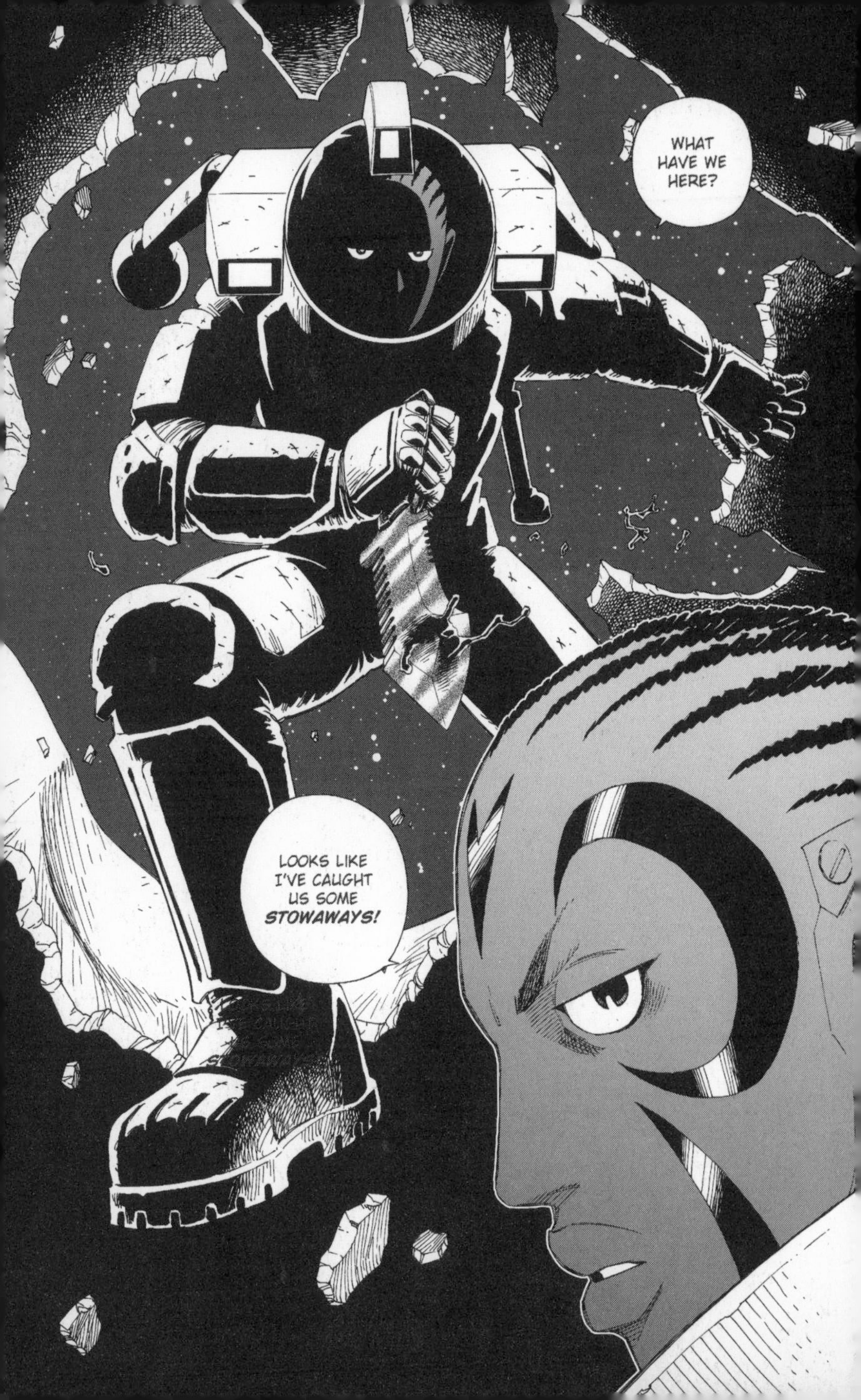
WHAT HAVE WE HERE?
LOOKS LIKE I'VE CAUGHT US SOME STOWAWAYS!

PHASE 17

And When Their Day Comes…

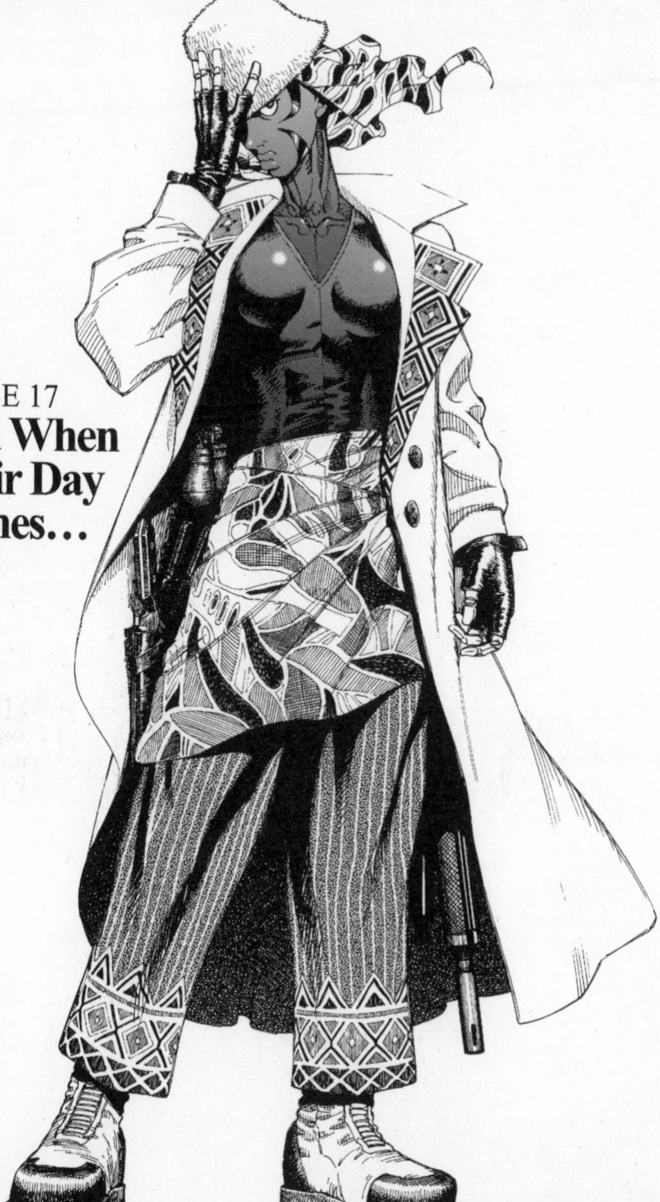

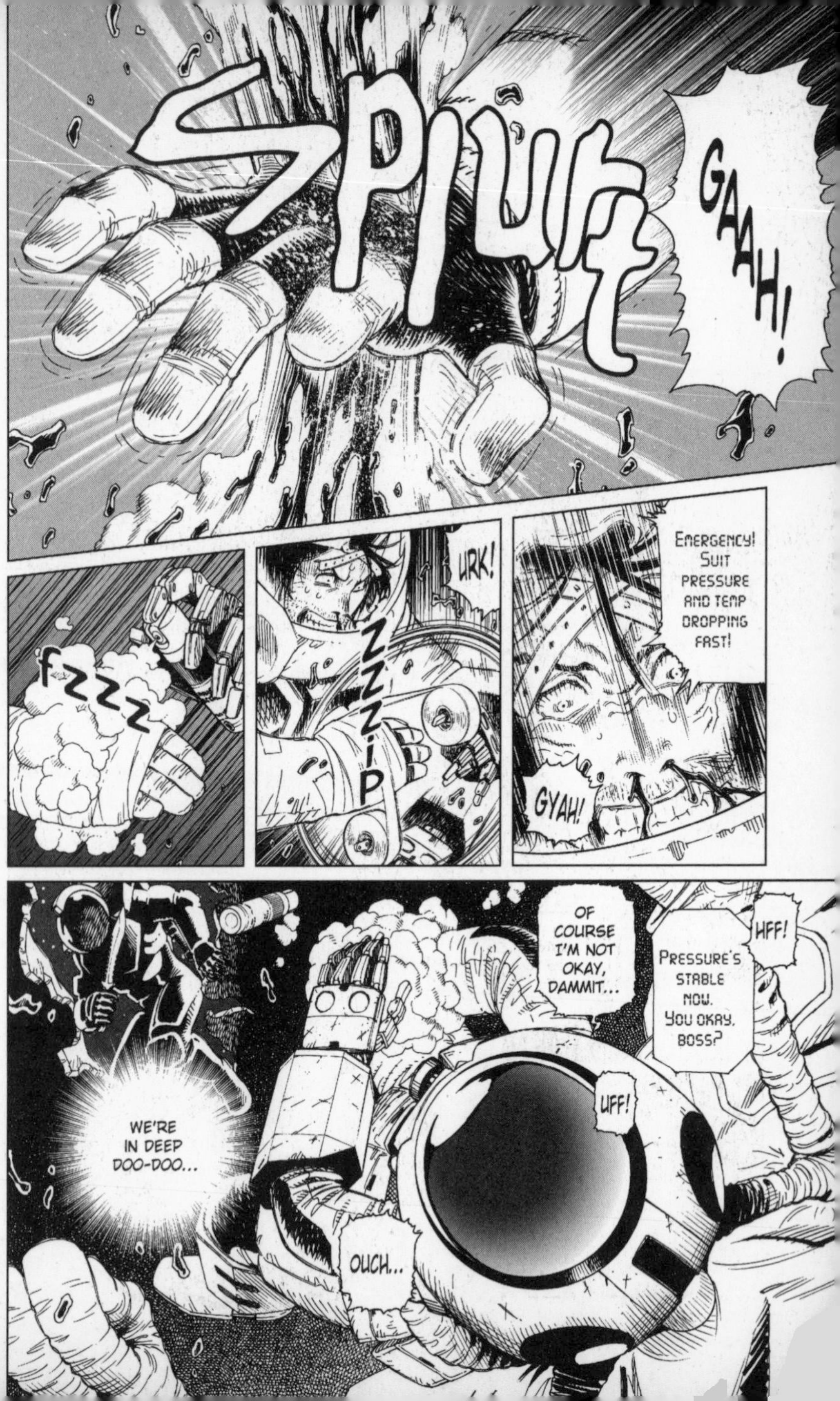
GAAAH!
SPLURT
Emergency! Suit pressure and temp dropping fast!
GYAH!
URK!
ZZZZIP
fZZZZ
HFF!
Pressure's stable now. You okay, boss?
Of course I'm not okay, dammit...
UFF!
OUCH...
WE'RE IN DEEP DOO-DOO...

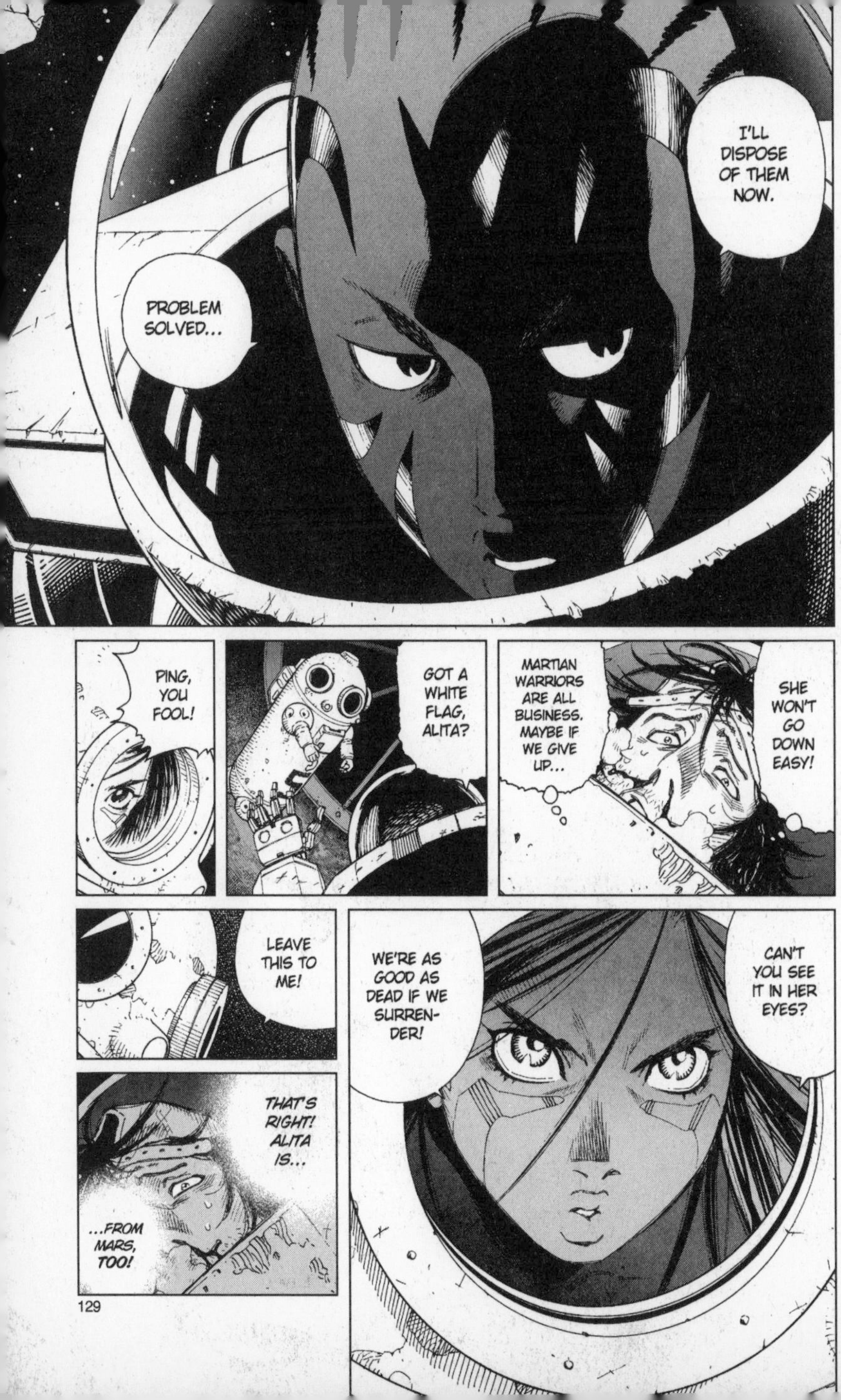
I'LL DISPOSE OF THEM NOW.
PROBLEM SOLVED...
SHE WON'T GO DOWN EASY!
MARTIAN WARRIORS ARE ALL BUSINESS. MAYBE IF WE GIVE UP...
GOT A WHITE FLAG, ALITA?
PING, YOU FOOL!
CAN'T YOU SEE IT IN HER EYES?
WE'RE AS GOOD AS DEAD IF WE SURRENDER!
LEAVE THIS TO ME!
THAT'S RIGHT! ALITA IS...
...FROM MARS, TOO!

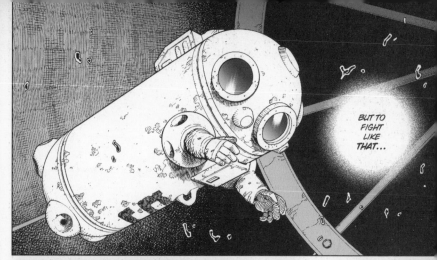

BUT TO FIGHT LIKE THAT...
...AGAINST HER?
ALITA'S GREAT AND ALL BUT... GIMME A BREAK!
DAMN. I-I'M PASSING OUT...
... ...
Boss!

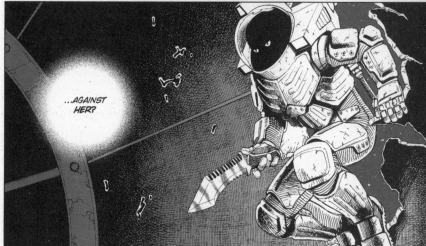

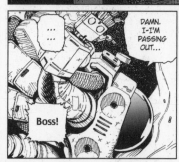

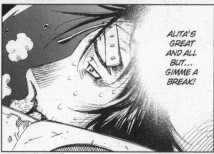

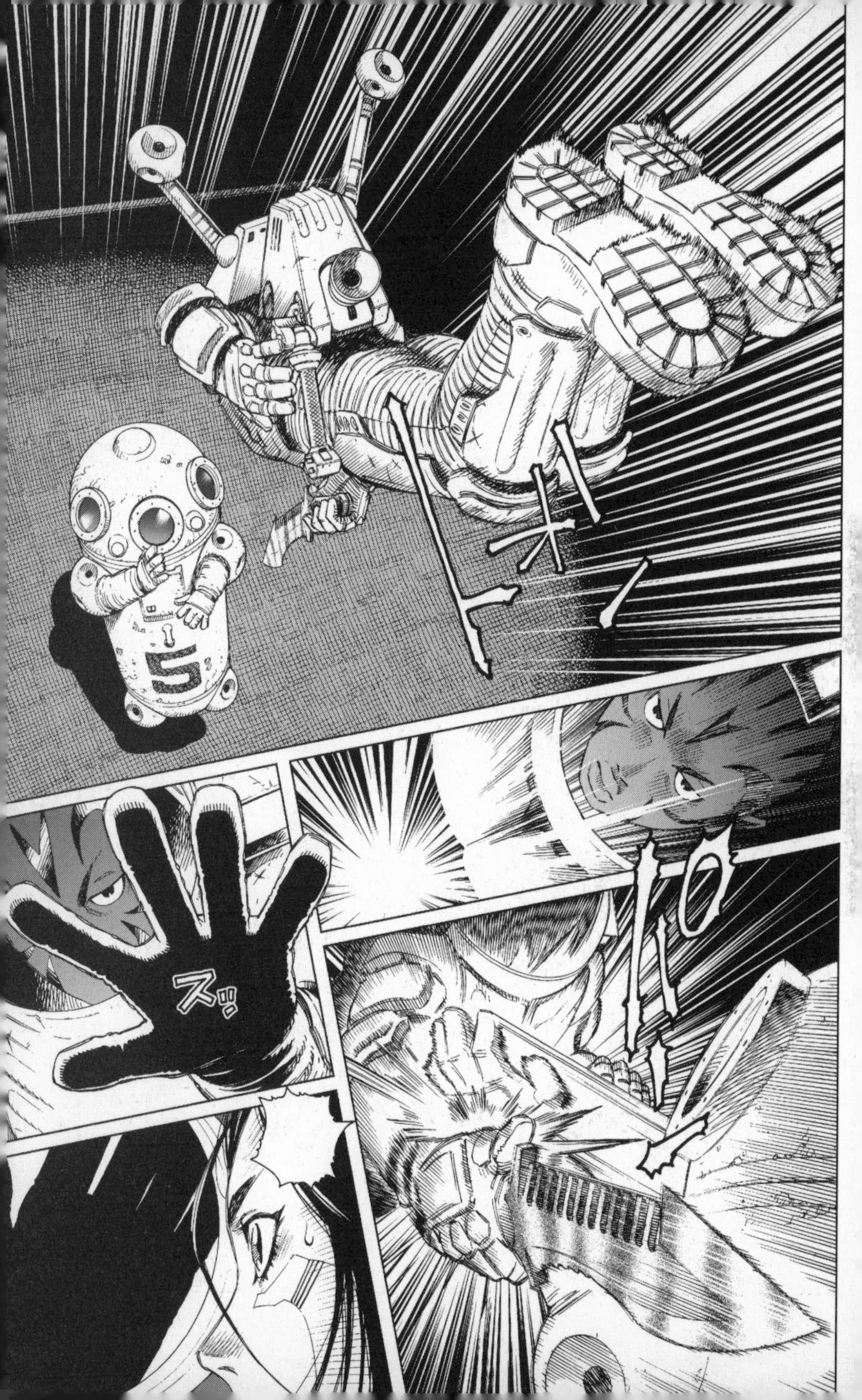
ス!!

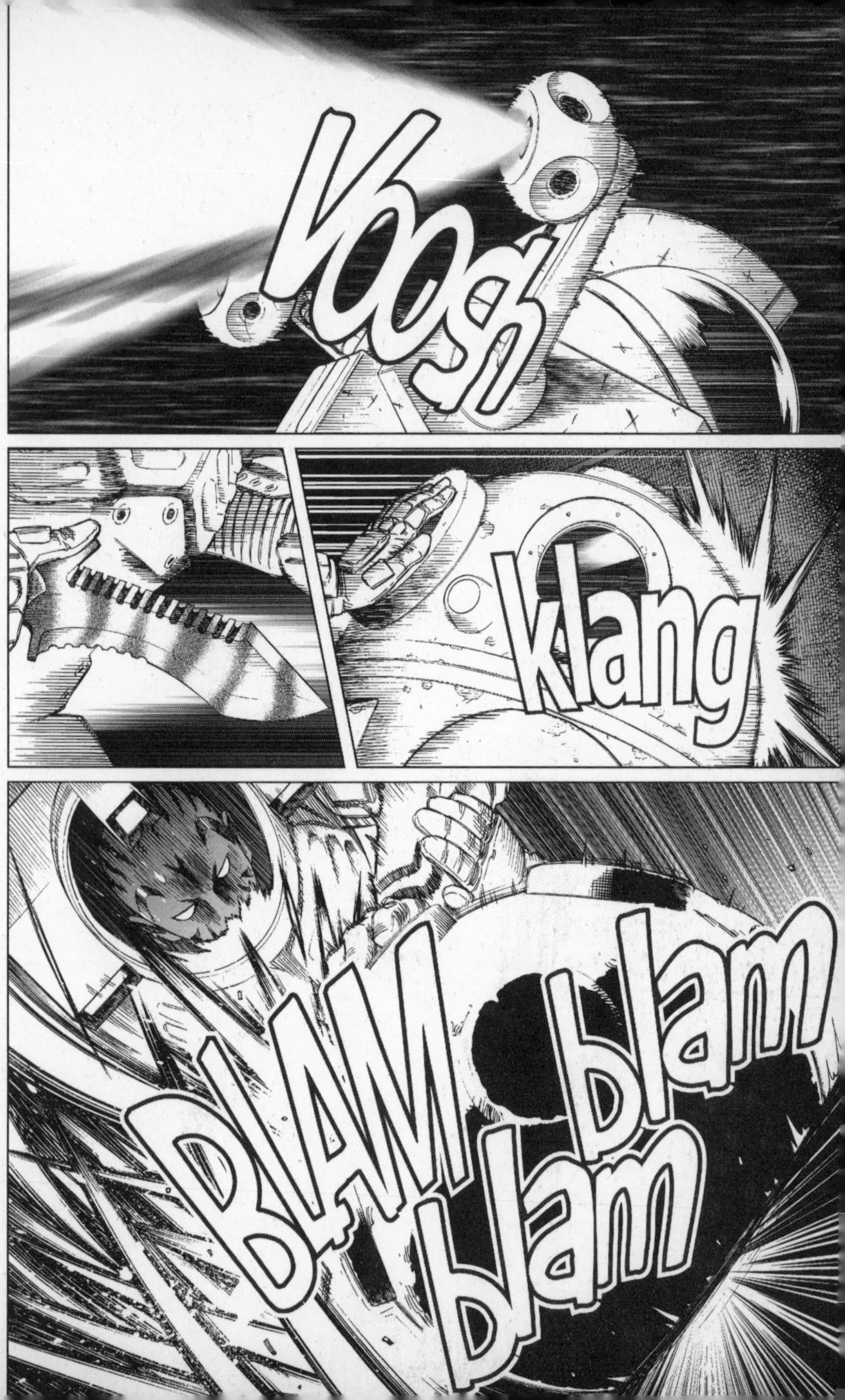
Voosh
klang
BLAM
blam
blam

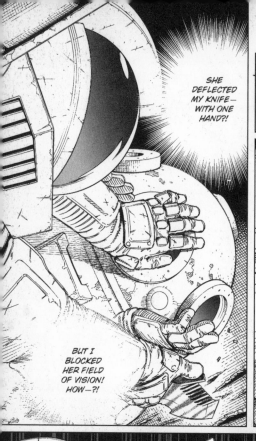

SHE DEFLECTED MY KNIFE— WITH ONE HAND?!

BUT I BLOCKED HER FIELD OF VISION! HOW—?!

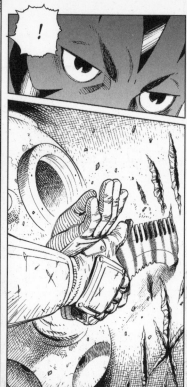

!

fwap

TING JING... CHINESE MARTIAL ART OF "LISTENING"!

SHE PREDICTED MY MOVES THROUGH THE CONTACT POINT!

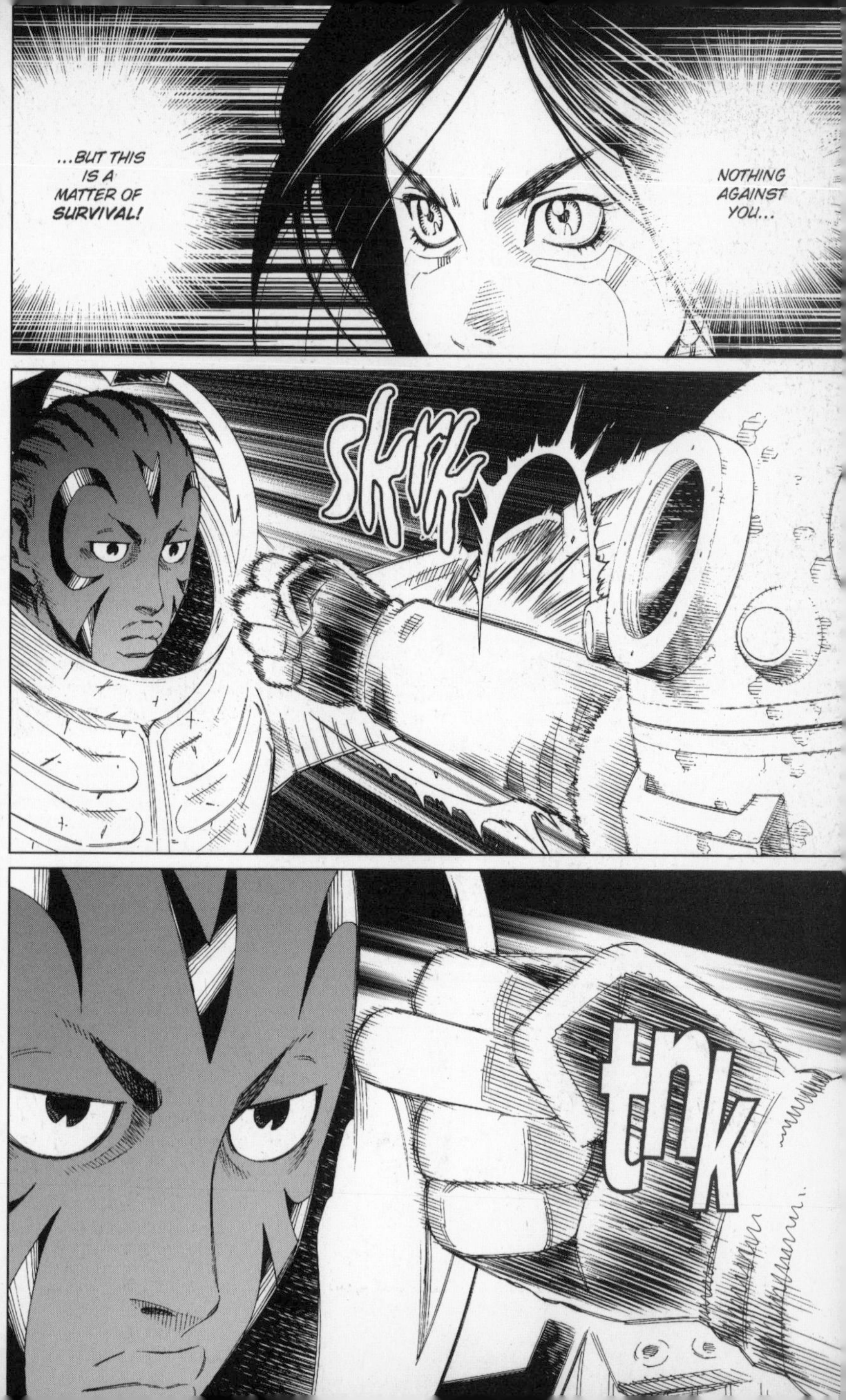
NOTHING AGAINST YOU...
...BUT THIS IS A MATTER OF SURVIVAL!
skrk
tnk

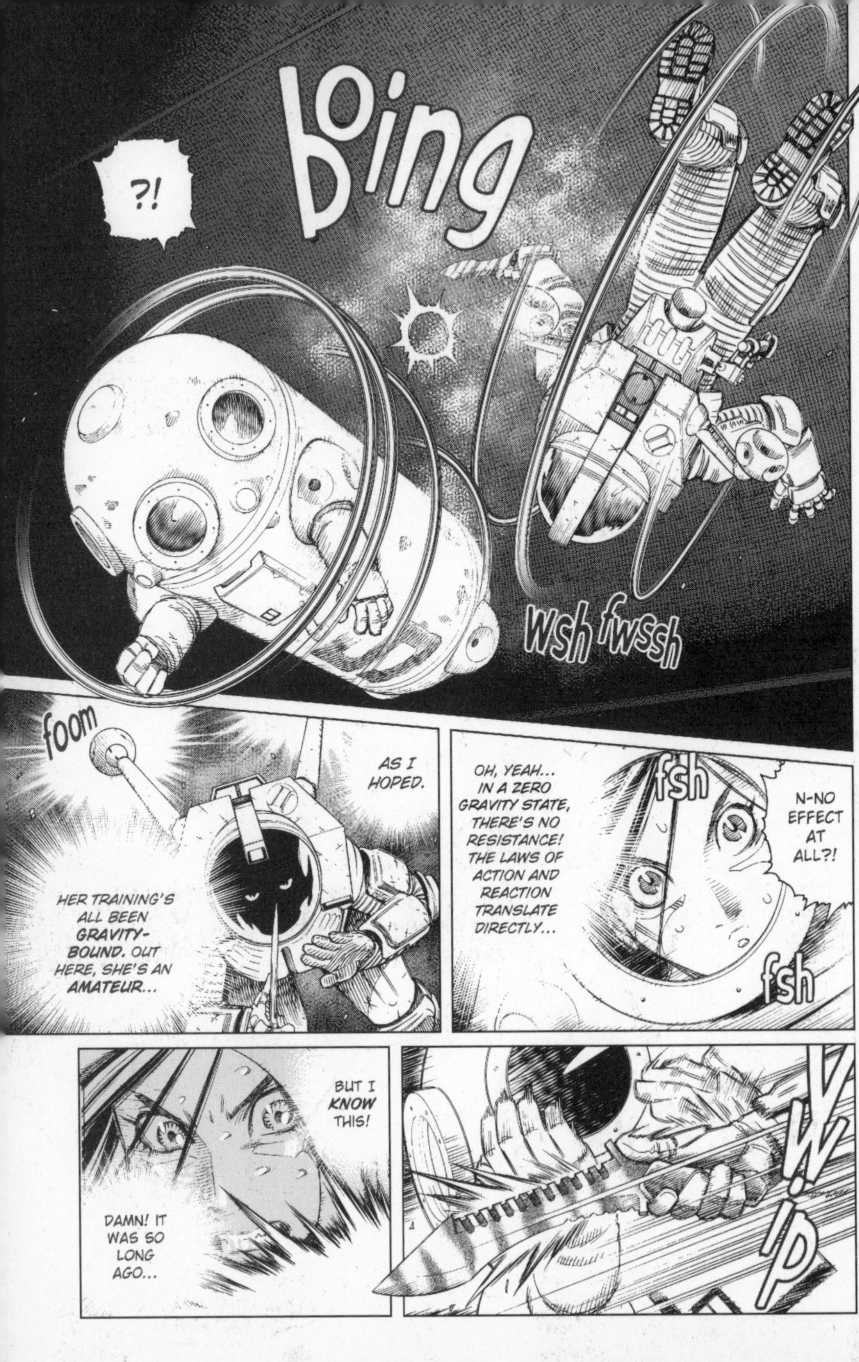
boing
?!
wsh fwssh
fsh
N-NO EFFECT AT ALL?!
OH, YEAH... IN A ZERO GRAVITY STATE, THERE'S NO RESISTANCE! THE LAWS OF ACTION AND REACTION TRANSLATE DIRECTLY...
fsh
AS I HOPED.
foom
HER TRAINING'S ALL BEEN **GRAVITY-BOUND.** OUT HERE, SHE'S AN **AMATEUR...**
Wip
BUT I ***KNOW*** THIS!
DAMN! IT WAS SO LONG AGO...

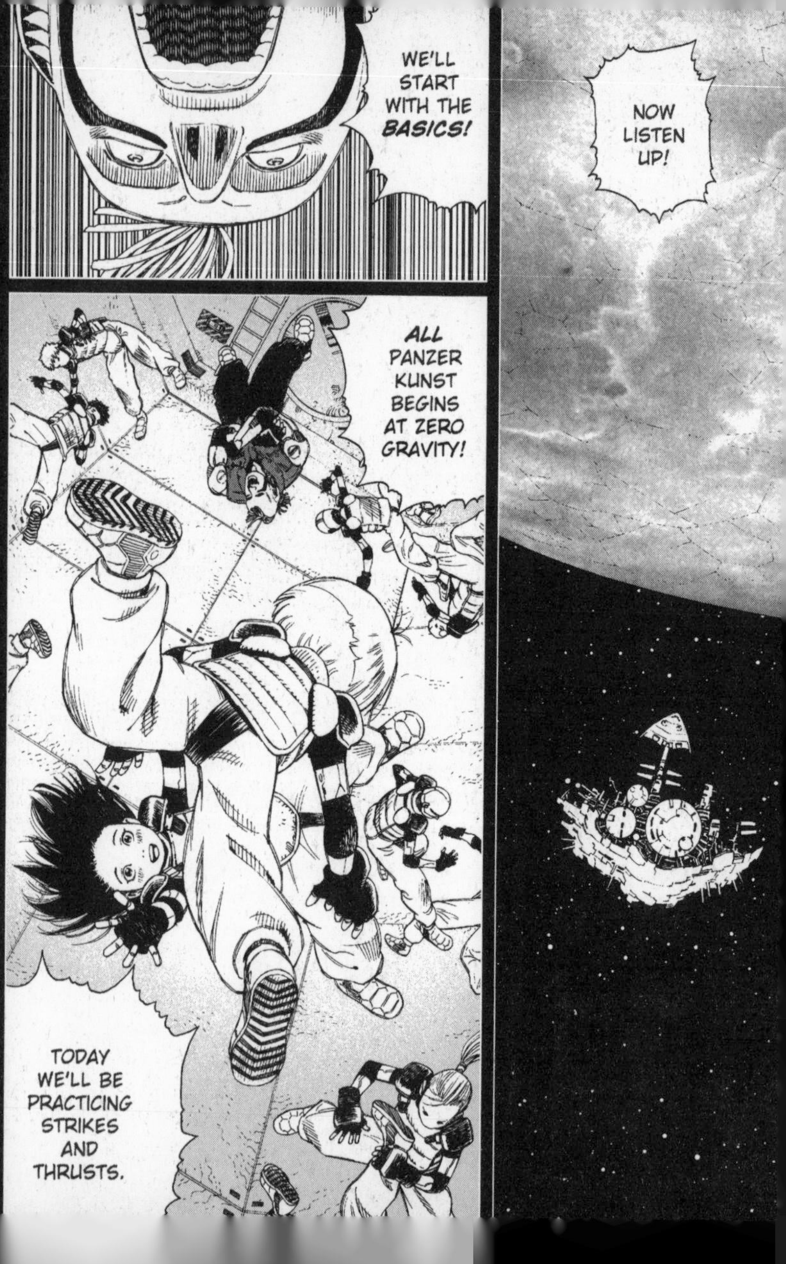
NOW LISTEN UP!
WE'LL START WITH THE BASICS!
ALL PANZER KUNST BEGINS AT ZERO GRAVITY!
TODAY WE'LL BE PRACTICING STRIKES AND THRUSTS.

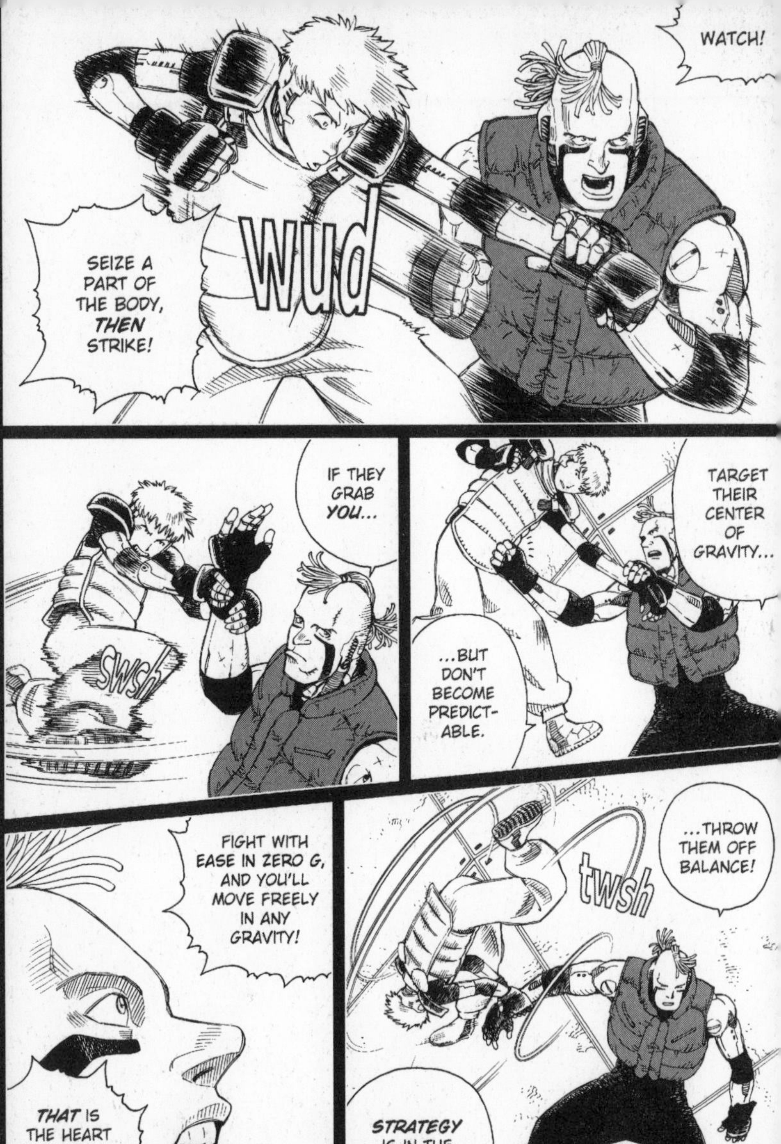
WATCH!
wud
SEIZE A PART OF THE BODY, *THEN* STRIKE!
TARGET THEIR CENTER OF GRAVITY...
...BUT DON'T BECOME PREDICT-ABLE.
IF THEY GRAB *YOU*...
swsh
...THROW THEM OFF BALANCE!
twsh
STRATEGY IS IN THE CONTACT POINTS.
FIGHT WITH EASE IN ZERO G, AND YOU'LL MOVE FREELY IN ANY GRAVITY!
THAT IS THE HEART OF THE PANZER KUNST!

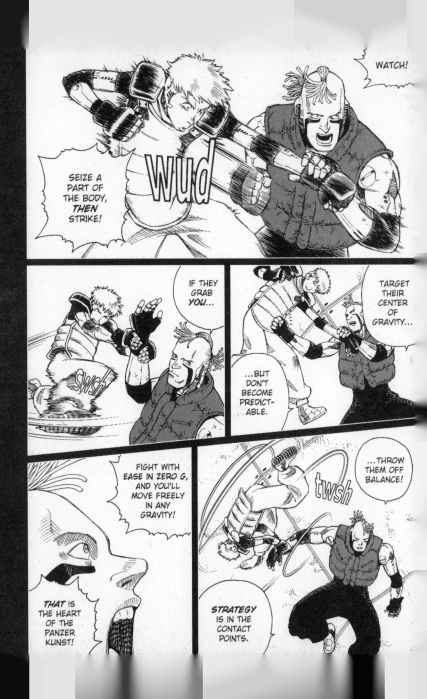

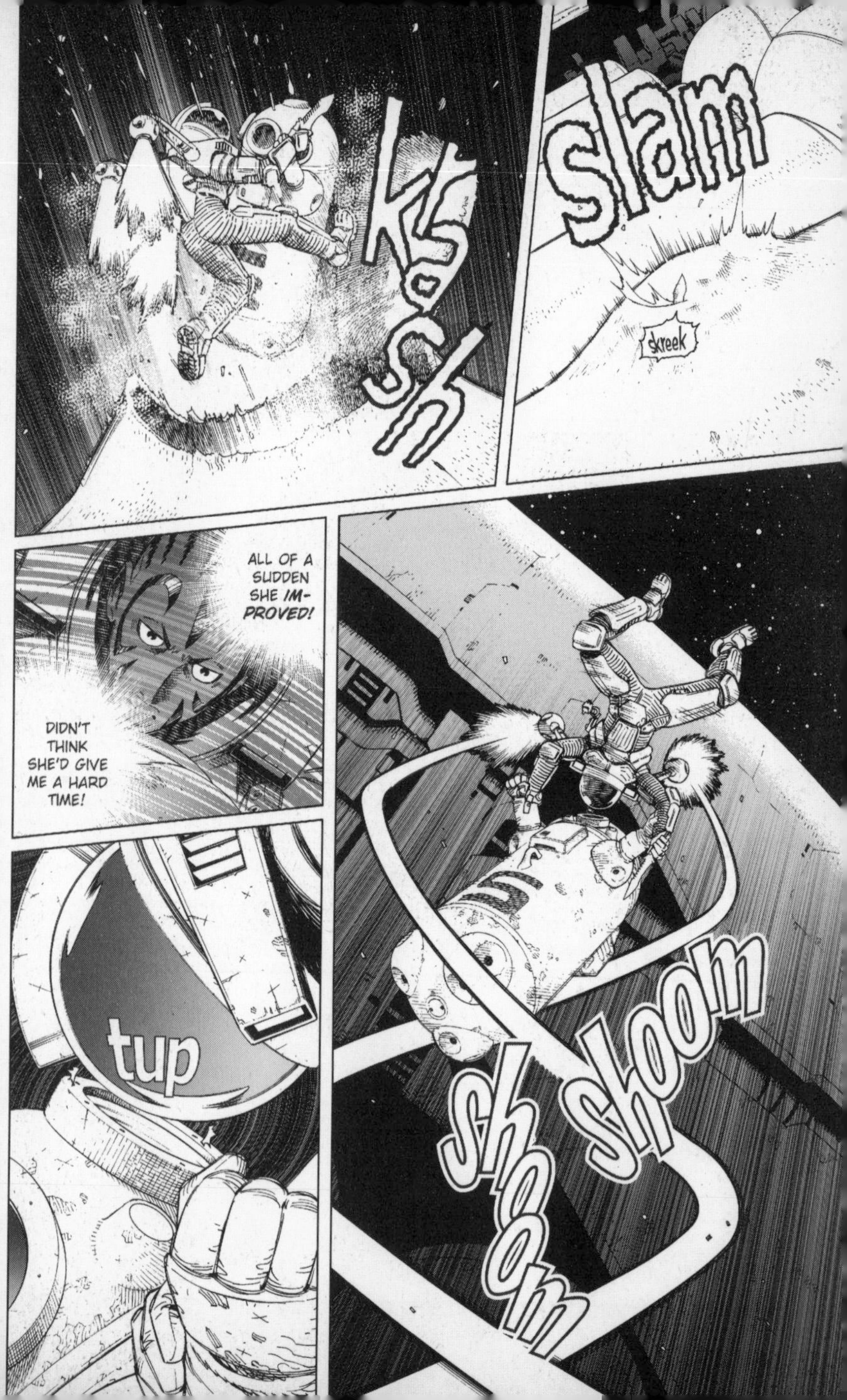
slam
skreek
krash
shoom
shoom
ALL OF A SUDDEN SHE *IM-PROVED!*
DIDN'T THINK SHE'D GIVE ME A HARD TIME!
tup

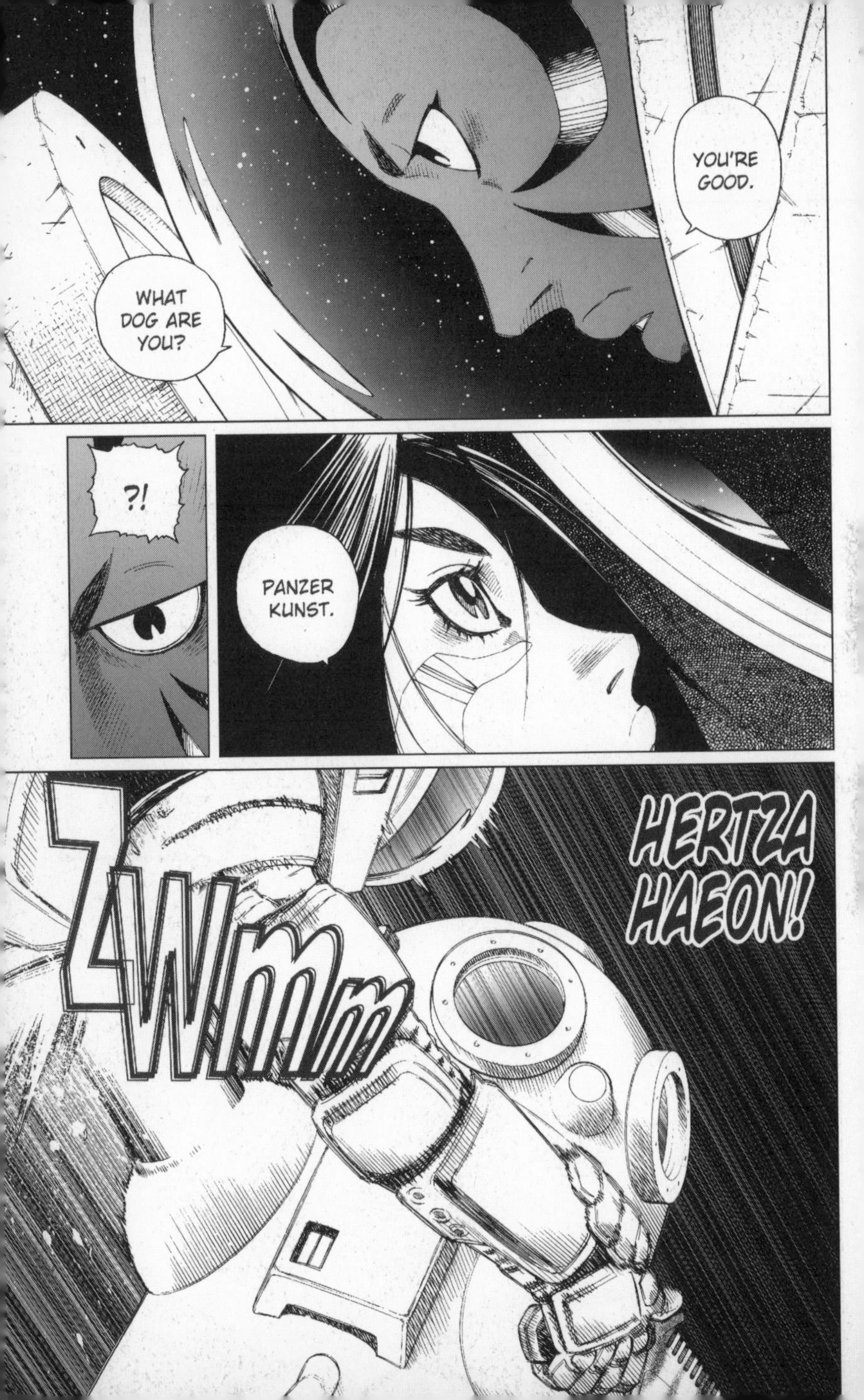
YOU'RE GOOD.
WHAT DOG ARE YOU?
PANZER KUNST.
?!
HERTZA HAEON!
ZWMMM

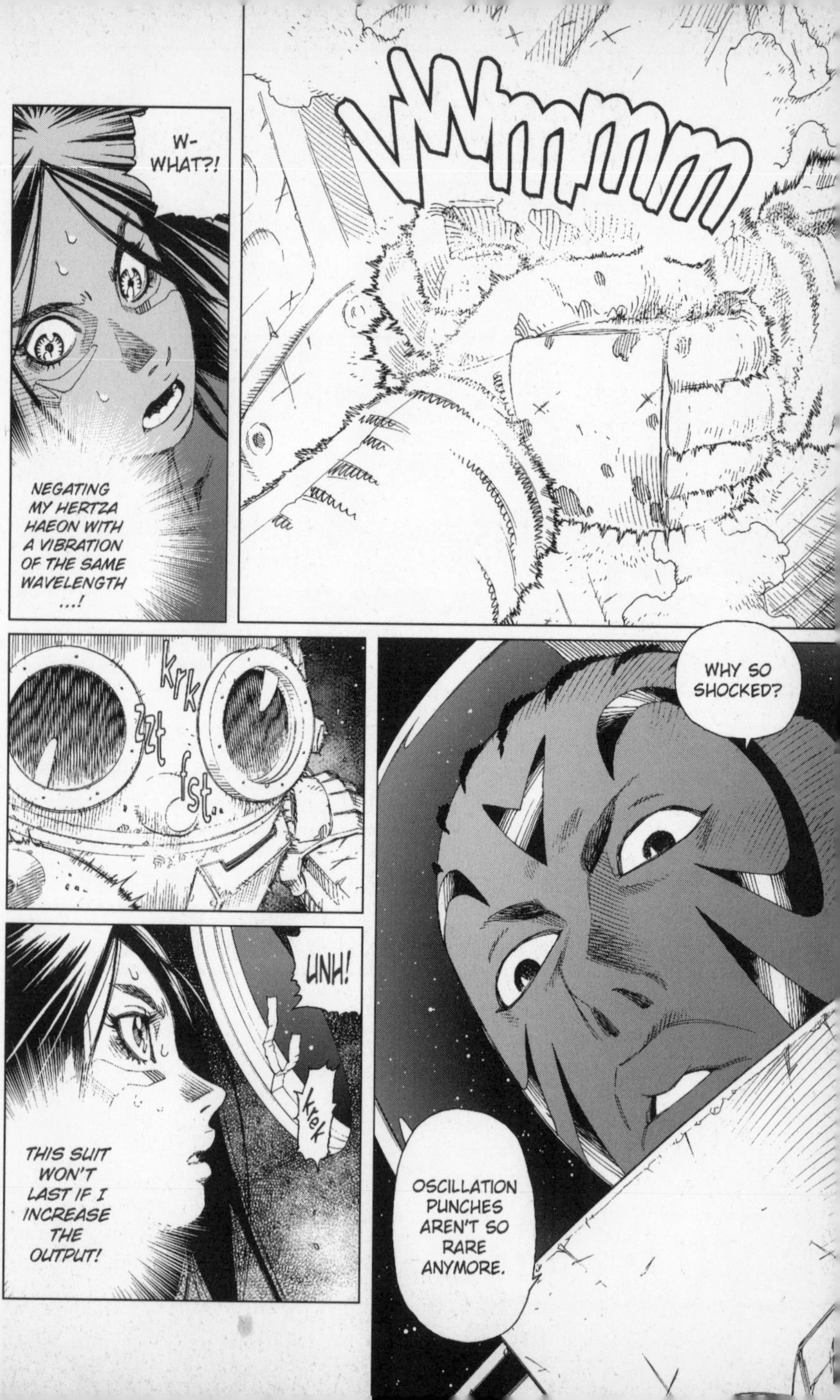
VVVmmm
W-WHAT?!
NEGATING MY HERTZA HAEON WITH A VIBRATION OF THE SAME WAVELENGTH ...!
WHY SO SHOCKED?
OSCILLATION PUNCHES AREN'T SO RARE ANYMORE.
krk
zzt
fst
UNH!
krek
THIS SUIT WON'T LAST IF I INCREASE THE OUTPUT!

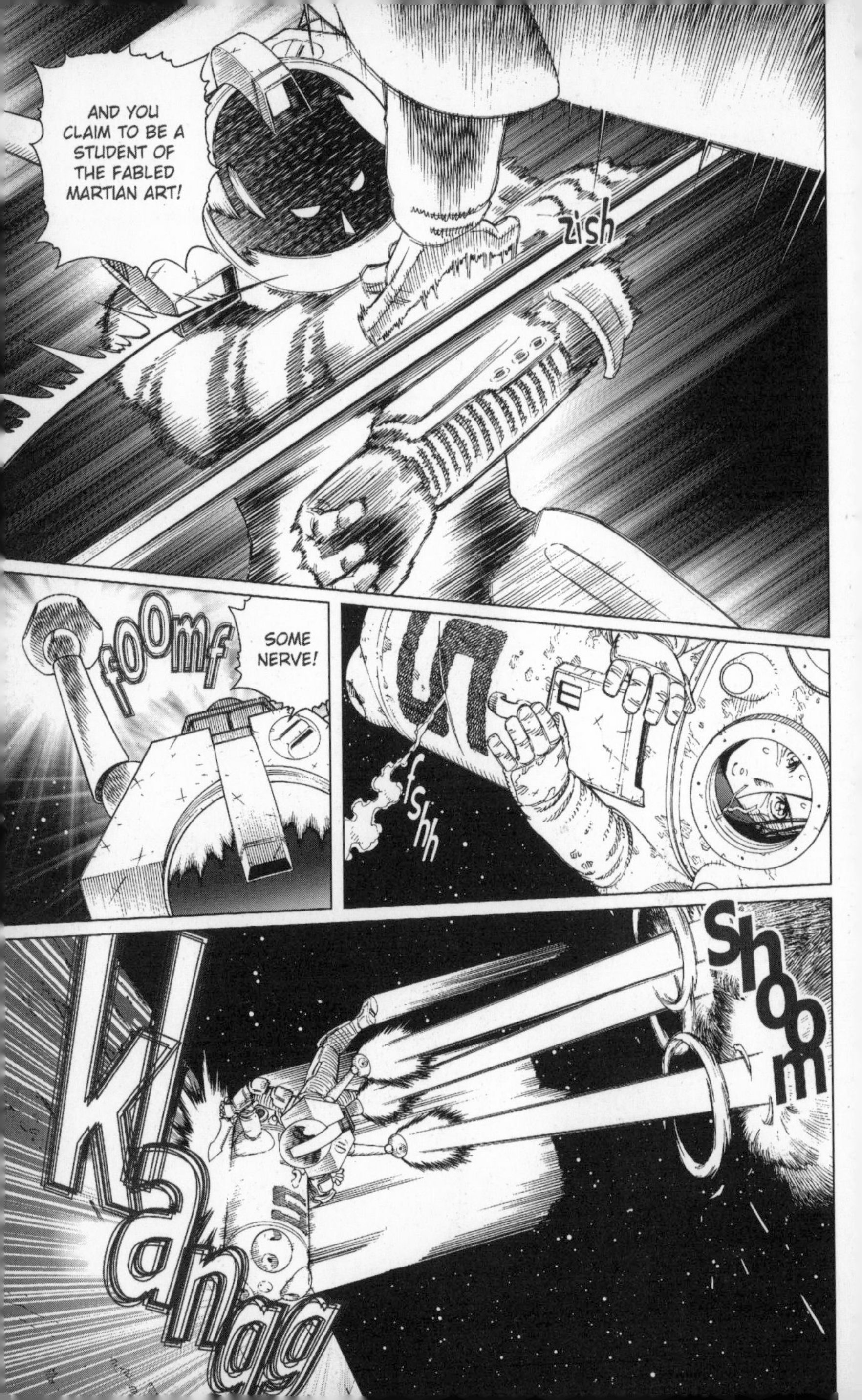
AND YOU CLAIM TO BE A STUDENT OF THE FABLED MARTIAN ART!
zish
fshh
SOME NERVE!
fOOmf
Shoom
Kanaag

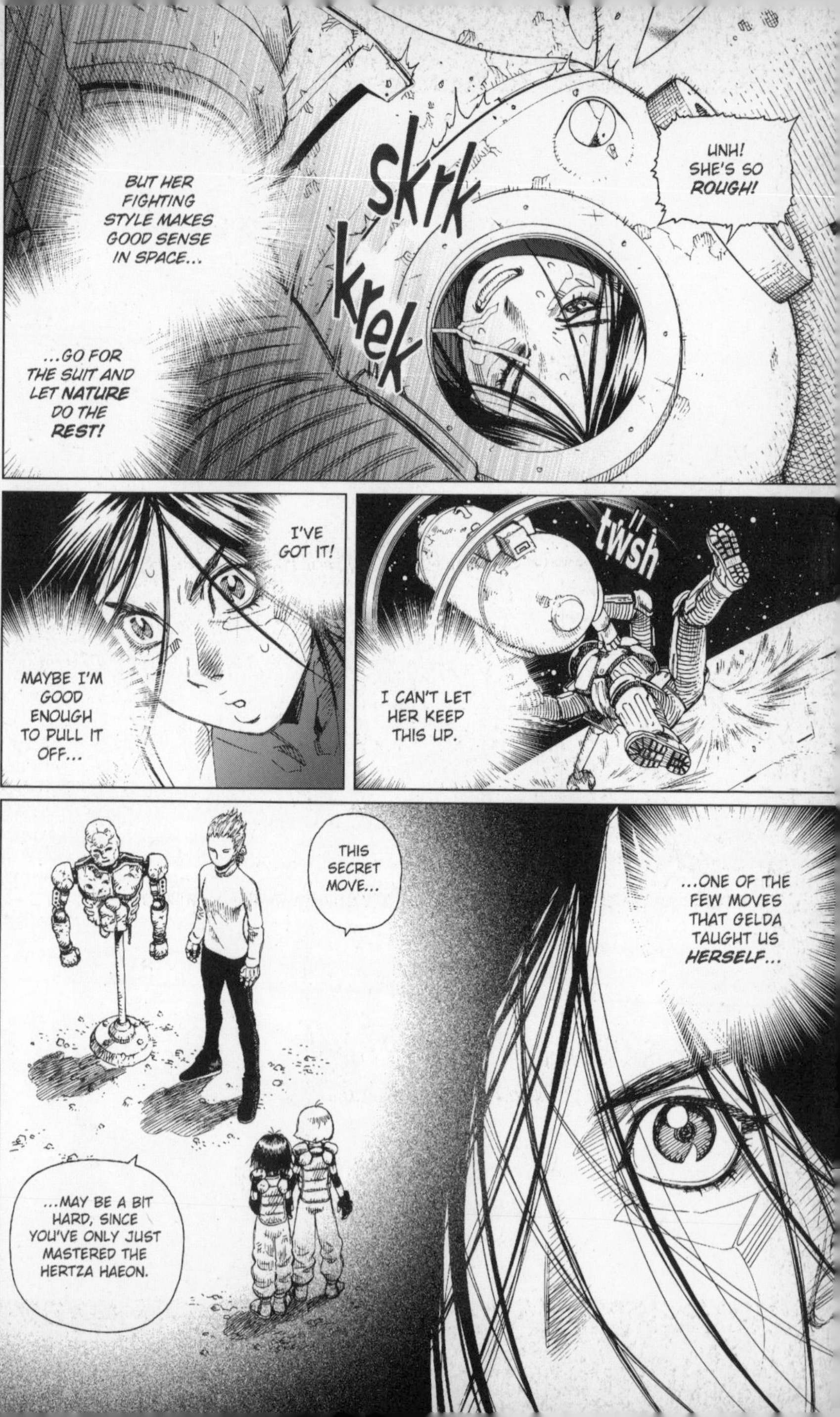

UNH! SHE'S SO ROUGH!
skrk
krek
BUT HER FIGHTING STYLE MAKES GOOD SENSE IN SPACE...
...GO FOR THE SUIT AND LET NATURE DO THE REST!
twsh
I CAN'T LET HER KEEP THIS UP.
I'VE GOT IT!
MAYBE I'M GOOD ENOUGH TO PULL IT OFF...
...ONE OF THE FEW MOVES THAT GELDA TAUGHT US HERSELF...
THIS SECRET MOVE...
...MAY BE A BIT HARD, SINCE YOU'VE ONLY JUST MASTERED THE HERTZA HAEON.

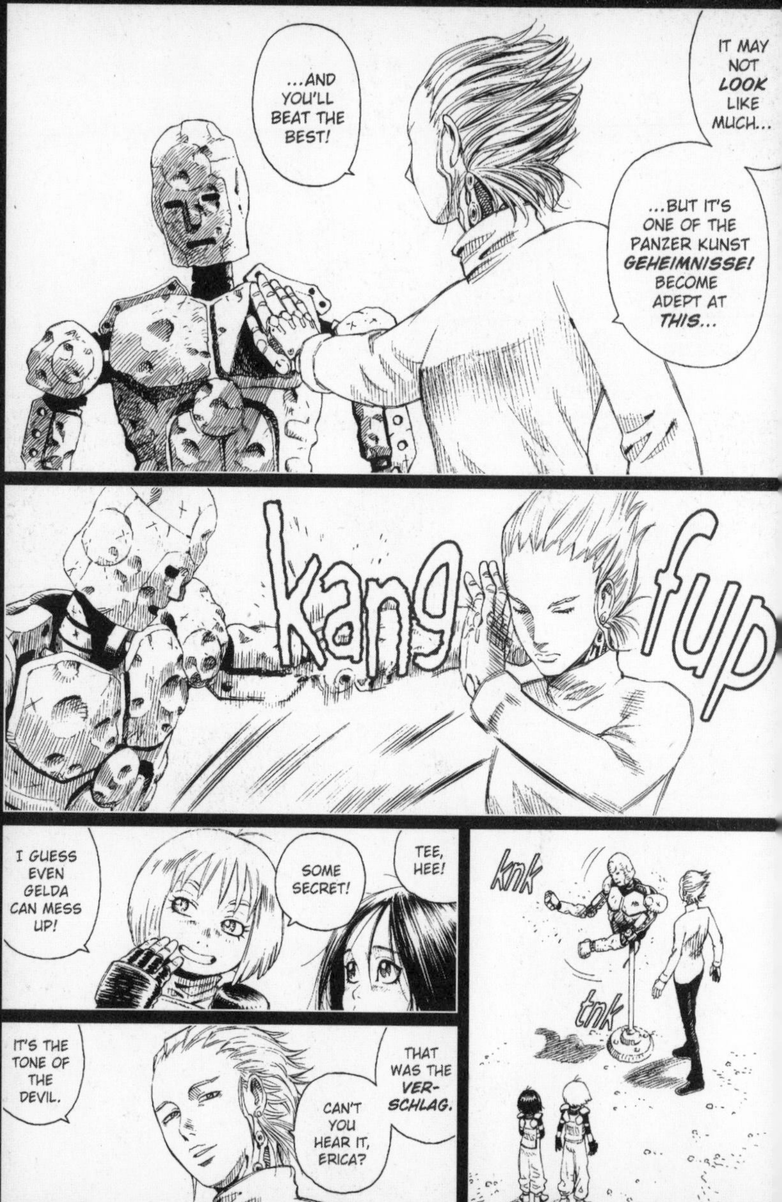
IT MAY NOT ***LOOK*** LIKE MUCH...
...BUT IT'S ONE OF THE PANZER KUNST ***GEHEIMNISSE!*** BECOME ADEPT AT ***THIS...***
...AND YOU'LL BEAT THE BEST!
fup
kang
knk
tnk
TEE, HEE!
SOME SECRET!
I GUESS EVEN GELDA CAN MESS UP!
THAT WAS THE ***VER-SCHLAG.***
CAN'T YOU HEAR IT, ERICA?
IT'S THE TONE OF THE DEVIL.

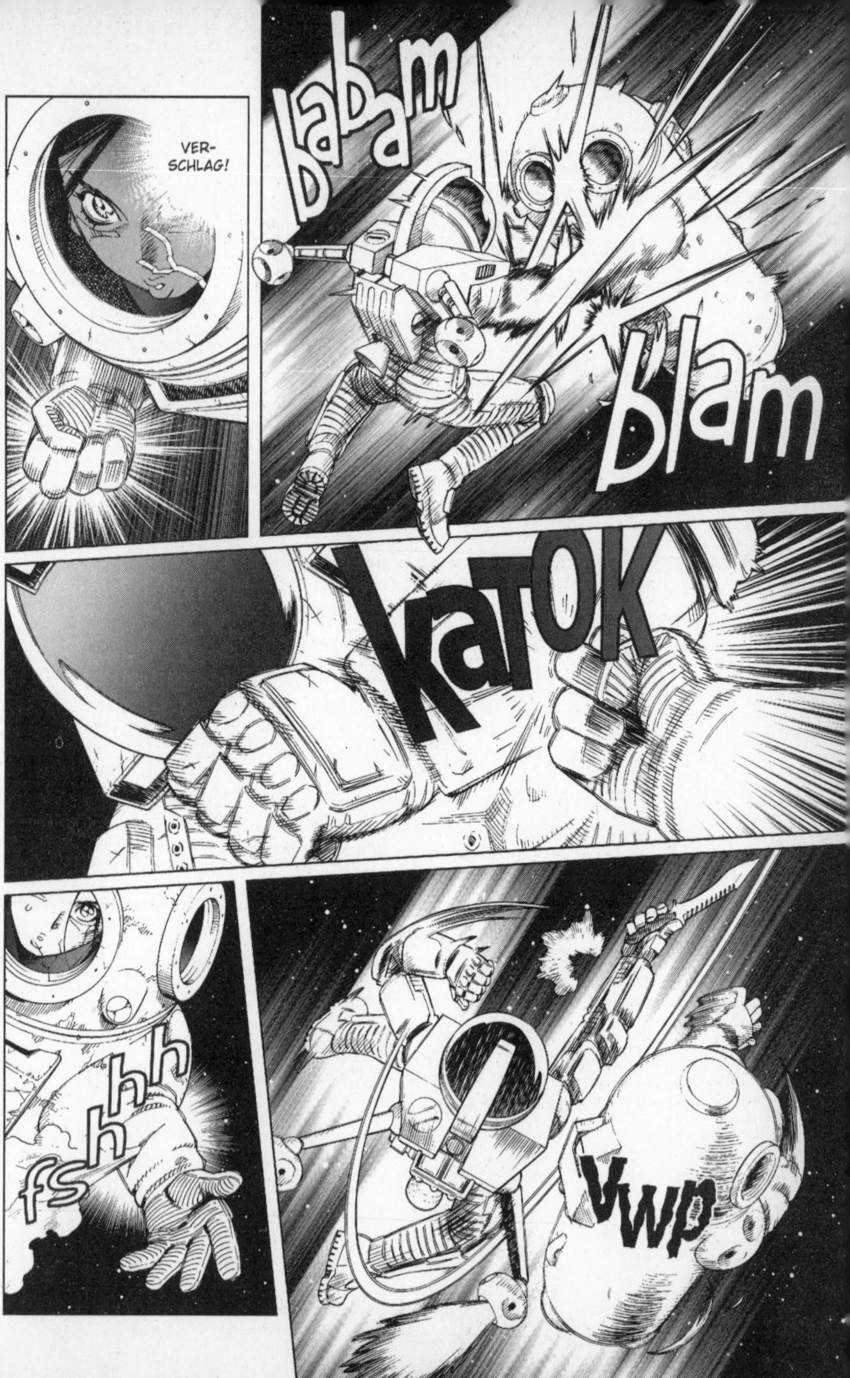
babam
b'lam
VER-
SCHLAG!
katOK
vwp
fshhh

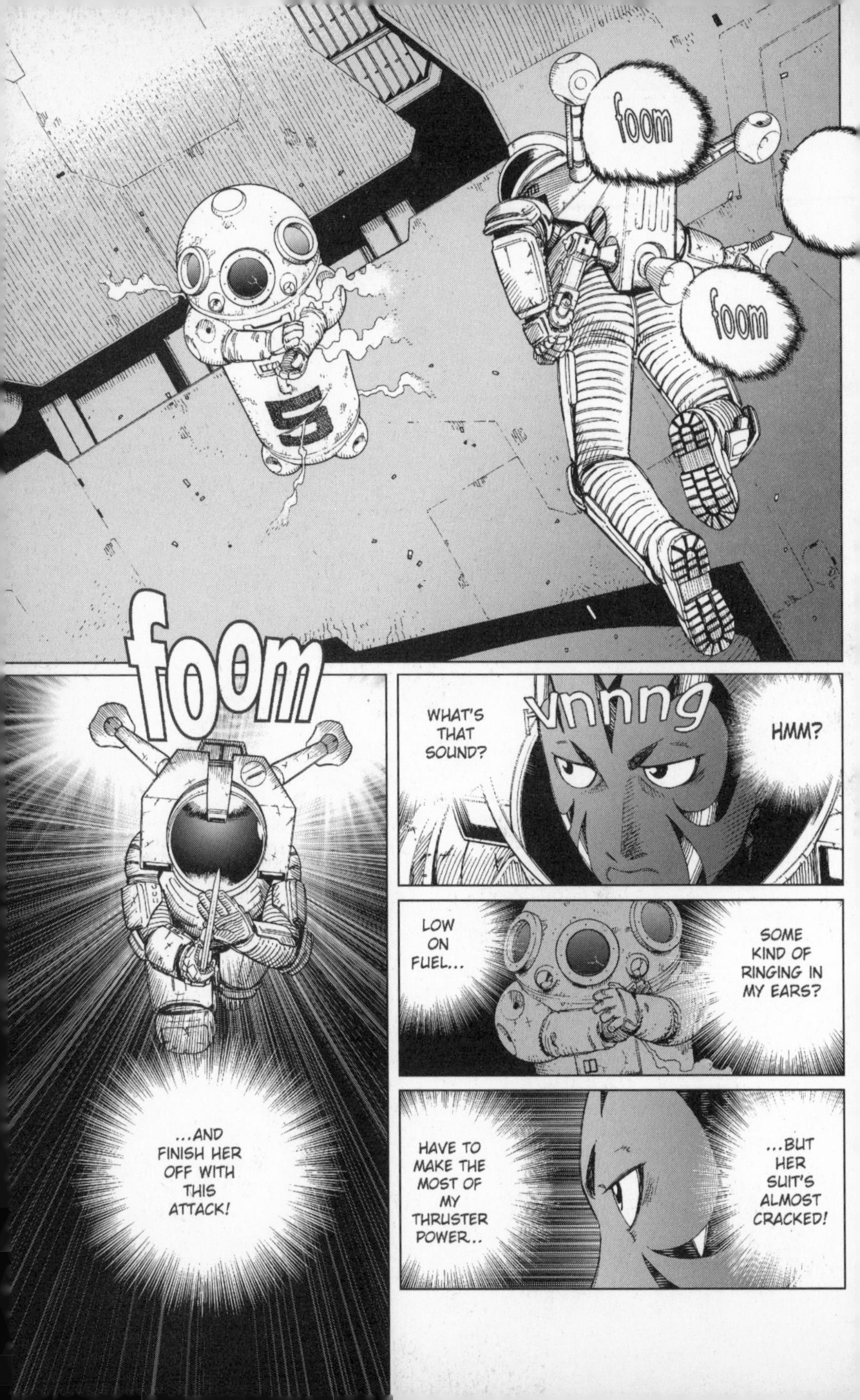
foom
foom
vnnng
HMM?
WHAT'S THAT SOUND?
SOME KIND OF RINGING IN MY EARS?
LOW ON FUEL...
...BUT HER SUIT'S ALMOST CRACKED!
HAVE TO MAKE THE MOST OF MY THRUSTER POWER...
foom
...AND FINISH HER OFF WITH THIS ATTACK!

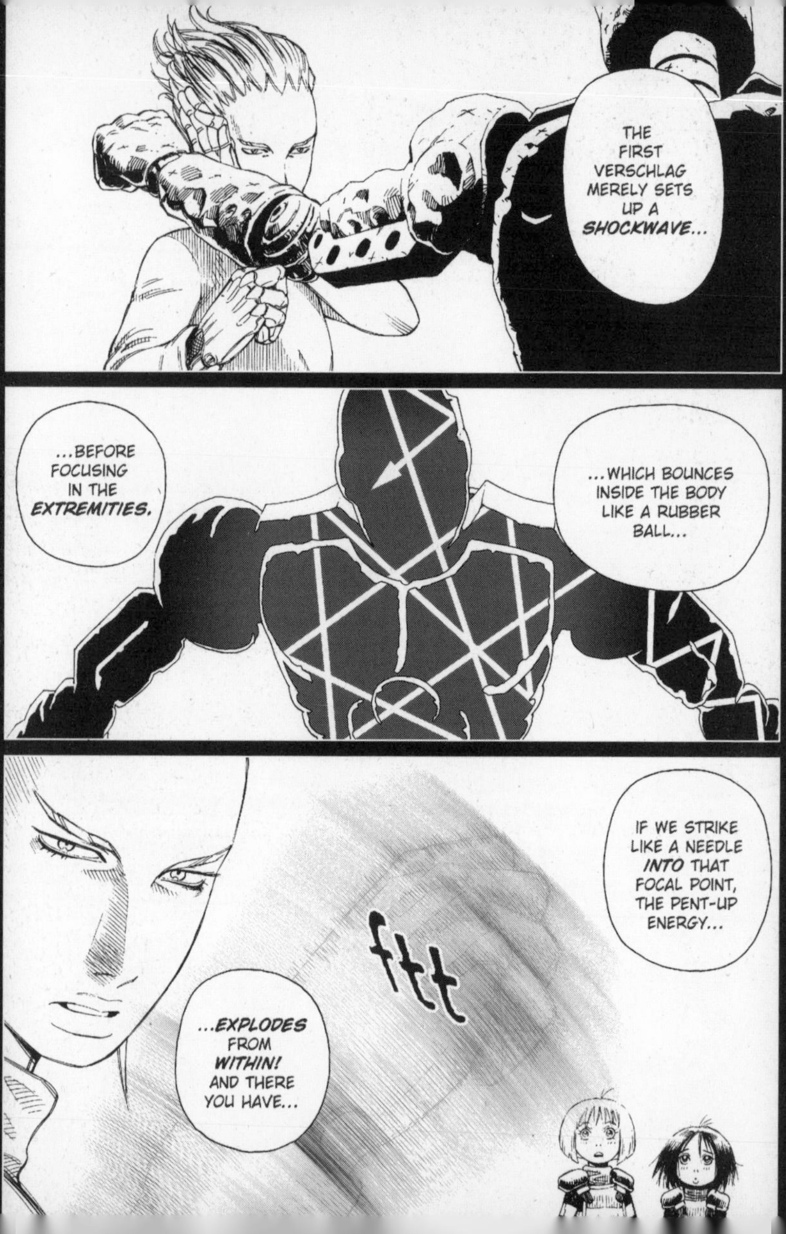

THE FIRST VERSCHLAG MERELY SETS UP A SHOCKWAVE...
...WHICH BOUNCES INSIDE THE BODY LIKE A RUBBER BALL...
...BEFORE FOCUSING IN THE EXTREMITIES.
IF WE STRIKE LIKE A NEEDLE INTO THAT FOCAL POINT, THE PENT-UP ENERGY...
ftt
...EXPLODES FROM WITHIN! AND THERE YOU HAVE...

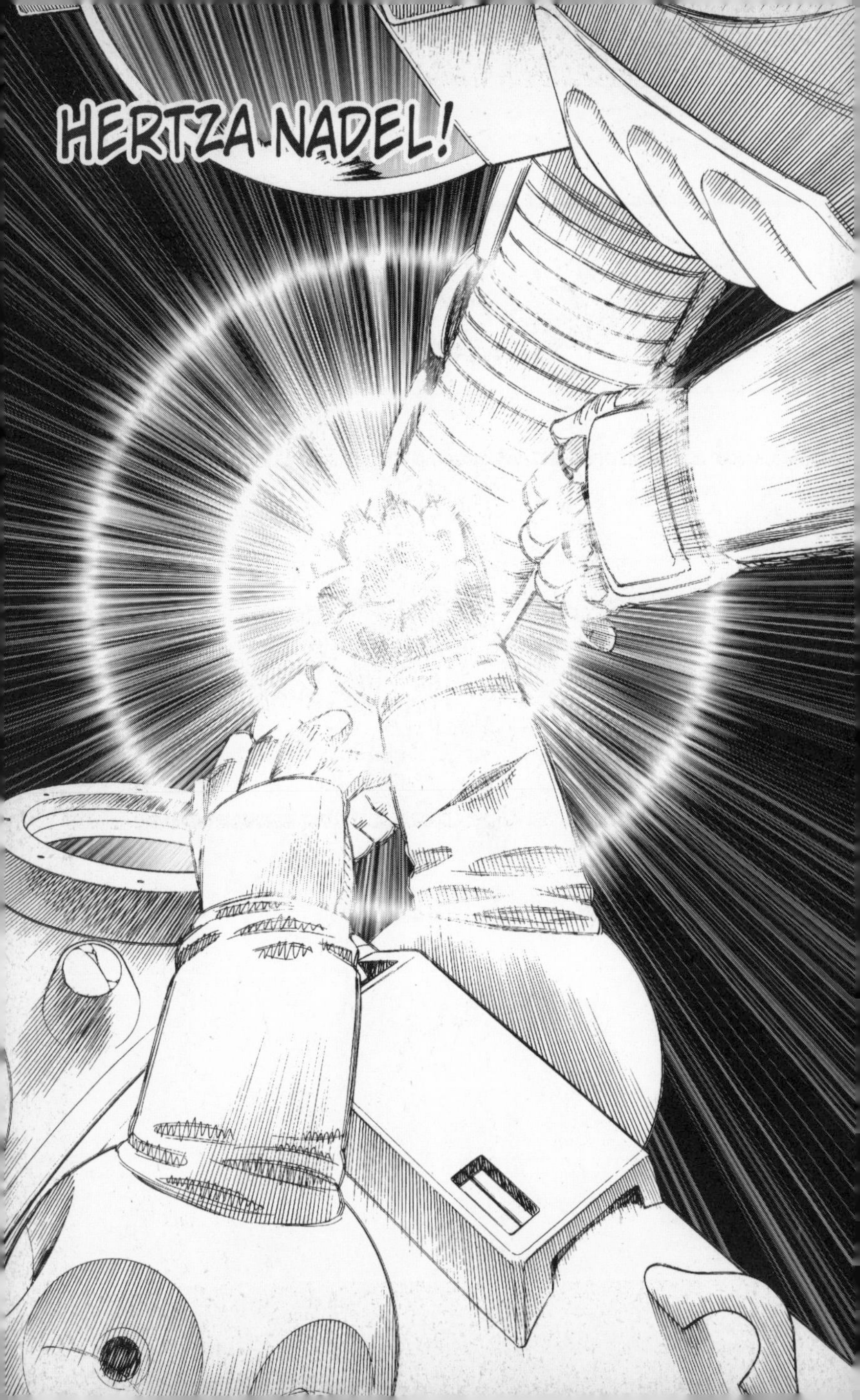
HERTZA NADEL!

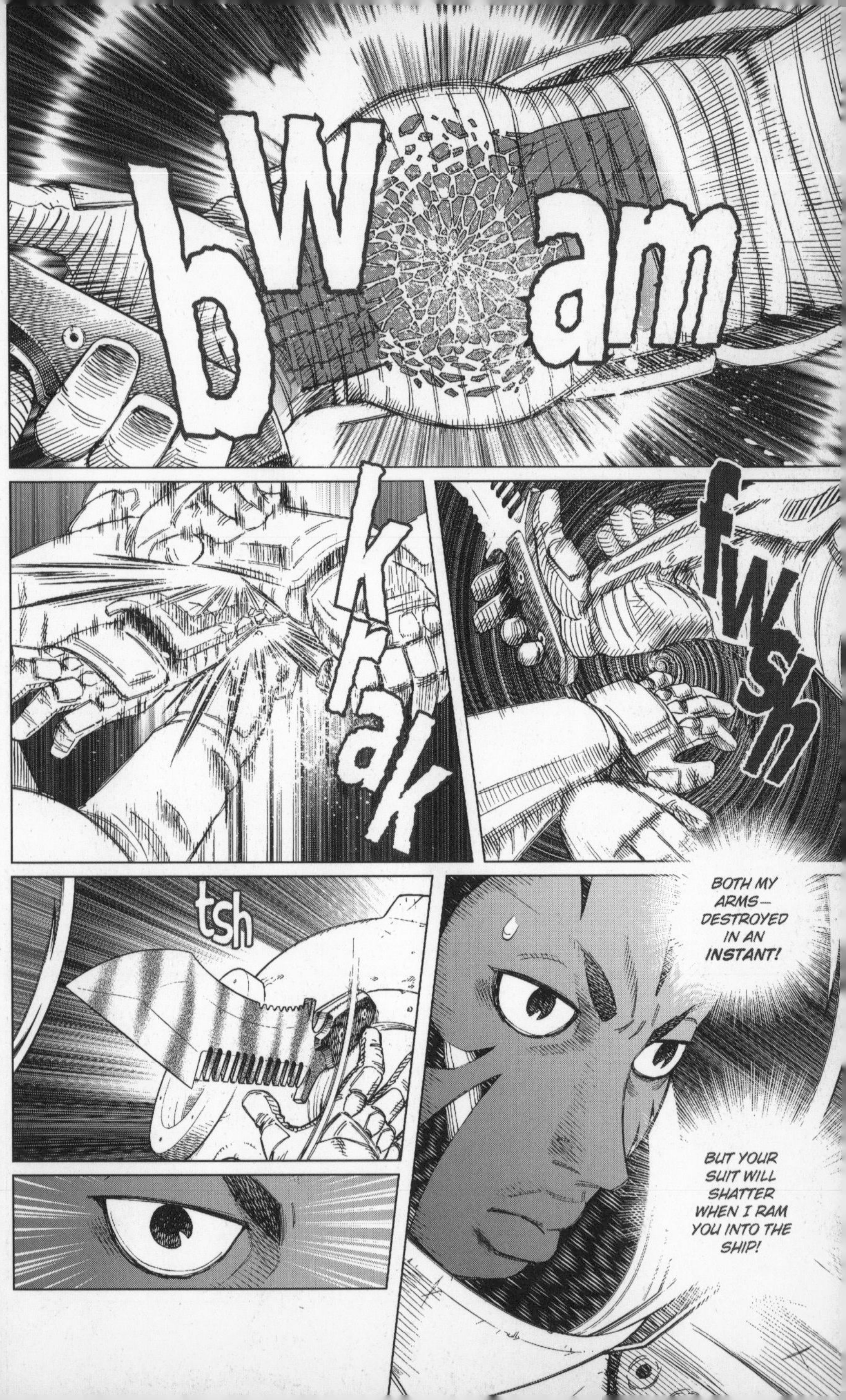
bWam
fwsh
krak
BOTH MY ARMS—DESTROYED IN AN INSTANT!
BUT YOUR SUIT WILL SHATTER WHEN I RAM YOU INTO THE SHIP!
tsh

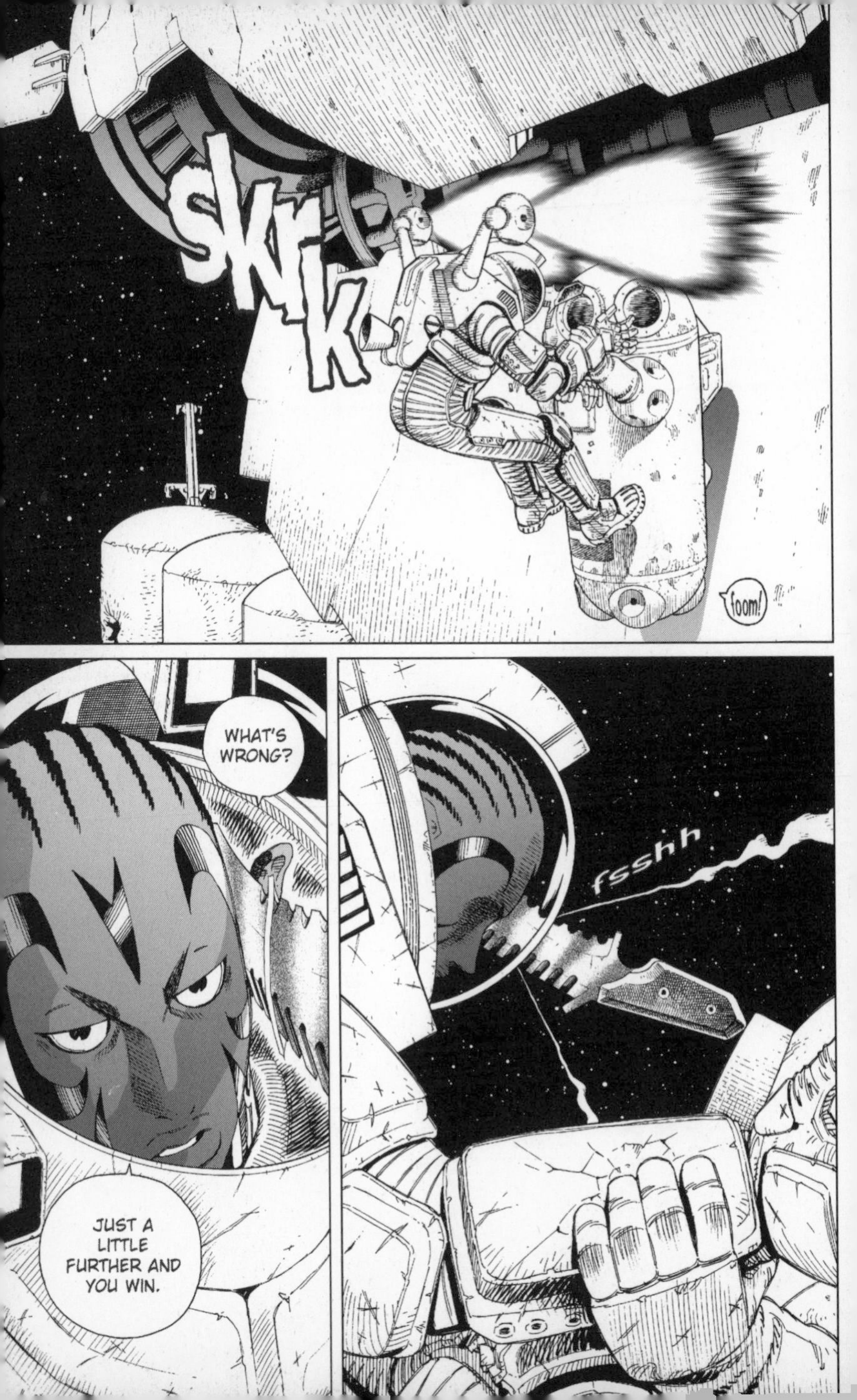
SKK
foom!
fsshh
WHAT'S WRONG?
JUST A LITTLE FURTHER AND YOU WIN.

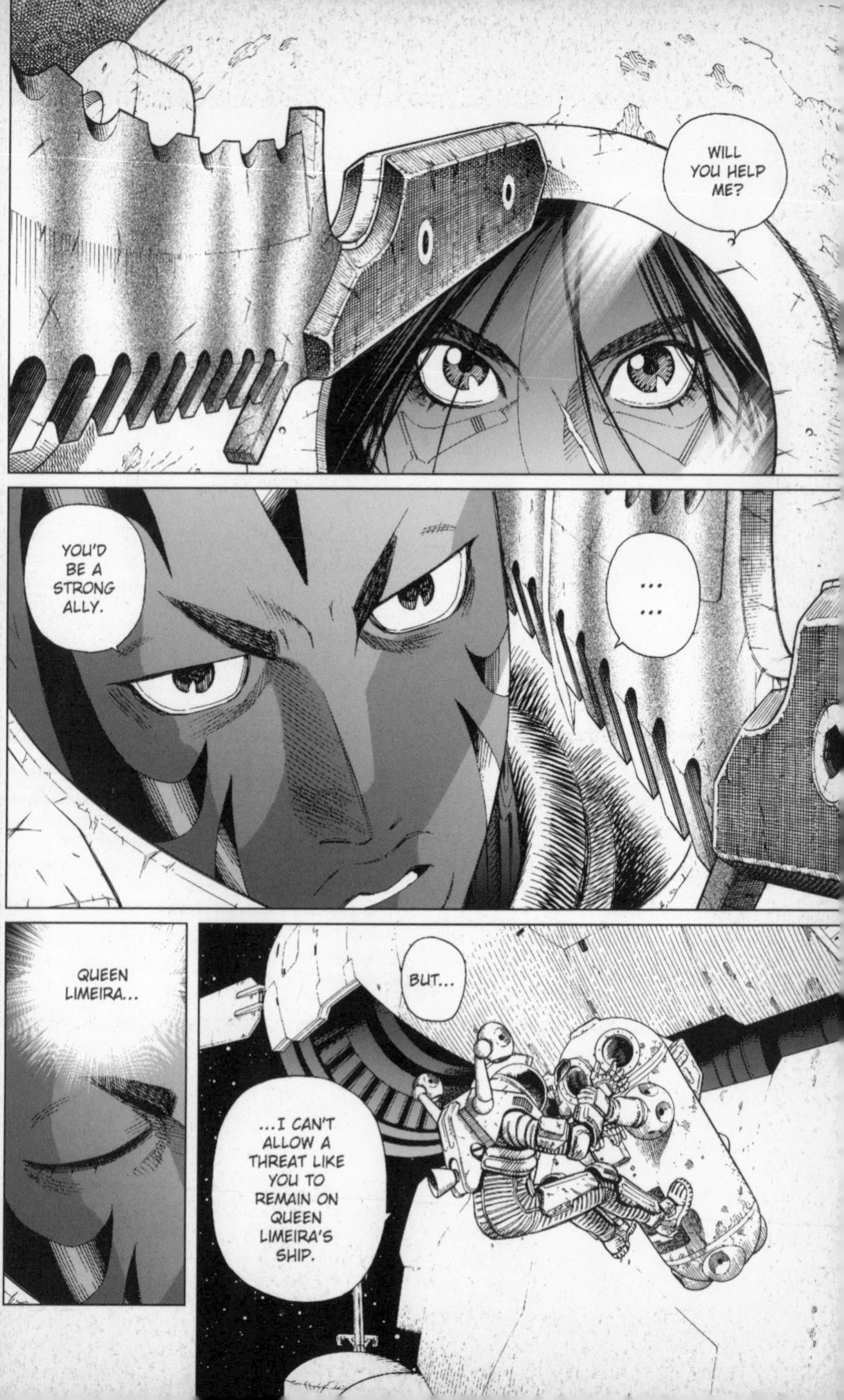
WILL YOU HELP ME?
...
...
YOU'D BE A STRONG ALLY.
BUT...
QUEEN LIMEIRA...
...I CAN'T ALLOW A THREAT LIKE YOU TO REMAIN ON QUEEN LIMEIRA'S SHIP.

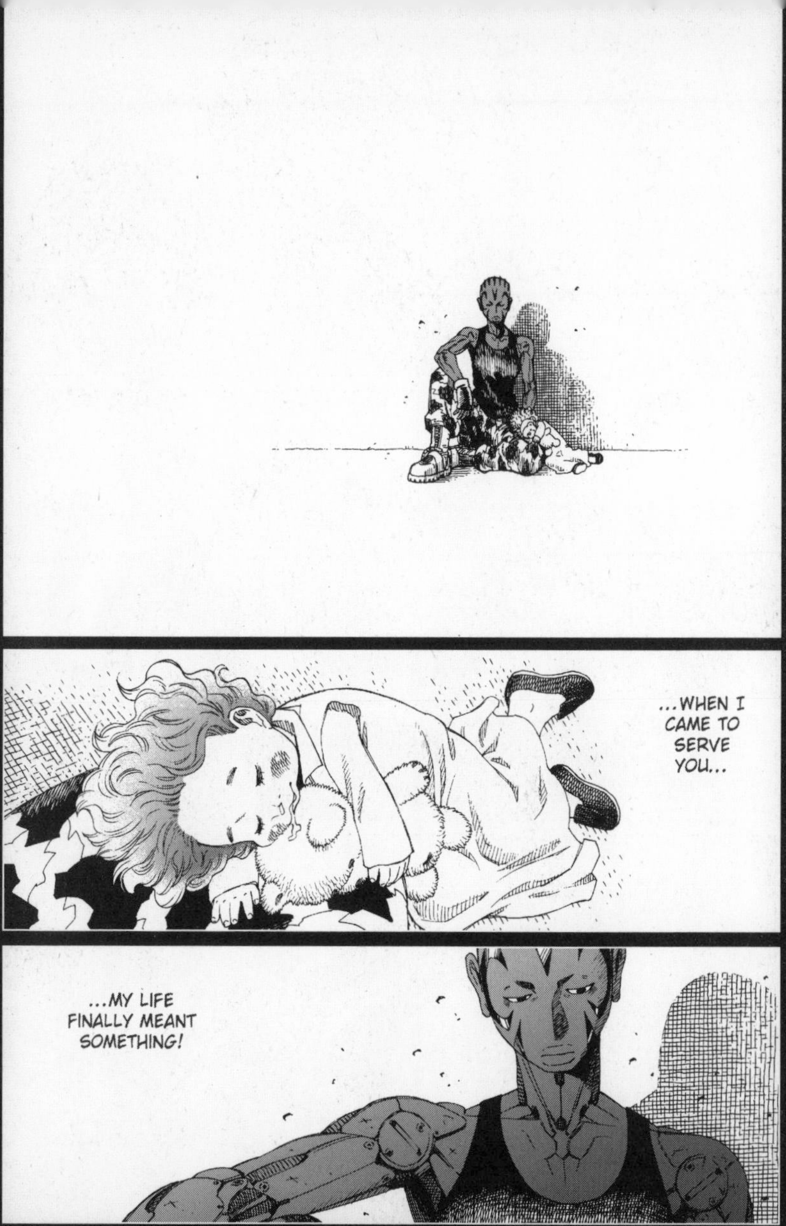
...WHEN I CAME TO SERVE YOU...
...MY LIFE FINALLY MEANT SOMETHING!

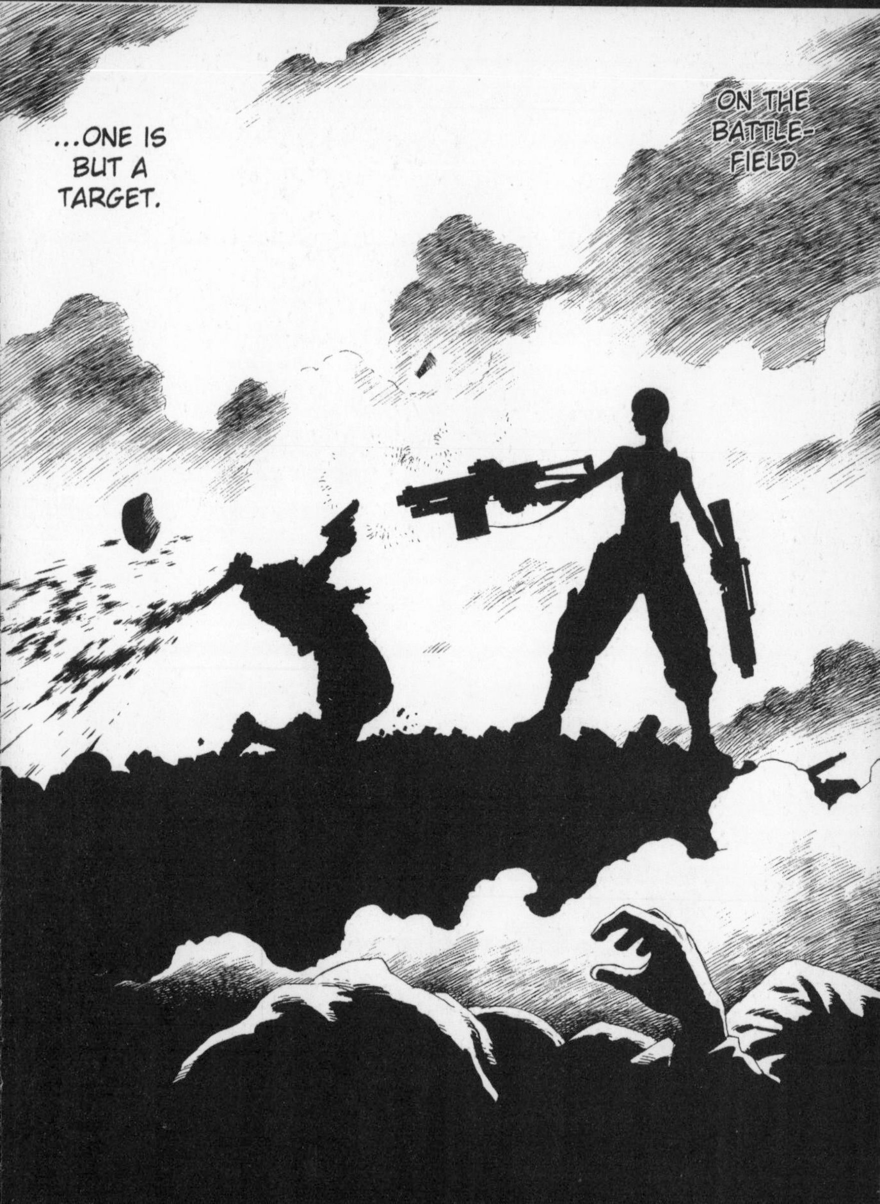
ON THE BATTLE-FIELD
...ONE IS BUT A TARGET.

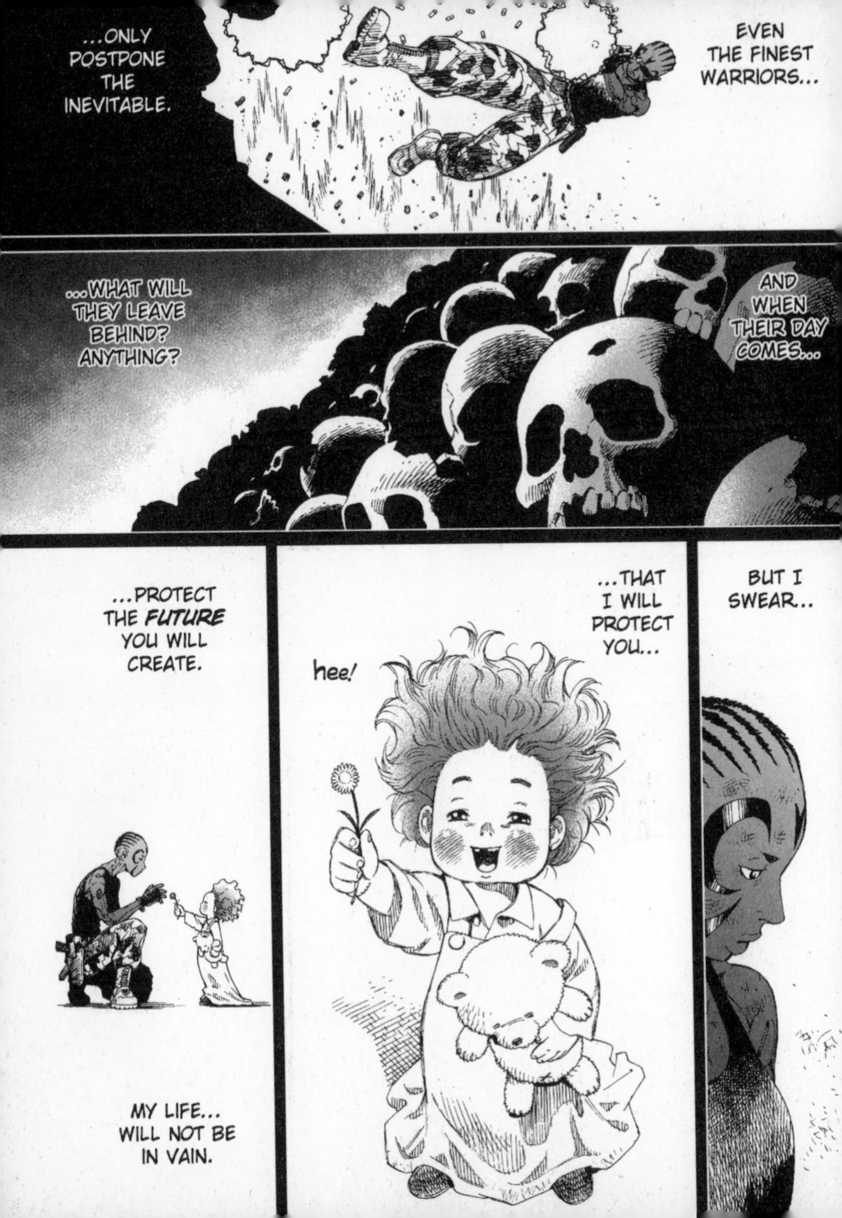
EVEN THE FINEST WARRIORS...
...ONLY POSTPONE THE INEVITABLE.
AND WHEN THEIR DAY COMES...
...WHAT WILL THEY LEAVE BEHIND? ANYTHING?
BUT I SWEAR..
...THAT I WILL PROTECT YOU...
hee!
...PROTECT THE *FUTURE* YOU WILL CREATE.
MY LIFE... WILL NOT BE IN VAIN.

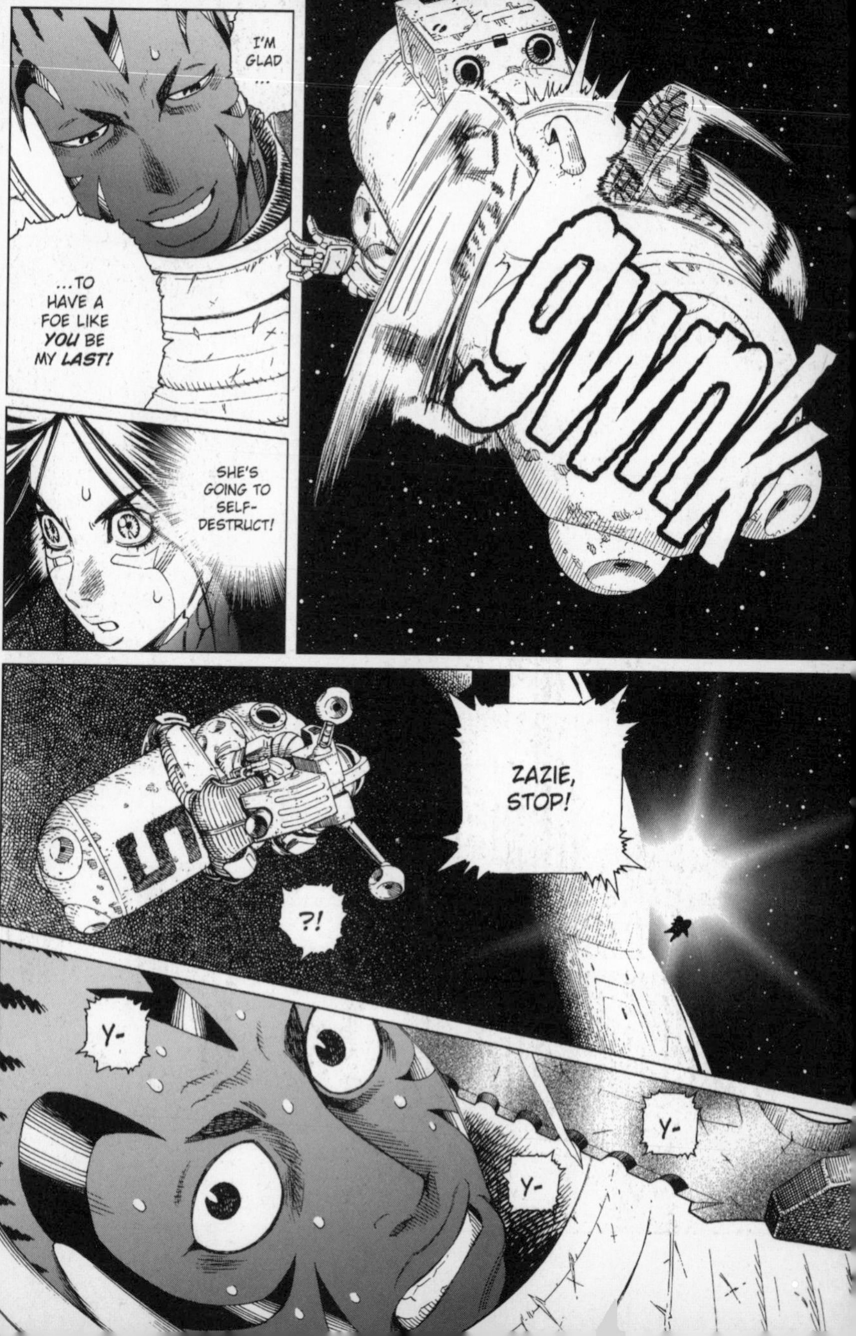
GUNK!
I'M GLAD ...
...TO HAVE A FOE LIKE *YOU* BE MY *LAST!*
SHE'S GOING TO SELF-DESTRUCT!
ZAZIE, STOP!
?!
Y-
Y-
Y-

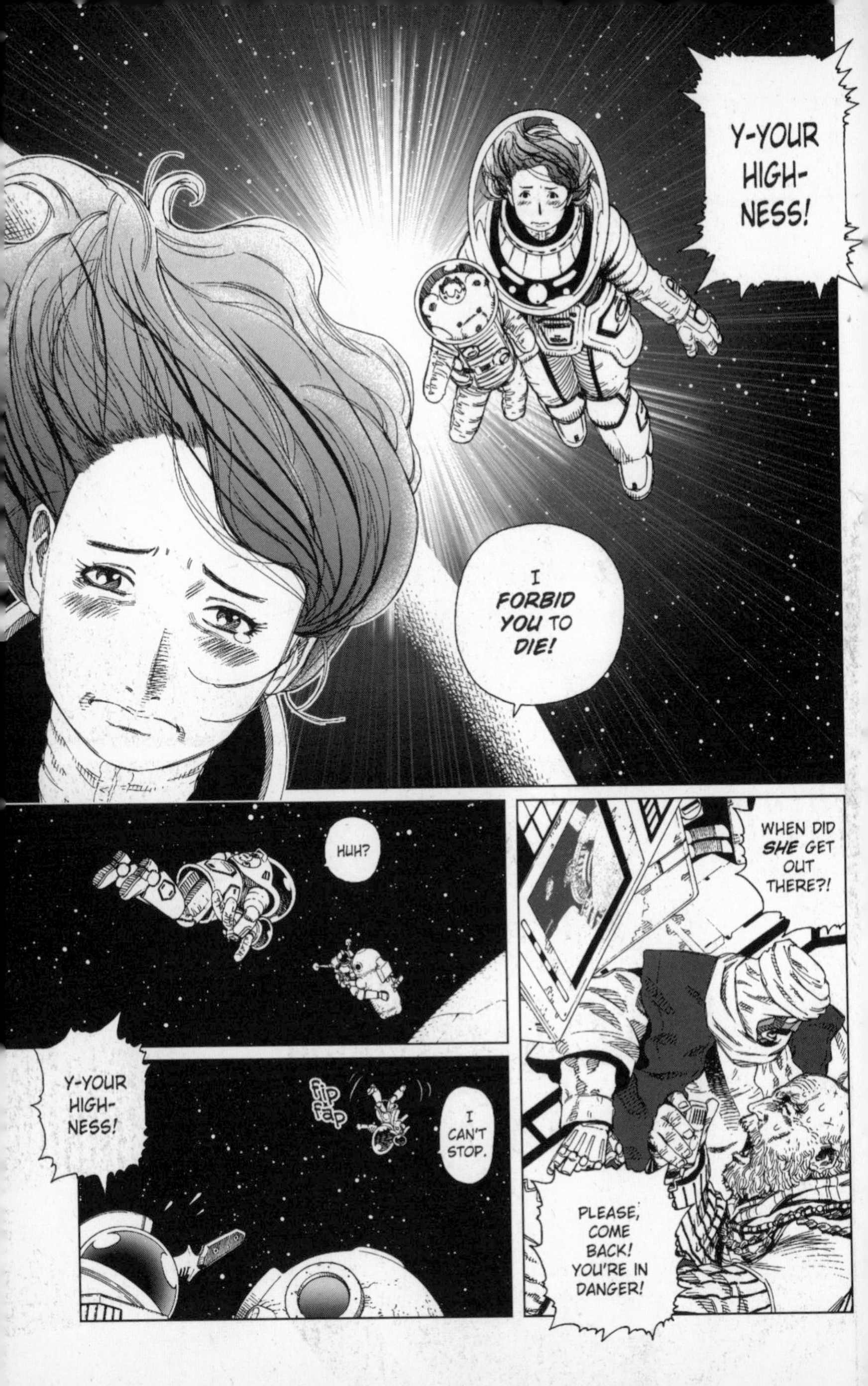
Y-YOUR HIGH-NESS!
I FORBID YOU TO DIE!
WHEN DID SHE GET OUT THERE?!
PLEASE, COME BACK! YOU'RE IN DANGER!
HUH?
I CAN'T STOP.
flip flap
Y-YOUR HIGH-NESS!

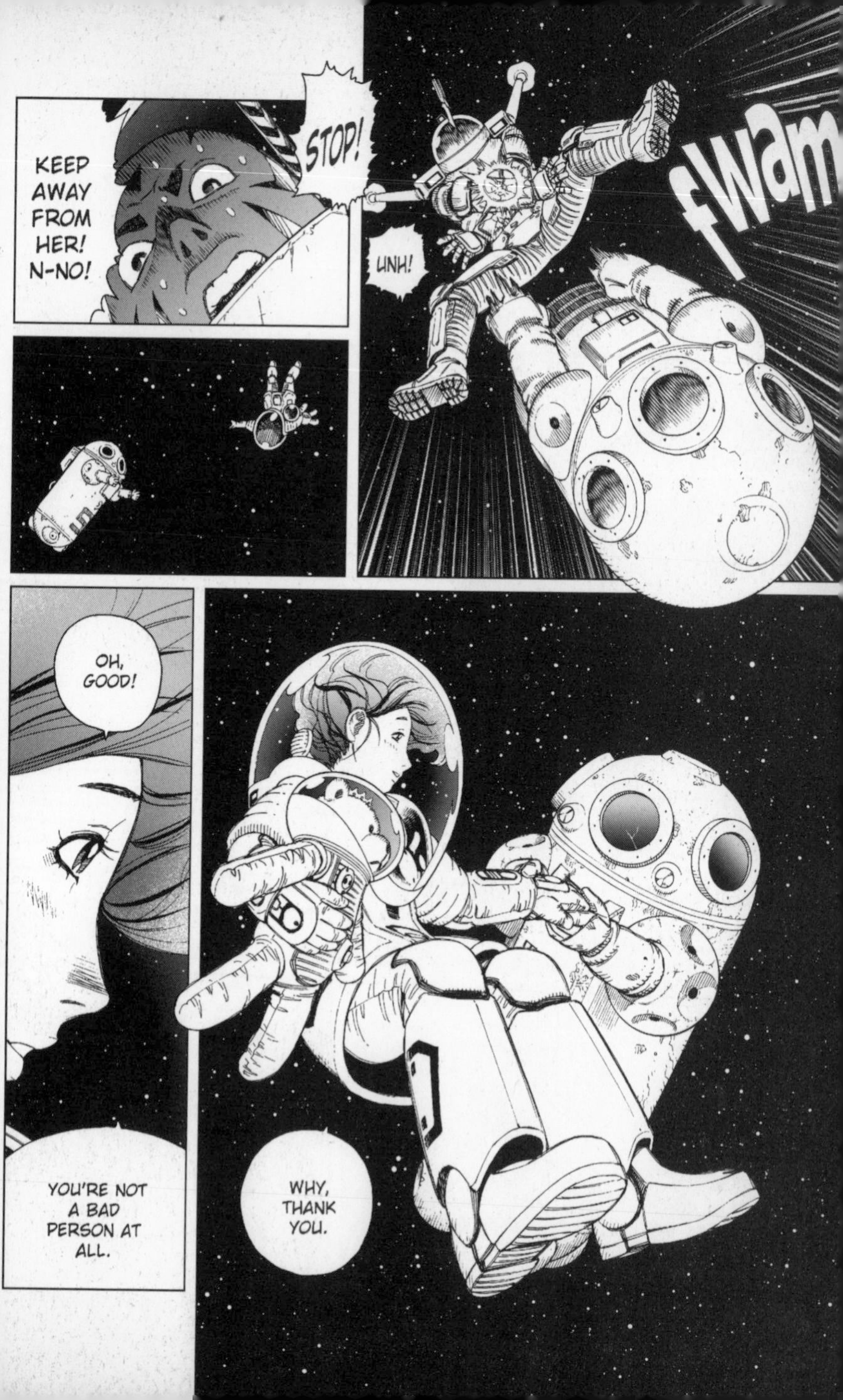
STOP!
UNH!
fwam
KEEP AWAY FROM HER! N-NO!
WHY, THANK YOU.
OH, GOOD!
YOU'RE NOT A BAD PERSON AT ALL.

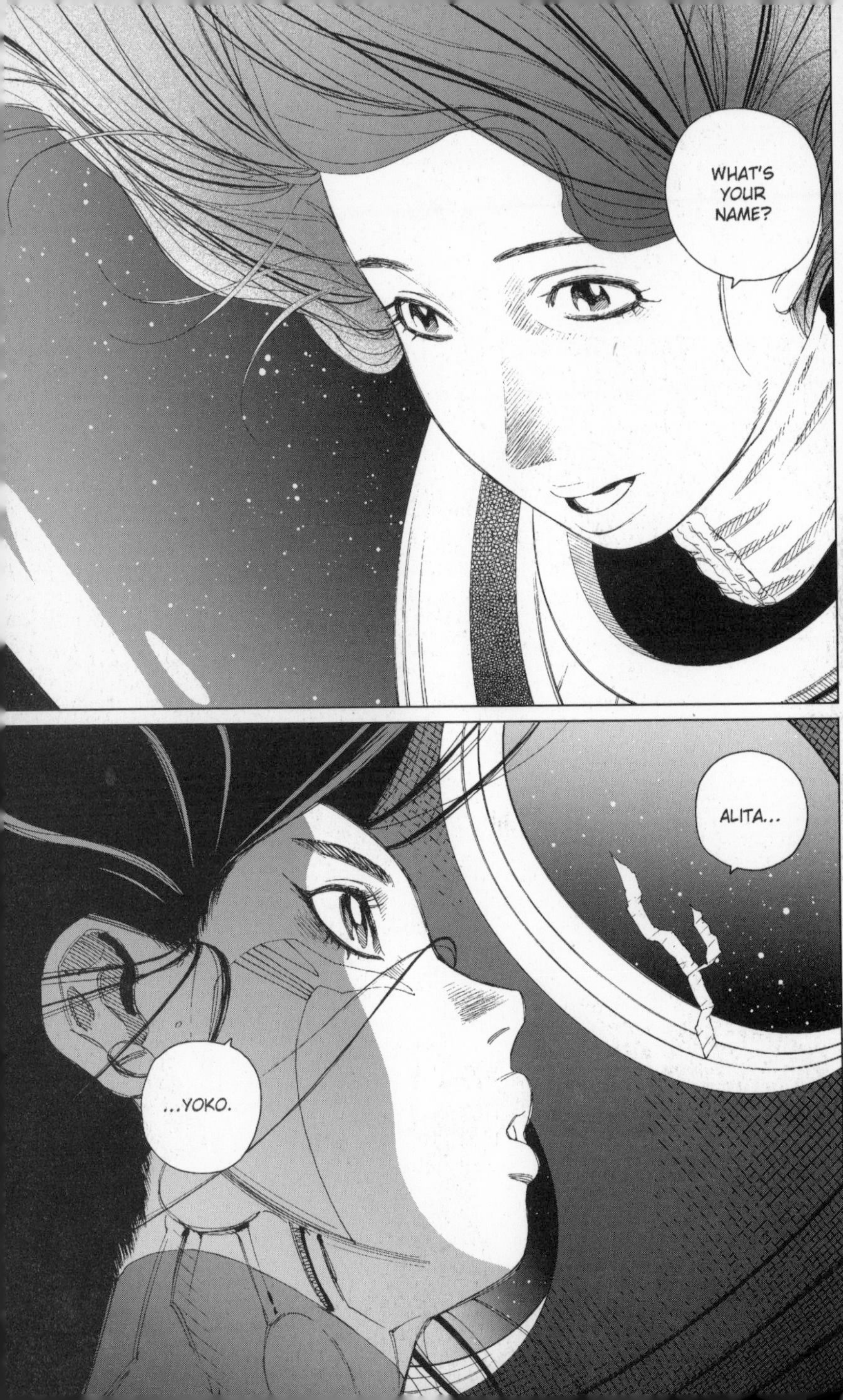
WHAT'S YOUR NAME?
ALITA...
...YOKO.

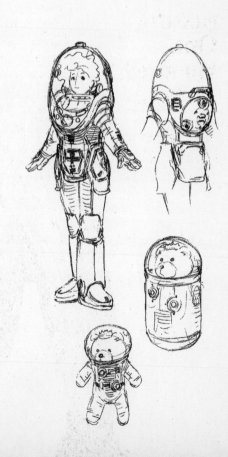

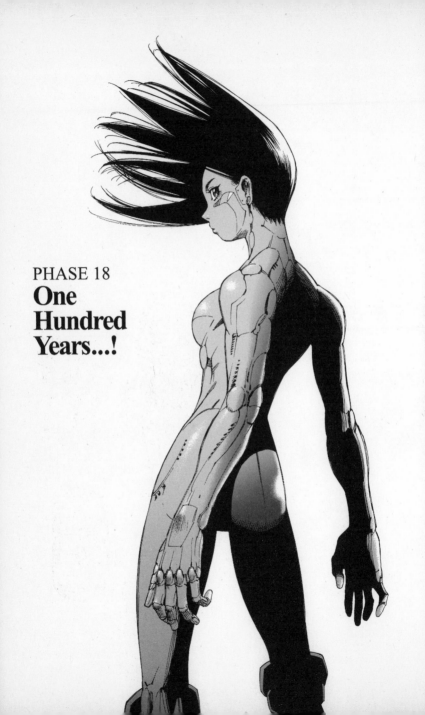

PHASE 18
One
Hundred
Years...!

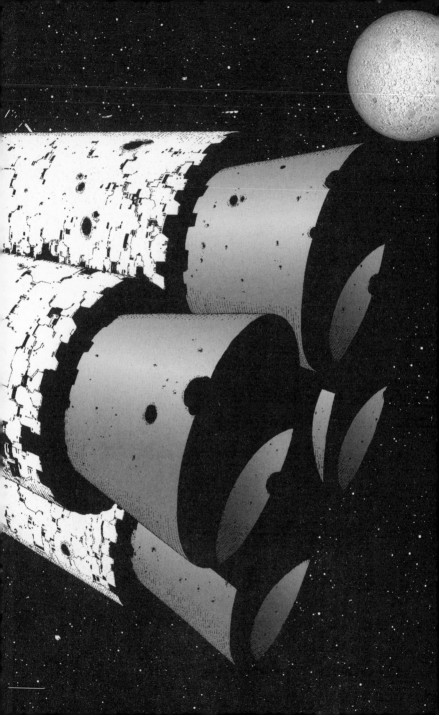

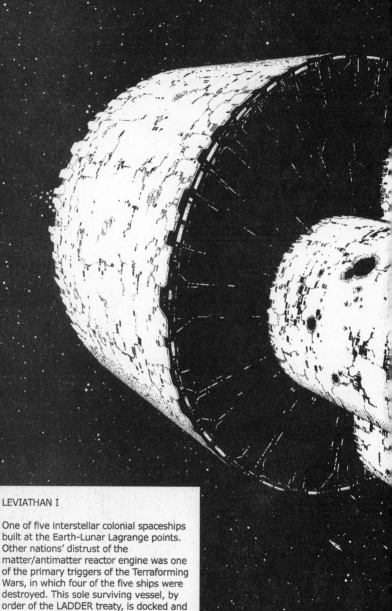

LEVIATHAN I

One of five interstellar colonial spaceships
built at the Earth-Lunar Lagrange points.
Other nations' distrust of the
matter/antimatter reactor engine was one
of the primary triggers of the Terraforming
Wars, in which four of the five ships were
destroyed. This sole surviving vessel, by
order of the LADDER treaty, is docked and
serves as a space colony.

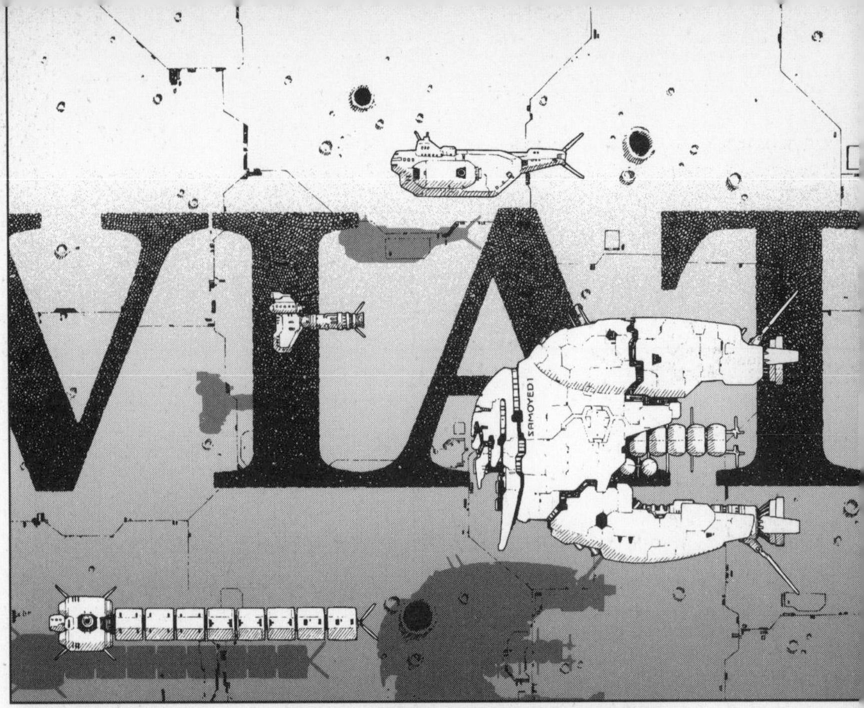
VIAT
SAMOYED 1
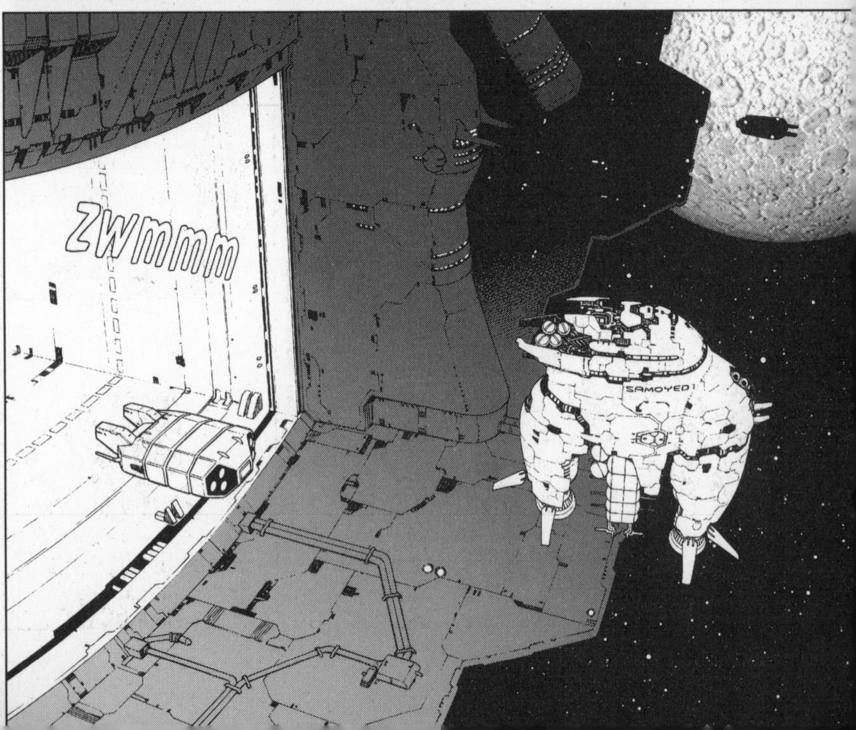
ZWMMM
SAMOYED 1

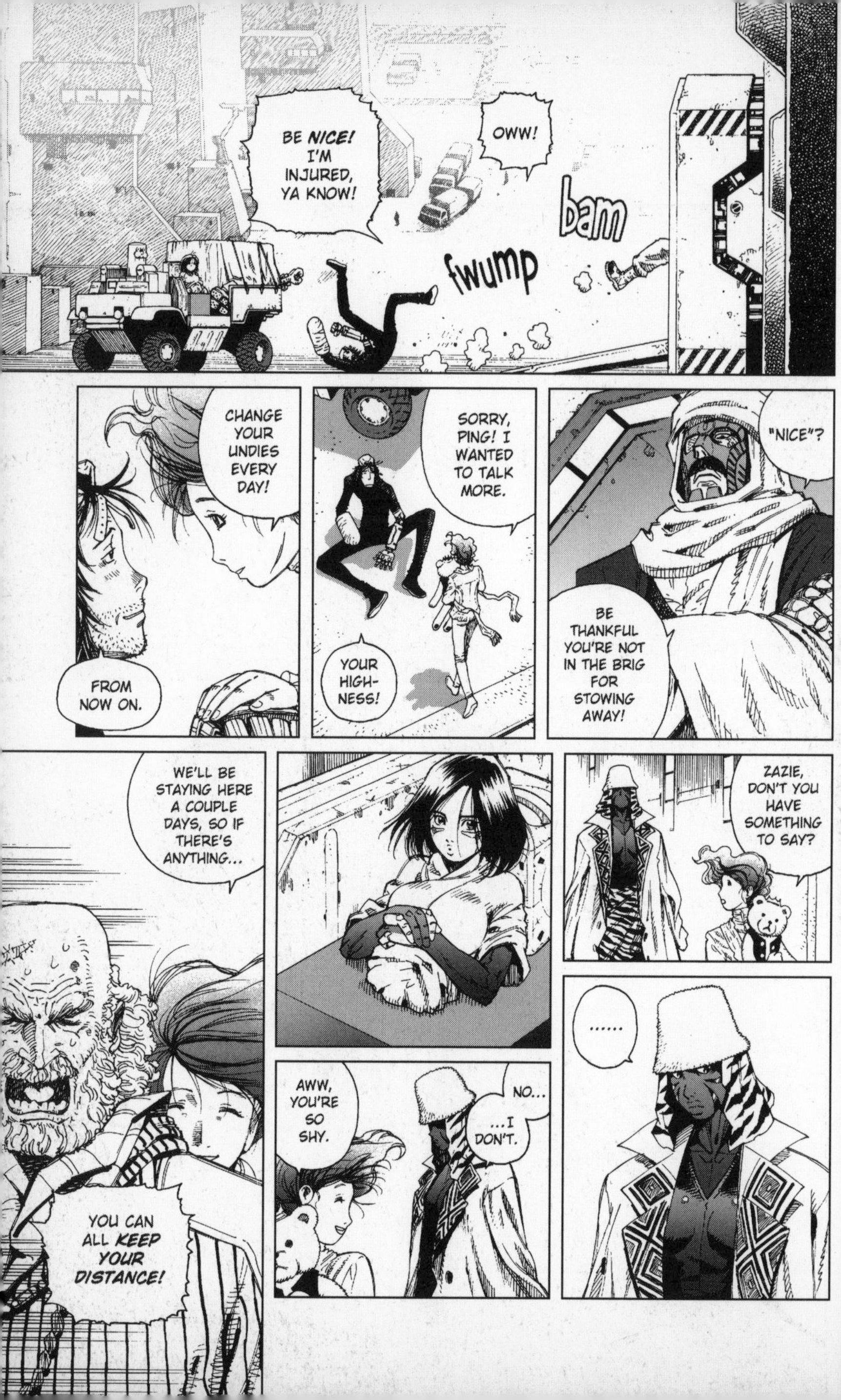
bam
fwump
OWW!
BE NICE! I'M INJURED, YA KNOW!
"NICE"?
BE THANKFUL YOU'RE NOT IN THE BRIG FOR STOWING AWAY!
SORRY, PING! I WANTED TO TALK MORE.
YOUR HIGHNESS!
CHANGE YOUR UNDIES EVERY DAY!
FROM NOW ON.
ZAZIE, DON'T YOU HAVE SOMETHING TO SAY?
......
NO...
...I DON'T.
AWW, YOU'RE SO SHY.
WE'LL BE STAYING HERE A COUPLE DAYS, SO IF THERE'S ANYTHING...
YOU CAN ALL KEEP YOUR DISTANCE!

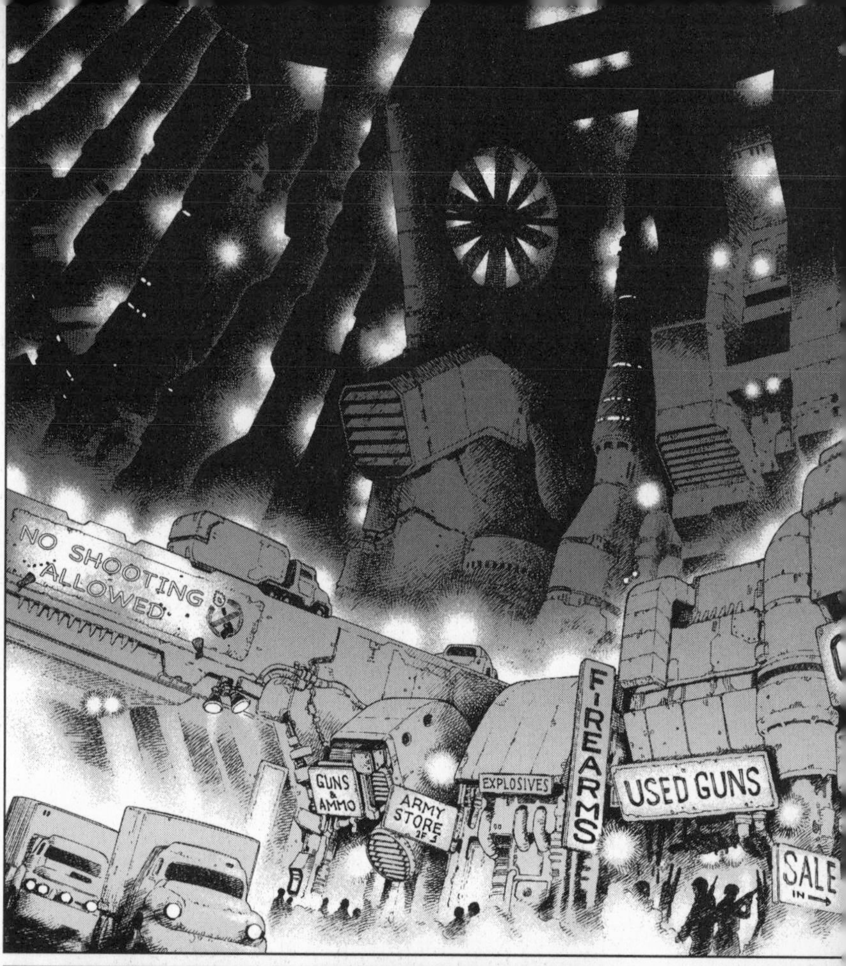
SALE
IN
USED GUNS
FIREARMS
EXPLOSIVES
ARMY STORE
GUNS & AMMO
NO SHOOTING ALLOWED

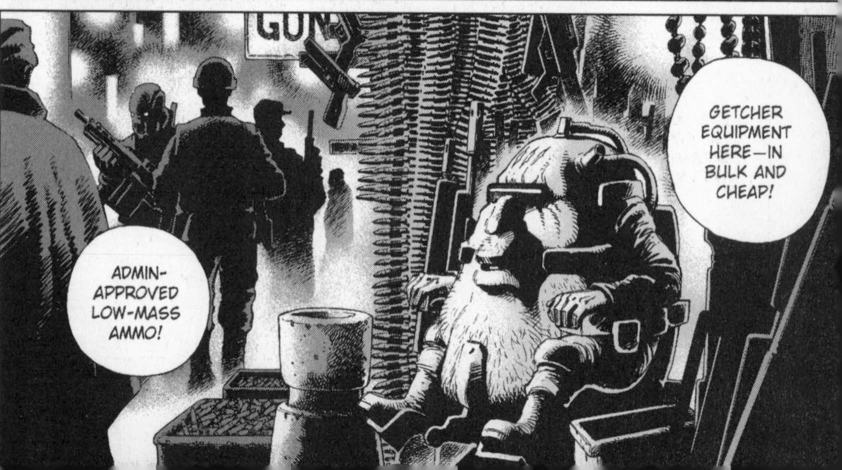
GETCHER EQUIPMENT HERE—IN BULK AND CHEAP!
ADMIN-APPROVED LOW-MASS AMMO!

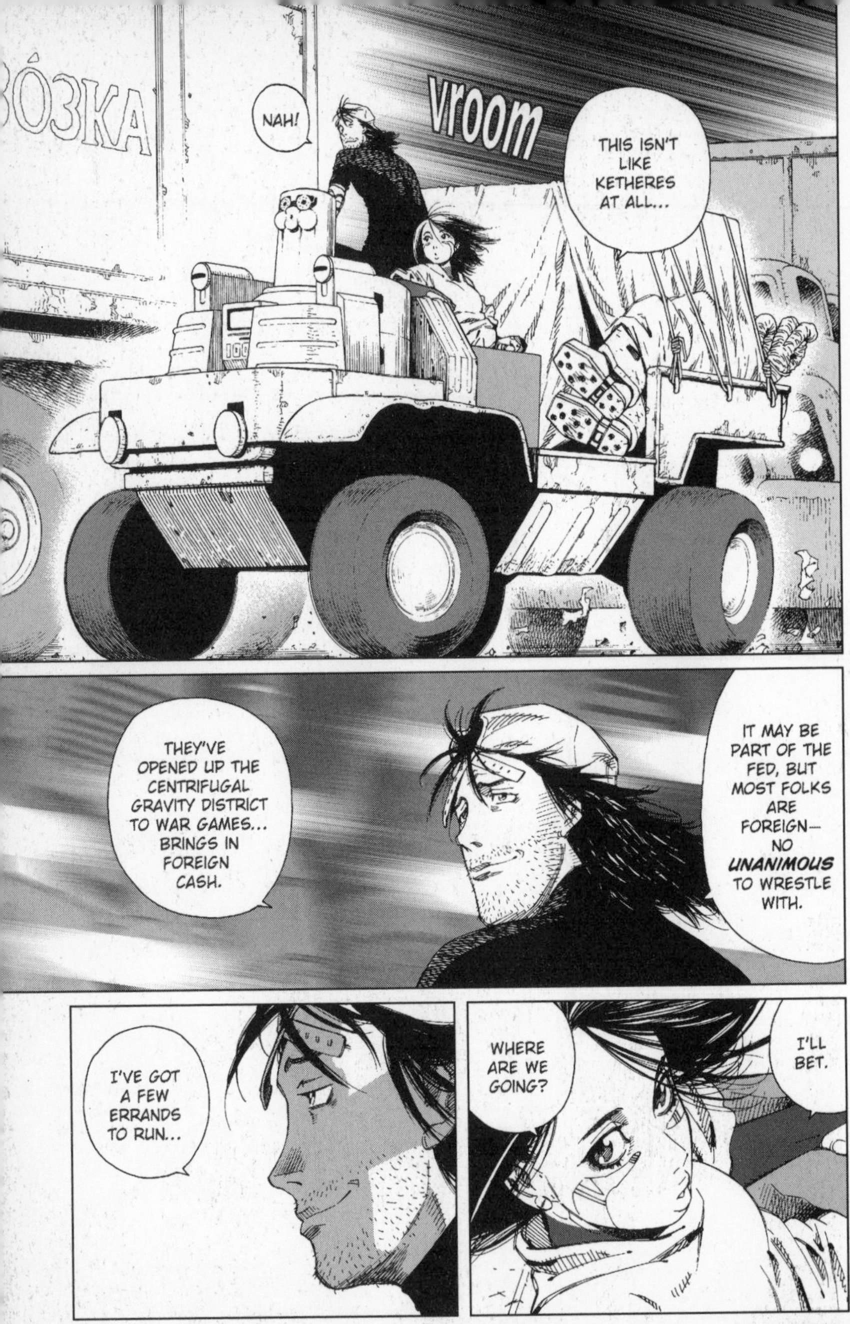
THIS ISN'T LIKE KETHERES AT ALL...
vroom
NAH!
IT MAY BE PART OF THE FED, BUT MOST FOLKS ARE FOREIGN— NO *UNANIMOUS* TO WRESTLE WITH.
THEY'VE OPENED UP THE CENTRIFUGAL GRAVITY DISTRICT TO WAR GAMES... BRINGS IN FOREIGN CASH.
I'LL BET.
WHERE ARE WE GOING?
I'VE GOT A FEW ERRANDS TO RUN...

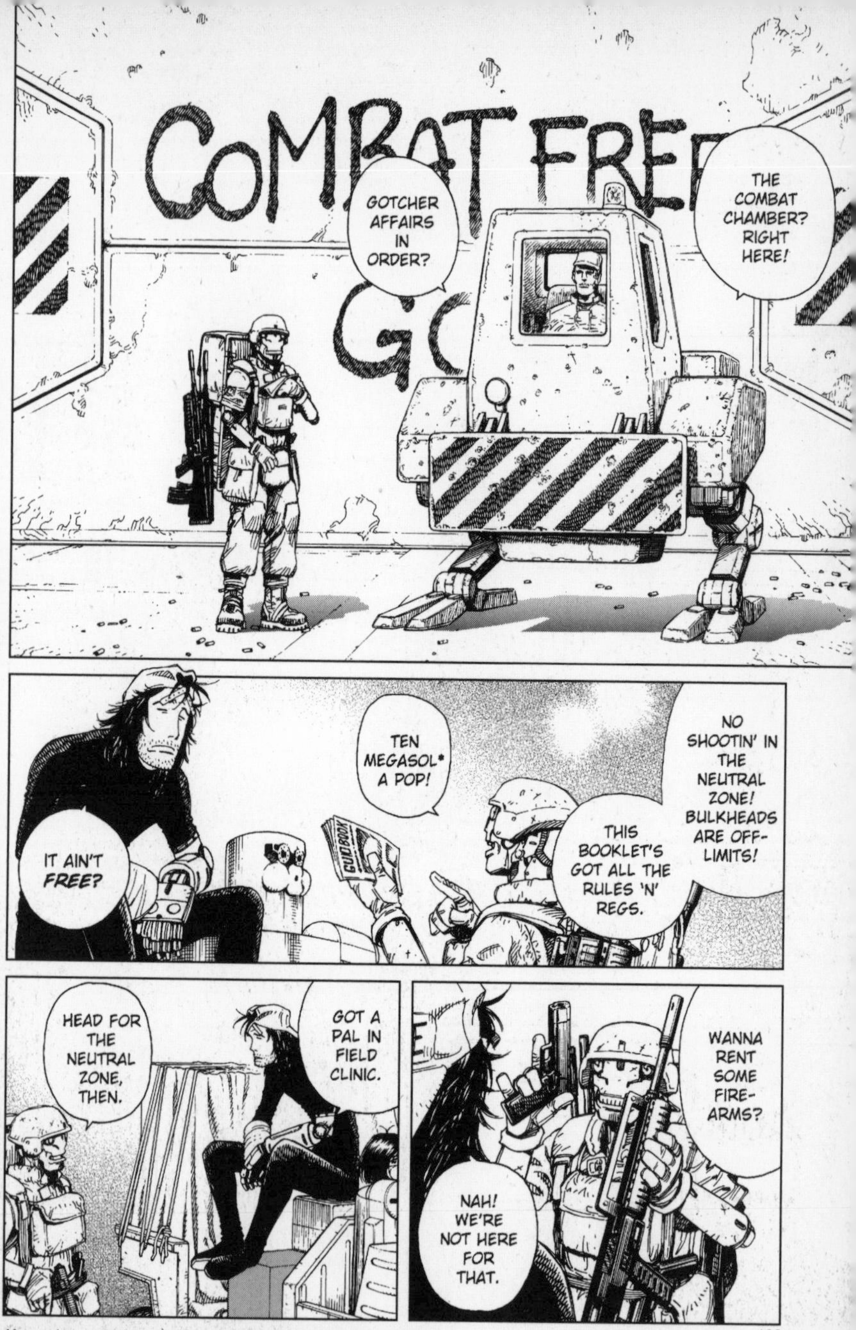
COMBAT FRE
THE COMBAT CHAMBER? RIGHT HERE!
GOTCHER AFFAIRS IN ORDER?
NO SHOOTIN' IN THE NEUTRAL ZONE! BULKHEADS ARE OFF-LIMITS!
THIS BOOKLET'S GOT ALL THE RULES 'N' REGS.
GUIDEBOOK
TEN MEGASOL* A POP!
IT AIN'T *FREE?*
WANNA RENT SOME FIRE-ARMS?
NAH! WE'RE NOT HERE FOR THAT.
GOT A PAL IN FIELD CLINIC.
HEAD FOR THE NEUTRAL ZONE, THEN.

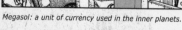

Megasol: a unit of currency used in the inner planets.

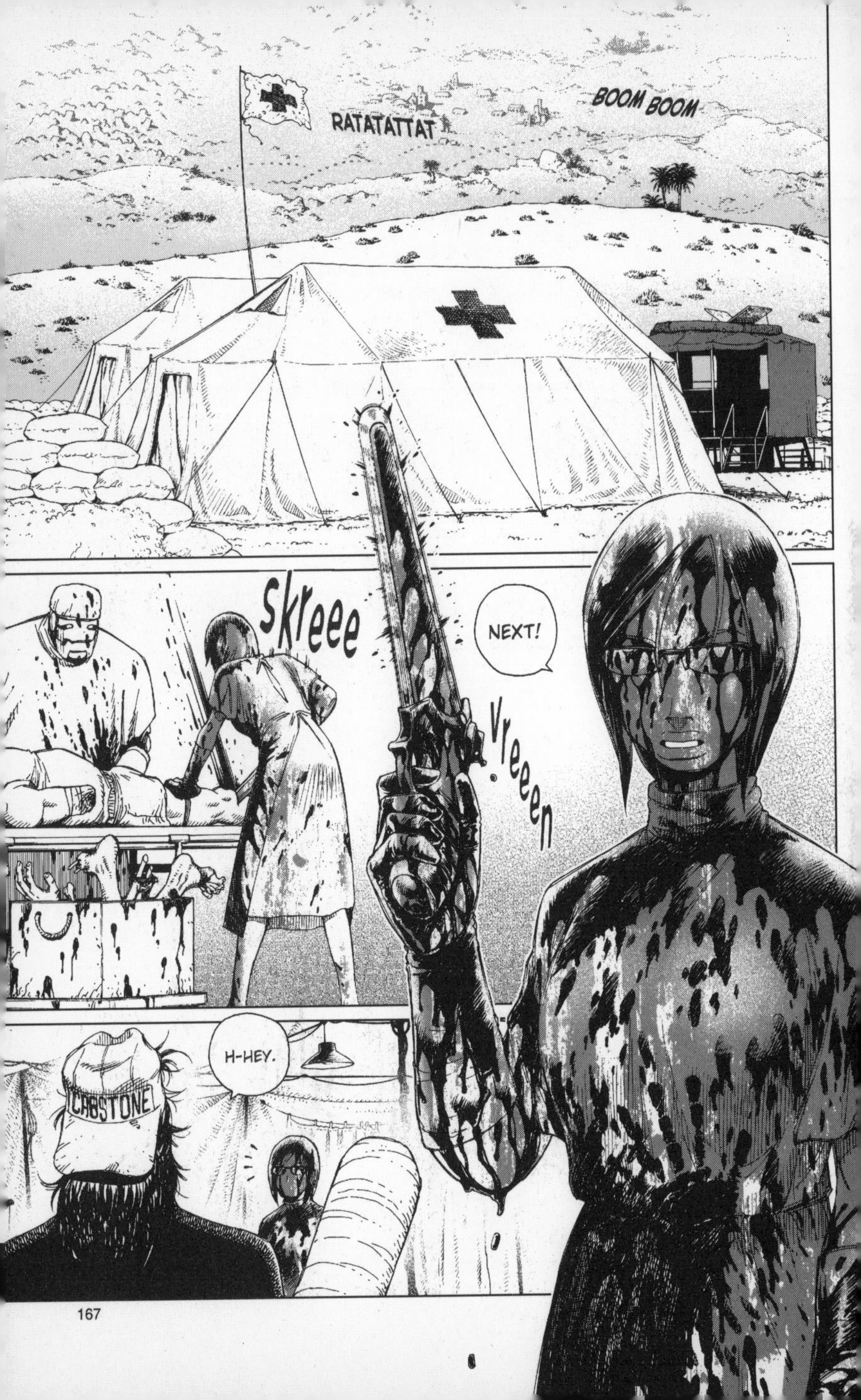
BOOM BOOM
RATATATTAT
NEXT!
Vreeeen
Skreee
H-HEY.
CABSTONE

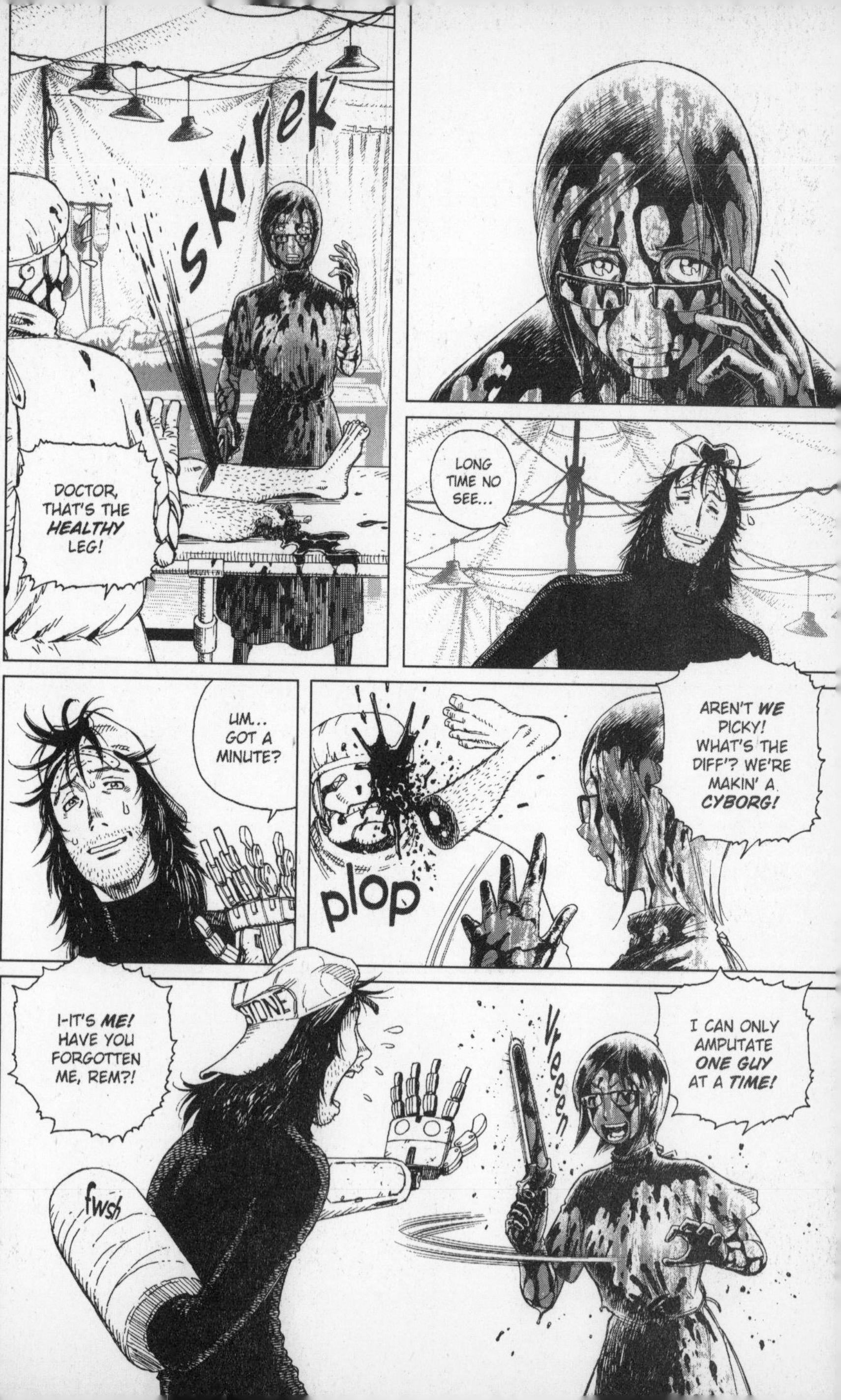
LONG TIME NO SEE...
skrrek
DOCTOR, THAT'S THE *HEALTHY* LEG!
AREN'T *WE* PICKY! WHAT'S THE DIFF'? WE'RE MAKIN' A *CYBORG!*
plop
UM.. GOT A MINUTE?
I CAN ONLY AMPUTATE *ONE GUY* AT A *TIME!*
Vreeen
I-IT'S *ME!* HAVE YOU FORGOTTEN ME, REM?!
fwsh

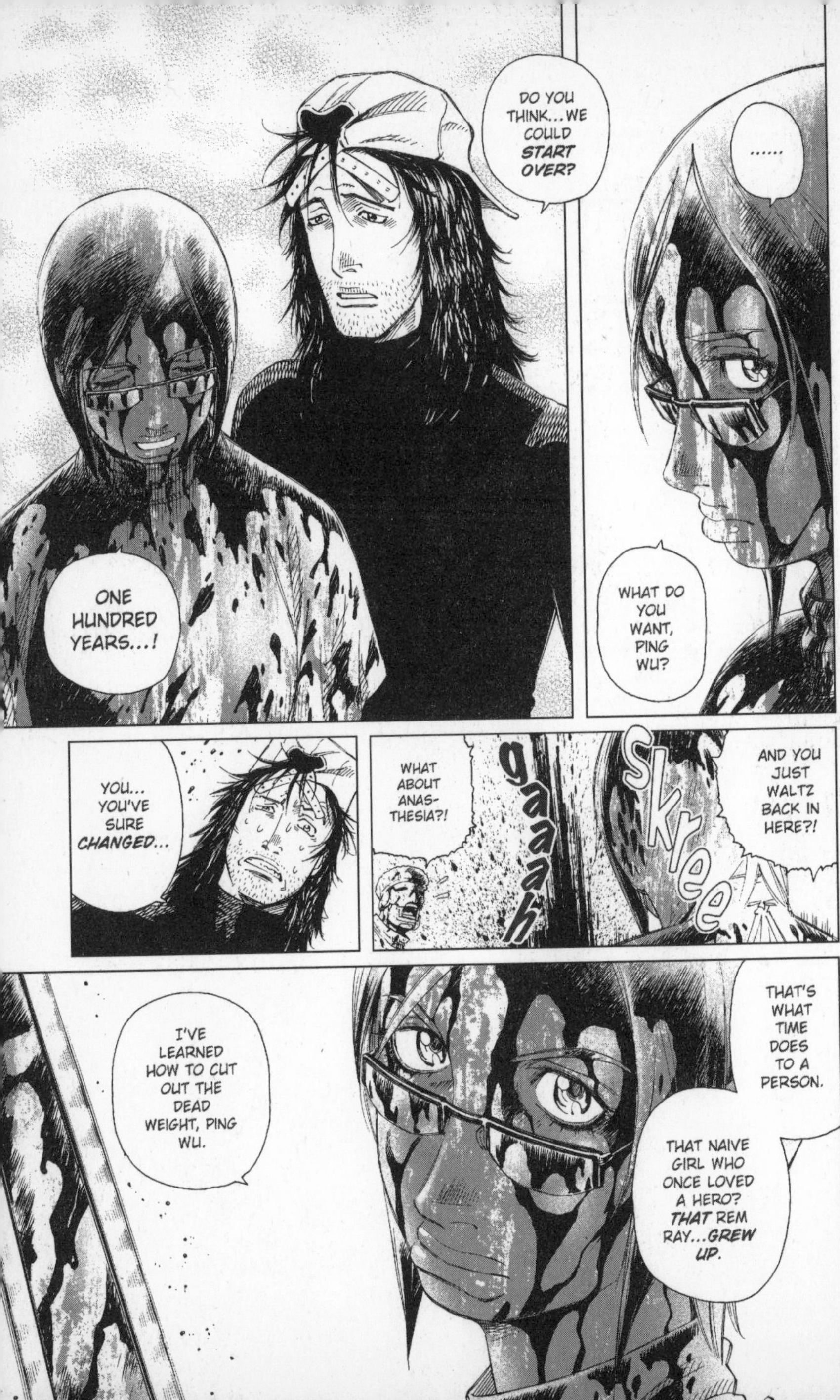
......
WHAT DO YOU WANT, PING WU?
DO YOU THINK...WE COULD START OVER?
ONE HUNDRED YEARS...!
AND YOU JUST WALTZ BACK IN HERE?!
skree
gaaaah
WHAT ABOUT ANAS-THESIA?!
YOU... YOU'VE SURE CHANGED...
THAT'S WHAT TIME DOES TO A PERSON.
THAT NAIVE GIRL WHO ONCE LOVED A HERO? THAT REM RAY...GREW UP.
I'VE LEARNED HOW TO CUT OUT THE DEAD WEIGHT, PING WU.

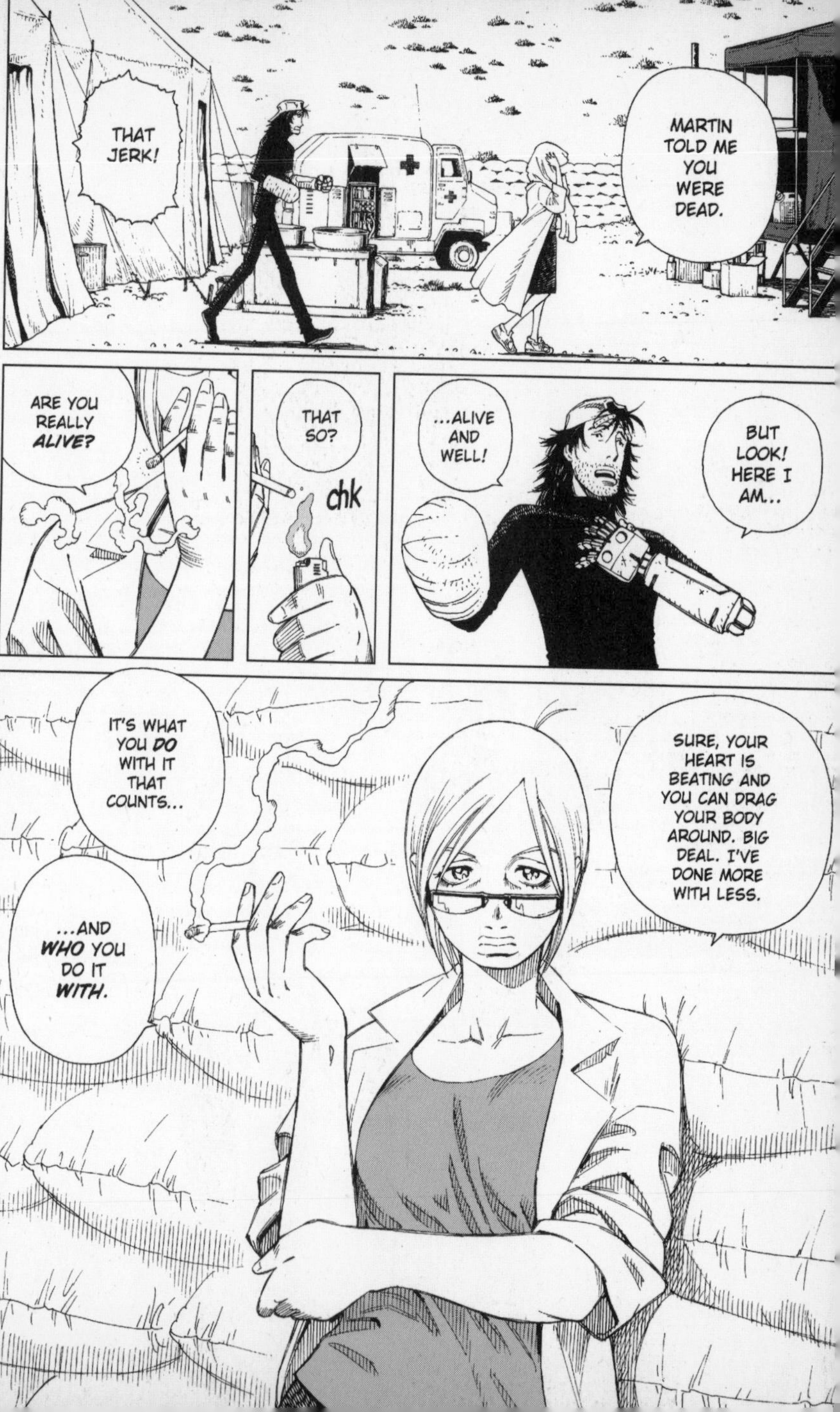
MARTIN TOLD ME YOU WERE DEAD.
THAT JERK!
BUT LOOK! HERE I AM..
...ALIVE AND WELL!
THAT SO?
chk
ARE YOU REALLY *ALIVE?*
SURE, YOUR HEART IS BEATING AND YOU CAN DRAG YOUR BODY AROUND. BIG DEAL. I'VE DONE MORE WITH LESS.
IT'S WHAT YOU *DO* WITH IT THAT COUNTS...
...AND *WHO* YOU DO IT *WITH*.

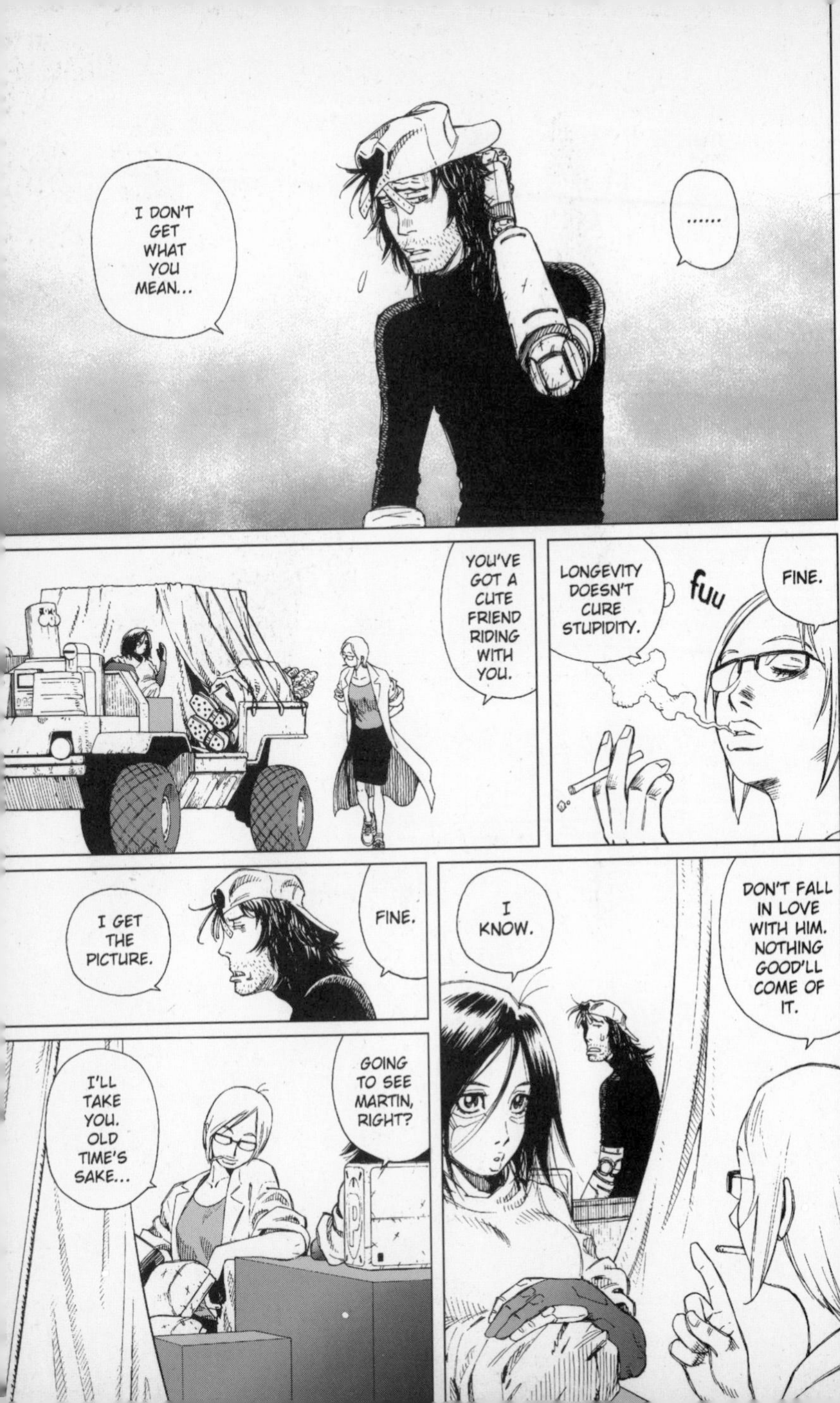
......
I DON'T GET WHAT YOU MEAN...
FINE.
fuu
LONGEVITY DOESN'T CURE STUPIDITY.
YOU'VE GOT A CUTE FRIEND RIDING WITH YOU.
DON'T FALL IN LOVE WITH HIM. NOTHING GOOD'LL COME OF IT.
I KNOW.
FINE.
I GET THE PICTURE.
GOING TO SEE MARTIN, RIGHT?
I'LL TAKE YOU. OLD TIME'S SAKE...

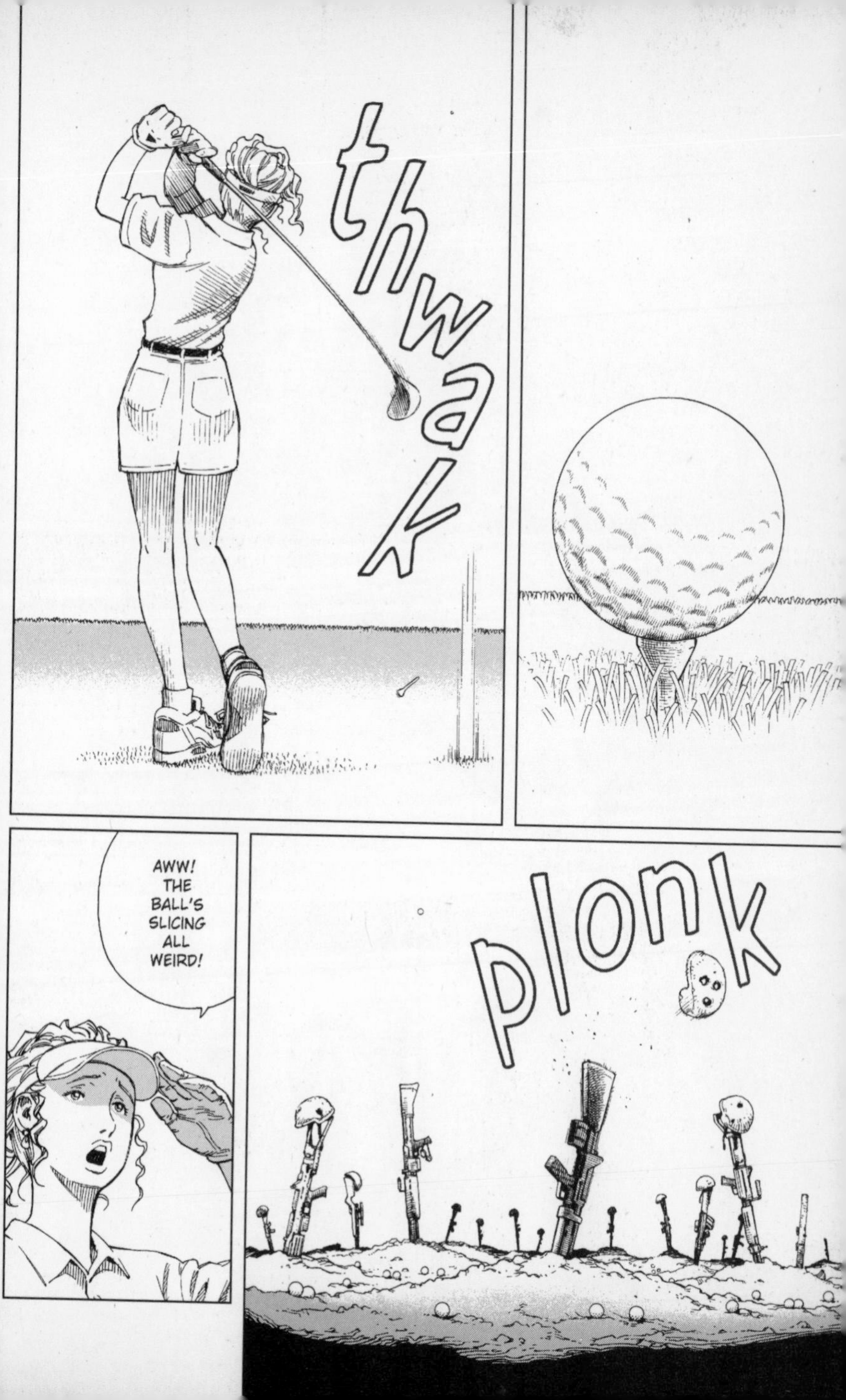
thwak
plonk
AWW! THE BALL'S SLICING ALL WEIRD!

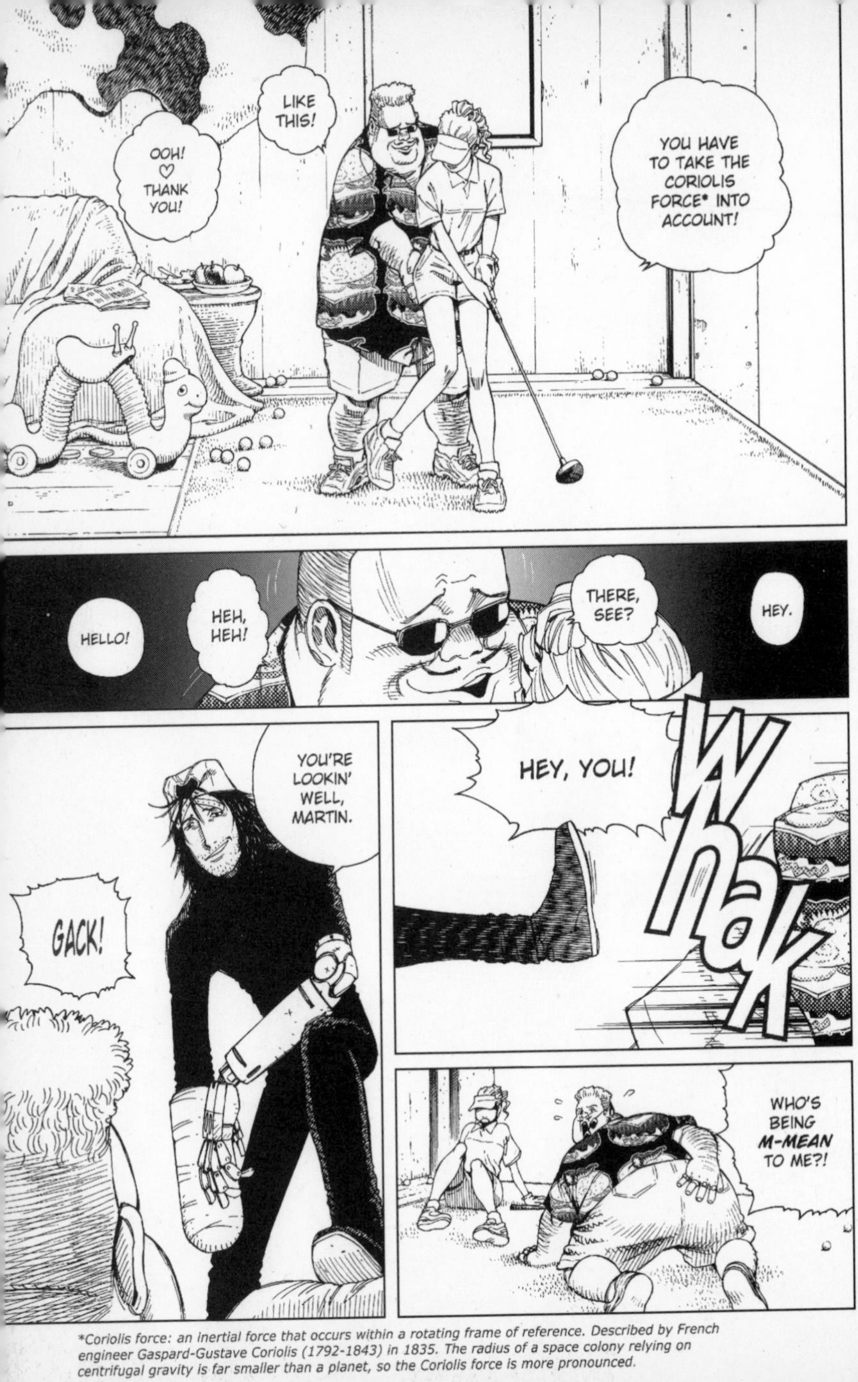
YOU HAVE TO TAKE THE CORIOLIS FORCE* INTO ACCOUNT!
LIKE THIS!
OOH! ♡ THANK YOU!
HEY.
THERE, SEE?
HEH, HEH!
HELLO!
WHAK
HEY, YOU!
WHO'S BEING *M-MEAN* TO ME?!
YOU'RE LOOKIN' WELL, MARTIN.
GACK!

**Coriolis force: an inertial force that occurs within a rotating frame of reference. Described by French engineer Gaspard-Gustave Coriolis (1792-1843) in 1835. The radius of a space colony relying on centrifugal gravity is far smaller than a planet, so the Coriolis force is more pronounced.*

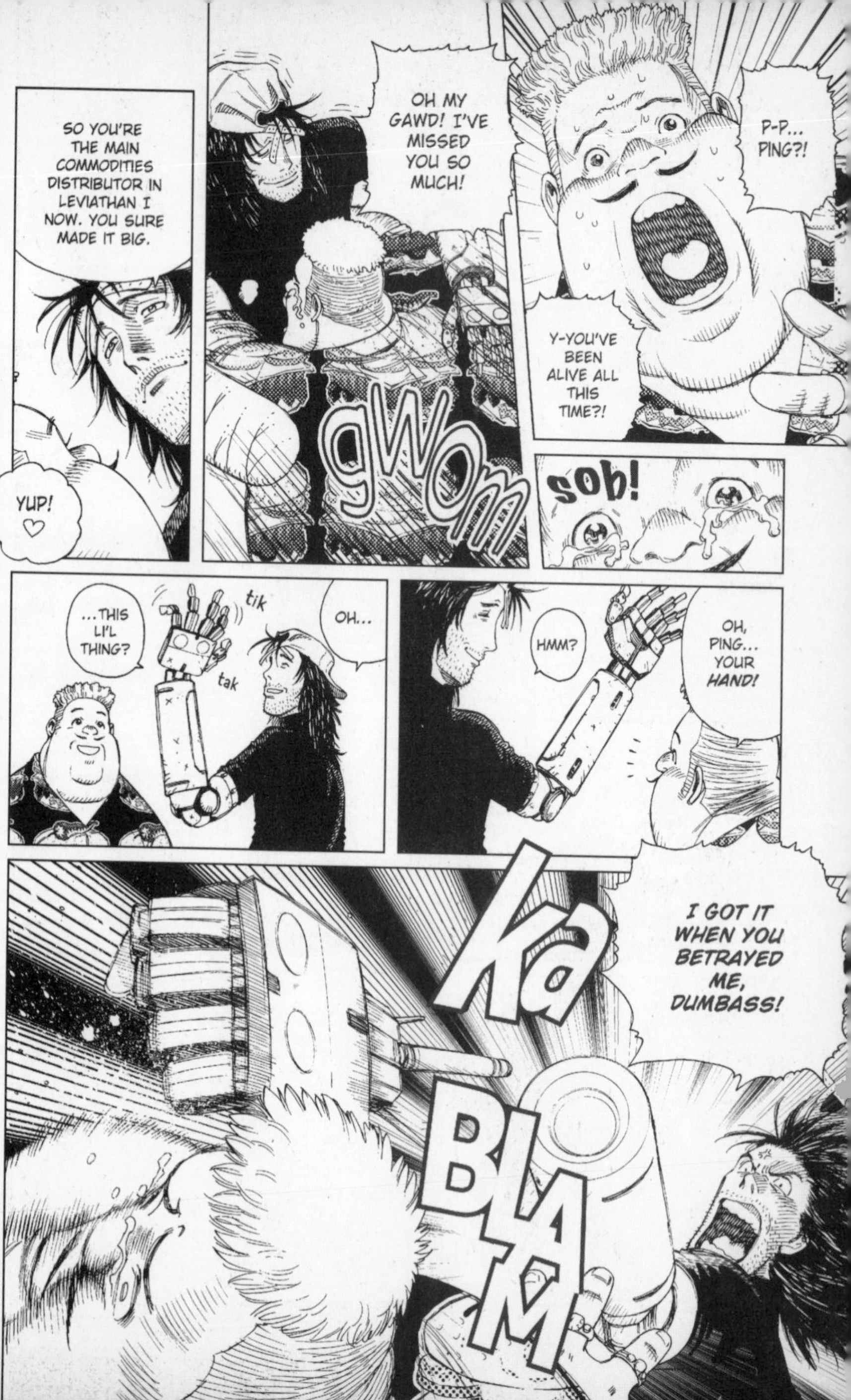
P-P... PING?!
Y-YOU'VE BEEN ALIVE ALL THIS TIME?!
sob!
OH MY GAWD! I'VE MISSED YOU SO MUCH!
gWom
SO YOU'RE THE MAIN COMMODITIES DISTRIBUTOR IN LEVIATHAN I NOW. YOU SURE MADE IT BIG.
YUP! ♡
OH, PING... YOUR HAND!
HMM?
OH...
...THIS LI'L THING?
tik
tak
I GOT IT WHEN YOU BETRAYED ME, DUMBASS!
Ka
BLAM

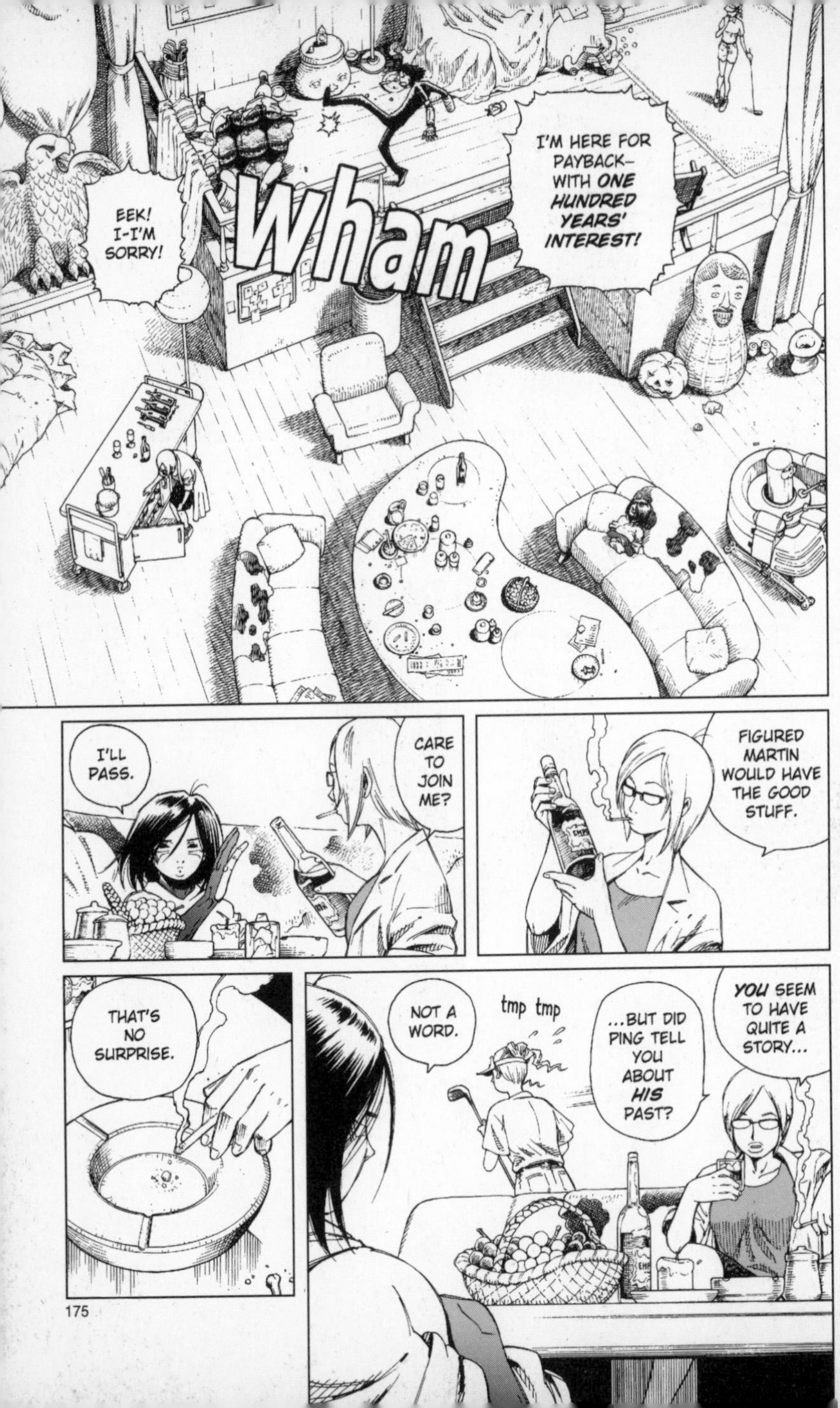
I'M HERE FOR PAYBACK—WITH *ONE HUNDRED YEARS'* INTEREST!
Wham
EEK! I-I'M SORRY!
FIGURED MARTIN WOULD HAVE THE GOOD STUFF.
CARE TO JOIN ME?
I'LL PASS.
YOU SEEM TO HAVE QUITE A STORY...
...BUT DID PING TELL YOU ABOUT *HIS* PAST?
tmp tmp
NOT A WORD.
THAT'S NO SURPRISE.

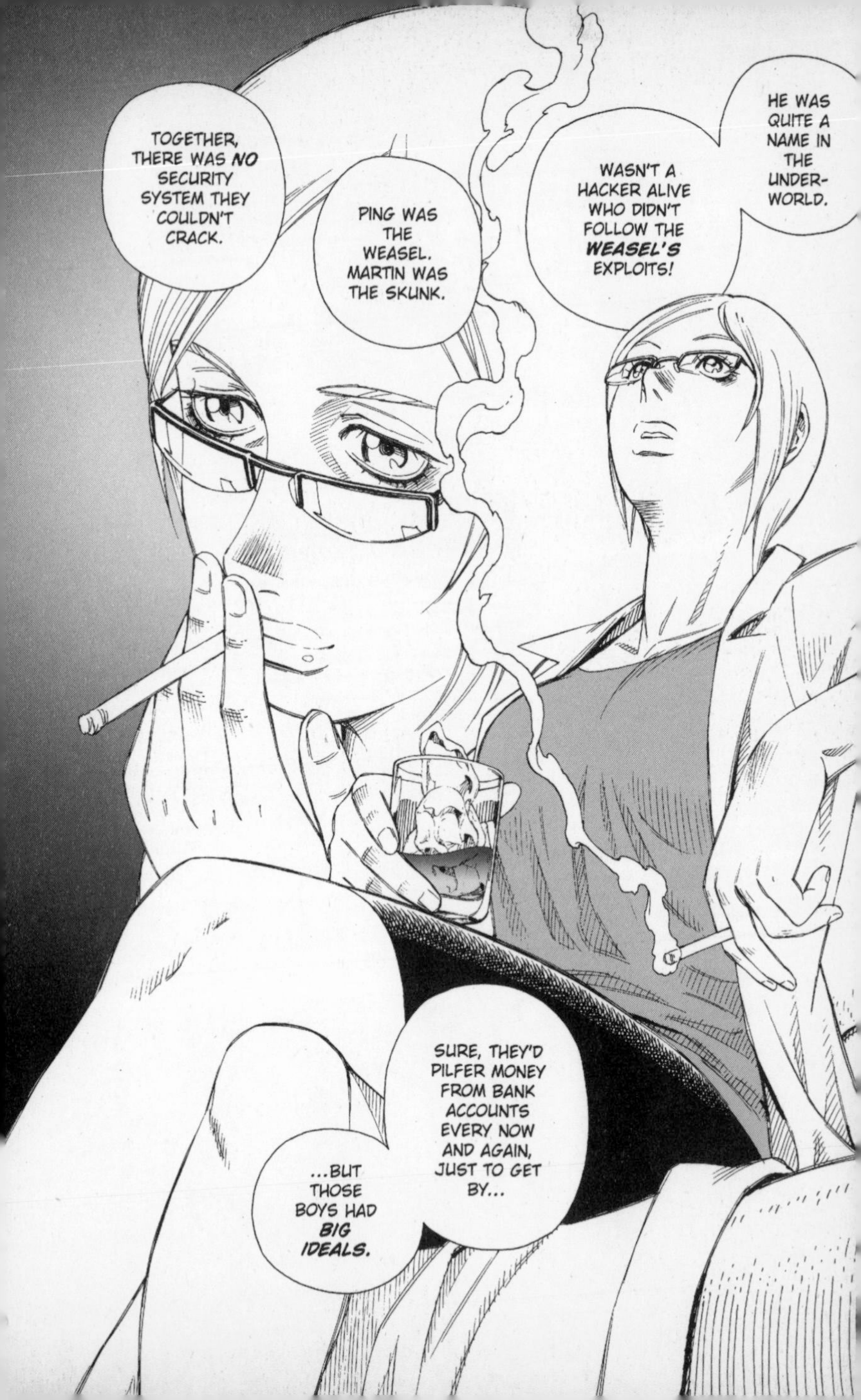
HE WAS QUITE A NAME IN THE UNDERWORLD.
WASN'T A HACKER ALIVE WHO DIDN'T FOLLOW THE WEASEL'S EXPLOITS!
PING WAS THE WEASEL. MARTIN WAS THE SKUNK.
TOGETHER, THERE WAS NO SECURITY SYSTEM THEY COULDN'T CRACK.
SURE, THEY'D PILFER MONEY FROM BANK ACCOUNTS EVERY NOW AND AGAIN, JUST TO GET BY...
...BUT THOSE BOYS HAD BIG IDEALS.

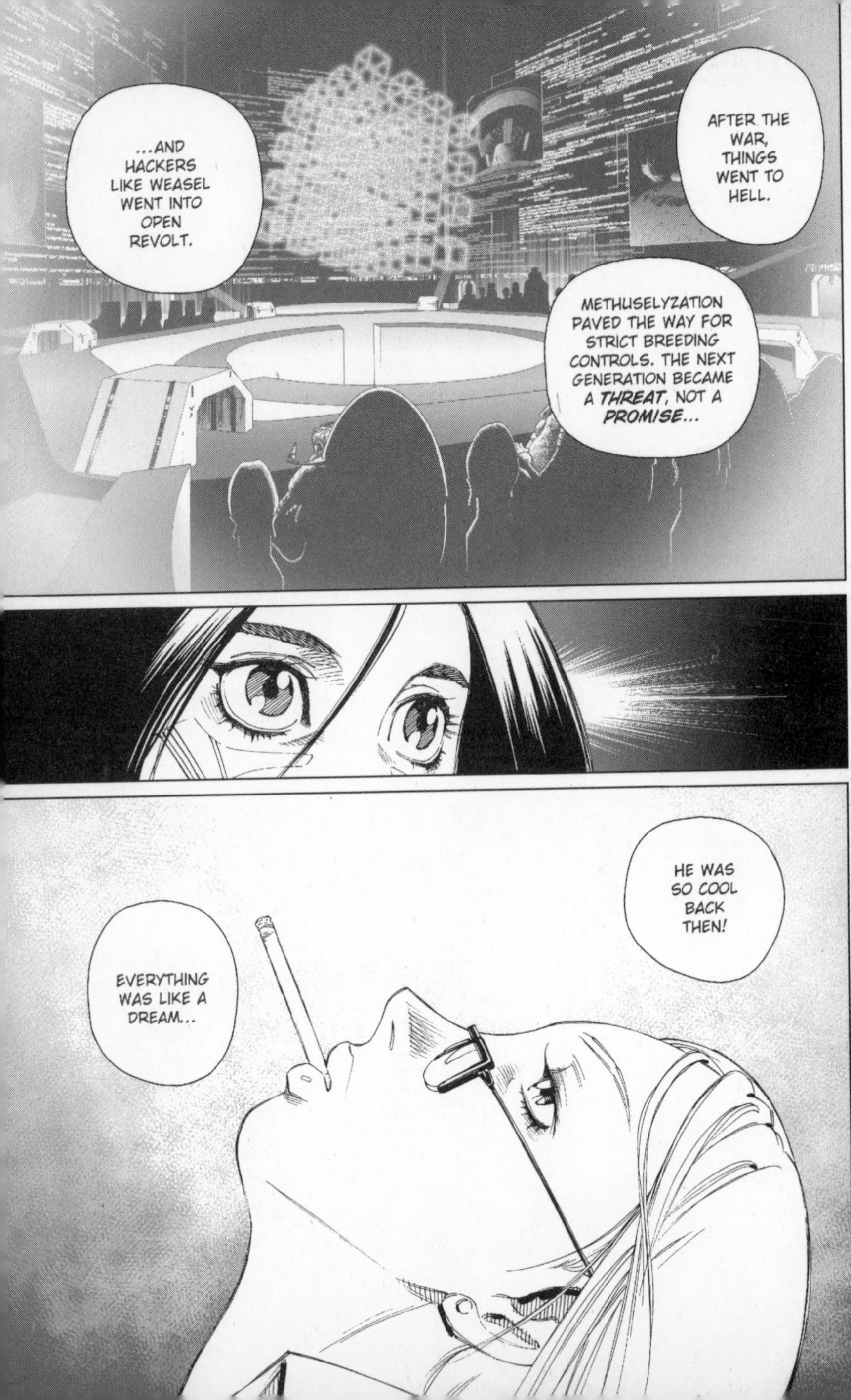
AFTER THE WAR, THINGS WENT TO HELL.
...AND HACKERS LIKE WEASEL WENT INTO OPEN REVOLT.
METHUSELYZATION PAVED THE WAY FOR STRICT BREEDING CONTROLS. THE NEXT GENERATION BECAME A *THREAT*, NOT A *PROMISE*...
HE WAS SO COOL BACK THEN!
EVERYTHING WAS LIKE A DREAM...

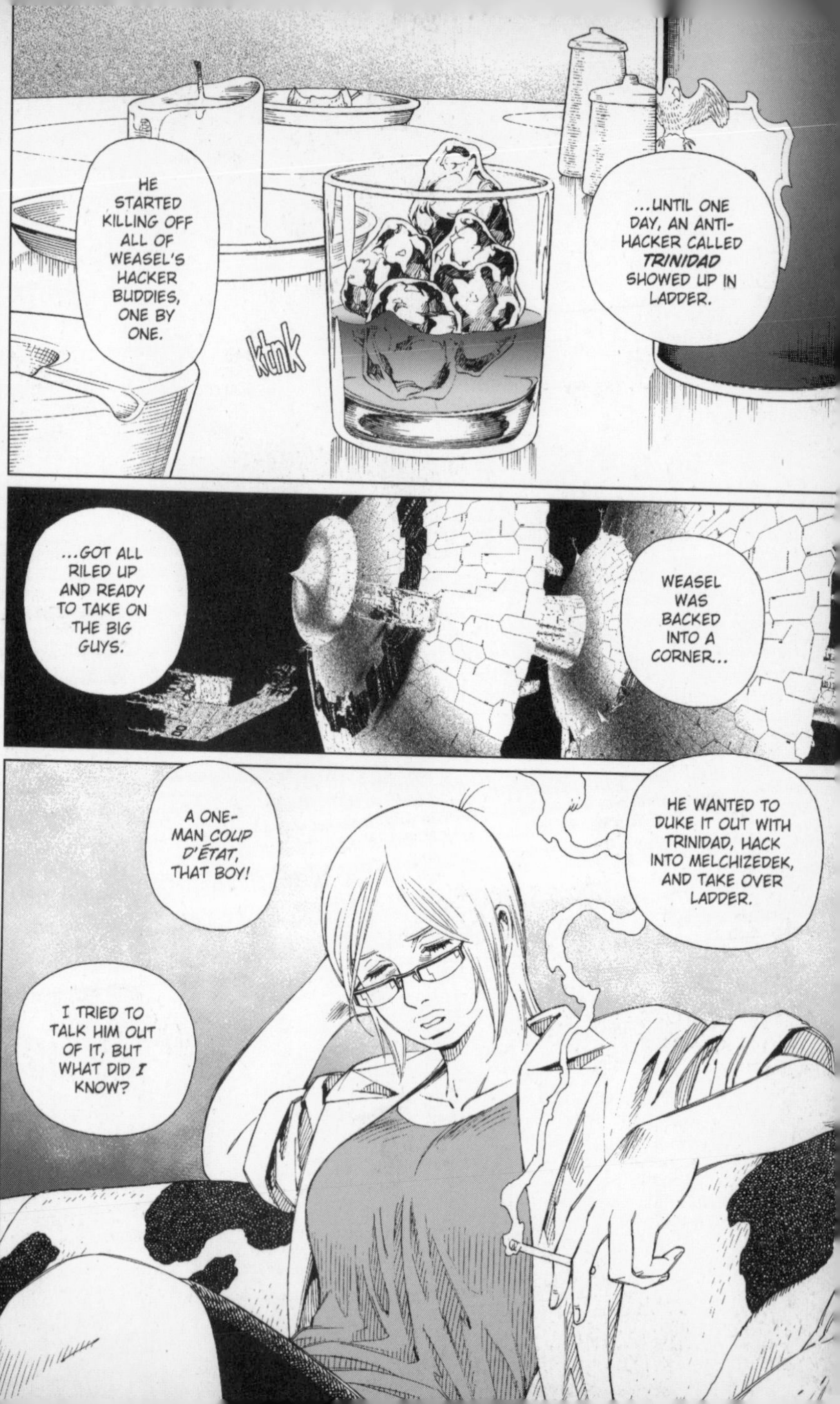
...UNTIL ONE DAY, AN ANTI-HACKER CALLED *TRINIDAD* SHOWED UP IN LADDER.
HE STARTED KILLING OFF ALL OF WEASEL'S HACKER BUDDIES, ONE BY ONE.
ktnk
WEASEL WAS BACKED INTO A CORNER...
...GOT ALL RILED UP AND READY TO TAKE ON THE BIG GUYS.
HE WANTED TO DUKE IT OUT WITH TRINIDAD, HACK INTO MELCHIZEDEK, AND TAKE OVER LADDER.
A ONE-MAN *COUP D'ÉTAT*, THAT BOY!
I TRIED TO TALK HIM OUT OF IT, BUT WHAT DID *I* KNOW?

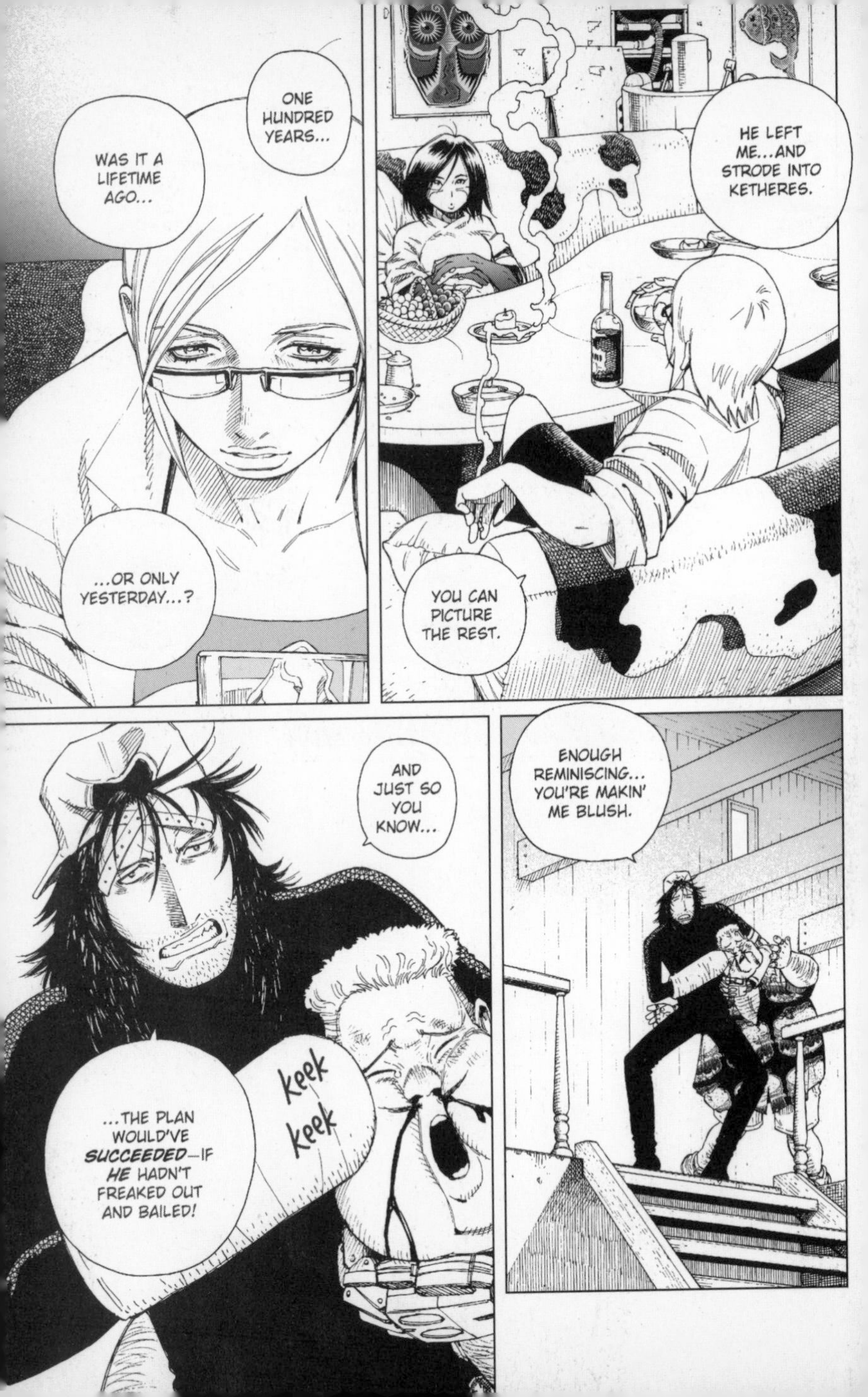
HE LEFT ME...AND STRODE INTO KETHERES.
YOU CAN PICTURE THE REST.
ONE HUNDRED YEARS...
WAS IT A LIFETIME AGO...
...OR ONLY YESTERDAY...?
ENOUGH REMINISCING... YOU'RE MAKIN' ME BLUSH.
AND JUST SO YOU KNOW...
keek keek
...THE PLAN WOULD'VE SUCCEEDED—IF HE HADN'T FREAKED OUT AND BAILED!

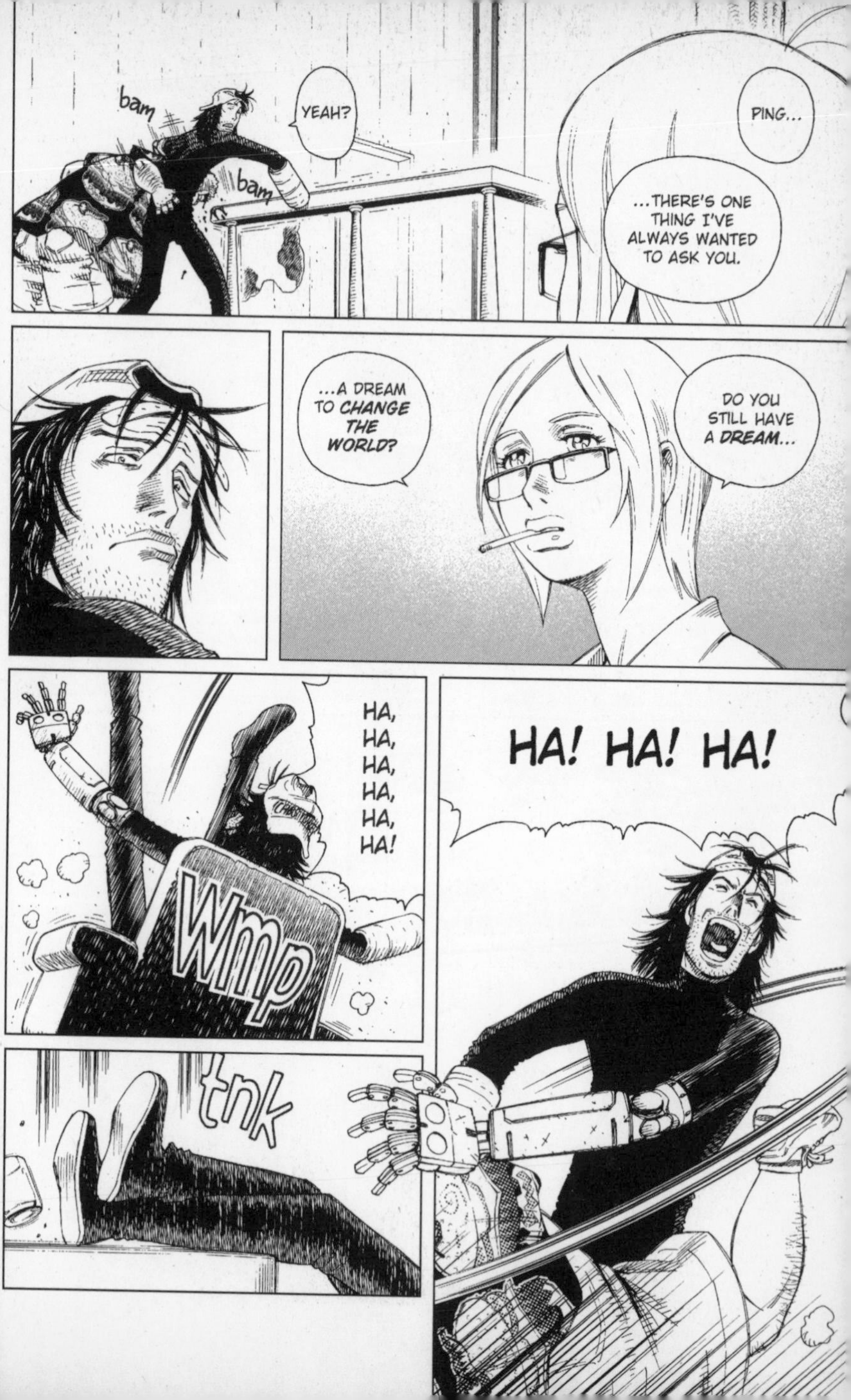
PING...
...THERE'S ONE THING I'VE ALWAYS WANTED TO ASK YOU.
YEAH?
bam
bam
DO YOU STILL HAVE A *DREAM*...
...A DREAM TO *CHANGE THE WORLD?*
HA! HA! HA!
HA, HA, HA, HA, HA, HA!
Wmp
tnk

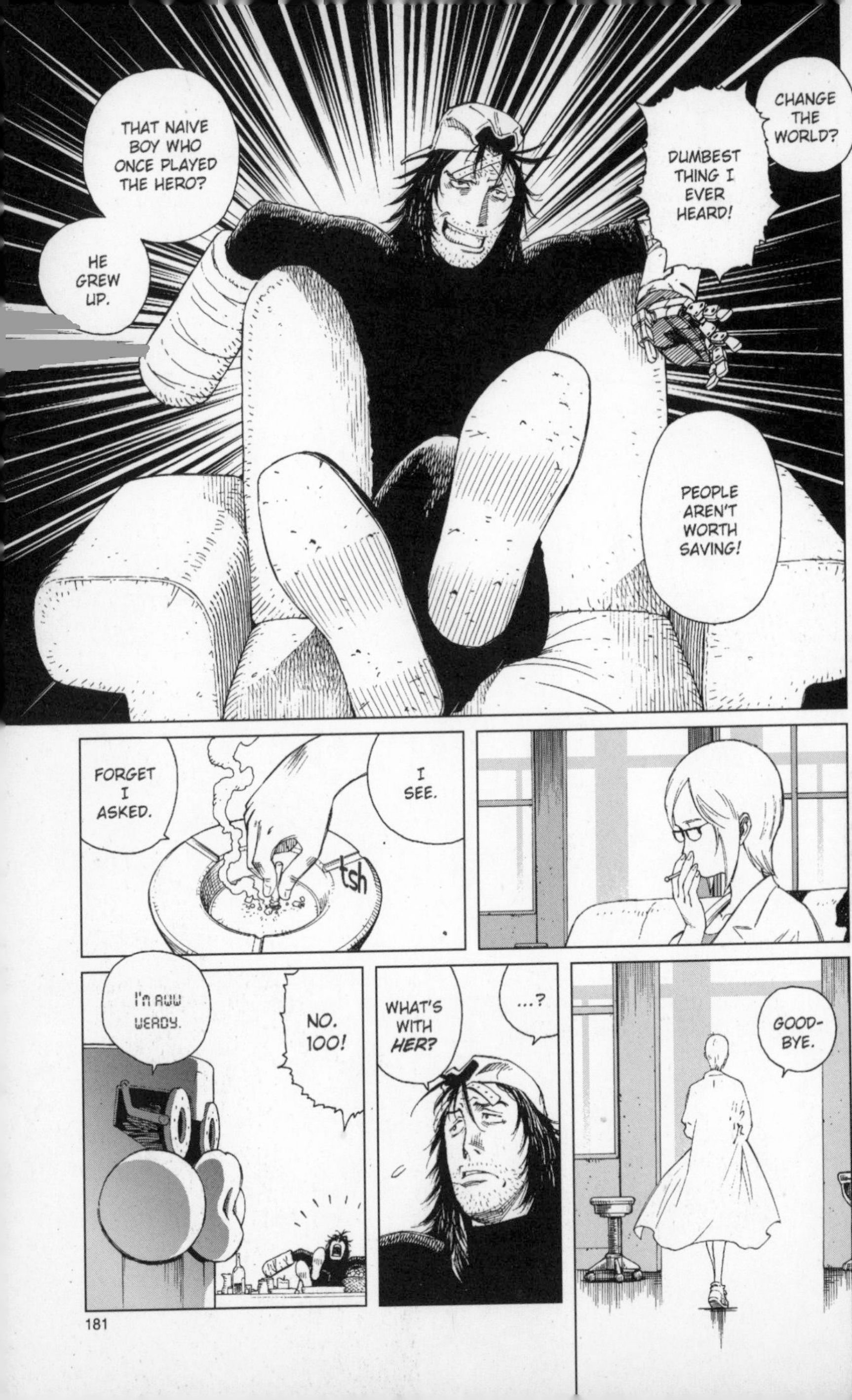
CHANGE THE WORLD?
DUMBEST THING I EVER HEARD!
THAT NAIVE BOY WHO ONCE PLAYED THE HERO?
HE GREW UP.
PEOPLE AREN'T WORTH SAVING!
I SEE.
FORGET I ASKED.
tsh
GOOD-BYE.
...?
WHAT'S WITH *HER?*
NO. 100!
I'm AWW WERDY.

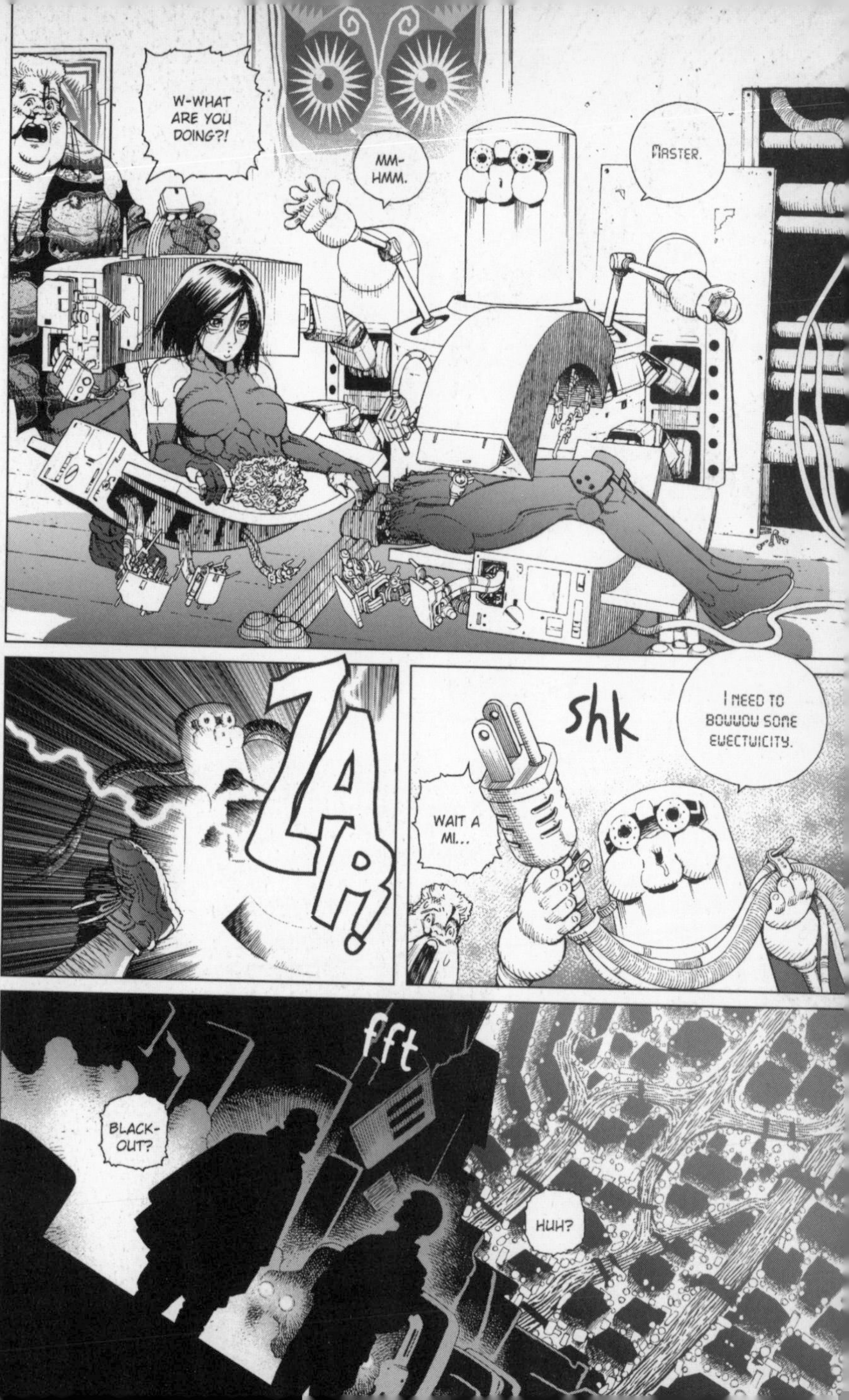
MASTER.
MM-HMM.
W-WHAT ARE YOU DOING?!
I NEED TO BOWWOW SOME EWECTWICITY.
shk
WAIT A MI...
ZAP!
fft
HUH?
BLACK-OUT?

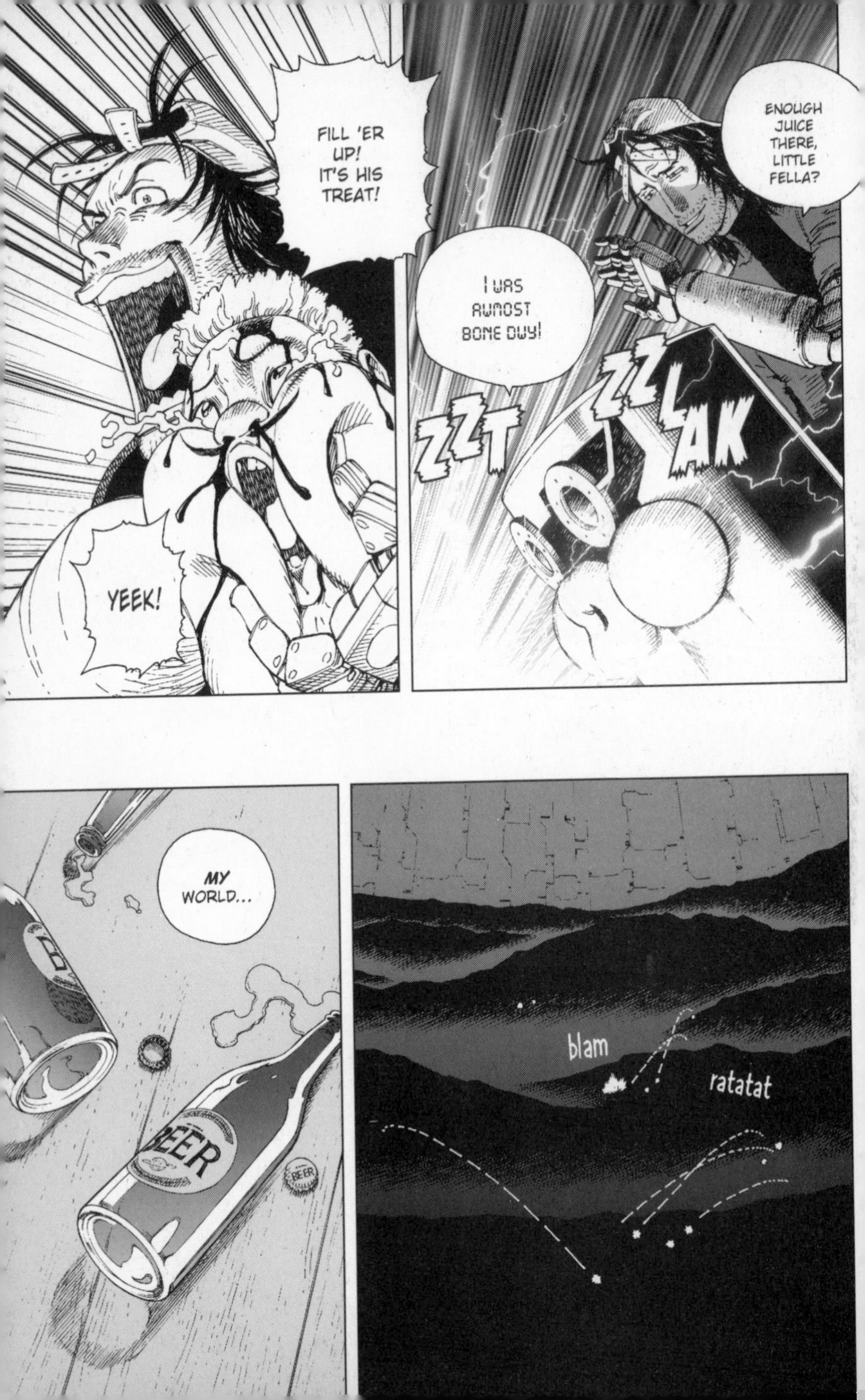
ENOUGH JUICE THERE, LITTLE FELLA?
I WAS AWMOST BONE DWY!
ZZLAK
ZZT
FILL 'ER UP! IT'S HIS TREAT!
YEEK!
blam
ratatat
MY WORLD...
BEER

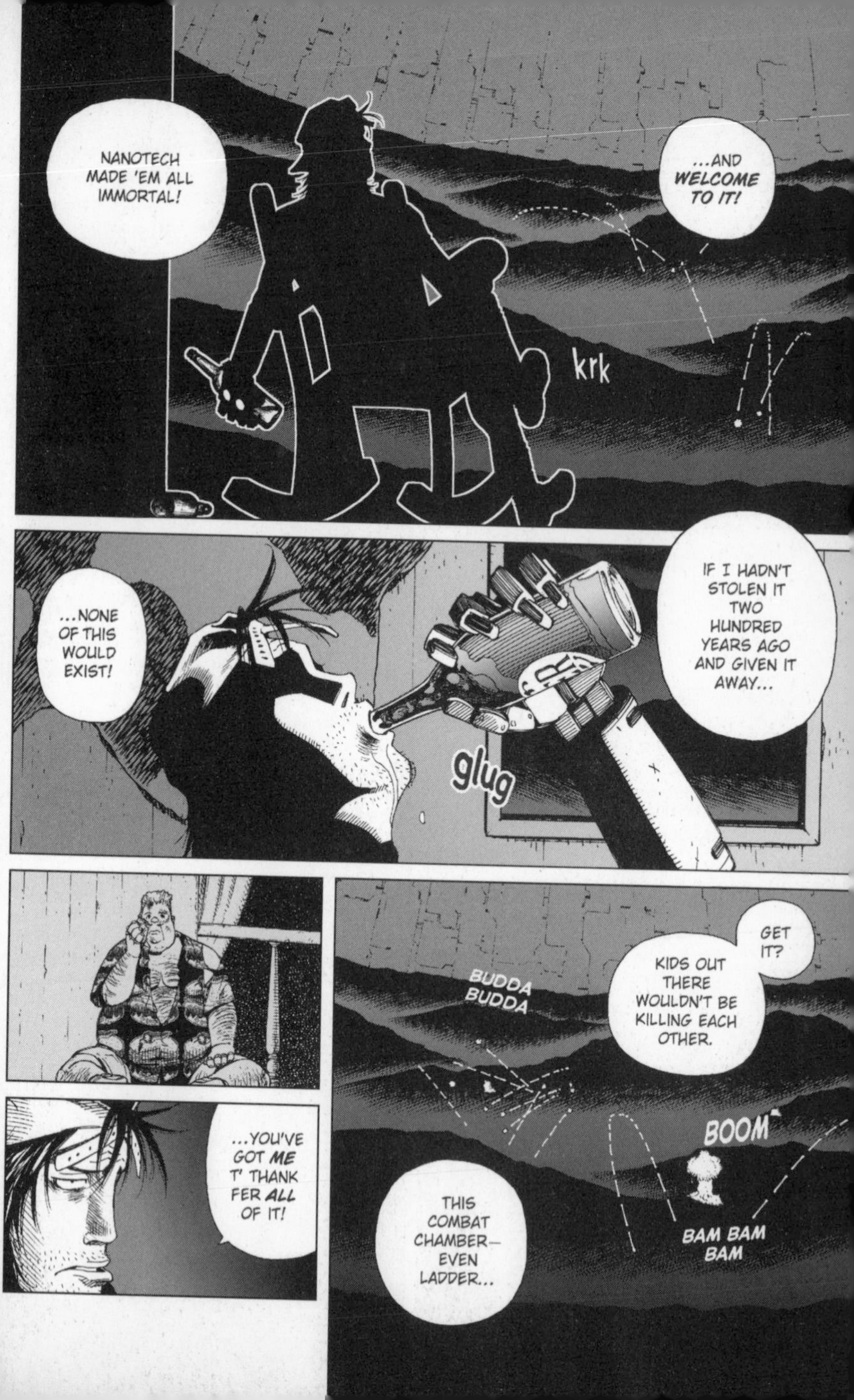

...AND WELCOME TO IT!
krk
NANOTECH MADE 'EM ALL IMMORTAL!
IF I HADN'T STOLEN IT TWO HUNDRED YEARS AGO AND GIVEN IT AWAY...
...NONE OF THIS WOULD EXIST!
glug
GET IT?
KIDS OUT THERE WOULDN'T BE KILLING EACH OTHER.
BUDDA BUDDA
BOOM
BAM BAM BAM
THIS COMBAT CHAMBER— EVEN LADDER...
...YOU'VE GOT ME T' THANK FER ALL OF IT!

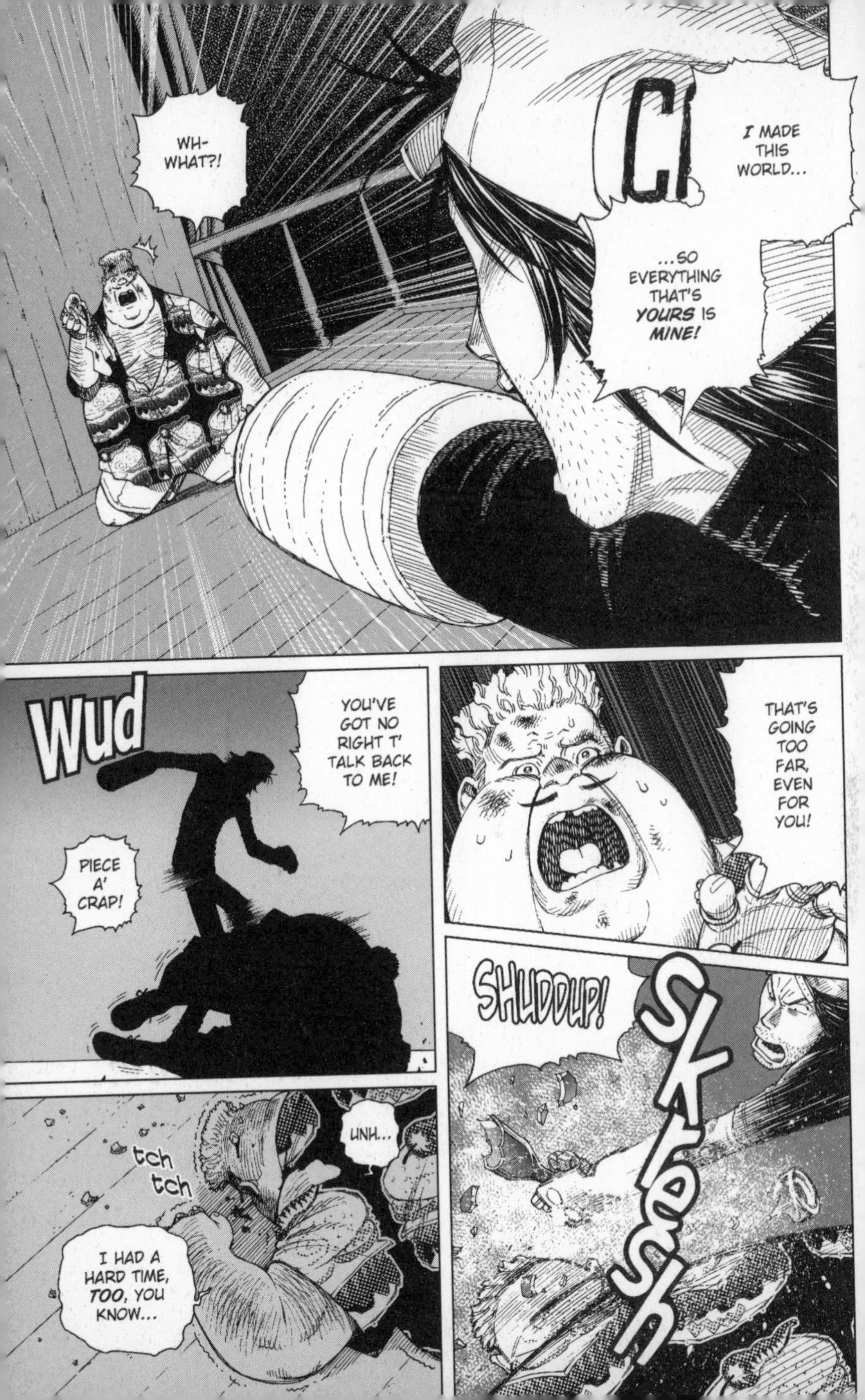

CI
I MADE THIS WORLD...
...SO EVERYTHING THAT'S YOURS IS MINE!
WH- WHAT?!
THAT'S GOING TOO FAR, EVEN FOR YOU!
SHUDDUP!
Skresh
Wud
YOU'VE GOT NO RIGHT T' TALK BACK TO ME!
PIECE A' CRAP!
UNH...
tch tch
I HAD A HARD TIME, TOO, YOU KNOW...

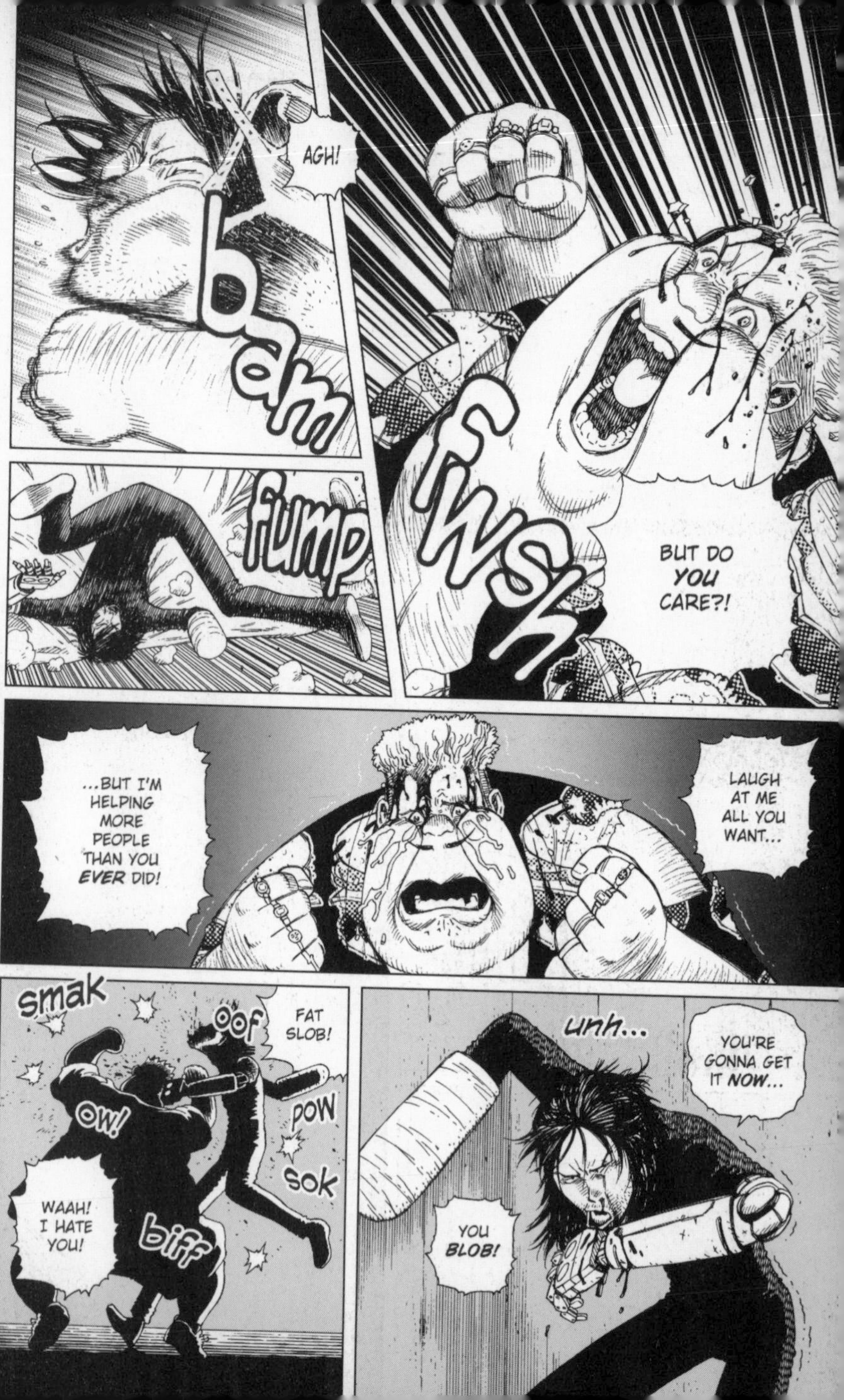
fwsh
BUT DO YOU CARE?!
AGH!
bam
fump
LAUGH AT ME ALL YOU WANT...
...BUT I'M HELPING MORE PEOPLE THAN YOU EVER DID!
YOU'RE GONNA GET IT NOW...
unh...
YOU BLOB!
FAT SLOB!
oof
smak
pow
ow!
sok
WAAH! I HATE YOU!
biff

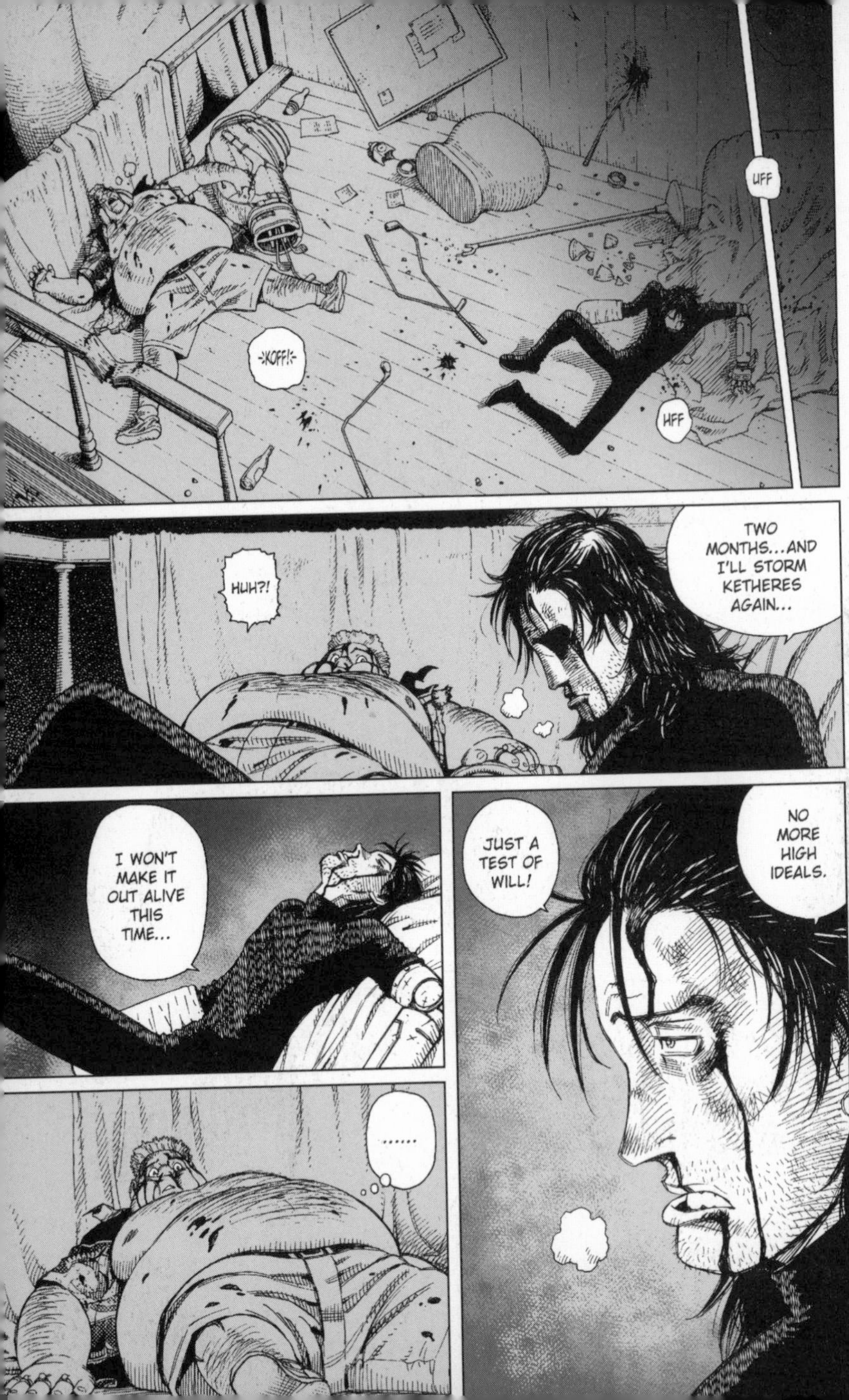
UFF
-KOFF!-
HFF
TWO MONTHS...AND I'LL STORM KETHERES AGAIN...
HUH?!
NO MORE HIGH IDEALS.
JUST A TEST OF WILL!
I WON'T MAKE IT OUT ALIVE THIS TIME...
......

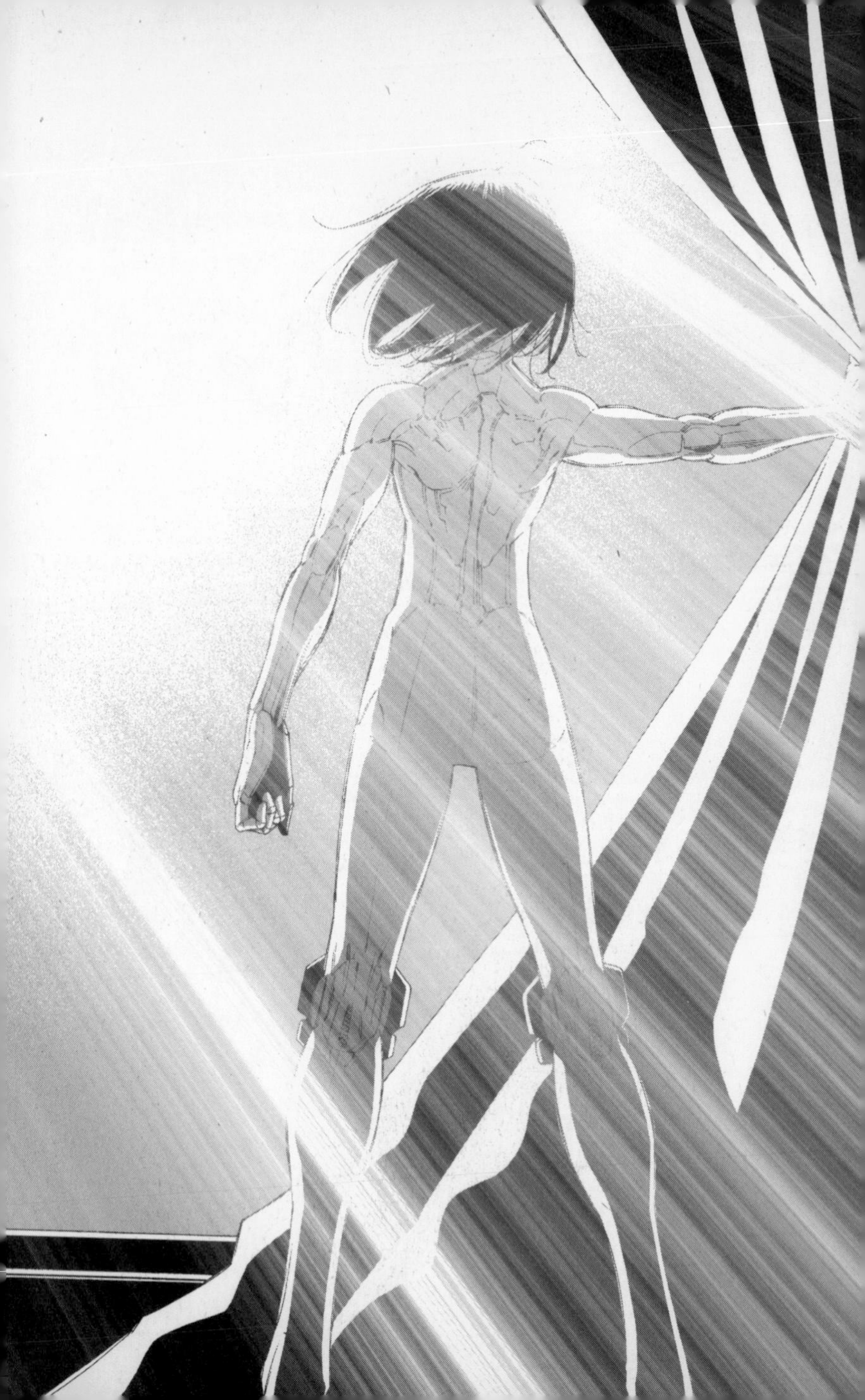

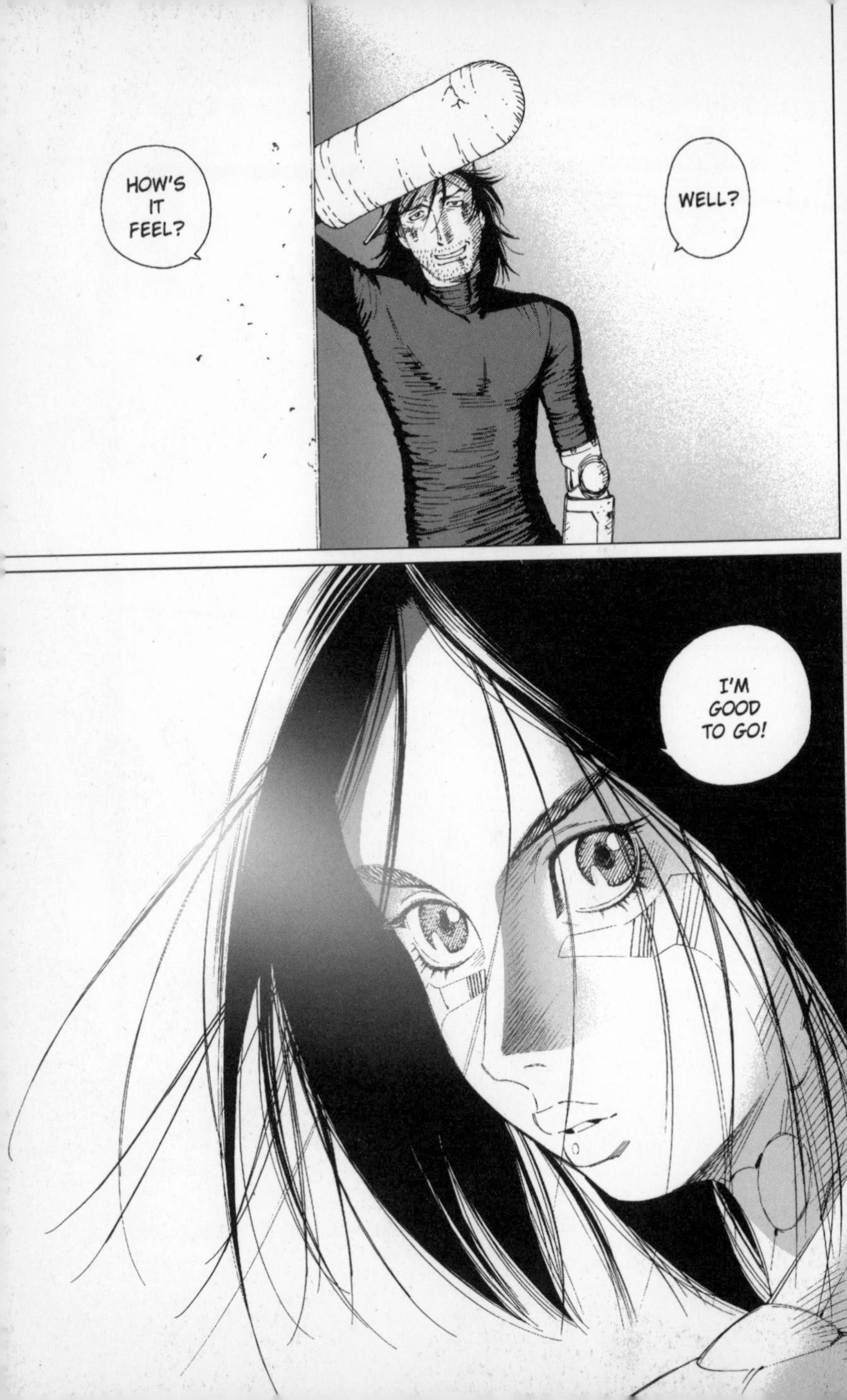
WELL?
HOW'S IT FEEL?
I'M GOOD TO GO!

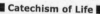

Catechism of Life

Catechism of Life!!

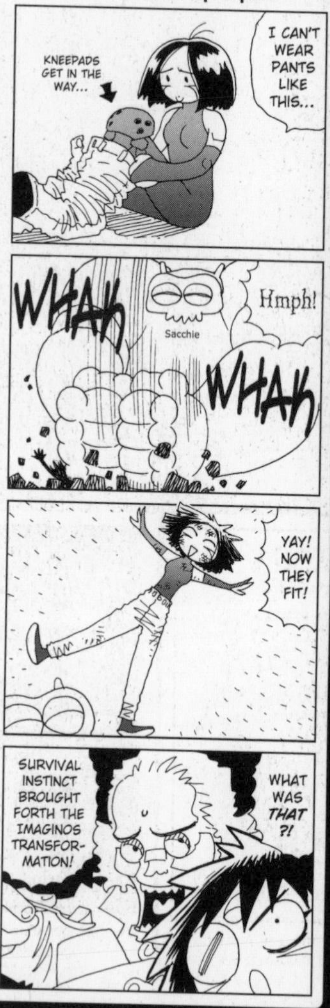
I CAN'T WEAR PANTS LIKE THIS...
KNEEPADS GET IN THE WAY...
Hmph!
WHAK
Sacchie
WHAK
YAY! NOW THEY FIT!
WHAT WAS *THAT*?!
SURVIVAL INSTINCT BROUGHT FORTH THE IMAGINOS TRANSFORMATION!

Midnight Battle!!

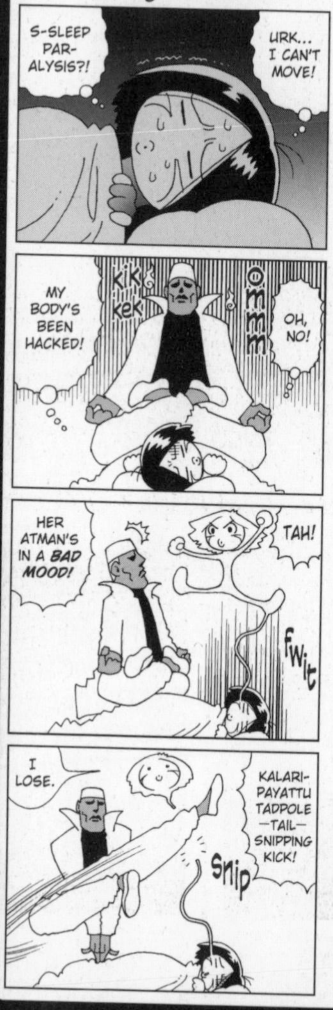
URK... I CAN'T MOVE!
S-SLEEP PAR-ALYSIS?!
OH, NO!
ommm
KIK KEK
MY BODY'S BEEN HACKED!
TAH!
HER ATMAN'S IN A *BAD MOOD!*
fWit
KALARI-PAYATTU TADPOLE —TAIL— SNIPPING KICK!
Snip
I LOSE.

For those lamenting the paucity of Alita combat in Volume 3, we bring you two battle-oriented comic strips!

ITOR'S RECOMMENDATIONS

Search **viz.com** for hard-to-find, not-to-be-reprinted **Yukito Kishiro** graphic novels, before they're sold out. Warning: these editions will be more expensive than the copy of **Last Order** you're holding in your hands. Why? Because the books are printed BIGGER. The trend in graphic novels has been to downsize so readers can get more pages for their dollars. But **Yukito Kishiro**'s ***Aqua Knight*** and ***Ashen Victor*** are *only* available in the larger format…and with the complexity and delicacy of Kishiro's work, that's a good thing!

Meet Alita's friend Lou before her brain was removed! **Battle Angel Alita: Last Order** will make more sense and be all the richer when you've read the stories of struggle and heroism that led up to it. Reformatted volumes of the original nine-volume **Battle Angel Alita** series will all be reissued, with one hitting the stores every other month from December of 2003 through April of 2005, but if you can't wait and want the BIGGER original versions, they're all still available on our "backlist" at viz.com! As of this writing, at least…

See below for more details!

Annette Roman

Editor of ***Battle Angel Alita***

If you like *Battle Angel Alita: Last Order*, sample these other Viz titles!

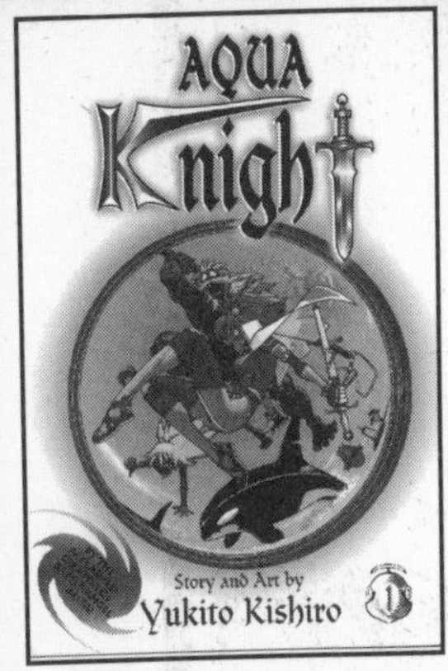

AQUA
Knight
Story and Art by
Yukito Kishiro

• ***Aqua Knight***: This fantasy tale by the creator of Alita also stars a female heroine and a mad genius, but is a tad more lighthearted and quirky. The action is set on a water world where Aqua Knights ride the high seas on the backs of orca steeds. Find the precious last available copies on our website viz.com under "backlist." These may never be reprinted!

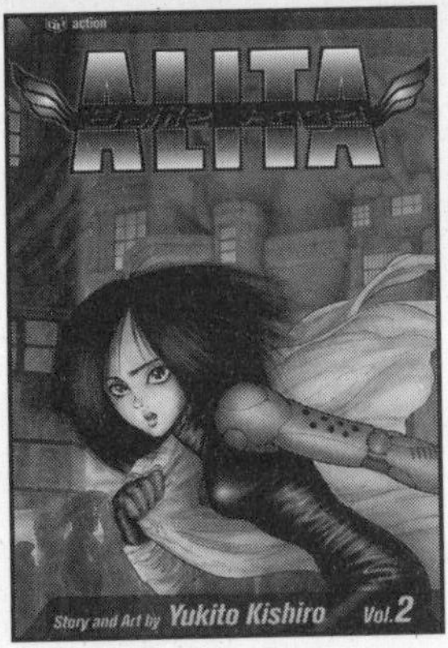

ALITA
Story and Art by Yukito Kishiro
Vol. 2

• ***Battle Angel Alita***: This 9-volume series tells the saga of Alita's early life after her *first* resurrection. Alita as heroine and defender of innocents! Alita as champion in the blood sport of Motorball! Alita in love!

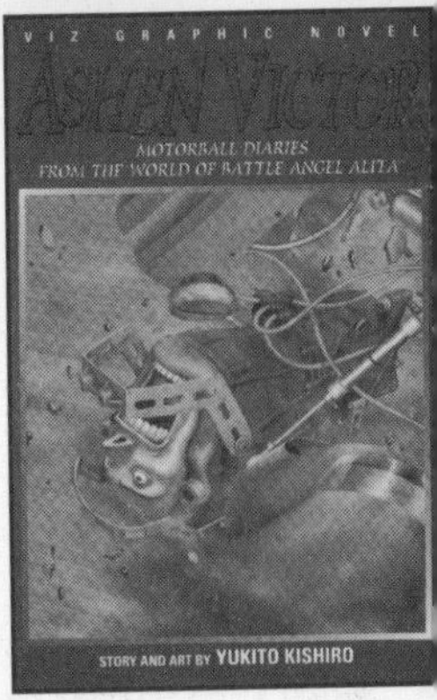

VIZ GRAPHIC NOVEL
ASHEN VICTOR
MOTORBALL DIARIES
FROM THE WORLD OF BATTLE ANGEL ALITA
STORY AND ART BY YUKITO KISHIRO

• ***Ashen Victor***: A one-volume Alita side story set in the Scrapyard and drawn in a *noir* style inspired by American comic artist Frank Miller Watching the blood-soaked sport of Motorba provides its fans with an escape—not so for Snev, a glum Motorball player nicknamed the "Crash King." As his teammates turn against him and his friends die one by one, will Snev's repressed fury save him or doom him? Again, get this volume while you can from our backl *now*, as this title is very unlikely to be reprinte in any form…. (Manga fans nowadays seem t prefer lighter fare, more's the pity.)

COMPLETE OUR SURVEY AND LET US KNOW WHAT YOU THINK!

☐ Please do NOT send me information about VIZ products, news and events, special offers, or other information.

☐ Please do NOT send me information from VIZ's trusted business partners.

Name: _____

Address: _____

City: _____ **State:** _____ **Zip:** _____

E-mail: _____

☐ Male ☐ Female   Date of Birth (mm/dd/yyyy): ___ / ___ / ___   (Under 13? Parental consent required)

What race/ethnicity do you consider yourself? (please check one)

☐ Asian/Pacific Islander   ☐ Black/African American   ☐ Hispanic/Latino

☐ Native American/Alaskan Native ☐ White/Caucasian   ☐ Other: _____

What VIZ product did you purchase? (check all that apply and indicate title purchased)

☐ DVD/VHS _____

☐ Graphic Novel _____

☐ Magazines _____

☐ Merchandise _____

Reason for purchase: (check all that apply)

☐ Special offer   ☐ Favorite title   ☐ Gift

☐ Recommendation   ☐ Other _____

Where did you make your purchase? (please check one)

☐ Comic store   ☐ Bookstore   ☐ Mass/Grocery Store

☐ Newsstand   ☐ Video/Video Game Store ☐ Other: _____

☐ Online (site: _____)

What other VIZ properties have you purchased/own? _____

_____

How many anime and/or manga titles have you purchased in the last year? How many were VIZ titles? (please check one from each column)

ANIME	MANGA	VIZ
☐ None	☐ None	☐ None
☐ 1-4	☐ 1-4	☐ 1-4
☐ 5-10	☐ 5-10	☐ 5-10
☐ 11+	☐ 11+	☐ 11+

I find the pricing of VIZ products to be: (please check one)

☐ Cheap ☐ Reasonable ☐ Expensive

What genre of manga and anime would you like to see from VIZ? (please check two)

☐ Adventure ☐ Comic Strip ☐ Science Fiction ☐ Fighting

☐ Horror ☐ Romance ☐ Fantasy ☐ Sports

What do you think of VIZ's new look?

☐ Love It ☐ It's OK ☐ Hate It ☐ Didn't Notice ☐ No Opinion

Which do you prefer? (please check one)

☐ Reading right-to-left

☐ Reading left-to-right

Which do you prefer? (please check one)

☐ Sound effects in English

☐ Sound effects in Japanese with English captions

☐ Sound effects in Japanese only with a glossary at the back

THANK YOU! Please send the completed form to:

NJW Research
42 Catharine St.
Poughkeepsie, NY 12601

All information provided will be used for internal purposes only. We promise not to sell or otherwise divulge your information.